D0762360

Style, Character and Language

VICTOR H. ROSEN, M.D.

Style, Character and Language

Victor H. Rosen, M.D.

edited by

SAMUEL ATKIN, M.D.
and
MILTON E. JUCOVY, M.D.

Jason Aronson, Inc.
New York

ISBN: 0-87668-251-4

Library of Congress Catalog Number: 77-70332

Manufactured in the United States of America

Acknowledgments

Any volume which brings together much of the scientific work of one man inevitably reflects the cooperative efforts of many people whose dedication and sense of commitment are deeply appreciated. The editors especially wish to thank Dr. Elise W. Snyder for her gracious and generous permission to reprint her husband's articles and for her keen and insightful contributions to the editorial comment. Members of Dr. Victor H. Rosen's family provided vital inspiration and valuable biographical detail. For this we wish to thank Mrs. Elizabeth Rosen Fraenkel, his daughters, Barbara and Winifred, and his sister, Mrs. Norma Starobin. For secretarial and other technical help in the preparation of the manuscript we wish to express our gratitude to Miss Helen Atkin and Mrs. Florence Snow. We want also to thank our wives, Shirley Jucovy and Edith Atkin, and Dr. Peter M. Jucovy for their helpful and creative comments after reading the manuscript. For their confidence in this work we are grateful to Dr. Robert Langs and Dr. Jason Aronson, whose consistent and loyal interest in the project never faltered.

Finally, we express our deepest appreciation to the editors and publishers of the various journals and volumes from which have been culled the individual papers that constitute this volume. For permission to reprint the following materials by Victor H. Rosen, M.D., we would like to thank the copyright holders. Articles have been slightly adapted for book use.

Chapter 1: from "On Mathematical Illumination and the Mathematical Thought Process," *The Psychoanalytic Study of the Child*, Vol. 3, ed. by Ruth S. Eissler et al. (New York: International Universities Press, 1953). Presented to the New York Psychoanalytic Society, June 23, 1953.

Chapter 2: from "Strephosymbolia: An Intrasystemic Disturbance of the Synthetic Function of the Ego," *The Psychoanalytic Study of the Child*, Vol. 10, ed. by Ruth S. Eissler et al. (New York: International Universities Press, 1955). Presented to the New York Psychoanalytic Society, January 11, 1955.

Chapter 3: from "Abstract Thinking and Object Relations," *Journal of the American Psychoanalytic Association* 6, no. 4 (October 1958), International Universities Press. Presented at the annual meeting of the American Psychoanalytic Association, May 11, 1957, as part of the panel on the Psychoanalytic Theory of Thinking.

Chapter 4: from "Disturbances of Representations and Reference in Ego Deviations," in Rudolph Loewenstein, *Psychoanalysis—A General Psychology* (New York: International Universities Press, 1966).

Chapter 5: from "Disorders of Communication in Psychoanalysis," *Journal of the American Psychoanalytic Association* 5, no. 3 (July, 1967), International Universities Press. Presented at the Plenary Session of the fall meeting of the American Psychoanalytic Association, December 17, 1966.

Chapter 6: from "A Re-examination of Some Aspects of Freud's Theory of Schizophrenic Language Disturbance," *Journal of the Hillside Hospital* 17, nos. 2 and 3 (April-July 1968), International Universities Press.

Chapter 7: from "Sign Phenomena and Their Relationship to Unconscious Meaning," *The International Journal of Psycho-Analysis* 50 (1969). Presented to the New York Psychoanalytic Society, October 29, 1968.

Chapter 8: from "Introduction to Panel on Language and Psychoanalysis," *International Journal of Psycho-Analysis* 50 (1969). Presented to the Twenty-Sixth International Psychoanalytical Congress, Rome, 1969.

Chapter 9: from "The Role of Metapsychology in Therapeutic Interpretation," *Currents in Psychoanalysis*, ed. Irwin Marcus (New York: International Universities Press, 1971).

Chapter 10: from "The Nature of Verbal Interventions in Psychoanalysis," *Psychoanalysis and Contemporary Science*, Vol. 3, ed. by Leo Goldberger and Victor Rosen (New York: International Universities Press, 1974).

Chapter 11: from "Some Aspects of the Role of the Imagination in the Analytic Process," *Journal of the American Psychoanalytic Association* 8, no. 2 (April 1960), International Universities Press. Presented at the spring meeting of the American Psychoanalytic Association, April 25, 1959, as part of the panel discussion on Imagination.

Chapter 12: from "The Relevance of 'Style' to Certain Aspects of Defence and the Synthetic Function of the Ego," *International Journal of Psycho-Analysis* 42 (1961). Presented to the New York Psychoanalytic Society, December 20, 1960.

Chapter 13: from "Variants of Comic Caricature and Their Relationship to Obsessive-Compulsive Phenomena," *Journal of the American Psychoanalytic Association* 11, no. 4 (October 1963), International Universities Press. Presented at the annual meeting of the American Psychoanalytic Association, May 5, 1962, as part of the panel on Symptom Formation.

Chapter 14: from "Some Effects of Artistic Talent on Character Style," *The Psychoanalytic Quarterly* 33 (1964). Presented as the Fifth Sophia Mirviss Memorial Lecture, March 4, 1963, to the San Francisco Psychoanalytic Society and Institute and the Mount Zion Hospital and Medical Center of San Francisco.

Classical Psychoanalysis and Its Applications:
A Series of Books
Edited by Robert Langs, M.D.

Langs, Robert
THE TECHNIQUE OF PSYCHOANALYTIC PSYCHOTHERAPY, VOLS. I AND II

THE THERAPEUTIC INTERACTION, TWO-VOLUME SET

THE BIPERSONAL FIELD

Kestenberg, Judith
CHILDREN AND PARENTS: PSYCHOANALYTIC STUDIES IN DEVELOPMENT

Sperling, Melitta
THE MAJOR NEUROSES AND BEHAVIOR DISORDERS IN CHILDREN

Giovacchini, Peter L.
PSYCHOANALYSIS OF CHARACTER DISORDERS

Kernberg, Otto
BORDERLINE CONDITIONS AND PATHOLOGICAL NARCISSISM

OBJECT-RELATIONS THEORY AND CLINICAL PSYCHOANALYSIS

Console, William A.
Simons, Richard C.
Rubinstein, Mark
THE FIRST ENCOUNTER

Nagera, Humberto
FEMALE SEXUALITY AND THE OEDIPUS COMPLEX

OBSESSIONAL NEUROSES: DEVELOPMENTAL PSYCHOPATHOLOGY

Hoffer, Willi
THE EARLY DEVELOPMENT AND EDUCATION OF THE CHILD

Meissner, William
THE PARANOID PROCESS

Horowitz, Mardi
STRESS RESPONSE SYNDROMES

Rosen, Victor
STYLE, CHARACTER AND LANGUAGE

Sarnoff, Charles
LATENCY

Series Introduction

There is an exquisite concordance between the qualities of a man and those of his life's work. Nowhere is this more evident than in the case of Victor Rosen. In this extraordinary volume, one finds not only the writings and ideas of an unusually gifted psychoanalyst, but also three essays that evaluate Rosen's lasting contribution to psychoanalysis and pay tribute to his creativity and humanity. Victor Rosen was one of the first psychaonalysts to seriously attempt to expand the boundaries of psychoanalysis within the confines of its own theory and techniques, and to clarify its basic concepts through the examination of related disciplines, linguistics in particular. In recognizing that language has a central place in the expression of psychopathology and in the communicative interaction between the analyst and analysand, Rosen shed considerable light on the therapeutic and adaptive functions of language and on its many disturbances. By broadening his investigations into such areas as thinking, schizophrenia, interpretation, imagination, and character, Rosen's efforts have added to our basic understanding of the mind and to many aspects of the therapeutic process. His unusual capacity to integrate theory and practice is more than evident in these pages. Rosen was a bold adventurer among psychoanalysts, and he leaves behind him the many rewards of his searches. Psychoanalysis has been greatly enhanced by his original and insightful work, and all who are concerned with understanding human behavior and its disturbances will remain indebted to his memory for many years to come.

Robert Langs, M.D.

Contents

PART I
LANGUAGE AND PSYCHOANALYTIC TECHNIQUE

LANGUAGE AND PSYCHOANALYTIC TECHNIQUE

Introduction

by SAMUEL ATKIN, M.D.

The evolution and progress of psychoanalytic science—its basic assumptions, its methods, its realized and unrealized potentialities, and the nature of its unsolved problems—can be studied from the viewpoint of the philosophy of science. Another avenue of approach might be through the scrutiny of the career and achievements of a special kind of theoretician and practitioner. Such a man was Victor Rosen.

The writings of Victor Rosen over the last two decades unfold an intellectual autobiography that can be read not only as the history of one man's intellectual journey but also as a chapter in the evolution of the science of psychoanalysis. His matchless intellectual integrity and power, his passion for exactitude, his extraordinary critical faculty, his courage produced a great intellectual harvest. Although no intellectual rebel—for all his ambition, he stood firmly on home ground—Rosen, in his research of ideas, was a great innovator, a creative doer, creating new forms to replace those he considered erroneous.

The depth and subtlety of his comprehension of Freud's ideas made it possible for Rosen to retain Freud's insights even while criticizing the ambiguities he found in them. He took pride (no false modesty, his) in being able to stand on Freud's shoulders to peer ambitiously and with sterling talents into the unexplored expanse of Freudian science. His pride was well warranted. Through his venture into psycholinguistics and the bridge he built between that science and psychoanalysis, Rosen made a major contribution to the development of psychoanalysis as a science.

In this essay I shall present a summary of Rosen's work on the relationship of psychoanalysis and psycholinguistics, primarily to orient readers unacquainted with the latter. My estimate of his impact on psychoanalysis, as well as any implied blueprint of his work in this field, is my own interpretation and evaluation, derived from a consecutive reading of his work, his tutelage in the Language Study Group, of which I was a member, and my long association with him. I take a biographer's and critic's responsibility for them.

In 1953 and 1955 Rosen wrote two papers (Chapters 1 and 2) on the case of a young man gifted with "mathematical illumination" who suffered from strephosymbolia, a disability in the recognition of the printed word and in reproducing the printed word in writing. Here the theme of language appears for the first time. (Rosen was not to return to it until almost ten years later.) In those two early papers he noted the analogy with the "phylogenetic phases of orthographic evolution"; that is, "a transitional stage between ideographic script and the syllabary alphabet." This linguistic observation conformed to the Freudian evolutionary concept, by which Freud postulated an analogy between the development of culture and language with the evolutionary progression from child to adult or from savage to modern man.

Rosen, a trained neurologist, referred to Schilder's psychophysiological explanation only to dismiss it. He did not pursue an examination of either the "process" psychology or the physiology of the "mathematical illumination" or of the reading disturbance. Nor did he pursue the psycholinguistic challenge at that time, but turned rather to a psychoanalytic id interpretation for a dynamic formulation of the case. He attributed the source of the patient's "illumination" to a reunion with his father, from whom he received permission for gratification of his scoptophilic and epistomophilic wishes. With the reappearance of the primal scene, "the illumination condensed at least three acts of seeing in the light of day and the creation of a child in both the masculine and feminine roles."

He also posed the problem of strephosymbolia as arising in an autonomous ego function. But again he solved it by recourse to the patient's inability to handle the anxiety arising from the conflict-ridden primal scene constellation. In the primal scene, father is associated with "active" and "visual," mother with "passive" and "auditory." Because of conflict they fail to be united to produce a child. Rosen concludes that the failure to produce the synthetic product is due to its primal scene significance, with consequent conflicts and defenses.

It can be conjectured that in bringing in language in these early papers, Rosen had an "illumination" of the idea that the development of the language faculty enters into the development of the ego. It may well be that such considerations led him to the decision to study psycholinguistics.

The publication of those two papers was followed by Rosen's active participation in the Gifted Adolescent Project of the New York Psychoanalytic Institute, led by his preparatory psychoanalyst, Ernst Kris. In his studies of special talent and even of abstract thought (Chapter 3), he stated forthrightly that it was not the "process" that was under study but the gifted individual and his psychopathology. The studies remained within the confines of classical psychoanalysis, taking for granted the self-sufficiency and all-inclusiveness of psychoanalytic theory and methods. What came to the fore in these studies was the application of the then new concept, initiated by Kris, of regression in the service of the ego.

The themes of Rosen's studies, particularly his studies of style and artistic creativity, evidenced his preoccupation with the synthetic and integrative aspects of the ego, especially as they were manifested in artistic products that were configurative and contextual.

Although there was little indication in this interim period of a preoccupation with the process psychology of the ego functions in general or of language in particular, in his paper on style (Chapter 12) Rosen advanced the following formulation: "We talk about entity in terms of style and of products, whether artistic or conceptual products, and I think this is an important step toward the next most important development in Language Theory and its relationship to concept formation." A statement of Freud's (1921) on language as an artistic product seems appropriate at this point: "A language is a work of art, but it is an artistic product of the group mind. . . . Its group mind is capable of creative genius . . . as shown by language itself."

In his Introduction to Part II, Milton Jucovy bears witness that Rosen was concerned at all times with the enhancement of analytic technique, and that for the greatest therapeutic effectiveness a minute comprehension of the ego's functions was essential. The psychoanalytic method comes more easily to grips with the content of thought and the psychology of motivation and mental conflict than with the mediation processes. It can bring ego defenses under observation and work with them. However, we may pause to ask whether a fuller understanding of the working process of the ego's instruments is nonetheless essential to an adequate psychoanalytic comprehension of the operation of the ego. If this is so, this can be done through an interdisciplinary application of such other psychological sciences as psycholinguistics, sciences which lend themselves better than psychoanalysis to the study of the mediation processes.

Although Rosen did not articulate this question during this interim period, one must assume that he asked it, since in his subsequent work he proceeds to seek the answer. In 1963, when he founded the Language Study Group, he was already an advanced student in psycholinguistics and was doing research into its possibilities for the extension of psychoanalytic theory.

In 1966 Rosen published the first major product of his application of psycholinguistics to psychoanalysis—"Disturbances in Representation and Reference in Ego Deviations" (Chapter 4). This was followed by a monumental series of contributions in quick succession—papers and organization of panels on psychoanalysis and psycholinguistics at the American Psychoanalytic Association meetings and at the International, while continuing his teaching and collaboration with the Language Study Group. His papers were reports of his attempts to apply psycholinguistics in the investigation of discrete psychoanalytic problems of theory and clinical application.

I shall divide Rosen's research in psychoanalysis and psycholinguistics into four categories: (1) the application of psycholinguistics to special problems of ego psychology; (2) developmental psychology, in which he attempted to demonstrate the interactive and correlated development of the language faculty and the psychological phases of personality development; (3) information that psychoanalysis and psycholinguistics can share with each other; and (4) a critique of psychoanalysis and psycholinguistics as sciences and the conceptualization of a theoretical model that fitted them both in the same field.

1. Before introducing the subject of the *application of language theory* to psychoanalytic ego psychology, let me first give a general definition of language: Language is a means of coding (i.e. using word symbols) that enables people to think of the same things, to have concepts in common, and to verify concepts jointly. It consists of symbols (code) which carry the meaning of things in the common environment of all individuals and of communicating the environment "secondhand."

Edward Sapir (1921, 1960) gives a more comprehensive definition: Language is a "fully formed function system, a perfect self-contained *configurative* creation of the human mind, capable of the full expression of all thought, feeling, emotion. It is a non-intuitive method of communication among every known people . . . a perfect symbolic system for handling all references or meanings in a given culture . . . in actual communications or . . . such ideal substitutes of communication as thought. . . . It symbolizes actual meanings . . . can discover meanings for its speakers not traceable . . . to experience, but [behaving] as projections. . . . Language completely interpenetrates [and] directs experience. . . . Speech as behavior is a wonderfully complex blend of the two pattern systems, the symbolic and the expressive [and communicative]. . . . Language has evolved from the symbolic tendency, the uniquely human one, and has then become language. . . . The historical nucleus of language, is, curiously . . . how *vocal articulations become dissociated from their original expressive power.*"

Addressing himself to the psychoanalytic study of language, Rosen posits language as "the prime example of a rule-directed organization of the Ego. It may even be that the internalized language system constitute[s] a supraordinate regulating system of the Ego. . . . The process of [language] pattern development both reflects and influences psychic differentiation . . . [and] plays a fundamental role in the emergence of consciousness, the development of a sense of self and the establishment of conscience. . . . An examination of the ontogenesis of speech can illuminate the process of Ego and Superego formation" (Edelheit, 1968).

Here psychoanalysis and psycholinguistics intersect in four areas. The rules of language enter into (a) the operation of the ego functions; (b) superego development; (c) social rules; and (d) the relationship of language and thought. All of these are surely interdependent.

Correlating psycholinguistics and ego psychology, Rosen offers examples of how the language faculty enters into the operation of the ego. "It provides a special opportunity for mapping detailed structures in early ego organization and later ego development." It is through language that man has "the capacity to symbolize transitive actions" (Edelheit, 1972). Along these same lines, Lidz states, "Through the medium of words man is able to think and to 'fragment the past,' remember it, learn from it and think upon it" (Edelheit, 1968).

In the capacity for self-observation and self-consciousness, language also operates in many ways. Lili Peller, a member of the Language Study Group, averred that language is our main tool in the construction of a symbolically organized universe. She said, "Words are signifiers and symbolizers . . . they make possible a different organization of the mental apparatus." Language makes possible a "distance" from our physical and mental acts which contributes to "self-awareness and a new intimacy with ourselves" (Peller, 1967).

Words fix meanings of events. They make possible prolonged attention to a meaning. Words differ from other products of thought in that they are "responses" at the same time that they are "stimuli," and as such they are realities of a social group. Words as language thus become a social event and in this sense they enable events to reach consciousness (Atkin, 1969).

In time Rosen arrived at the point of making large claims for the importance of psycholinguistics for psychoanalysis. Let me cite an example: In interpersonal and intrapersonal communication, the auditory sphere is paramount. Rosen writes (Chapter 10), "In the psychoanalytic situation the 'idiolect' of body language (Symptom) needs to be translated into the 'dialect' of everyday speech and this requires a method more analagous to psycholinguistics than any other discipline." He proceeds to explain how this method applies. Meaning, "the mutual evocability of name and sense," is the prime concern of psychoanalysis, and this extends outstandingly to finding meaning in the apparently meaningless, a distinctive achievement of psychoanalysis. There the psycholinguistic theory of signs, signals and symbols complements psychoanalytic primary process theory. "The primary process is largely a signalizing and signifying activity, although [it] uses conventional symbols by converting them into signs and signals."

Rosen demonstrated the process of the interpretation of the unconscious meaning of "meaninglessness" by applying this transliteration of the psychoanalytic primary process system into psycholinguistic semiotics—in the "meaning" of a parapraxis. In the psychoanalytic situation he does with a parapraxis, a linguistic type of "idiolect," what he has just outlined as the process of the translation or interpretation of an "idiolect" into the dialect of everyday speech. This transliteration of primary process into semiotics and then into secondary process symbolism applies to most psychoanalytic interpretations.

No better example can be offered of the need Rosen saw for the investigation of the ego function as *process* than his critique (Chapter 6) of Freud's hypothesis of language disturbance in schizophrenia: "In the attempt to regain the lost object (the thing) the verbal part of it is cathected and is all that is retained." Rosen finds the following "ambiguities" in Freud's concept: Freud makes no distinction between speech and language; he doesn't define the link between words and things; and he makes no distinction between language and thought. Rosen points out that Freud's "thing" would be less likely to connote a tangible object if it would be called *referent* linguistically, and he suggests that Freud's "ambiguity," as expressed in the slurring of the study of language per se, resulted from his wish to fit the speech disturbances of schizophrenia as another spoke in the wheel of his topographical model. In the revision along structural lines Rosen would replace "word thing presentation" with "manifest meaning" or "linguistic reference." "Reference is a synthetic product including speech, syntax, and conceptual categories of meaning, none of which are completely independent of the complex self, object and environmental representation of the ego." (Heretofore syntax, grammar and the conceptual process generally had been largely neglected by psychoanalysis.)

The hypothesis of the *absolute* interdependence of language and thought is of great interest to psychoanalytic ego psychology because it would establish the language faculty as an ego function of first rank. This hypothesis, formulated as the Sapir-Whorf Relativity Principle, posits that the study of language "shows that the form of a person's thoughts (thinking) is controlled by inexorable laws of pattern [which] are the unperceived intricate systematization of his own language" (Whorf, 1956).

The correctness of the Sapir-Whorf Relativity Principle can be verified only by psychoanalytic methods, according to Rosen (Chapter 8). Here is Rosen's first claim of the dependence of psycholinguistics upon psychoanalysis.

It should be noted that Rosen remained unconvinced by the Sapir-Whorf Relativity Principle and found support for his stand in Freud, who defined thought as "trial action" which need not be verbalized (Edelheit, 1972). Rosen believed that the unconscious contains the faculty of abstract thought. (The unconscious he is referring to here is the topographical concept of the unconscious, which he questioned elsewhere.) In elaborating his idea, Rosen made the following observation: "With ideas that have no sensory modalities, like 'space' or 'justice' or the relationship of A to B, the word provides an acoustic-visual hitching post in consciousness which makes it possible for us to communicate or think about the abstraction" (personal communication).

Rosen hypothesized that two separate processes become fused. He said, "Thought is polarized around the vicissitudes of the drives and their frustration-gratification phenomena are predominantly narcissistic, while language is polarized around the development of object libido and object relations and the need to communicate." Shapiro (in a personal communication) pointed out, "Here is one of Rosen's important ideas in that it brings the psychoanalytic vantage point to language development in a way that had not been done before."

Reflecting upon Rosen's view of linguistic relativity, I would like to interpose a metapsychological speculation of my own, namely, that the purely thought aspects of language can be conceived of as having a developmental root of their own and as being of narcissistic derivation. So conceived, the symbolizing-categorizing function may then be primarily a faculty of the thought function. In the interpersonal communication of thought, language also tends to become libido cathected. In its feedback, such social functions of language process as "inner speech" promote the thought function.

Thought, then, in psychoanalytic terms, operates along a spectrum ranging from primary process activity to secondary process activity (an idea proposed by Jacob Arlow) with the structuralized and configurative aspects probably increasing as the thought function progresses along the spectrum. We might expect, then, that the preponderant imagery would be auditory (language bound at the secondary process end) but the imagery would be visual or in other sensory modalities at the primary process end. We might also place at the primary process end of the spectrum the affective and expressive factors in language. The sign and signal symbolism at the early stage of language is involved at this functional level. At the secondary process end we have the symbolizing-categorizing component of language which is functionally involved with logical, abstract and reality-bound thought. This would accord with Ogden and Richards's (1923) classification of language into its semantic (symbolizing-categorizing function) and expressive-affective-poetic phases (intercommunications).

Whether or not thought operates apart from language function, we see that much that is structured and configurative in both thought and language occurs reciprocally. This is the substance of the idea that language is the groove of thought.

In his 1966 paper, "Disturbances of Representations and Reference in Ego Deviations" (Chapter 4), Rosen offers the thought that a careful delineation of psycholinguistic norms would give us a primary rather than a post hoc classification of the elementary ego functions as obtained from psychopathology. He says that the identifying of language disturbance should thus prove a less ambiguous sign of ego disturbance than the customary psychoanalytic case.

2. In the recent phase of psychoanalysis as a science, inquiry into child development has become of paramount importance. Rosen found and demonstrated a striking *correlation between the ontogenesis of personality development and the development of language* in the child ontogenetically, and probably in the evolution of language phylogenetically.

Man is nurtured in a language-permeated environment. He does not exist as a human outside the human community. The recent view of the genetic transmission of the language faculty, or more exactly, the grammatic faculty, is an impressive datum (Lennenberg, 1964; Wolff, 1967). Rosen sought to demonstrate that the maturation process along the lines of individuation, object relations, and the development of secondary process autonomy goes hand in hand with the progression of the language faculty as developed within the mother-child interaction and social interaction, resulting in the acquisition of speech and language.

In the context of the mother-child relationship, the world of objects is cathected and reality is internalized and integrated. The speech of the mother in the communicative and training activity is instrumental in the growth of the child's intelligence as it increasingly perceives the symbolic and syntactic components of the mother's speech. Thus, "earliest word symbols are fused not only with the referent but with the mother" (Chapter 6).

Here Rosen refers to the formulation of Werner and Kaplan (1963). They present two hypotheses that may make this point more concrete. First, regarding the genesis of the language symbol, they see the symbol "formed when mother, child, and referential object become differentiated out of an initially undifferentiated matrix (from the infant's point of view). By going through a similar and parallel process of tripartite differentiation, the 'designation' of the object subsequently becomes a full-fledged representation, i.e., a symbol." Secondly, "out of the common matrix with a shared object . . . follows not only a progressive polarization or distancing between mother and child, but simultaneously a *distancing* between symbolic vehicle (word) and the object for which it stands. . . ."

Individuation—the differentiation between self and object in the developmental process—goes hand in hand with the highest and solely human development of the language faculty, which is characterized by the symbolizing-categorizing function. By this we mean "the representation of classes and relations in linguistic symbols" (Rapaport, 1951a) and also the categorization of "the world of everyday objects" (Cofer, 1961). Furthermore, the socializing implication of the use of language symbols rather than signs and signals is "the prodigious increase in the number of individuals reached and . . . in the range and precision of information" (Chapter 5).

The defective language development in symbiotic children suggests "the extent to which mother-child separation and language development are interdependent" (Chapter 5). The mother, through the prominent role of language in her relationship to and communication with the child, communicates to it the social essence of membership in the community. Withdrawal from object is tantamount to withdrawal from the language community, the regression to preintellectual language and preverbal thought (untying the "Vygotsky knot"). This effect is the schizophrenic process as it operates in the language function, as discussed in Rosen's reexamination (Chapter 6) of Freud's theory of schizophrenic language.

3. Rosen's work is replete with clinical investigations from which he derives clinical theory based on concepts stemming from the *integration of psychoanalytic and psycholinguistic observations and explanations*. As might be expected, his most impressive formulations are based on the communication process in the psychoanalytic situation. Here reoccur the early stages of language learning, with the patient and analyst seeking clues to each other's meaning, in which is reflected and recapitulated the progression from the prestage of language—that is, from the utilization of signs and signals in parent-infant communication to the advanced stage of the use of words with the ability to use "similes." To use Rosen's illustration: "That one (over there) is also a dog like the one in the picture book." In the early stage the ability to use "contiguity" is attained. To use Rosen's example again: "This one (here) is a dog" establishes an "ostensive contiguity." Rosen also indicates that this progression in language development corresponds to the maturation of the personality in the individuation process.

In the psychoanalytic situation there is a reciprocal intercommunication between teacher and pupil or patient and analyst. This reciprocity in communication, conditioned as it is by the language-thought relativity, in some ways also affects transference-countertransference. Rosen writes: "The communication styles as well as disturbances of communication . . . stem from preoedipal influences—frequently rigid patterns indicative of early fixations or 'developmental conflicts' which occurred during individuation struggles."

The communication style is likewise bound to the language style, so that some patients (and analysts) are deficient in "similes" in the encoding-decoding process, the similes corresponding "to the speaker's act of encoding thoughts into words." These individuals are "active" in the psychoanalytic situation in the sense that they want to do the analysing themselves. They are consequently less receptive in the learning situation. For these patients episodic narrative cannot exist when links are based solely on "similarity."

Rosen contrasts this group to a group deficient in "contiguities". These patients are "passive" in the analytic situation. They are deficient in their ability to tell a story clearly (Chapter 5). This is one instance in which omission of information, rather than being defensive, is a built-in characteristic of communication. Lack of awareness of language styles in the patient or in himself would blind the analyst in a way comparable to his scotomata due to his repression of emotional conflicts.

The preceding is meant merely to serve as an illustration of the heuristic value of focusing psycholinguistic and psychoanalytic theory on the same psychological problem. Amazingly, what Rosen achieves here is the *core* of psychoanalytic learning theory.

Elsewhere Rosen notes that in analysis it may be possible to reconstruct the process of language learning in early childhood, a process which cannot be investigated by direct observation. Psychoanalysis would in this way pay its debt to psycholinguistics.

Rosen wrote much on psychoanalytic interpretation throughout his career. It is in this area (listening to and decoding free association), which was his greatest interest as a psychoanalyst, that he tested the usefulness of language theory and psycholinguistics to psychoanalysis. In his 1967 paper he omits, regretfully, a psycholinguistic treatment of free association, a language phenomenon empirically well known to analysts, the "process" psychology of which, however, has received little study. Rosen said that only in free association do we observe certain kinds of verbal communication in which the defects are in the language function rather than in ego defenses. Comprehending this would increase our therapeutic effectiveness as well as extend our knowledge of the ontogenesis of language and communication. "All analyses seem to . . . partake of the early experiences in the development of verbal communication" (Chapter 5).

Rosen gives clinical illustrations of the linguistic styles that mold, limit, and condition the patient's free association. But challenging the art and science of interpretation is "the intimate connection between language and thought, distinguishing language structured by an idea from an idea that is given its form by language" (Chapter 5). (Note here Rosen's limited acceptance of the Sapir-Whorf concept of language relativity, in which language is primary.)

4. Rosen's last papers were a bold and penetrating *epistemological inquiry into psychoanalysis as a scientific theory*. His is a compelling and powerful critique. He focused primarily on an evaluation of interpretation, using language theory as a testing ground. Psychology deals not with stimuli as causes, as they are dealt with in the natural sciences, but rather with the mental representation, above all with the "meaning" of stimuli, "meaning" in the sense of what is "purposed" or "intended."

Psychoanalysis and psycholinguistics are based on the principle of "entailment" or experiential data of observation, rather than on causality. Thus true statements in psychoanalysis are not causal propositions but "entailment propositions"—that is, statements about historical or symbolic events that can be tested by the rules of definition or classification. For example, "the paralysis is caused by hysteria" has the form of a causal proposition but is incorrect because it can only be stated as an entailment proposition. However, "the paralysis is caused by peripheral neuritis" is properly cast as a causal proposition (Chapter 10). Here is another example: a psychoanalyst studying the intensity of the orgasm in dreams would properly deal with the subject-aim-object fantasies rather than with the physiological stimuli that produced the cognitive experience of orgastic pleasure (Chapter 9).

I would say that the distinction between the focus of psychoanalysis on the one hand and of academic psychology and psycholinguistics on the other is that the former concerns itself with *wishing* and the latter with *knowing*. With the exception of behaviorism, academic psychology and psycholinguistics lend themselves to the study of cognition and semantics, whereas psychoanalysis offers the best approach to the study of such intercommunicative aspects as the emotive. As Rosen emphasized, both ultimately deal with "meaning." The exclusion of either approach limits a full comprehension of the subject. Rosen has done much to put them under the same roof and in many respects to integrate them.

This confluence of psychoanalysis and psycholinguistics together with other sciences seeking to comprehend man as a social being would bring us to a fuller comprehension of the human situation, as well as to the achievement of a psychoanalytic social psychology.

In his humorous essay, "Psychoanalysis and the Community,"

Rosen worte, "If I have conveyed the impression that there could be more relating between the analytic and the nonanalytic community than now exists I will have achieved my purpose." Victor Rosen took a great stride toward attaining that goal.

But he has done more than promote interdisciplinary study. Earlier we had asked whether psychoanalytic ego psychology stands to gain from greater knowledge of the mediation processes, which needs the help of other psychological disciplines. Victor Rosen has not only demonstrated that the necessity exists but he has done much to fulfill that need. His work proclaims psychoanalysis as an open-ended science that stands on the threshold of posing ever new questions and, if necessary, introduces new means to find the answers. A new era lies ahead for psychoanalysis if we can follow his example.

Notes

1. I take responsibility also for that part of this essay in which I try to convey Rosen's theses in my own words and in introducing my own concepts, derived largely from my participation in the Language Study Group.

2. Shapiro points out that the language of the group is a determinant in the form of the thought of the group, and this has an important bearing in the transformation of the idiolect into the dialect of a member of the linguistic group.

3. Levi-Strauss (1966) puts linguistic relativity and its possible connection with psychoanalysis thus: "Language is human reasons which has its reasons of which man knows nothing."

4. Shapiro demurs that "trial action" is an ontogenetic principle with relation to primitive reflex arc reactions. (This theory relates psychoanalysis to behaviorism.)

5. Language Study Group minutes, October 30, 1966 (unpublished).

6. According to Vygotsky (1934), "egocentric speech" is a transition from the interpsychic (social communication) to the intrapsychic (individual action-thinking process), a pattern of development common to all the higher psychological functions. "Speech for oneself originates from speech for others." Note the correlation between the process of introjection-identification and the socialization facts and the process alluded to in this brief quotation. This formulation of the developmental transition from social communication (interpsychic speech) to intrapsychic (inner) speech parallels the psychoanalytic proposition of internalization (introjection, identification), and the establishment of such internal discourse suggests differentiation within the ego (intrasystemic) and communication between the ego and superego (intersystemic).

7. Allowing that the psychoanalytic use of id symbols is appropriate to primary process thinking, there still remains a gaping discrepancy between psychoanalytic id symbolism and

language symbolism. It may help to offer several definitions of psychoanalytic id symbolism: Lili Peller states, "A symbol in the psychoanalytic sense refers to an image carrying an affect that in the deepest strata belongs to something else." These she called "primordial symbols." Ferenczi states, "Only such things (or ideas) are symbols in the sense of psychoanalysis as are invested in consciousness with a logically inexplicable and unfounded affect . . . which they owe . . . to unconscious identification with another thing (or idea) to which the surplus of affect really belongs." Henry Edelheit adds further clarification. He states, "*Primordial* symbols are seemingly derived from body parts and body functions, especially the functions of the erotic zones. We associate them with primary process and see them spontaneously coming into being in dreams, fantasies, and symptoms. They are concrete, nonarbitrary, and remarkably limited in form and content (through subject to infinite variation in detail)."

8. Edelheit (1968), reporting on Edward Stankiewics, writes, "Language serves to communicate affect in a uniquely human way through the 'emotive' (as distinct from the emotional) utilization of situationally independent symbols." These two aspects of language must be kept in mind, although they are synthesized into a fully formed functional system serving a gamut of psychic uses.

9. This guide proved useful in demonstrating a specific language manifestation of the disturbed cognitive faculty in a borderline case (Atkin, 1974, 1975).

10. Language Study Group minutes September, 29, 1964 (unpublished).

11. Language Study Group minutes January 11, 1965 (unpublished).

12. Vygotsky (1934) posits a preverbal and a preintellectual stage in early development which become fused—Hence the "Vygotsky knot."

13. This idea finds expression in Freud's statement: "No influence . . . can ever enable us to think without purposive ideas" (Freud, 1900, p. 528). Shapiro informed us that recently psycholinguistics and psychoanalysis have converged in their concepts in "the current growing interest of psycholinguistics in speech acts with its accordant interest in intentionality."

CHAPTER ONE

Mathematical Thought Process and Abstract Thinking

Fontenelle has said: "Mathematicians are like lovers. . . . Grant a mathematician the least principle, and he will draw from it a consequence which you must also grant him and from this consequence another." Ernst Mach in a less poetic vein adds: "The power of mathematics rests on its evasion of all unnecessary thought and on its wonderful saving of mental operations" (Bell, 1937).

The present chapter is an attempt to bring together certain observations concerning the psychological process of "pure" mathematics and to formulate them in terms of the economic and structural concepts of psychoanalytic theory. That data is derived largely from the analysis of a gifted young graduate student in mathematics who is also suffering from a so-called strephosymbolia in reading and writing. The analysis of several episodes of mathematical "illumination" has given rise to the present thesis.

Pure mathematics is a creative process that stands midway between the arts and sciences. It attempts to conceptualize according to its own set of rigorous rules the properties of number and space that are too complex or beyond the ken of immediate apprehension by the sensory-perceptual apparatus. The following theoretical concepts will be developed: The concept of number arises normally in connection with certain stages of the maturation of the perception apparatus during the oedipal period. In those with a special mathematical "gift" it is probable that this maturational sequence takes place at an earlier period in ego development so that along with the precocious concepts of number and quantity there remain certain archaic ego defense mechanisms which later are utilized in the creative aspect of the process. A large part of the ordinary process of mathematical thought in these gifted individuals is preconscious and utilizes a capacity for decathexis of the conscious perceptual system. The illumination experience is a creative act, as is inspiration in other fields, and utilizes the ego's capacity for controlled regression to unformalized, infantile modes of perceiving space and number. It is a highly overdetermined psychic event which involves all three structural systems as well as the subject's historical individuality.

The author is in no way specially prepared to deal either with the content of mathematics itself nor with the philosophical problems that surround this field. Within the scope of the present formulation this is not a major barrier. It places some limits upon assessing the objective importance of any work done in the field of mathematics by the patient. The evidence that at very least he is highly gifted has been his winning of a mathematics prize and his enrollment for his doctorate in a leading university where requirements in this field are stringent. One can feel sure of these minimal attainments on his part, although the future may prove that his gifts should be rated more highly.

The term *pure* as a modifier of mathematics deserves some attention. It is used here in the obvious sense of denoting one whose interest, like that of Archimedes (Bell, 1937), is centered only upon the properties of number and space, within the framework of necessity imposed by the logic of mathematics itself, without any concern for how, or by whom, it may be utilized. It is also applicable in the psychological sense in which it is referred to by Ella Sharpe (1950) when she states that "the pinnacles of genius . . . are only attained by those who, if the circumstances so fell out, would pursue their unconsciously determined goals to the verge of starvation. . . . The 'pure' scientist is as detached from the exigences of practical life as is the 'pure' artist."

As so often happens in other attempts to separate elements in a highly complex function, the best glimpse is often afforded when a pathological specimen of the phenomenon is studied. In the case about to be reported, the mathematical function stands out as a figure against a background of symptom formation. A similar study has been made by Hermann (1924, 1926, 1929, 1949, 1950) without recourse to analytic case material. Jones (1931) has studied a comparable problem in his fascinating reconstruction of the case of the chess player, Paul Morphy, but with interest centering primarily upon the instinctual contributions rather than the ego aspects of chess.

Case Report

In the case about to be reported there were two episodes of sudden illumination of mathematical problems. These occurred in contexts that made it possible to analyze some of the genetic and economic factors involved. The first was connected with a term thesis that dealt with a certain aspect of Reimannian geometry. The patient needed a certain book on mathematics which was out of print in order to find a forgotten theorem that was necessary for his proof. Instead of going to the university mathematics library (where he was not a student at the time) he wrote to his father in a distant city requesting that he send him the book. When the package arrived one morning in the mail he had a sudden inspiration for a short-cut method of reaching the same result by an original method without even removing the wrapping. On another occasion the patient had been disappointed by his girl friend at the last minute in a date to go to the theater on his birthday. While brooding about this episode one night shortly before going to sleep, it suddenly occurred to him that the interval integer for all Goldbach's pairs over the number five were divisible by six. (A Goldbach pair consists of two prime numbers separated by one integer, e.g., 5 and 7; 11 and 13, etc.) The pair of dreams following this episode of minor illumination will be discussed later in the case report. The history of the patient follows:

When the patient was first seen three years ago he was a twenty-one-year-old student of mathematics who was about to enter graduate school for his doctoral training. He first became aware of psychological difficulties in the winter of 1950 when he was declared ineligible for the draft because of "neurotic difficulties." At that time he expressed his difficulties as follows: "I seem to get periods of panic. I have a confusion about life values. I am particularly concerned about my failure to talk to girls on an ordinary human level. I seem to keep a great distance from them. It gives me a sense of social isolation. I seem to want to idealize women and get to know them better, but if a girl begins to like me I seem to do everything possible to make her feel that I am detached and uninterested. At other times I get all mixed up with women I don't really care for." In addition he felt that a rather severe reading and spelling difficulty that dated from his earliest school years might also be of psychological origin. It had been called on several occasions during his childhood, "a strephosymbolia due to a double reading center." It had always been implied that this was an inborn defect that could only be overcome by training. Without being able to read more quickly or to spell more accurately he feared that he might be held back from achieving his academic goals.

The patient was referred for analysis following a consultation with a colleague and a painstaking diagnostic workup. The result of this study, however, left the precise diagnostic classification in doubt. Some of the data in the psychological test battery suggested a latent psychosis. In spite of the malignant potentialities suggested, it was felt after several weeks of vis-a-vis sessions, that a classical analytic technique could be tolerated. In three years of this procedure there has been no evidence of any disturbance of reality testing.

The patient is the youngest of three siblings, coming from an old American family of wealth and respected standing in the community in which he was born. For two generations before the patient's birth, the men on the paternal side of the family have been able to follow rather specialized and narrow fields of scientific endeavor without any concern for the practical problems of earning a living because of the wealth handed down by the paternal grandfather in a carefully guarded trust of "gilt-edge securities." Several members of the family, including the father, have high academic rank in leading universities. The tradition among them is to return their salaries as donations to the university.

The patient grew up with the feeling that the opportunity to pursue scholarly research is sufficient compensation in itself and that the possession of wealth places a great burden of social responsibility for the contribution of creative or original work. At the age of twenty-one he had come into an income which could be expected to make him financially secure for all ordinary eventualities for the rest of his life.

From early infancy the patient is said to have been a very sensitive child. At an early age he had shown extreme intolerance of loud noises. There has been a lifelong interest in music and the building of high fidelity record players of ever increasing refinement. At the age of three he was subjected to a flashbulb exposure during the taking of an indoor family photograph. It is said that his eyes teared and appeared reddened for several days thereafter. One of his present complaints is still a marked photophobia especially on awakening in the morning. At the age of fourteen he complained of being able to see floating specks in his peripheral areas of vision and a diagnosis of "drusen" due to floating vitreous opacities was made by an opthalmologist. Glasses are worn for myopia. A curious game of "playing with his visual accommodation" was also recounted during the analysis. This consists of being able to make both near and fairly distant objects blur and come back into sharp focus at will. (This data is presented because it is felt that it has a bearing upon the selectivity of attention which is part of the precocious acquiring of the number concept. This will be discussed below.) On one occasion it was a source of almost missing an analytic session when he failed to read the street numbers correctly from the bus.

The patient's first dream was reported in this third session on the couch:

> I am lying on a bed in a darkened room with a window at one end of it which is lighted as if from the street. I am considering whether I should masturbate. Suddenly from behind the drape next to the window, I see silhouetted against the light the figure of my father.

The patient recalled that as a child around the age of four or five, he had had a severe pavor nocturnus. A night light used to be left burning in his room. He recalled that on many occasions when he was about five years of age he was suddenly no longer allowed into his mother's bed and the night terrors disappeared shortly after this. Different versions of this experience presented themselves at various times. In one which had the clearest implications of a screen memory, he finds his mother's bed is empty except for a pillow left under the covers to simulate a body. The dream appeared to focus upon several problems. The appearance of the father from behind a drape refers to scoptophilic primal scene interests with special reference to father's erection (the silhouette). The light from the street and the window to direct primal scene curiosity and its replacement by curiosity in the intellectual sphere. This latter is suggested in the reference to the delay in instinctual gratification. "I am *considering* whether I should masturbate." The dream appears to refer, therefore, to the process of sublimation and the turning of the night light of the pavor nocturnus into intellectual light.

In the early phase of the analysis, the patient presented the picture of an aloof, inhibited, young man with an exaggerated elegant politeness and a somewhat unbending aristocratic bearing. There was considerable loosening up of his behavior as the treatment progressed so that he became capable of laughter and occasional humor. He is tall and thin with what can best be described as a typical "scholar's pallor." He speaks with a full varied vocabulary and expresses himself well. Intellectualization was a favorite defense with a preference for generalizations on philosophical and aesthetic themes. Specific data concerning events and persons were obtained at first with the greatest difficulty. The patient's polite tones took on a disparaging quality whenever he had occasion to refer to his parents, particularly his father. His older sisters were always treated with considerable sympathy as if they were all companions in misery and objects of parental misunderstanding like himself. The first picture of the father obtained was that of a cold, detached scientist, closeted in his study with little time for his children. His field of study dealt with inanimate objects for which he is said to have had a greater affection than for his children. The patient says of him: "I am certain that he neither knew how, nor had time, to beget children—we were probably conceived by artificial insemination." Although this disparagement appeared on the surface to be directed toward the father's many idiosyncrasies and petty foibles the underlying feeling was one of having been rejected by him. He accused his father of paying little attention to his (the patient's) mathematical attainments. This he attributed to his father's envy and his inability to countenance an intellectual rival in his home. He took pains to read me his father's letters to demonstrate the commonplace quality of the content and the failure on his father's part to attempt any interchange of ideas with him. He complained frequently of his father's inability to listen to him because of preoccupation with his own thoughts. "We only speak to each other in terse phrases about immediate everyday matters." Later in the analysis the father began to appear as a man given to violent outbursts of temper, toward whom the rest of the family was forced to adopt a constant placating and conciliatory attitude. The mother has appeared variously as a good woman without any intellectual interests; as a woman interested in poetry, gardening, and literature; and at other times as a bustling, inefficient creature who expended her energy on too many tasks and who, in attempting to organize the lives of her relatives, produced great disorganization in her own life. Although expressing great concern for his physical needs, she usually forgot his specific requests. During one winter, he had written home requesting a pair of woolen gloves (it is quite possible that parts of the letter were not legible). When his mother failed to supply the gloves he went around for the rest of the winter with exposed hands pointing out the fact that his knuckles had become reddened and cracked. He seemed to enjoy the Spartan quality of his suffering and preferred the mute testimony to his mother's neglect to the procuring of gloves. It has always angered him to have to remind his mother to do something for him.

During the first few sessions of the treatment the patient brought small samples of his creative productions: poems in free verse, small drawings and abstract sculpture, made with wire and solder. An example of one of his poems, with his spelling errors retained, follows:

> Community! We honor the community,
> It is a bit of stale bred and some red wine.
> They speak of things earnestly, long and tedes.
> There heds all wage in unisen, community.
> Democracy and ruls of order fill their minds.
> Edicts are reaffermed by the majority.
> The word that rattle's on thick lips: community.

In all of these offerings the patient had the conscious purpose of saying that, to him, aside from mathematics only art was important. In all of his artistic productions sound and form take precedence over meaning. Along with his interest in poetry and art went a great love of music, particularly Bach. On several occasions he described the marked hypnagogic effect which listening to music had upon him. "It was like sinking back into a soft wave." With the cessation of the sound he often found himself "coming to, with a feeling of being startled." There was considerable sensitivity to the timbre and quality of voice sounds and the literary style of speech. The unconscious purpose of bringing his artistic productions was to elicit in me the interest his father withheld from him.

There appeared to be a close connection between his artistic interests and his falling in love. His first crush occurred in the last year in high school. The girl was an intellectual, somewhat older than the patient for whom he had a "pure and tender love from a great distance." He never revealed his feelings and it was some time before he could get up the courage to talk to this young woman at all. His second romantic attachment occurred in the first year of college. This girl was also older; a statistician who cared very little for the usual college social life. Their relationship consisted of long walks and was nurtured on concerts, philosophy, and art exhibits. Part of her attraction for the patient was that "she did not make me feel as if I were in competition with the usual 'Ivy League' stereotype." The patient became depressed and felt himself betrayed when the girl announced her engagement to another boy. A second similar attempted romance with a classmate whom he considered an intellectual equal, although in a different field from his own, also ended in an acute disappointment. This was followed by a series of minor romances with "empty-headed girls" whom the patient succeeded in "overpowering with my mind," quickly losing interest when the girls showed any evidence of responding to him.

The patient began his schooling with kindergarten in his fifth year. It took several months before his mother was able to leave him alone in school. The first and second grades of school seem to have gone fairly well. He has a relative amnesia for the third and fourth grades. These were apparently the years in which subsequent reading and spelling performance tests reveal that he had the greatest learning difficulty. From his fifth year on the patient left school during the other children's play period and was driven in his chauffeured car across town, where a special tutor attempted to help him catch up in his reading and spelling without much success. These attempts continued in college where the patient spent two summers at a reading clinic. The test curves in reading and spelling performance (Blanchard, 1947; Pearson, 1952) reveal an initial average level with a sharp drop at the third and fourth year levels and a gradual rise in the spelling and reading of eighth and ninth grade words. First attempts to teach him to read were by the word and picture recognition method. Later it was found that he could do somewhat better when the phonetic method was substituted.

The patient's arithmetical abilities were well in advance of his years. At the age of nine he could use a slide rule accurately for complex arithmetical computations. He has very little recollection of being taught arithmetic and his talent in this field was unnoticed and more or less overshadowed by the reading deficit. His mathematical ability was not discovered until the eighth grade when the patient was allowed to go ahead of the class in plane geometry and later in algebra, both of which he mastered in an unusually short time. During this period of his schooling a striking character change was also noted. Previously a shy and timid child who was usually found on the periphery of the group, he became more assertive in his class relationships and was sometimes thought of as arrogant toward the less advanced students with a tendency to use his learning in an overbearing manner.

Mathematical and alphabetical content have appeared rather frequently in his dreams. The first such dream was reported after the patient had begun his first overtly sexual affair with a young woman who was also in analysis. This consisted of mutual masturbation. He felt a great deal of guilt over this affair and had constant arguments and disagreements with the young woman. Although he talked freely about his partner, he refused for a long time to disclose the name of her analyst. Subsequent material indicated clearly that the girl represented a sister figure (the younger and belittled sister) while the other analyst clearly represented a maternal figure. She was in fact a woman. The clear wish in this acting out was to prevent the sexual union of the parental figures behind the backs of their children. In this setting the following dream was recounted:

> I am sitting on the floor and see a snapping turtle through a crack in the door of a room. It is my job to keep the turtle in the room, but it seemed to force its way out despite my vigilance.

In a second dream the same night:

> I see a small "e" to the "x" power times an equation. I realize that I should factor it out and that "e" to the "x" power is a psychoanalyst which must be taken into account in each factor.

This dream occurred shortly after the episode of sudden illumination of the problem in Reimannian geometry when his father's book came in the mail. This solution had in fact involved the sudden realization that a factoring operation was involved. (It is important to recall that factoring is, in effect, the recognition of two or more antecedent quantities which produce a certain product by multiplication.)

As a child the patient had thought that all turtles were snapping turtles but was fascinated by them and liked to keep one in a pail. The turtle also reminded him of an individual who retires into his own shell and shuts out the world (like father). He has noticed that turtles blink in the sun and has associated this to the darkness within their shells and to his own photophobia on exposure to bright light. Turtles can see the outside world while themselves remaining unseen. The crack in the door referred to early peeping experiences at his sisters. The room recalled his own bedroom at home, and his mother's practice of watching him through a crack in the door when he first went to kindergarten, because of his terror at being left by her. His vigilance at keeping something from coming out referred to recent sexual experiences. The revelation of his sexual urges could be tolerated within the privacy of my office. If I knew the name of his girl's analyst we might discuss him behind his back. This apparently referred to the frequently mentioned fantasy that his parents regard him as an asexual being and would be shocked to discover that he has erotic feelings (a complete reversal of the true state of affairs). In the second dream the small "e" is a constant, the base of the logarithmic table.

The "x" power in addition to the obvious "unknown quantity" referred to an X-ray examination and the penetrating power of X-rays. The radiologist had walked around his office wearing a pair of red goggles. He felt that this was either an exhibitionistic affection on his part or for the purpose of protecting the physician's eyes from the noxious effects of radiation. Although he had made the observation that the radiologist removed the red goggles while doing fluoroscopy, he had forgotten this detail because it would have necessitated a revision of his hypothesis in a direction that was unacceptable; namely that the goggles were for the purpose of obviating the need for reaccommodation each time the radiologist went from the light into the dark room. The suppressed observation later led to problems of seeing in the dark, his early pavor nocturnus and primal scene fantasies. The dream is presented to indicate the relationship of the illumination experience to the primal scene problem. " 'e' to the 'x' power is a psychoanalyst who must be taken into account in each factor." In the transference two analysts must be kept separate and unknown to each other. In the solution to the problem it is suddenly realized that two factors go into the formation of a certain product.

Two themes are referred to which are of importance for the development of the theoretical formulations which will follow: the first refers to the selective use of perception in the service of drive and defense in scoptophilic fantasies, and the second to the narcissistic withdrawal from the real darkness and light surrounding the functional relationships of parental objects and their investment in the neutral symbols and relationships of mathematical invention.

The use of projection and narcissistic withdrawal was illustrated by a series of mirror dreams. The following is an example:

> I am in the garden at home with B. A woman's voice is directing me. She is short and blonde. She was walking on a stone path away from me. I find myself looking through a glass window which is also a mirror. She appears to have a disease and the glass indicates that it is verboten to get closer. I write to her on the window backwards and to the left so that she can read it without having to reverse the words. I recall the letters "e," "r" and "w." It is like writing with soap on a looking glass. On the other side there is a garden party. The garden is filled with elegant people. Someone is commenting about my parents in French and Russian.

The letters remind him of his reading and spelling defect. These are some of the letters that he most frequently omits or inserts in the errors encountered in both reading and spelling. The looking glass reminds him of Lewis Carroll who was also a mathematician. When Alice looked through the glass one room was warm and homey and the other side of the glass was cold and strange. As a child he was very much interested in women's clothes and liked to watch his mother's dressmaker put things on the dressmaker's dummy. The soap refers to masturbatory practices. Coldness is one of his complaints against his mother. The written word is for communication with people who are gone or at a distance. Writing refers to his love letters which are elegant but devoid of any real warmth. Written words are like eternal things. The two rooms also refer to his parents' bedrooms. As long as the patient could remember they always occupied separate rooms. Elegance refers to a mathematical proof which excludes unnecessary steps and to a quality which he attributes to his paternal grandparents and which he feels is lacking in his own parents.

This and other "mirror" dreams suggested one of the central meanings of this pavor nocturnus: At the age of two or three the patient's care was given over largely to a *Fraulein*, the short blonde woman of the dream. This must have been experienced as a rejection by his mother, and his clinging to his mother was intensified thereafter. The experience of awakening in his mother's bed after a nightmare to find not his mother but a pillow lying next to him under the covers was the screen memory covering his feeling of rejection by her. He referred to this as "a shameful hoax to play on a small child." The night terror consisted of a sudden awakening and rushing down the hall to his mother's room. During the oedipal phase the object of the visit was to determine that each parent was safe in his respective bedroom. The reserve of the parents with each other and the children and the absence of any overt display of physical tenderness were all woven by the patient into a sadistic masturbatory fantasy of parental intercourse as an act performed at a distance "by artificial insemination." This fantasy is reproduced in his own complaint of distance from women and the "inability to meet them on an ordinary human level."

The complex interrelation of his positive and negative oedipal strivings is further elaborated in another series of dreams which bears upon another episode of mathematical illumination. During the second year of the analysis the patient had begun to have intercourse with a young woman who also had "rather overt manifestations of Lesbian tendencies." He was remarkably tolerant of her relations with other women, however. Several months after the beginning of this affair the young woman refused to continue their sexual relationship. On one occasion she had "stood him up" on his birthday. The patient became depressed and sought solace in attempting to work out a problem in number theory which eluded him. He had a series of dreams following this episode. These dreams illustrate among other problems his selective lack of attention to details of feminine importance, his rejection of his own femininity, his rejection by women because of this inattention and his defense against the affects produced by a retreat into mathematical thinking.

> I am lying on an operating table. There is a rubber tube in my urethra. Some nurses are pouring plaster of paris into the tube to make a cast of the urethra. I am afraid that when they pull it out it will be very painful and there will be a destruction of tissue.

On the previous day the patient had had an impression taken of his mouth for some dental work. The rubber tube referred to a description he had once heard of a catherization which always made him shudder. He is amazed at how unabashed he feels when exposed in front of nurses. This is in marked contrast to his difficulty in talking to me about sexual problems. The white cast was associated to tampax that he had seen in his girl's bathroom the previous week but only after I had suggested the similarity. The patient was reminded of his almost total unawareness of the female menstrual cycle, although he could discuss it learnedly from courses in biology.

During this period of the analysis the patient had been coming to his session immediately following another patient who was in her eighth month of pregnancy. On the day following the "urethral" dream he reported the following pair of dreams:

> I am lying on a bed next to a woman. We are both naked and reading books. The woman has a cold and we feel no sexual

> attraction for each other. I am reading the "Gospel According to St. John" from the Bible.
>
> In the second dream there are no visual images. There are thoughts about number theory. I realize that numbers can be divided into three groups on the basis of the sum of their divisors.

The patient had been reading the "Gospel According to St. John" that evening. It had also occurred to him suddenly on this same evening that the number between a "Goldbach pair" beginning with five was always divisible by six. Although this was not a particularly productive illumination it made him feel "contented" when the proof "gradually unfolded" itself for him. He wanted to tell me about it on the following day, since it was "too small a matter" to bring to his professor of mathematics. His association to St. John was that he counseled meditation and told the parable of Christ's protection of the adulterous woman. He had noticed that the patient who came before him had a cold. He speculated humorously on the source of her infection. Grouping numbers on the basis of the sum of their divisors produces three number groups; those where the sum is less than the number, more than the number, or equal to the number itself. The numbers in this last group are called "pure" numbers. He had not felt so bitter about "L.'s" refusal of sexual relations after the solution of the number theorem. He associated the Goldbach pair and the intervening number to the family triangle (the former are the parents, the latter the child). The third presents three pairing possibilities: father and mother; mother and child, and father and child. At the end of the session the patient was startled when I pointed out to him that he had completely suppressed the observation of the previous patient's pregnancy.

Both dreams refer to passive feminine wishes which play a large role in the illumination process. The rejection of his own femininity plays an important role in his distance from love objects. It had never occurred to the patient that when his girl friend had denied him intercourse, she might have been menstruating. The substitution of thinking (the "meditation" of St. John[1]) for erotic feeling is illustrated in the theorem concerning the Goldbach's pairs. This was interpreted as a gift to the analyst (in this case a paternal figure) in which the patient plays the feminine role.

The patient's study habits are also of considerable interest and have a relationship to the structure of the childhood pavor nocturnus. He has a marked preference for doing his mathematical work during the hours of darkness. On many occasions he has begun to work in the early evening and has had the experience of suddenly noticing that it was morning. It is not unusual for him to have intense periods of concentration on mathematical work lasting as long as fourteen hours during which he is unaware of hunger, fatigue, or the stimuli arising from a full bladder. He is unaware of any desire to sleep during such periods and has a mild elation. In part his study habits are an identification with his father who worked late into the night. But the marked inhibition of any desire to work at mathematics during the daylight hours suggests an association between the resolution of the early pavor nocturnus and the hypercathexis of intellectual functioning.

The results of the patient's analysis to date can be summarized as follows: There has been a greater capacity for spontaneity in personal relationships. He has been able to engage in an active, although disturbed, heterosexual relationship. There has been definite improvement in his reading and writing ability, especially in the speed of reading and the accuracy of spelling which was his most burdensome academic handicap.

Lastly, I would like to extract a few pertinent details from the observations made in the psychological test battery.[2] In the subtests the patient revealed a considerable scatter of his abilities from perfect arithmetic ability to an extrememly low score on the similarities which related to his insistence on handling each answer in a highly personalized and, in some cases, symbolic manner. In the Rorschach material "three extremely unusual features in his actual perceptual experience" are noted. The first is "so rare that it has been noted by the tester in only two cases examined by the stress tolerance test among battle casualties." This is a synesthesia involving visual stimuli and sound. The patient hears the sound given by the impression of "fighting cats" in one of the cards. In the second type of dysesthetic response he sees a bright yellow sky on a card which presents only black and white stimuli. A third unusual dysesthesia is seen in the attributing the quality of darkness to the white spaces of some of the cards. Over and above these perceptual deviations the tester finds a bizarre quality to the content of the Rorschach material. The patient takes great pains to give unusual responses. There is an emphasis on oral and anal characteristics (see Brill, 1940). An animal is seen eating and defecating at the same time (cf. also Strachey, 1930) or "breaking through portals and leaving something behind it on its trail." The response to color is described as "symbolic." The patient sees "day and night" in the red and blue of one card. The tester felt that there was a marked insufficiency of "garden variety" responses. The tests were interpreted as containing potentialities for unusual talents as well as psychosis.

The Role of the Preconscious Process

Of necessity the data derived from the patient is presented in outline and in fragmentary form. In order not to be taken too far afield, the reading and spelling disability, which constitutes a fascinating clinical problem in its own right, is only being considered in so far as it bears upon the present problem.

Most of academic psychology in the past has attempted to study calculation and mathematical thinking at a purely conscious and descriptive level (Adler, 1933; Barlow, 1952; Binet, 1894; Grau, 1937; Hahn, 1927; Ioteyko, 1910; Jakobsson, 1944; Kommerell, 1928; LaFora, 1935; Menzerath, 1913; Moebus, 1907; Oehl, 1952; Scherer, Rothman, and Goldstein, 1945; Ravina, 1946). This usually leads to a reworking of the content of the mathematical process itself into verbal form or an attempt to find a qualitatively different use of perceptual imagery and memory in calculators or mathematicians (Binet, 1894; Scherer et al., 1945).

The observations concerning the preconscious aspects of the mathematical process came first not from the psychologists but from the introspective observations of the mathematicians themselves. Helmholtz and Gauss first spoke of the quality of "revelation" in mathematical creation. Poincaré's (1952, 1952a) ideas in this connection are of particular interest. The mathematician Hadamard (1945) was stimulated by these observations to attempt an organized theory of the psychology of mathematical invention. He implicitly recognizes the preconscious aspects of much goal-directed problem-solving activity, as did Poincaré.

Kris (1950), in considering the problem-solving functions of ego, says,

> The automatic functions of the ego are commonly considered to include a special kind of preconscious process which becomes conscious only in case of danger or under other special requirements. Consciousness in these instances is no guarantee of improved function; on the contrary, automatic (habit) responses in driving automobiles, or the use of tools for instance, seem to have undoubted advantages. Similarly the shift from consciousness to preconsciousness may account for the experience of clarification that occurs when after intense concentration the solution to an insoluble problem suddenly presents itself following a period of rest. *Briefly, we suggest that hypercathexis of preconscious mental activity with some quantity of energy withdrawn from the object world to the ego—from the system pcpt. to preconscious thinking—* accounts for some of the extraordinary achievements of mentation.

Piaget (1952) in a most beautiful experimental study of the stages of the development of the conception of number demonstrates several facts of considerable importance. The true conceptualization of number is quite distinct from the process of the mere verbal reproduction of integers (see also Costa, 1950; Hermann, 1949; and Schilder, 1936, 1942). The ability to comprehend the crude notion of quantity begins at about the age of four and proceeds in three fairly definite stages. The final stage in which the quantitatively exact notion of number is finally fixed is usually at about the age of six years.

In children of average intelligence the three stages of conceptualization are primarily dependent upon the maturation of the processes of perception. In the first stage, if a child is asked to place in front of a series of saucers a series of cups so that there is one cup for each saucer, he will be able to make only a crudely qualitative attempt. In the second stage, he will be successful at the first task, but if now one or another row of objects is disturbed in its spatial arrangement, the child no longer realizes that each row contains the same number of objects. In the third stage, after placing the objects in a one-to-one relationship, no matter how the row of cups is spread out or compressed in relation to the row of saucers, the child will always realize that numerically they are the same. Piaget also expresses this another way. In the first stage perception is "global" and cannot take in enough data for a precise estimate. In the second stage perception is more selective, and two aspects of a group of objects can be attended to so that the notion of quantity is possible but irrelevant data cannot be excluded so that the concept cannot remain fixed. In the third stage the processes of perception are capable not only of including more than one aspect of the group of objects so that a quantitative estimate can be made but also of excluding the irrelevant data (so far as counting is concerned) that the objects have been rearranged.

Translated into the framework of the cathexis of attention, the first stage would correspond to that period when the total cathexis of attention is involved in one direction at a given moment. The cups and saucers can only be perceived as a group of objects. In the second stage the cathexis of attention is capable of being divided between two aspects of the group of objects, i.e., the saucers as discrete objects and the interval between each saucer. In the third stage once the child has placed the cups and saucers in their one-to-one correspondence, he retains the concept of their numerical equivalence, as long as no objects are removed or added, whatever other rearrangements are made. The decisive change at this stage appears to be the ability to utilize a mobile countercathectic energy which excludes the irrelevant aspects of the new data presented to the process of perception.

The investigations of Bergman and Escalona (1949) and Leitch and Escalona (1949) afford some interesting data for further speculation concerning some of the genetic aspects of the problem. These workers support Hartmann's formulations (1939, 1951, 1952) concerning the simultaneous origin of ego and id with differentiation occurring as a maturational as well as a reactive process to the reality principle (see also Hartmann, Kris, and Loewenstein, 1949, and the Symposium on "The Mutual Influences in the Development of Ego and Id," *Psychoanalytic Study of the Child* 7). The perception-motility apparatuses are part of the inborn structure of the ego and as such contribute to the formation of the mature ego. Bergman and Escalona's observations on infants with unusual sensitivities have given rise to the hypothesis that precocious ego development, which is related both to the development of susceptibility to psychosis and of unusual intellectual or artistic talents, may get its initial impetus from processes set in motion by the low threshold of the stimulus barrier in certain infants. The variations in threshold may be of organic hereditary origin, or may be due to insufficient maternal protection in the broadest sense of this term. Their observations and the hypotheses arising from them provide some helpful links in the chain of evidence that is being proposed. It is suggested by them that the need to erect secondary protective barriers against excessive external stimuli produces the capacity for certain ego functions that would ordinarily mature at a later date. It is suggested here that these secondary barriers thus erected are precursors of the process of selective countercathexis of perceptual data as described above. In these infants, therefore, an ego process is available precociously, for the decisive third stage, described by Piaget. Some of the clinical data in the patient are also consistent with this hypothesis: There are suggestive borderline features as far as psychosis is concerned. Sensory hypersensitivity is still evident in his startle reaction to commonplace auditory stimuli and in his photophobia. Music has played a prominent role in his life and is still capable of producing in him a kind of hypnagogic state. (It is to be recalled in this connection how prominent a role music, both in its melodic and rhythmic aspects, plays in the description of cases of so-called "infantile autism.") The peculiar sensory synesthesias and dysesthesias of the Rorschach and the over-all resemblance to certain responses in the "stress tolerance test" in the traumatic battle neurosis are also significant. The precocious character of the patient's arithmetical achievements should also be recalled in this connection. He achieves a perfect score in the psychological battery and apparently came to his first-grade work with a well-developed arithmetical capacity. During the time that the other children were engaged in learning about numbers the patient was being given special tutoring in reading. He has very little sense of ever having been taught arithmetic. When he was finally exposed to elementary algebra and geometry, he encompassed these subjects in a short time and again has little recollection of a learning process in the sense of the expenditure of attention energy in these fields.

Precocity in mathematics is perhaps a more outstanding quality of genius in this field than in any other with the exception perhaps of music. It is unmatched in any other area of intellectual endeavor.

Ordinary mathematical ability does not have this characteristic (Beke, 1933). Pascal discovered his projective geometry at the age of sixteen (Bell, 1937). It is also noted that he suffered from severe hypochondriasis and occasional hallucinatory experiences. Newton had a premature birth and is described as a "sensitive child" who could not engage in physical activities but revealed prodigious intellectual endowments in childhood (Bell, 1937). By the age of twenty-one he had laid the basis for all his later mathematical work. It may be of some significance that at the age of fifty he suffered from an involutional melancholia with paranoid features. The Bernouilli family are often adduced as evidence of the constitutional origin (Bieberbach, 1934; Moebus, 1907; Poponoe, 1930-31) of intellectual genius having produced eight mathematicians of the first rank in four generations. Monge,[3] the author of descriptive geometry, became a professor of physics at the University of Lyons at the age of sixteen. Fourrier began his mathematical work at the age of thirteen after a childhood that is described as being "wayward, petulant and destructive." Gauss was an infant prodigy at the age of two and is said to have shown a highly original capacity for arithmetization at the age of three. He is also described as having "a constitutional predisposition to hypochondria." Cauchy, another child phenomenon, was always considered sensitive and eccentric by his associates. Jacobi began his original mathematical work at the age of twelve. Hamilton is said to have had a complete mastery of arithmetical operations at the age of three. His life was characterized by a marked tendency to withdraw from social relationships. Galois, whose life is worth a special study in this connection, wrote down a summary of years of creative mathematical thinking at the age of twenty on the night before he was killed in a senseless duel (Infeld, 1948). His short paper on the theory of equations which survived for posterity marked him as one of the greatest mathematicians of all time. Cayley, another sensitive child, is described as having been a "wizard at calculation" at the age of eight years. This is but a fragmentary list that could be expanded in the same vein for several pages.

A curious group of rare individuals, known as the lightning calculators (Ameline, 1913; Barlow, 1952; Binet, 1894; Brill, 1940; Ioteyko, 1910; Jakobsson, 1944; LaFora, 1935; Menzerath, 1913;

Scherer, Rothmann, and Goldstein, 1945; Ravina, 1946) will also bear scrutiny. In the past many of these individuals have been described as "feeble-minded." This is a difficult description to evaluate in the absence of our current methods of psychological testing. Feats of purely mental computation are recorded in them that rival the operations of mechanical calculating machines. Several phenomena stand out in these individuals which further support certain aspects of the present formulation:

1. Precocity is a striking feature of this capacity. It was never a development of their adult lives.

2. The speed of the mental operation defies description in terms of any mere dissection of the arithmetical steps involved. For example a lightning calculator by the name of Colburn at the age of six could give correct responses in four seconds to such problems as "what number multiplied by itself is equal to a given number of six integers" (Barlow, 1952; Poponoe, 1930-31). It had been asserted for centuries that the number four billion, two hundred and ninety four million, nine hundred and sixty seven thousand, two hundred and ninety four million, nine hundred and sixty seven thousand, two hundred and ninety-seven (4,294,967,297, or 2 to the 32 power plus one) was a prime number. Euler had discovered by complex mathematical means that this was incorrect and that it could be factored into 641 times 6,700,417. Colburn came to the same result in less than a minute by a purely mental process. Bidder was being exhibited as a lightning calculator at the age of four. At the age of ten he could respond in a few seconds to such problems as how many times does 1728 go into the cube of 36. Safford, another calculating prodigy who later became professor of astronomy, gave the correct answer in less than a minute to the following problem: What number is it that being divided by the product of its digits, the quotient will be 3 and if 18 be added to the quotient the digits will be reversed?" In solving these kinds of problems Safford is described as going through a series of bizzare and complex postures and movements (see also Jones, 1943). Many similar feats among others are recorded.

3. Practically none of the subjects studied have ever been able to give satisfactory accounts of the speed of the process, although some could give the conscious operations. Inaudi, a famous Italian

calculator who was completely illiterate, stated that he heard the answers as if spoken by an outside voice (Barlow, 1952; Bieberbach, 1934). In this connection we should recall Kris's (1950) statement concerning states of inspiration where the preconscious process is felt as coming from outside of the ego. Diamandi, another lightning calculator, claimed that he saw colors during the mental process and that he associated a different color to each of the integers (Barlow, 1952; Bieberbach, 1934; Ioteyko, 1910). Colburn and Arumogani, the latter another so-called feeble-minded calculating genius, each had supernumerary digits and toes (six on each hand and foot) (Barlow, 1952). It has been suggested that in their cases a duodecimal system, which has certain advantages for rapid multiplication and division, arose on a body-image basis. Shakuntala Devi, a young Indian woman described as the "human Comptometer," recently gave a television performance in England. She is unable to give an account of her mental processes and has a deep religious conviction that they are a gift from God. She usually spends twenty-four hours immediately preceding a demonstration in what she describes as a state of "concentration." The state of concentration consists of making her mind a blank screen as far as possible, thinking of nothing at all (Barlow, 1952). This exercise would appear to be an excellent example of an attempt to decathect all conscious perceptual images. Some of the more educated calculators are no more sucessful in the process of self-observation than the illiterate and unsophisticated ones.

4. Almost as curious as the ability itself is the large number of lightning calculators who appear to be feeble-minded (Barlow, 1952; LaFora, 1935; Menzerath, 1913; Poponoe, 1930-31), as did the "Idiot Savant" studied by Scherer, Rothman, and Goldstein (1945). Verhaege, a Dutch boy, was said to have had a mental age of two years (Barlow, 1952). Yet from the types of problems that he was able to comprehend and respond to, it is difficult to believe that this was a true case of mental defect. One may hazard a guess that a closer study of such cases, according to our present concepts, would rather place these individuals in the category of childhood schizophrenia or so-called infantile autism.

5. Lastly, and most interesting, is the repeated observation on the frequency with which these prodigies lose their capacities as they mature, often becoming even rather average paper computers. It

has been proposed by several observers (Barlow, 1952; Scherer et al., 1945) that this is related to education and to the loss of interest in the narrow field of arithmetical computation. In the general sense this is probably correct, and yet it does not explain the retention of the ability by some of the most distinguished and educated members of this group of individuals who retain their infantile abilities throughout life. An infant calculating prodigy George Parker Bidder, born in 1805 in Devonshire, retained his calculating ability in spite of education and sophistication; he has the following to say about his mental processes:

> Suppose I had to multiply 89 by 73, I should say exactly 6497. If I read the figures written out before me I could not express a result more correctly or more rapidly. This facility has however tended to deceive me, for I fancied that I possessed a multiplication table up to 100 x 100, and when in full practice, even beyond that; but I was in error. The fact that I go through the whole operation of the computation in that short interval of time, which it takes me to announce the result . . . the velocity of the mental processes cannot be adequately expressed; the utterances of words cannot equal it. . . . Were my powers of registration at all equal to the powers of reasoning or execution, I should have no difficulty in an inconceivably short time, in composing a voluminous table of logarithms. [In another place he states:] The reason for my obtaining the peculiar power of dealing with numbers may be attributed to the fact that *I knew the value of numbers have always had a significance and a meaning for me very different from that which figures convey to children in general* [Barlow, 1952].[4]

It would appear that Bidder might well be saying that for him the concept of number is not indissolubly bound up with the visual image of the arabic numerals. The riddle of the retention or loss of the lightning calculating ability may depend primarily for its explanation upon the persistence or loss of the capacity to decathect numbers as written figures or visual images. It is also postulated that this quality must have an important bearing upon the reading and writing defect in this patient, where it would act as a deterrent to the learning process.

Hadamard (1945) provides other examples of the same process in pure mathematics from his own subjective observations. In repeating the proof of the classic proposition that the sequel of prime numbers is unlimited he says "a group of vague unstructured spots of different cluster qualities stand out at each decisive stage of the proof before the state (itself) comes clearly to mind." Also concerning the problem of considering a sum of infinite numbers of terms intending to valuate its order of magnitude, he states: "When I think of that question I see not the formula itself, but the space it would take if written; a kind of ribbon which is thicker or darker at the place corresponding to the possible important terms . . . or as I should see it, being strongly farsighted, if I had no glasses on." Hadamard also confides that he makes many errors in writing.

In mathematical thought, in contradistinction to purely arithmetical operations, we are constantly struck by this same relationship between the purely operational process and that portion of it which is capable of becoming part of the system pcpt-cs, in the relationship between algebra and geometry. Algebra is the highest expression of the decathected process, while geometry deals with spatial relationships in their most attenuated form but still in a guise which is capable of visual representation. Throughout the history of mathematics the algebraist has recourse to geometry when it is necessary for him to conceptualize abstract quantitative relationships that have become too complex, as in Descartes' analytic geometry. The geometer, on the other hand, utilizes algebra for an advance in the level of his conceptualization when the formal aspects of the space he is working with become too complex for visual cathexis, as in Einstein's theory of relativity (Black, 1952; Ramsey, 1950).

The Role of the Primary Process

Up to this point the mathematical process has been discussed as if it could be explained entirely in terms of autonomous ego functioning with decathexis of that portion of the system pcpt-cs, which is concerned with space and quantity, and hypercathexis of the preconscious process, as its essential components. Several examples can be extracted from the historical literature to illustrate the quality of what Kris (1950) has referred to as "controlled regression" before returning to the data from the patient. This would appear to be the decisive feature of the mental event described as an "illumination." The preconscious process, as with wit, humor, fantasy, etc., is permitted a momentary domicile behind the barrier of repression to be reinforced with id energy for its emergence as the solution (and not always the correct one) of the frustrating problem (Kris, 1950).

Bell (1937) states that

> . . . part of the riddle of Gauss is answered by his *involuntary* preoccupation with mathematical ideas. . . . As a young man Gauss would be "seized by mathematics." Conversing with his friends he would go silent, overwhelmed by thoughts beyond his control, and stand rigidly oblivious of his surroundings. Later he controlled his thoughts—or they lost their control over him—and he consciously directed his energies to the solution of a difficulty until he succeeded.

The relationship of the primary process to the meaning of numbers and the mathematical process is also discussed by Baker (1951), Hermann (1924, 1926, 1929, 1949, 1950), Hug-Hellmuth (1915), Schilder (1936, 1942), Sharpe (1950) in relation to the "pure scientist," Saussure (1926), Voelmy (1949), and Wisdom (1947), in various connections.

In the structure of the mathematical discovery itself it is often possible to see the imprint, so to speak, of the momentary passage through the barrier of repression. Lobatchowsky, for example, builds a systematic geometry, later expanded by Reimann, upon a negation of sensory reality testing, namely that parallel lines can meet (Bell, 1937). Non-Euclidean geometry has become an important adjunct to modern physics and astronomy. Cayley's algebra of matrices stood for many years as a kind of bizarre oddity in the field of higher algebra. It begins with a postulate, in "paranoiac" fashion, which appears to be an absurd negation of the self-evident, namely that the products of "x" and "y" are different depending upon the order in which the multiplication is performed. From the year 1858, when his first memoir on the subject was written, until 1925 the algebra of matrices was a mathematical curiosity. In 1925 Heisenberg recognized in it exactly the tool which he needed for the development of his revolutionary work in quantum mechanics (Bell, 1937).

The subjective observations of Poincaré (1952, 1952a) on mathematical illumination contain a brilliant intuition of the relationship of the conscious work, the preconscious activity, and the suddenly becoming conscious of the new creative idea. Unfortunately the details do not permit any reconstruction of the unconscious contribution to the experience. Poincaré conceives of the mathematical process not as a simple set of syllogisms, *but as a construction of aggregates under the guiding influence of the necessity to exclude contradictions, and to conform to the ideals of mathematical elegance.*

In our patient the illumination experiences while in analysis permit of a more detailed psychological observation of the process. In the first experience recounted, the book from his father represented a gratification of his passive feminine strivings and a moment of access to unconscious fantasy. It also appears to represent in the form of reunion with his father permission for scoptophilic and epistemophilic gratification in which the repressed fantasy of the primal scene reappears in the realization that a product can be factored into two antecedent quantities. The event added useful material to a reconstruction of the content of the early pavor nocturnus which now appeared as a wakeful vigil on the part of the child to ensure the possession of his parents individually by preventing the union of the parents in their separate bedrooms. At the same time his sexual curiosity had elaborated a fantasy of genital contact at a distance, with marked sadomasochistic features. In the transference situation the separation of the parental figures was reenacted by keeping the name of the female analyst of his girl friend secret from me. This was further borne out by his fantasy that his parents were asexual beings and that his father's union with his mother must have been accomplished by artificial insemination. The frequent references to the dark and the denial of the process of dark accommodation point to the wish and defense against scoptophilic drives. Behind the screen memory of the pillow lay the patient's rage against both parents for their frustration of the oedipal drives. The receipt of the book from father allows him to see the forbidden relationship between the parents, assures him that father will not retaliate against his active oedipal strivings nor deny him his passive feminine ones. Thus in the illumination are condensed at least three acts of seeing in the full light of day and the creation of a child in both the masculine and feminine roles.

It was most striking throughout the analysis that the patient was trying to find a way back to an object relationship without having to recognize his impulses to possess the parental objects and to be possessed by them. For this reason he must either be given things without asking for them or having asked he must find a way to show that what he asked for was denied to him. To receive from his parents meant to him to be bound by the obligation of acknowledging himself as their child and to reexperience the frustration of the struggle for possession and the disappointment in ideal figures experienced in the primal scene. In addition to other meanings the illumination experience has also the quality of the frustration of the paternal wish. By receiving the book from his father he is reassured that he is still his father's son, but by experiencing the original idea as his own he is also reassured that he owes nothing to his father. This undoubtedly played a large part in his reading difficulty (Blanchard, 1947; Pearson, 1952; Strachey, 1930) which, unlike the arithmetic, had its origin during the early latency period with the oedipal conflicts still unresolved. To learn to read from his parents or their tutorial representatives would run the risk of undoing his hostile defenses, as an act of taking something from them. It is of interest, in this connection to recall Strachey's (1930) theoretical formulations on reading as a sublimation of oral ambivalent drives. "In obsessional reading symptoms," he states, "we see the vulnerability of the reading process to the invasion of oral ambivalence."[5] In both examples of the process of "illumination" cited in the case report, the primary defense appears to be against feelings of frustration or disappointment at the hands of objects to whom he previously had positive libidinal ties. In the patient's character this was seen as an acceptance of traditionalism in dress, bearing, and manner (which he only acknowledged as a legacy of his paternal grandparents), while maintaining a complete bohemianism in thought (see patient's poem on "The Community" above), and a capacity for original mathematical thinking which was felt as something completely outside the stream of family inheritance.

In 1926 Einstein asked the rather surprising question: "How can it be that mathematics being after all a product of human thought independent of experience is so admirably adapted to the objects of reality?" (Bell, 1937). It is interesting to speculate on the mechanism of this highly condensed process of illumination with its contribution of narcissistic defense in the service of the reality principle. Although pure mathematics certainly does not have any self-conscious goal beyond the investigation of the properties of its own internally consistent operations, it seems to have its most dramatic usefulness in the description of those aspects of the universe that are beyond the range of observation of the human sensory apparatus and must be studied through mechanical instruments. Is it perhaps the personality with sufficient intelligence, most capable of the controlled use of primitive ego mechanisms such as projection and introjection, who is also most likely to be capable of creative mathematical thinking? In his paper on "Negation" Freud (1925) states:

> The function of judgment is concerned ultimately with two sorts of decision. It may assert or deny that a thing has a particular property; or it may affirm or dispute that a particular image exists in reality. Originally the property to be decided about might either be good or bad, useful or harmful. Expressed in the language of the oldest, that of the oral instinctual impulses, the alternative runs thus: "I should like to eat that, or I should like to spit it out" . . . that is to say it is to be either inside me or outside me . . . the original pleasure-ego tries to introject into itself everything that is good and to reject from itself everything that is bad. From this point of view what is bad, what is alien to the ego, and what is external, are to begin with, identical.
>
> The other sort of decision made by the function of judgment, namely as to the real existence of something imagined, is a concern of the final reality-ego. ... It is now no longer a question of whether something perceived (a thing) shall be taken into the Ego or not, but of whether something which is present in the Ego as an image can also be rediscovered in perception (that is, in reality). Once more it will be seen that the question is one of external and internal. What is not real, what is

> merely imagined or subjective, is only internal; while on the other hand what is real is also present externally. . . . In order to understand this step forward we must recollect that all images originate from perceptions and are repetitions of them. So that originally the mere existence of the image serves as a guarantee of the reality of what is imagined. The contrast between what is subjective and what is objective does not exist from the first. It only arises from the faculty which thought possesses for reviving a thing that has once been perceived, by reproducing it as an image, without its being necessary for the external object still to be present . . . [as in the recognition of words in reading, or the reproducing of them in writing.]

The mathematician avoids the ambivalence conflict inherent in all the other sciences that deal with external objects, which in a sense must go through a continuous process of retesting what is an internal and what is an external perception. He does this as suggested above by decathexis of the image of the object. (This process apparently reaches its epitome in Cantor's set theory, which the limitations of the present writer preclude from this discussion.) By the process of a continuous substitution of symbols for images the question of what is internal or external need never be faced. It is necessary only to answer the question whether the new "aggregate" of symbols is consistent with the previous step and this in turn with the one before, reaching back to the original axiom. This axiom can, with impunity then, as in the examples given above of Lobatchevsky's geometry and Cayley's algebra, begin with what appears to be a direct negation of reality. Freud (1925) also says of negation, "a negative judgment is the intellectual substitute for repression; the 'No' in which it is expressed is the hallmark of repression, a certificate of origin. . . . By the help of the symbol of negation, the thinking process frees itself from the limitations of repression and enriches itself with the subject-matter without which it could not work efficiently." In the patient's illumination this has been expressed in another way. The negation of the repressed wish to be possessed by his father or to possess the mother allows the merging of two ideas in the preconscious which had previously been kept in isolation like the parental images. Where the task demands full cathexis of the image of the external object, as in reading or writing, the ambivalence can no longer be evaded behind the mask of the mathematical process and breaks through (in this case) in the form of distortion of the word picture.

The Mathematical Process as a Sublimation

A critical comment by a colleague to the foregoing formulation draws attention to the fact that it does not explicitly point out the relationship of the patient's distance from his aggressive as well as libidinal drives in fixing the mathematical creativity as a sublimatory process. The patient's striking capacity for deferring the release of physiological tensions during periods of mathematical work is certainly one aspect of this. Both of the examples of illumination emphasize the substitution of mathematical thinking for aggressive feelings: in the first case toward his father, and in the second instance toward the frustrating "girl friend."

In the transference situation this was more specifically illustrated, when on several occasions of prolonged silence on the couch, the patient was asked about his thoughts and replied "nothing very much—I was just imagining that I had an instrument in my hand that was capable of shooting a projectile of perfect elasticity. I begin with each wall, then the floor and the ceiling, trying to figure out from the position in which I am lying what the angle of incidence has to be to make the projectile ricochet from various surfaces until it flies out of the window." There was considerable evidence that this was a childhood game which had its onset following his exclusion from his mother's bed. In the analysis it was a substitute for an expression of annoyed boredom as it probably was in childhood. Instead of attacking the analyst verbally, the patient resorts to a trigonometric ballistic exercise which combines an aggressive fantasy with a problem-solving activity. It appears pertinent that in the solution to the problem the projectile does not damage but flies harmlessly into space through the window.

To summarize, "pure" mathematics is a consistent corrective process against both projection and introjection. It utilizes the preconscious problem-solving capacity of the ego in hypercathected form. This is made possible by the exclusion of the ambivalence problem concerning what is internal and what is external by the use of a mobile countercathectic energy which is probably an outcome of precocious maturation of some phases of the processes of perception. Negation is utilized to allow the emergence of repressed representatives of the primary process. These do not require reality testing but are utilized or discarded only in so far as they coincide with the rules of mathematical consistency and economy of energy expenditure which the mathematician experiences as an aesthetic feeling to which he gives the name *elegance* (Poincaré, 1952) (perhaps a reaction formation to the primal scene). The sublimatory fixing of the whole process is ensured by the high degree of "neutralization" of both libidinal and aggressive drives. Thus the creative act in mathematics ("illumination") has its counterpart in the arts while the secondary elaborative process is continuous with those of the sciences.

Notes

1. The "Gospel According to St. John" emphasizes the mystic union of father and son. "There was a man sent from God whose name was John. The same came for a witness, to bear witness of the Light, that all men through him might believe. He was not that Light but was sent to bear witness of that Light" (Bates, E.S., 1937, pp. 1006-1007).

2. The psychological testing was done by Dr. Molly Harrower. I am indebted to her for permission to utilize her material in this report.

3. For the following biographical data, see Bell (1937).

4. Also see Wiener (1953). In Brill's (1940) observations of the six-year-old calculating prodigy, Jungreis, the preconscious aspects of the process are also mentioned. Brill, however, is more interested in the hereditary tendency in this talent and in the possibility of the reawakening of "phylogenetic memories" by libidinal regression to an oral-anal phase.

Jungreis, the lightning calculator observed by Brill, is described as follows: "He can give instantly the totals of formidable columns of figures and his answers are invariably correct yet strangely enough he cannot distinguish one written arabic numeral from another. When I saw the boy he still knew only the written number '3.' "

5. In this connection, see also Freud's examples (1904) of lapses in reading and writing.

CHAPTER TWO

Strephosymbolia

It is probable that symptomatic disturbances of reading and spelling are of multiple etiology.[1] This chapter, however, is concerned with a fairly discrete, well-recognized disability in the recognition of printed words and the reproduction of words in writing. This disability is usually characterized by normal intelligence and normal learning capacity in other areas. It is found about four times as frequently among males (Blanchard, 1947). Reversal of letters as individual symbols and in their sequence within the word is the most frequent source of error in both reading and writing, but it is not the only error encountered. This gives rise to an impression of a right-left disorientation in these patients which, however, has no counterpart in their orientation in general (see Cole, 1951; Bender and Schilder, 1951; and Schilder, 1944; Orton, 1939; to the contrary).

These cases were first systematically described by Hinshelwood (1917) under the title of "Congenital Word Blindness." Orton (1937, 1939) continued this structural concept in more definitive form, introducing the term *strephosymbolia* to denote a failure to achieve complete right-left orientation through what he conceived to be a conflict between the memory images of the two cerebral hemispheres, one of which had failed to establish complete dominance in organizing visuomotor patterns. Dearborn (1933, 1938) proposes a similar concept based upon learned rather than congenitally determined patterns of sensorimotor function. Many investigators have since thrown considerable doubt upon both of these hypotheses from clinical and experimental considerations. Young (1938), Tulchin (1935), and Hincks (1926) first stressed emotional difficulty and personality problems as general determinants of reading disabilities. Blanchard (1947) was first to investigate the problem psychoanalytically. She stresses the use of a phonetic "speech writing" in one case as a form of revenge against the female teacher who stood for the mother who had abandoned the patient. She also discusses the disability in relation to the symbolic meaning of the alphabet where letters are often conceived as threatening, orally aggressive wild animals. Bender and Schilder (1951) and Schilder (1944) studied graphic art in children with reading disabilities. They utilize a Gestalt approach and attempt a synthesis of structural and dynamic concepts. They see the defect as an isolated disorder in gnostic intellectual functioning in which written words and letters cannot be integrated and differentiated in terms of the spoken word due to disturbances of brain development. (Psychoanalytic problems connected with spelling are also discussed by Freud, 1904; Sterba, 1943; and Knight, 1952.)

The present paper will attempt to demonstrate that the so-called strephosymbolic disturbance consists of a failure to synthesize the ordinal aspect of the word, which is a function of its phonetic qualities, with the visual elements of the word. This is especially evident where one finds different visual elements standing for identical phonemes. An attempt will also be made to demonstrate that this disturbance resembles a phylogenetic phase in orthographic evolution, namely, the transitional stage between idiographic scripts and the syllabary alphabet. In the present case, the failure of synthesis of the higher discriminatory functions of the auditory and visual spheres has its analogue in the patient's primal scene fantasies and in the pattern of his object relationships. It is contended, although the evidence for this is by its nature somewhat inconclusive, that precocity of the "reading readiness stage" of ego-apparatus development plays a decisive role in its genesis.

Case Report

This patient has already been reported in some detail in a previous paper on mathematical illumination (Chapter 1). The present summary, therefore, will be merely a brief recapitulation of this history with some additions which are pertinent here and were not directly pertinent to the material then under consideration.

The patient was a twenty-one-year-old graduate student of mathematics when he first came for analysis. He was about to enter graduate school to become a candidate for a doctoral degree. He sought analysis for two seemingly separate problems. The first was his inability to form any lasting relationships with women, and the second was a disability in reading and spelling of the so-called strephosymbolic type which threatened to interfere with the fulfillment of his academic ambitions. His arithmetical and mathematical ability was of the highest order. There were no speech problems as far as verbalization was concerned. The patient had managed to compensate for a good deal of his reading deficit by an excellent auditory retentive memory which enabled him to pass courses at the college level in all subjects. He was the youngest of three children. Both parents held scholarly achievements in high esteem. The father held a high academic position in a leading university. From earliest infancy the patient is said to have been a very sensitive child. At an early age he had shown an extreme intolerance of loud noises. At the age of three he was subjected to a flashbulb exposure during the taking of an indoor family photograph. It is said that his eyes teared and appeared reddened for several days thereafter. One of his present complaints is still a marked photophobia, especially on awakening in the morning. At the age of fourteen, he complained of being able to see floating specks in his peripheral areas of vision and a diagnosis of "drusen" due to floating viterous opacities was made by an ophthalmologist. Glasses are worn for myopia. The curious game of playing with his visual accommodation was also recounted during his analysis. The patient suffered from a severe pavor nocturnus at about the age of four to five years, whose disappearance is covered by a screen memory of finding that his mother had left a pillow in bed next to him to simulate a body after one of his visits to her bed following a nightmare. He still talks of this event as a "shameful hoax to play on a small child." The patient began his schooling with kindergarten in his fifth year. It took several months before his mother was able to leave him alone in school. The first and second grade of school seemed to have gone fairly well. He has a relative amnesia for the third and fourth grade. These were the years in which subsequent reading and spelling tests revealed that he had the greatest learning difficulty. They are perhaps also the years of greatest emphasis on these subjects. Attempts to tutor him in reading and spelling began in the fifth grade and continued in college where the patient spent two summers at a reading clinic. In his fifth grade a diagnosis of "strephosymbolia" was made. His mother was told that it was due to a congenital failure of one side of his brain to achieve dominance.[2] The test curve in reading and spelling performance reveals an initial average level with a sharp drop at the third and fourth year levels and a gradual improvement in the spelling of eighth and ninth grade words. First attempts to teach him to read were by the tachistoscopic word and picture recognition method. Later it was found that he could do somewhat better when the "old-fashioned" phonetic method was substituted. The patient's arithmetical ability was well in advance of his years. At the age of nine he could use a slide rule accurately for complex arithmetical computations. He had very little recollection of being taught arithmetic. His talent in this field was unnoticed at first and more or less overshadowed by the reading deficit. His mathematical ability was not discovered until the eighth grade when the patient was allowed to go ahead of the class in plain geometry and later algebra, both of which he mastered in an unusually short time. During this period of his schooling a striking character change was noted. Previously a shy and timid child who was usually found on the periphery of the group, he became more assertive in class relationships and was sometimes thought of as arrogant toward the less advanced students with a tendency to use his learning in an overbearing manner. His progress in mathematics in college was rapid and he was recognized as having a superior talent in this area. In graduate school he has done some original work in mathematics. He is mainly interested in rather esoteric fields of pure mathematics. He is also interested in symbolic logic. His work has shown a high degree of a capacity for "illumination" in regard to difficult problems, which is the mark of the creative mathematician. The strephosymbolia was not discussed in the previous communication (Chapter 1) in order to keep the problem from being unduly complicated. However, it was present as a symptom requiring dynamic understanding from the very beginning and at all stages during the analysis. It was stated in the previous communication that the patient had had a series of mirror dreams in which the unconscious meaning of the reversal of letters in words began to emerge. The full meaning of one of these dreams in connection with his strephosymbolic symptom did not become clear until very late in his analysis. This dream was reported as follows:

> I am in the garden at home with B. A women's voice is directing me. She is short and blond. She was walking on a stone path away from me. I find myself looking through a glass window which is also a mirror. She appears to have a disease and the glass indicates that it is "verboten" to get closer. I write to her on the window backwards and to the left so that she can read it without having to reverse the words. I recall the letters, E, R, and W. It is like writing with soap on a looking glass. On the other side, there is a garden party. The garden is filled with elegant people. Someone is commenting about my parents in French and Russian.

The letters in the dream reminded him of his reading and spelling defects. The looking glass reminded him of Lewis Carroll who was also a mathematician. When Alice looked through the glass, one room was warm and homey. The other side of the glass was cold and strange. At the age of two or three the patient's care was given over largely to a "Fraulein," the short blond woman of the dream. (Later it was found that this lady was really from one of the Slavic countries which is probably another determinant of the reference to Russian.) The arrangement was partly due to the illness of an older sister, which necessitated a good deal of the mother's attention. This was experienced by the patient as a severe rejection by his mother, and his clinging to her was intensified thereafter. The soap in the dream referred to masturbatory practices. Coldness is one of his complaints against his mother and represents his feelings concerning the relationship between his parents who sleep in different rooms. It also represents his feelings about both parents' inability to have sexual desires or to create children. He conceived of his father, particularly, as an asexual being. In his own words, "My father must have conceived us by artificial insemination." The written word is for communication with people who are at a distance. Writing also refers to his love letters which are elegant but devoid of any real warmth. This complaint of the distance between his parents and their artificiality with each other is reproduced in his own complaint, i.e., "the inability to meet women on an ordinary human level." The meaning of the foreign languages in the dream did not become clear for some time. Later it became apparent that French is a language that he must learn in order to complete his Ph.D. requirements. He is fearful of the difficulty that he will encounter in learning to read and spell in French. Russian stands for the cold war and the distance between the Eastern and Western hemispheres. They are both meaningless to him by ear. Russian is meaningless both auditorally and visually since it utilizes an unfamiliar alphabet.

Other aspects of the patient's history revealed his concern about the creative process, his denial of the pregnancy of a young woman in her eighth month, and his interest in artistic production. It was pointed out in the previous communication that for some time in the analysis the patient brought small samples of his creative production, mostly poems in free verse, small drawings and abstract sculpture. The bringing of written productions continued for some time, and fortunately for the present study it was not interpreted until a fairly large number of samples of his writings had been collected. It seemed on one occasion that these written productions represented not only the presentation of his creative work to the analyst but also a request for more direct help in the problem of his spelling. The patient confirmed this transference wish on a subsequent occasion.

The following list of misspelled words were encountered at random in a series of uncorrected hand-written poems and essays which the patient handed to me. For a considerable period of time there did not appear to be any principle involved. The first impression of his spelling errors had a random quality. Later it was found that the misspelled words could be placed in two groups, the significance of which will be discussed in more detail below. For the present it will be sufficient to note that one type of error arises from an attempt to revisualize the word without recourse to its phonetic attributes while in the other group, the phonetic qualities are retained but one would expect the writer to be disturbed by the visual inaccuracies:

Attempts at Visual Reproduction (idiographic)	*Attempts at Phonetic Reproduction (phonographic)*
Piviot (pivot)	Inmoast (inmost)
Truning (turning)	Growning (groaning)
Retalion (relation)	Cloke (cloak)
Thoery (theory)	Theery (theory)
Turnes (turns)	Gross (grows)
Metadates (meditates)	Stachure (stature)
Bouyant (buoyant)	Brest (breast)
Eygipt (Egypt)	Wherels (whirls)

It is more difficult to elicit the comparable data from reading, since direct observation of the patient's reading habits were not readily available. However, one experience recounted in the analysis serves as a clue. The patient was in the habit of taking a bus for his appointment from a certain corner. There was a grocery store on this corner whose name was unknown to the patient. On several occasions he caught himself trying to remember the sequence of the letters in the name. The letters were "G-R-I-S-T-E-D-E-S." On comparison, the following day he found that he had made various errors in the order of the letters but that he recalled the individual letters correctly. He confessed in recounting the following experience that he would have been ashamed to ask the pronunciation of the name, although he frequently bought groceries there. One Lincoln's Birthday while waiting for his bus, a lady tried the door of the store and he overheard her say to a companion, "I didn't know that Gristedes was closed on Lincoln's Birthday." The patient suddenly realized how the name was pronounced and said it to himself several times on his trip to his session. (He had introduced the session by saying that several passengers on the bus had looked at him oddly since he seemed to be talking to himself.) At this time I asked him if he could now spell the word that he had just discovered how to read. He suddenly realized that he no longer could picture the correct letters and had only a hazy notion of the appearance of the word. In his first attempt he now spelled it "GRISTEADY'S," a better phonetic equivalent of the word he had learned than an idiographic one.

During the course of the analysis there was a very striking improvement in the patient's reading. As far as one can tell at the present time he reads at an average speed. No such comparable improvement has occurred in his spelling, although he notes that he can frequently tell when a word "looks" wrong and in contrast to his former state he is able to proofread and correct his own written productions to a large extent.

Discussion

Hinshelwood's (1917) theory of congenital alexia and dysgraphia has been unable to withstand the neuroanatomical and neuropathological objections of subsequent findings in acquired and congenital aphasic defects. The lesions postulated by Hinshelwood to explain so-called congenital alexia would have to be not only miraculously selective but bilaterally symmetrical as well, to fulfill the criteria of clinical experience.

Orton's (1939) hypothesis still finds wide acceptance in many circles today (Gates and Bond, 1936; Hildreth, 1934; Kirk, 1934; Phillips, 1934; Selzer, 1933; Woody and Phillips, 1934), although much work among experimental and educational psychologists is opposed to it (see McFie, 1952; Ketcham, 1951; Witty, 1936; Kopel, 1936). Orton bases his theory of conflicting memory images in equipotential cerebral hemispheres upon several observations with strephosymbolics, namely, the tendency to sinestrad reversals which he calls "static reversals" (see also Davidson, 1935) when they occur in letters alone, and "kinetic reversals" when they occur in the order of letters within the word, and the relatively greater speed of learning of mirror writing and mirror reading that is found in these patients. Orton also evokes evidence of at least latent ambidexterity[3] in regard to other functions that tend ordinarily to be lateralized such as to use of a dominant eye or a dominant leg, etc. Orton (1937) makes interesting and astute observations in regard to these patients but formulates the problem in what would appear to be hypotheses from which psychological considerations are largely excluded.

A consideration of the evolution of writing has yielded some interesting data which appear to be relevant to the present problem. These data are largely derived from Diringer (1948) and Ogg (1948). Recorded communication probably takes its origin from the cave painting of the paleolithic period, although it is probable that this early cave painting had a magical-religious rather than an aesthetic or communicative function. The earliest written records with a clearly communicative motivation are the pictographic scripts found among many primitive peoples. These used direct representation of objects themselves in a story sequence. With the progress of civilization, pictographs gradually gave way to idiographic writing where the representation of the object comes to stand for an idea rather than for the object itself. Idiographic writing is still a prominent element in ancient alphabets such as the Chinese. Idiograms are an important part of early Egyptian hieroglyphics. The decisive stage in the transition from idiographic writing to the phonetic alphabet comes by way of phonograms where the visual representation of an object is no longer utilized to convey an idea but denotes the sound of a verbal syllable. Alphabets making use of such phonograms are known as syllabary alphabets. Of these Japanese, Kana and ancient Sumerian cuneiform are usually cited as examples. The phonetic alphabet in which a single symbol or combination of discrete symbols (the diphthongs) comes to stand for a speech sound is the last stage in the evolution of the modern alphabet. This is an obvious "economy of energy expenditure" compared to the syllabary alphabet in that it reduces the number of visual symbols that have to be remembered in order to reproduce the same range and variety of speech sounds. Early Egyptian hieroglyphics contain all elements of the various stages of the evolution of the writing process. Idiographic and phonographic symbols appear in succession and combinations.

The direction of writing has been an important corollary of the evolution from pictography to phonetic script. In *hieroglyphics*, Diringer says, "the direction of writing was normally from right to left, the signs facing the beginning of the line. Sometimes, however, inscriptions were written from left to right, and sometimes for purposes of symmetry, in both directions. In the latter case, each of the two parts usually faces toward the center reading from there outward." Early *hieratic* writing which followed *hieroglyphics* was usually vertical. The direction of writing was probably a further synthesis with kinesthetic phenomena. Actually, sinestrality and dextrality of script is a later development than even the phonetic alphabet. Early Greek writing which is clearly alphabetical still utilizes the principle of "boustrophaedon" or "ox turning" (i.e., like an ox plowing a field). If one line reads from left to right then the next would read from right to left with complete reversal of all alphabetical symbols. Other directional peculiarities recorded by Diringer are the following: An ancient script discovered in 1929 in Syria known as *Ugarit* consists of a cuneiform alphabet which is apparently unrelated to the ancient Sumerian or Assyrian languages. One tablet has been found in this script where the letters appear to be a kind of mirror writing or analogous to what today would be called printer's "offset type." The *Bataks*, a primitive group in Sumatra, use a syllabary script. They begin at the bottom of the page on the left hand side and place letter above letter in a vertical column until they reach the top. They then return to the bottom again in the next column to the right. *Pictish Oghamic*, an ancient Druid script discovered in Ireland, is read vertically from bottom upward. The *Phaistos* disc, an undeciphered script from Crete and Asia Minor, utilizes a spiral sequence of symbols reading from right to left and from the interior of the disc toward its periphery. Paleographers are of the opinion that the kinesthetic peculiarities of writing were most often determined by the properties of writing instruments and the media used in a particular culture. These they believe gradually became assimilated into the symbolic characters. Whatever the truth of the matter, it is easily observed that the closer one comes to a phonetic alphabet, the more consistent are the conventions concerning a strict directional character to writing. The more primitive the script, the greater the latitude in this regard. It is quite obvious that less confusion would be introduced by varying the direction of pictograms as long as a sequence was maintained than a similar flexibility in regard to phonetic symbols.

Pedagogy (Durrell, 1940; Harris, 1948) is well aware of the analogous stages in the learning process of the child in regard to reading and writing from pictography to phonetic concepts. The tachistoscopic teaching method is an implicit recognition of the transitional stages of development in this regard. What would appear to be relevant here is the similarity between the transitional character of the patient's reading and writing pattern and similar transitional phases in the evolution of the written word.[4] The early Egyptians, who read or wrote in hieroglyphic characters had to be prepared to oscillate between an idiographic visual system and a phonographic auditory set of symbols as the conventions of their writing demanded. One has a hunch that the first step in Champollion's historic deciphering of the Rosetta Stone must have been a triumph of the capacity for a kind of "controlled regression" (Kris, 1950) in reading and writing patterns. The sudden realization that some symbols were to be read as phonograms and others, the so-called determinatives, were to be read as idiograms led to the unraveling of the hitherto undecipherable secrets of ancient hieroglyphics. The patient seems to perform in the same manner. His spelling errors and similar, but not as clearly demonstrated, slips of reading can be understood as alternating attempts to reproduce or understand the word either purely as a visual configuration of symbols or as a phonetic sequence of syllables. Orton gives an interesting example of a similar process in a fourteen-year-old girl who read the word *phenomena* as "fmonia." When she was asked what was meant by "fmonia," she parried the question with the query: "Do you mean the liquid or the disease?" Obviously, her interchange of "phenomena" and "pneumonia," according to Orton, was the result of the visual similarity of the words, while that of "pneumonia" and "ammonia" rested on their auditory likeness. In normals, a similar disturbance may occur occasionally. It is to be noted how frequently when the spelling of a word seems to be forgotten it will be spelled "by ear" and then written to discover if it looks right.

In his discussion of the synthetic functions of the ego, Nunberg (1931) states: "The ego's capacity for synthesis manifests itself during the formation of the superego, not only in its mediation between the inner and outer world and its assimilation of the two, but also in the manner in which it unites, modifies, and fuses the separate psychic elements within itself." Nunberg goes on to suggest that the synthetic function derives its energy from the erotic components of the id and is the ego process which represents the creative process, which in its most elemental form is seen as the fusion of male and female elements to form a new human being. Also relevant in this connection is a statement (Hartmann (1951): "So far we have come to see ego development as a result of three sets of factors: inherited ego characteristics, influences of the instinctual drives and influences of external reality; to these we have to add as a fourth factor the influences different functions of the ego exert on each other."[5]

In this case we seem to be dealing with an individual whose development of idiographic ego functions is seen to be intact as evidenced by his extraordinary capacity to utilize mathematical symbols and concepts.[6] Functions that are elaborated upon the auditory sphere and have a purely phonographic pattern are likewise intact and highly developed. This patient speaks well. He has a large vocabulary. His diction is excellent. He is addicted to classical music and, as was noted in the previous history, has a hobby which consists of building high fidelity recording sets of unusual sensitivity. He has also in the past had a fair aptitude at playing a woodwind musical instrument (but was unable to play from written musical notation). Why then should his defect show itself in that one area of ego functioning where a high degree of integration between idiographic and phonographic symbolization is required? The present thesis suggests that these functions, as long as they can be utilized separately, fall within the sphere of ego functions utilizing neutralized energies, or what Hartmann (1939, 1950a, 1950b, 1951) has also called "secondary autonomies" (see also Hartmann, Kris, Loewenstein, 1946) but that in combination they become invaded by the primary process and fall victim to the patient's basic conflict.

It is to be recalled to what extent the parental figures in this patient represented for him auditory and visual functions (Chapter 1). Mother was a poetess. She had been an English major at college. She was a great lover of music. One of the patient's complaints about his mother is that as a small boy she used to talk to him too much about her troubles—"things that should have been reserved for adults." In this respect he was utilized as a listening post to compensate his mother for his father's inadequacy as a companion. There were times when his mother's talking went to such lengths that he found himself listening to her tones and inflections, removing his attention from the content of what she was saying. In identification with his mother, the patient still writes poetry, listens for long periods of time to music and builds high fidelity record players. The patient's father was a man "closeted in his study." His complaint against his father is: "We never had anything to say to each other." His father's profession was connected with a microscope. The familiar image of his father is a man sitting in his study peering into a microscope. Father is also a camera "fan." He has a large film library. He annoys the rest of the family with his propensity to break in on all occasions with his flashbulb or movie camera. At the age of three it was his father's flashbulb, while taking a family picture, that allegedly produced the patient's photophobic response. When the patient was eight, his father suffered from a detached retina of one eye. At the age of fourteen, the patient suffered from visual disturbance diagnosed by an ophthalmologist as "drusen." The patient's scoptophilic impulses were detailed in the previous report in connection with his pavor nocturnus at the age of five. At this time it was necessary to keep a light burning in his room at night. It is also noted that the patient's first dream in analysis (Chapter 1) represented a scoptophilic wish to see father's erection. In brief, then, father is associated with the idiographic processes. Mother is represented in the area of auditory integrations. The two fail to be synthesized in the same manner that it is difficult for the patient to conceive of father and mother in terms of any kind of togetherness or in a mutual creative function. This had also shown itself in the transference when for some time the patient had withheld from me the name of the woman analyst who was treating his "girl friend," for fear that we would "get together behind his back."

In this connection, it is interesting to refer back to some Rorschach material that was reported also in the previous paper and which appeared quite inexplicable at that time. It was reported that the tester noted three extremely unusual features in the patient's actual perceptual experience.[7] The first she described as so rare that it had been noted by the tester in only two cases examined by the Stress Tolerance Test among battle casualties. This she described as a synesthesia involving visual stimuli and sound. She stated that the patient heard the sound given by the impression of "fighting cats" in one of the cards. The other dysesthetic responses described are not relevant in the present context. The failure of synthesis between visual and auditory functions in the written word appears as a primitive synesthesia to the unstructured visual percepts of the Rorschach patterns, i.e., in the form in which it probably exists at an early stage in object conceptualization (Piaget, 1954).

The question can now be asked why, in spite of the identification of these two ego-apparatus functions with parental figures, should failure of the synthetic process take place? One feels that it is necessary here to invoke a highly theoretical speculation which, however, was already implicit in the previous report on this case. Here it was pointed out that there was an extraordinary precocity in the mathematical talent of the patient which was also a rather consistent feature in the history of mathematical geniuses and lightning calculators who had been previously studied. Some speculation on this problem was offered, based upon the investigations of Bergman and Escalona (1949), concerning the probability of precocious ego development, in certain cases of infantile psychosis and also cases of unusual talents, which derives its initial impetus from processes set in motion by the congenitally low threshold of the stimulus barrier in certain infants.[8] Reference should also be made to Hartmann's formulation (1939, 1951, 1952; see also Hartmann and Kris, 1945) concerning the possibility of having to consider uneven advances in the maturation not only of the ego as a total structure but also in regard to various sectors within the ego in relation to each other. To explain the involvement of the idiographic and phonógraphic functions of the ego in the area of conflict in this patient one might suppose that as with his mathematical ability these apparatuses had matured to a greater degree than would ordinarily be found in a child of similar age. There is some evidence that the patient's Slavic governess, who was herself studying English when he was three years of age, had also managed to teach the patient to read and write a few simple words. At least such a legend exists in the family. It would then be possible that a maturational phase for synthetic auditory and visual functions—the so-called reading readiness stage (Harrison, 1939) which ordinarily does not occur until the latency period in most children—would in this patient have been ready to function at the height of the Oedipus complex during the period of the pavor nocturnus. One of the standard genetic hypotheses of psychoanalysis has been that the taming of the instinctual drives of the preoedipal and oedipal phases ushers in the latency period, which makes possible the education of the child. It would seem that some revision of this formulation is necessary. The maturation of certain ego apparatuses is better described as the *sine qua non* for the child's acquiring of specific intellectual functions. These maturational phases usually coincide with certain stages of libidinal development under average conditions, but one is not necessarily dependent upon the other. Thus the optimal period for the education of the child in regard to language appears to be the period from about fifteen months to roughly five years (Gesell and Ilg, 1946). Thereafter language is continually acquired but at a greatly reduced rate of learning. In the case of reading, the maximum learning ability appears to begin at about the age of six years and to increase rapidly during the next two or three years, gradually leveling off in later childhood. Marked variations on either side of the norm are encountered according to the general principle of the "normal distribution curve." The vicissitudes of an ego function may well depend upon the id phase in which it appears. One would also expect mutual influences and modifications (A. Freud, 1952), but the appearance of the ego function must be considered relatively independent of the id phase. The reading readiness stage is, according to this hypothesis, a variable maturational phase of the synthesis of verbal-auditory and visual-ideographic ego functions.[9] It is characterized by the appearance of the child's capacity to grasp the concept of phonograms. By precocious development it may become involved in the oedipal conflict and thus fail to become part of the "conflict-free sphere" (Hartmann, 1939) as would be expected under average conditions.

Finally an attempt should be made to bring this formulation into a coherent relationship with the hypothesis developed in the study of the patient's successful mathematical sublimation (Chapter 1). At that time the importance of the capacity for decathexis of the image of the object (Kris, 1950), in enhancing the speed and mobility of the preconscious problem-solving function, was emphasized. Evidence was adduced to indicate that the child calculating prodigies who lose their special capacities as they mature, do so, in so far as they begin to "treat numbers as written symbols and become conscious paper computers rather than preconscious lightning calculators." Many lightning calculators, it was indicated, could not distinguish one written arabic numeral from another. Those who became educated and retained this ability did so by retaining the capacity to decathect the image of the written symbol. In other words, the capacity is possible in a child who has not developed a certain stage of "object concept" (the written symbol) or in the adult who has the capacity for a "controlled regression" (Kris, 1950) to this more primitive ego level. Piaget (1954), in studying the stages of the development of the concept of "object permanence" in the infant, stresses the importance of early intersensory coordinations: "In the case of sight and hearing, there exists at the outset no objective identity of the visual image with the auditory image [the development of these is then discussed]. . . . In short, intersensory co-ordinations contribute to the solidifying of the universe" (i.e., helping to give objects their external substantial character). The final stage of this process is, according to Piaget, the "concept" (image) of the object as a complex intersensory synthesis after the object itself has vanished. The written word is an advanced stage of such complex intersensory synthesis. In the case at hand a primitive level of this aspect of the process of "objectivation" has been demonstrated. It interferes demonstrably with the development and retention of visuophonetic word images. In the case of mathematical operations, however, it serves as a distinct advantage. The mathematician operating with abstractions or attenuated images has a shorter distance to traverse for his "controlled regression," if the intersensory syntheses of his object world are less "solid."

Summary

A case is presented involving the analysis of a young mathematician who suffers from a developmental dysgraphic and dyslexic defect or so-called strephosymbolia. Evidence is presented to indicate that his writing errors arise from oscillations between attempts to reproduce words in phonetic fashion without regard to their visual appearance or alternatively in idiographic fashion without regard to the ordering of phonemes necessitated by the sound of the word. It is suggested that phylogenetically his disturbance is similar to a transitional stage in the development of writing between idiographic forms and a syllabary alphabet with incomplete development of the concept of phonetic writing. It is suggested that the basic conflict in this case arises from the primal scene fantasy which associates father with visual activities, mother with auditory functions and which conceives of them as two separate unloving human beings who are incapable of producing a child except by artificial insemination. It is further suggested that secondary autonomy has been achieved in the visual and auditory perceptual functions of the ego when utilized separately, and that conflict invades these areas only in their synthetic function related to recognizing and evoking phonetic words and images. At this point their synthetic product becomes invested with primal scene significance. The genetic origin of the disability may be due to precocious maturation of certain ego sectors involved in visual and auditory perceptual processes so that they become involved in the oedipal conflict at a crucial stage in their development. Thus they are prevented in their synthetic relationship from forming a new, completely autonomous structure as they might have, had their maturation been somewhat delayed. An attempt is made to indicate the relationship between this disturbance of interperceptual synthesis and the enhancement of preconscious problem-solving operations in mathematics which utilize attenuated "unsolidified" images.

Notes

1. Blanchard (1928, 1935, 1947), Cole (1951), Crisp (1949), Dearborn (1933, 1938), Durrell (1940), Fernald and Keller (1921), Freud (1904), Gates (1941), Gates and Bennett (1933), Hincks (1926), Hinshelwood (1917), Hildreth (1934), Ketcham (1951), Kirk (1934), Knight (1952), Launay and Borel-Maisonny (1952), Orton (1937, 1939), Pearson (1952), Phillips (1934), Selzer (1933), Sterba (1943), Strachey (1930), Sylvester and Kunst (1943), Tulchin (1935), Witty (1936), Witty and Kopel (1936), Woody and Phillips (1934), Young (1938), and others.

2. The patient has been consistently right-handed throughout his development. Numerous tests of lateral dominance at various times are said to have confirmed this fact. However, the family pattern reveals that his father and oldest sister are both left-handed, while his mother and younger sister are right-handed.

3. The hypothesis presented here does not imply that functional lateralization is an irrelevant aspect of the problem, but would rather consider that such failures of lateralization, where they appear in cases of strephosymbolia, can also be explained as concomitant disturbances of intrasystemic synthesis rather than as a cause of the disability.

4. It is not intended here to suggest that the patient's disability has anything to do with the somewhat dubious concept of "phylogenetic regression" by comparing his defect with an incomplete stage in the development of the written word. Rather the similarity is meant to call attention to the analogy between the synthetic processes in the cultural evolution of a sublimation and its formation as an individual ego structure.

5. An example of this in almost pure culture would be the mutism or distortion of speech development secondary to varying degrees of early acquired or congenital deafness.

6. In this connection and also in relation to the formulations that follow, it is of some interest to note Kris's (1950) concept of decathexis of external objects in extraordinary feats of preconscious mentation, and Hermann's (1926) suggestion that in mathematics and logic there is a decathexis of objects and a hypercathexis of the relationship between objects.

7. The psychological testing was done by Dr. Molly Harrower.

8. In this connection also see Fries and Woolf (1953) in regard to the role of "congenital activity types" in ego development, particularly in its sensory functioning.

9. Schilder (1944) expresses a neurological point of view with certain similarities, although he does not view the ego disturbances in quite the same light nor relate it to id phases. "These variations are probably due to a different development of those parts of the brain which are indispensable for the process of reading. In the serious cases we probably deal with a dysfunction of a cortical apparatus. This dysfunction expresses itself in the integrating and differentiating difficulty, in optic mistakes concerning letters and in increased mirror tendencies. The inherent mirror tendencies as well as mirror tendencies originating from other sources, and intellectual difficulties, may alter and increase the primary trouble which is an isolated trouble of gnostic intellectual fashion."

CHAPTER THREE

Abstract Thinking and Object Relations

The tempo of technological advance in the present century has more than ever stimulated interest in abstract thought, a relatively neglected topic in psychoanalytic psychology. Perhaps the new emphasis in this psychological quest is less upon the process character of abstract theoretical thinking than upon the individual in whom it occurs (Chapter 1; Greenacre, 1957, 1958a; Jones, 1931, 1956; Roe, 1952; Savitt, 1957).

There is much popular mythology and folklore about such personalities (a subject so well treated by Ernest Jones (1956) in his Freud Anniversary address in New York.) Much of this folklore deserves attention for its fantasy character and has little further interest for the psychologist. The rather widespread view that individuals with unusual intellectual gifts have certain psychological differences from the rest of the population is at least a truism by the very nature of the gift itself although it may be contended that this is one of degree rather than of kind. Recent studies, however, and collateral data[1] do carry with them the suggestion that the unusual intellectual gift is often accompanied by a disturbance of ego functioning and/or of object relations in some other area. One such case, a highly gifted "pure" mathematician (Chapter 1) with strephosymbolia (Chapter 2) was reported two years ago by the present author (see also Ferenczi, 1955). Greenacre (1957) in a recent stimulating paper has discussed similar problems. The exploration of such phenomena appears to be important to the problem of a psychoanalytic theory of thinking since it holds out for us not only the possibility of greater comprehension of the psychology of talent, but also a promise of maturing some of our oversimplified and at times faintly moralistic notions concerning the development of sublimation and the secondary process: namely, the prevalent idea that the capacity to think is a reward *pari passu* with the renunciation of instinctual aims. What I am attempting here, however, is more of an attempt to underscore some of the phenomena encountered in the analysis of gifted individuals with a high degree of capacity for abstract conceptual thinking than to formulate any original addenda to our already rather complex design for a psychoanalytic theory of thought.

In Freud's formulation (1911; see also 1900, 1910b) regarding two principles in mental functioning, the thesis that the secondary process develops its special characteristics as a result of the reality-testing activities of the individual, and is thus in large part a reflection of the external world of objects (although drive motivated) is first clearly indicated (see also Ferenczi, 1916). The first stage of the development of the secondary process must therefore be conceived as consisting of images which are representations of the percepts of the animate and inanimate object world. In the later phase of language development, the gradual substitution of word symbols for images requires the withdrawal of some cahtectic energy from the mental image, as the development of the image in the first place required the withdrawal of certain quantities of libido from the external objects as "things in themselves." Abstract thought is, at least developmentally, the most advanced stage of the secondary process. It is made up of many elements. Some of those that can be most easily separated from the complex synthetic product that we call a theoretical concept are the ideas that deal with *class, quantity,* and *spatial relationships* (Piaget, 1953). The formation of these ideas requires an additional decathexis of the image-word representation of the external object. The economy of psychic energy expenditure appears to be one of the striking progressive gains for each stage of this process, and most particularly this final one.

Schilder (1942; see also Rapaport, 1951b) in his discussion of the development of thought, particularly in regard to concept formation, speaks of images as "way stations to meaning." One of the essential characteristics "in those experiences which play a crucial role in thinking," according to Schilder, "is their poverty in sensory material." He also suggests that the goal of concept formation is to gain insight into object relations and that the "checking effect" of an interposition that obstructs this goal is a return to thought in the form of manifest images.

In so far as this development requires the withdrawal of a certain quantity of libidinal cathexis from the object world, it would appear to be the antithesis of the mechanism by which reality testing and object relations were established in the first place. Thus it is necessary to conceive of two concurrent processes in this development which are in a sense the antithesis of each other. The process of reality testing implies the successive releasing of quantities of libido, formerly narcissistically directed, for the investment of external objects. The formation of certain aspects of the secondary process, on the other hand, seems to require the concurrent withdrawal of object libido for the cathexis successively of images, words and finally concepts. This could be described as essentially a process of narcissistic reinvestment. The delicate balance of this interchange has many implications for psychoanalytic theory and practice that have not yet been fully explored. For example, the observation that for many creative activities of thought, which utilize certain aspects of the primary process in the service of the ego (Kris, 1950), there are to be found analogous invasions of the secondary process which utilize certain aspects of its function in the service of the id (Gombrich and Kris, 1940), has frequently been overlooked as an almost regular clinical phenomenon (Kris, 1938, 1944). In this connection, for example, Kris says, "There are numerous conditions extending from the levels of normal life deep down into the realm of the pathological, in which the ego abandons its supremacy. . . . It seems that the ego finds its supremacy curtailed whenever it is overwhelmed by affects, irrespective of whether an excess of affect or the ego's own weakness is to be held responsible for the process. But the opposite case, where the ego enrolls the primary process in its service and makes use of it for its purposes is also of the widest significance. It is not confined to the sphere of wit and caricature but extends to the vast domain of aesthetic expression in general, and applies to the whole field of art and symbol formation, preconscious or unconscious, which beginning with cult and ritual, permeates the whole of human life" (Gombrich and Kris, 1940). The ancient shibboleth concerning the proximity of genius and psychosis may thus find a more refined expression in such metapsychological considerations.

If one examines the main categories of the elements of abstract thinking, it will be seen that they can be arranged in a hierarchical order of increasing withdrawal of object cathexis. Granting the oversimplification in the following statements: The process of *classification*, for example, when it is in the service of the ego, is essentially a sorting operation whose main purpose is to arrange objects in groups such that their similarities determine their arrangement while their irrelevant attributes or differences are excluded from consideration. Thus attention is withdrawn from only some of the attributes of the object while remaining invested in those that determine its class.

In the process of *quantification* on the other hand, all identifying special attributes of the object are ignored and attention is specifically directed to the object's position in its correspondence to a similarly decathected series of countable units. Thus discreteness alone becomes the main object of attention (Piaget, 1952).

In the most advanced concepts dealing with shape and the *special relationship* between objects, as in the non-Euclidean geometries for example, the object as such ceases to exist even in terms of discreteness and becomes merely a reference point for the demarcation of fragments of space. In this process the chief attention is directed to position, the intervals, the enclosures or to the blank spaces between objects, so to speak, rather than to the objects themselves (Dale, 1957; Piaget, 1956).

The use of the processes of abstract thinking, sometimes referred to as "intellectualization," as a defense is well known as a technical problem in analysis (Stein, 1958). Less well delineated are the roles of the specific elements of abstract thinking when they are utilized in the service of the primary process (Jones, 1931) as one of the many aspects of the complex defense that is subsumed under the concept of "regression" (Kasanin, 1944a; Savitt, 1957).

In the following case report, an attempt will be made to illustrate the utilization of the three elementary categories of abstraction as regressive defenses existing side by side with an unusual ability for the utilization of the same process in the service of the ego.

Case Report

The patient was a twenty-three-year-old, single female mathematician who had revealed unusual capacities for dealing with the mathematical problems of advanced experiments in nuclear physics on high-speed electronic computing devices. To her superiors, she seemed to display an uncanny ability for understanding the peculiarities of the mechanical devices and for translating the data most efficiently into the appropriate terms for machine handling. Even more striking was her ability to divine the source of insidious errors which held up the progress of calculation. This is known colloquially among univac technicians as "debugging." She was almost totally inarticulate, however, at explaining the steps by which her results were derived. The patient's main problems when she came for treatment were her dissatisfaction with her life, recurrent depressive moods, and an inability to form relationships of any intensity or permanence with others, but especially with members of the opposite sex. She confided in her first interview that she was living alone and that she still slept at night with a large teddy bear, now in a state of imminent dissolution. This had been going on for the past twenty years, the teddy bear having been the last gift of her father who had died when she was two years of age. On one occasion she had reported, "I live very happily alone with my teddy bear and my problems in variables as real functions." The father, according to a family myth, had an unusual ability for mental arithmetic. The patient had had two periods of analysis in childhood when she did poorly in her schoolwork and seemed to withdraw from the other children. She is described in the first of these as a case of "pseudo imbecility" (Mahler-Schoenberger, 1942).

The youngest of four children, her history reveals that an older sibling suffered from an acute paranoid episode several years before her present analysis had begun. The patient had also gone through a period of sexual seduction by an older male relative which began around the age of seven and seems to have terminated when she was about nine. The details of this did not emerge until rather late in her present analysis. In these episodes, the patient permitted him anal penetration in return for money. Her ineffectual mother, who had apparently become quite helpless in the face of the loss of her husband, could only cope with this situation by forbidding the child to take money from her seducer. According to the patient, this merely deprived her of her reward but did not interfere with the activity. She was also taken to sleep in the mother's bed for protection. An episodic symptom of derealization is also apparent retrospectively in the patient's childhood. One such episode seems to be characteristic. As a child of about seven, while sitting in church with her nurse, she had the impression that while her glance was removed, someone had changed the altar flowers, which now appeared to be of a different species and color. During the rest of the service, she paid attention to nothing else but the flowers, keeping her gaze fixed upon them. Nevertheless they appeared at intervals to change their character. The patient recalls having been tormented by the uncertainty as to whether her eyes were playing tricks upon her, or whether she was shifting her glance just long enough for someone to have substituted a different bouquet.[2]

The transference had two major aspects. The patient had been referred to me initially with the remark that I was particularly interested in mathematicians. Shortly after the analysis began she matriculated for an advanced degree in mathematics and then began to develop a variety of study blocks and a severe inhibition in regard to the completion of her thesis. Although apparently produced by her inability to be articulate about abstract concepts, at a deeper level this appeared to be a testing of her relationship with the therapist to see whether she would remain interesting to him even if she turned out to be "stupid" or a "hack". It was a repetition of the period of "pseudo imbecility" in childhood which also contained within it a condensation of many other meanings. It was also an appeal to be loved as "just an ordinary person." This was also expressed in frequent fantasies of leaving her academic research position and becoming an unskilled worker in some other field in a place where no one would know her. Another aspect of the transference seemed to represent a desire to establish a mutual relationship between two high-speed electronic computers into which the data could be fed and from which it could be elicited without the interference of any other feelings or any other form of object relationship. This would constitute a kind of telepathic cybernetic romance in which ideas of maximal complexity could be communicated by minimal signals.

The analysis of this patient was beset by unusual technical difficulties. One rather stubborn resistance was the use of long periods of silence during which the response to requests for information was usually, "I am thinking of nothing" or "My mind is a blank." During one phase of the analysis, when attempts were made to stimulate associations during these periods of "blankness," the patient exhibited a dramatic startle reaction which resembled a primitive "moro reflex." Other forms of what appeared in general to be regressive modes of "acting out" in the transference were tearfulness, petulance, unusual displays of anger and the constant threat, implied or explicit, of forsaking all of her responsibilities. During periods of more ordinary verbalization, more subtle defensive operations could be discerned. These were regressive analogues of some of her unusual capacities for abstract thinking.

Classifying Activity in the Service of the Primary Process

Categorizing of methods for handling data was an important part of the patient's work. The keeping of "library routines" was one example of this. These consisted of a file of various methods for handling different categories of data in the computing operation. The patient was very skilled in this branch of her work. On several occasions in situations in which there had been an increase in salary and an obvious promotion to a more responsible position, the patient was moved to a different office where she became associated with a new group of people. On each occasion she began to describe the various attributes of her new associates in order to find a common denominator which would enable her to uncover the motives of her superiors in ordering the relocation. There was a vaguely paranoid quality in this preoccupation. On each occasion, by sorting out irrelevant characteristics and overlooking the relevant ones, the patient was able to insist that she had been demoted and discovered to be a fraud. In the transference this meant that if the treatment were continued in spite of the discovery of her inferiority, it would prove that the therapist loved her for herself and not for her special capacity. On one occasion the distortion was so blatant that the patient was able to see through her own self-deception.

Arithmetical Computation in the Service of Defense

In their basic features, all computing machines are essentially the same in that they reduce higher mathematics to arithmetic and arithmetic to counting (von Neumann, 1956). The discovery of various imprecise notions of quantity in a computing automaton expert of such skill was felt to be of special significance. Shortly after the analysis had begun it was found that the patient had made two errors in her initial report concerning her finances. She had suppressed the information concerning a savings account, while at the same time reporting a sum of money several thousand dollars in excess of the actual amount that she had received as an inheritance. Although the patient felt that she was cheating by minimizing her assets, she overlooked the fact that the exaggeration of the inheritance more than balanced the failure to mention her savings account. Her net assets therefore were less than claimed. On another occasion, the patient began to spend a great deal of time in breeding Siamese kittens when she felt that the time should have been spent on her thesis. She claimed that she was doing this in order to earn some extra money. On the day that a litter of six kittens was born the patient announced that she was going to sell them for twenty dollars apiece and that the "hundred and fifty dollars that she would thus earn" would give her such and such a profit over her breeding expenses. Subsequent analysis of these distortions and others indicated that they were overdetermined events in the service of the ambivalent instinctual aspects of the transference. They indicated on the one hand that the patient was a true mathematician since real mathematicians are "notoriously poor at arithmetic." Insofar as the patient was only tolerated in the analysis on the basis of her mathematical talent (as she contended), this was her insurance against rejection. On the other hand as evidence of her stupidity it served the purposes of her wish to be loved as a female and/or child (more explicitly, as it turned out later, as a foolish teddy bear of the A. A. Milne "Pooh bear" variety). In the bisexual conflict it had been clear from the beginning that her mathematical talent was equated with masculinity.

Spatial Relationships Conceived Regressively

The ability to conceptualize positions in space is certainly an important aspect of geometrical thinking (Piaget, 1950, 1954, 1956). It also plays an important role in the development of the body image and concepts concerning anatomical relationships.[3] In so far as quantity and memory in the electronic computer are translated into positional relationships, the patient's knowledge of the machine demanded an ability to form such concepts of more than the usual degree. As the treatment progressed, the periods of silence and the reports of "mental blankness" decreased. This patient suffered from an extremely severe dysmenorrhea. During a large part of the analysis it was also found that she was engaged in secret sexual affairs which had never been reported. The mental "blankness" was usually found to be either a substitute for a statement concerning pelvic pain or for a report of a sexual experience on the day preceding the analytic session. Such matters could only be reported after a certain distance in time had been achieved from them. In one dream the patient suggested the analogy of this resistance to problems in abstract thought. The stimulus to the dream had apparently been the analyst's remark, when the patient had said that she was thinking "nothing," that "nothing must mean something" (see Lewin, 1948). In the dream "a series of zeros are emerging as an answer from a computing machine. The machine has been given its instructions in such a way that there is one missing element." The patient's only association to the dream was that zero stands for a definite position in the memory of the univac machine. An ability to translate concepts of quantity into positions in space was apparently a precondition of the patient's facility at "debugging" operations. As far as the patient's concept of her own genital anatomy was concerned, it appeared on several occasions that she retained childhood fantasies of the equivalence of the vagina and the anus and in her college biology courses had found it very difficult to retain any visual concepts of anatomical relationships. As far as the transference was concerned, the dream also indicated a reversible position of the patient and the analyst as "mind" and machine. In so far as the analyst occupied the position of the machine, she, the "mind," by omitting significant information, would get "nothing" as an answer. This defense served not only to hide her sexual relationships from the analyst, but its analysis first allowed the emergence of the information that the sexual play with her relative had been specifically an anal penetration. Her inability to visualize the actual physical aspects of this relationship had protected her against responsibility and guilt. The blank spells on the couch and the startle reaction appeared now to have been the fear of a comparable attack by the therapist. They also covered the terror and depression as well as the pleasurable aspects of the childhood event. One might generalize all this as follows: Insofar as she did not understand her own genital anatomy and what her seducer was doing behind her back, she was attempting through the blank spell to communicate the "nonrepresentational" aspects of the experience. It is of interest that the patient also reports that this is the way she "debugs" a problem and it also reminded her of one of her methods of studying a difficult subject. "One makes one's mind a blank until the information sinks in or until the answer to the problem comes out." The warding off of the concrete images of the experiences of childhood also served the purposes of isolation in its manifold forms.

A reconstruction of the classroom episodes of the period of "pseudo imbecility" in childhood reveals the relationship between her thinking patterns in her work and her recurrent inarticulateness in the analysis.

During the period of sexual seduction in childhood, the patient began to withdraw in class, sitting in the back of the room with a "cowlike" stare. She seemed oblivious of what was going on about her. She has recalled in the treatment that during these periods she was engaged in extensive daydreaming. She felt different from the other children and rejected by them. She ascribed this to the fact that she had no father. Her fantasies were frequently about her father who had not died as stated by the others, but who, as a famous man, still lived in other parts of the world. In these fantasies he was a great traveler who would one day return to his home to claim her.

Curiously, in spite of her withdrawal of attention, she was able to learn her arithmetic but had no *feeling* of having learned it or of knowing the steps by which she had arrived at the solution of a particular computation. In later years when she was "called" to the blackboard" to demonstrate a problem, she knew the answer but dreaded being asked to show how she arrived at it. Somehow to know the answer without the process meant the appropriation of something that did not belong to her.

It appears likely that the childhood learning, at least in the arithmetical area, had been able to proceed as part of a process of split attention. While the fantasy activity seemed central, a peripheral attention apparently continued to follow the teaching process. The analogy between this and certain aspects of the "thesis block" is most clearly demonstrated by her report that her chief difficulty in bringing her results to her advisor was the fear that he would say "how did you arrive at this?" or point out that certain essential steps were missing. The inability to reproduce the steps would lead to the discovery of the forbidden fantasy life (also equated with masturbation) and the illicit incestuous affair. This is similar to her behavior on the couch where the "thinking nothing" and unconscious fantasy activity coincide.

Another patient, studied as part of the same project, was a brilliant student of mathematics as well as a talented musician. This young man sought analysis because of his shyness, social anxiety, and inability to form any relationships with members of the opposite sex. One of the patient's complaints in the analysis was his inability to picture the anatomical relations involved in the act of intercourse. Although he had frequent nocturnal emissions and masturbatory fantasies, he had been unable, up to the current report, to achieve an emission by any means while in the waking state. A habit of sleeping at night with a pillow in his arms was reminiscent of the first patient's teddy bear. In his childhood, the family had to take along his special pillow when they traveled because he would refuse to sleep without it. Intercourse had never been attempted. During the course of his analysis it was also discovered that voyeuristic activities largely connected with pornographic pictures and magazines dominated his erotic life. On many occasions during the analysis he demonstrated the close economic connection between his regressive object relations and his intellectual life. These consisted of what he called "pseudo dreams" which were always followed by "real" dreams on falling asleep. By a "pseudo dream" the patient apparently meant a fantasy in a twilight state of consciousness. Almost invariably the "pseudo dream" was some variant of a sexual fantasy involving a faceless female form in which the patient was trying to solve the problem of "how is it done?" (i.e., the sex act), especially in regard to the physical positions of the two bodies in space. In the "real" dream that followed there was usually either a manifest mathematical problem or a reference to one which had existed as a day residue in the patient's study routine. The mathematical dream very frequently was accompanied by a nocturnal emission.

The Intermediate Stages of the Process of Concept Formation

Fisher's (1956, 1957) studies of the use by the dream process of subthreshold perceptual data has helped to elucidate some aspects of the intermediate stages of the development of the dream. An attempt will be made here to draw some of the threads of the present argument into a tighter pattern. A possible analogy between the regressive aspects of concept formation and the dream process is suggested. It should again be emphasized that the "progressive" development of object relations as well as the secondary process are dependent upon images and words (symbol formation) as a link between concrete objects and abstract concepts.

The use of abstract thought is a well-known form of "intellectual" defense, not only in the patient reported, but in the analytic treatment of many cases (Stein, 1958). In free association the analyst hopes to elicit primarily the word-image representations of the data of experience to counter this defense, since it is in these intermediate mental contents that the affects also reside and not in objects as such or in abstract ideas. If this intermediate stage in the development of concept formation is elided, two extreme possibilities present themselves. At one end of the scale one might expect an individual whose concepts are ephemeral, rote in character and lacking in a sense of emotional conviction (Bolles and Goldstein, 1938; Goldstein and Scheerer, 1941; Hanfmann and Kasanin, 1942; Kasanin, 1944a). At the other end one might predict the "object-bound" character or one of those personalities who are primitive in their modes of thought, expressing a restricted range of affect with ideas that are inordinately concrete and who reveal a relative or absolute inability to form abstract concepts. Most dramatically this is found in certain cases of brain damage (Goldstein, 1925; Goldstein and Scheerer, 1941), but it also has similarities to character traits of some fetishists and other perverse individuals. The "normal" individual is capable of cathecting the concrete object, representing it imagistically and verbally and then forming abstract concepts about its class, quantity and spatial-relational characteristics, from which more highly integrated concepts are finally built (Piaget, 1950, 1953).

In this discussion the dynamics and economics of a fourth possibility have been suggested for the highly "gifted" individual (see also Greenacre, 1957, 1958b). Essentially it is suggested that in such individuals the intermediate stages of object cathexis are not omitted but are dealt with preconsciously in the manner of the lightning calculator (Chapter 1) or the individual with perfect pitch. It is as if the transition from the concrete object to the abstract idea occurs in an image and word "blackout." This may account for that aspect of the patient's report that she is thinking "nothing" which is analogous to her inability to recount the steps by which she arrives at solutions for some of the most abstruse machine problems. Unlike the usual thought that has an intermediate link to words, this state of affairs produces an idea that appears to be anchored, so to speak, in only two places, the object world and the idea that can only be represented abstractly. Such ideas can be worn like reversible garments, the surface that remains close to the primary process producing in effect an individual who is often a surprising composite of the "object-bound" primitive personality and the brilliant theoretician or creative artist: or, as in this case, the colossal contrast between the small child who sleeps with a teddy bear at night and the adult who can operate a high-speed electronic computer by day.

It seems quite likely that Winnicott's concept (1953) of the "transitional object" has an important bearing, especially from the genetic point of view, on this aspect of the thought process. There can be little doubt that in this case the teddy bear is typical of such a "possession." Winicott says in this connection: "This intermediate area of experience, unchallenged in respect of its belonging to inner or external (shared) reality, constitutes the great part of the infant's experience and throughout life is retained in the intense experiencing that belongs to the arts and to religion, to imaginative living, and to creative scientific work."

In a childhood play fantasy around the age of six or seven, the teddy bear was conceived by the patient as a very extraordinary mental giant who knew everything but made very foolish mistakes. By balancing every achievement in computational brilliance with some single but foolish mistake, the patient also appeared to be enacting the early confusion of identity between herself and the teddy bear and the fear of separation from the "transitional" object with which the active and passive aims of cuddling could be simultaneously realized.

Greenacre has recently suggested several formulations that appear to bear upon this problem. She deals in greater detail with the genetic and economic aspects of creative thought than does this presentation. In "The Childhood of the Artist" (Greenacre, 1957), she says, "In the perverse individual the overlapping fusion, or at least too great communication between different phase drives, results in too easy substitution of one for another or sometimes in chaotic disorganization. Problems resulting from these states are frequently played out on the individual's own body. In the talented person, or one of genius, such a confusion may be obviated by the discharge through channels of developed or developing talent. . . ." In the other paper, entitled "The Family Romance of the Artist" (Greenacre, 1958a), she discusses this again in relation to the peculiarities of the gifted individual's sensory-perceptual organization: "Certain qualities which are precursors of creative ability are inborn, and these qualities produce a greater range of sensory responsiveness, together with a greater capacity to organize sensory impressions. . . . There is the possibility that personal relationships are, in the gifted individual, capable of heightened intensity and there may ben an extension of empathy with animation of related inanimate peripheral objects. It is this widened area of responsiveness with the inclusion of peripheral but 'high-lighted' objects [and the present writer would add: the exclusion of central but overshadowed ones] that has been referred to as the 'field of collective alternatives.' The effect of this would be to promote prematurity of the pregenital and genital phase development and to diminish the boundaries between phases. . . . In addition the heightened sensitivity reacting to body states and rhythms, as well as to the outer world, causes a continual searching for a harmony of balance between the two; and states of imbalance may be played out in disturbances of perception of the outer world and/or emotional relationships to other human beings."

It may be said that this is one way of describing the essential thought structure of schizophrenia. It may indeed account for the "borderline" clinical impression so often conveyed by such unusually gifted individuals. I think that there is one essential difference, although the dividing line may be a narrow one. In the true schizophrenic, objects and concepts are linked by word-image structures (as well as by the elements of the abstracting process) which are in the service of the primary process and *primarily for the facilitation of libidinal and aggressive discharge*. Thus the intermediate levels are rarely or only episodically available to the secondary process for ego services while the secondary process can be utilized for the services of the id. In the gifted, creative thinker on the other hand the proximity of these linkages between the external object and the abstract idea is primarily to facilitate the *mobility of cathexes* and the *economy of energy expenditure* inherent in this mobility. Thus although the psychic structures involved may be similar, the purposes are different. In the gifted individual these intermediate steps, or rather their results, are usually available to the secondary process and are in the service of the ego. But it is also the proximity of these elements to the primary process including the basic building blocks of abstract concepts, that apparently increases the possibility for their utilization as regressive defenses.

Conclusions

The foregoing schematic account has attempted to emphasize the following formulations:

1. That abstract thought consists of varying degrees of decathexis of objects in order to deal with nonrepresentational aspects of their attributes such as class, quantity, and physical spatial relationships.
2. This process can be in the service of the ego and reality testing or in the service of the primary process.
3. In the latter form it can be seen as one aspect of the more general use of regression as defense. The regressive defenses thus require more specific characterization in terms of their secondary process content than is ordinarily afforded to them.
4. In those individuals who have an unusual capacity for abstract thinking one can expect such "perversions" of abstraction to be particularly available for the defensive process and to leave its mark upon their personalities and their object relationships. Unlike the psychotic, however, who also keeps the intermediate stages of concept formation close to the primary process, they are particularly available to the secondary process in the gifted individual.
5. This is explained by the possibility that in the gifted individual

the proximity to the primary process of intermediate stages of concept development utilizes mainly its mobility of cathexis rather than its feature of availability to instinctual discharge. (The phase-developmental aspects of this process have been discussed by Greenacre, 1957, 1958b, and Winnicott, 1953).

6. Under the impact of the transference, however, and the increased drive pressure thus induced, the "controlled regressive" aspects of abstract thinking may be disturbed and thus bear a closer resemblance to the thought process of the psychotic. This appears to be a finding which has not only important consequences for the refinement of diagnosis and technique, but, when fully explored, may add to our understanding of the psychology of abstract thought.

Notes

1. The clinical material in this report was part of the study of gifted individuals undertaken under the auspices of the Treatment Center of the New York Psychoanalytic Institute, with funds made available by the generosity of the Arthur Davison Ficke Foundation. This project was initiated by, and was under the direction of, Dr. Ernst Kris until his death. I am greatly indebted to him and to the following members of the project for the opportunity that it has afforded for a mutual exchange of ideas: Drs. Marianne Kris (the present chairman), Phyllis Greenacre, Annie Reich, Edith Jacobson, Mary O'Neil Hawkins, Margaret Mahler, Leo Stone, Martin Stein, Samuel Ritvo, Leo Loomie, Allan Roos, and Mrs. Christine Olden. The views expressed in this paper are, of course, not necessarily subscribed to by the other members of the group.

2. See Winnicott (1953) on the problem of illusion in relation to transitional objects.

3. In *The Child's Conception of Space* Piaget (1956) states that even prior to organizing a projective and Euclidean space, "the child starts by building up and using certain primitive relationships such as proximity and separation, order and enclosure. Such relationships correspond to those termed 'topological' by geometicians . . ." Thus in the development of spatial concepts it is possible that a primitive "conceptual space" is antecedant to "perceptual space."

CHAPTER FOUR

Language Distortions in Ego Deviations

> "Do you mean that you can find the answer to it [the riddle]?" said the March Hare. "Exactly so," said Alice. "Then you should say what you mean," the March Hare went on. "I do," Alice hastily replied, "at least I mean what I say, that's the same thing, you know." "Not the same thing a bit," said the Hatter. "Why, you might just as well say that I see what I eat is the same as I eat what I see."
>
> —LEWIS CARROLL, 1865

This is a preliminary attempt to study the effect of ego deviations on language and to examine the possibility that some language distortions may be used to identify ego deviations. An effort will also be made to correlate current concepts of linguistic reference with Freud's theory (1915b) of "word-thing" presentations. The problem is vast, encompassing the whole range of language and

I am indebted to the members of a graduate study in linguistics and psychoanalysis, which has been meeting for several years in the New York Psychoanalytic Institute, for the exchange of many of the ideas that have led to this discussion. A special debt of gratitude is owed to Dr. Henry Edelheit who has served as the secretary to this group and often as its mentor. Without his diligent spade work and constant stimulation we would not have been able to proceed. I am also indebted to Dr. Elise Wechsler Snyder for editorial revision and valuable suggestions concerning the content of the paper.

communication theory within its sphere. I shall deal with only a fragment of this material through the analysis of a few clinical examples of the relationship between ego deviations and disturbances of linguistic reference.

Hartmann (1951) refers to these problems in discussing the "Technical Implications of Ego Psychology." He says, "Finally, the influence of the superego on speech and language is familiar to us, especially from psychopathology. This is to say that the different aspects of speech and language, as described by psychologists and philosophers, become coherent and meaningful if viewed from the angle of our structural model, and that in this case actually all the structural implications have today become relevant for our handling of the analytic situation. In trying to clarify the technical aspects of the problem involved, we are actually following the lead of structural psychology" (p. 150).

Encouraged to associate freely, the patient frequently "misunderstands" these directions as license for ambiguous and obscure reference. Not only is this a misinterpretation of the "basic rule" by the patient, but it exposes the therapist to the possibility of a technical error if he does not make clear that an understanding of the manifest meaning of an utterance is usually necessary before an interpretation of the latent meaning is possible. One may suspect an "ego deviation"[1] or at least an unconscious defensive maneuver when the patient is consistently unable to make the "reference" of his utterance explicit. Furthermore, the multiple choices and ambiguities inherent in the internal structure of language afford unconscious intentions, fantasies, and conflicts various opportunities for linguistic expression. The individual's representation of self object, and external world (Jacobson, 1964) determines in many cases the phonetic variant, the lexical alternatives, and the syntactic structures of words and sentences used in communicating ideas.[2]

Two extreme language phenomena encountered in the psychoanalytic situation cannot be understood simply as "defenses," but require a further examination of the language function itself. In one of these extreme forms of disturbed reference, the patient alludes to thoughts for which he cannot find adequate verbal expression and often assumes that they are too complex or too removed from shared experience to be verbalized. In the other extreme, words follow each other glibly and rapidly with few pauses and in bewildering profusion. One has the impression that the patient only knows what he is thinking by listening to what he says. This relationship between speech and thought was well summarized by an apocryphal elderly lady who, when asked her opinion about a certain matter, said that she did not know what it was until she heard what she had to say about it. Lewis Carroll's not-so-mad Hatter referred to the same problem.[3] Between the libidinized speech that is apparently empty of conceptual thought and the mental content that cannot be rendered in words lie a large variety of clinical phenomena which can be studied from a semantic viewpoint.

The process of communication in words, the one absolutely indispensable feature of psychoanalytic therapy, is itself often involved in the psychopathology that brings the patient to treatment. Part of the time consumed in any analysis is employed in developing a common vocabulary. When ordinary words cannot convey subtle idiosyncratic aspects of experience, despite a sufficient community of experience to share the idea if the right word or combination of words were available, difficulties in understanding arise. More often, however, the highly differentiated languages of man suffice for the communication of even the most uncommon event in the life of the individual (Sapir, 1921). Most commonly, the cause of disturbances in understanding the manifest meaning of an utterance lies in some distortion of the phonetic, syntactic, or semantic conventions of either the speaker's or the listener's linguistic code.

Ideally, when two individuals engaged in an ordinary dialogue[4] are "on the same wave length," they know that the arbitary meanings of the words they are using are the same, not only because they understand each other's idea, but also as a result of the opposite event. They know that they do not understand each other when the idea being expressed is unfamiliar as an experience, unfamiliar because of a logical ambiguity, or unfamiliar because a strange word is used or an unaccustomed meaning attached to a familiar word. Such a misunderstanding is often signaled by the listener's feeling that his attention has lapsed. At such times, the listener usually requests repetition of the statement. It is only when the repetition of the utterance fails to bring enlightenment, even with the aid of paraphrasing, word substitution, or examples, that the listener is sure that he has misunderstood or that the speaker has failed to make his meaning clear. When a speaker and listener are "on the same wave length," the meaning is clear to the listener, even when the experience described is recognized as an unfamiliar one.

In the "transference neuroses," the patient's referential utterances are usually unambiguous in their manifest content. Such precision in reference does not eliminate the possibility that some expressible thoughts are withheld and that some unconscious ideas are unavailable to language. The opposite case, typified by the florid psychoses, is one in which the language process is so severely disorganized that we know, without question and without the need for closer scrutiny, that failures of communication result from the use of unfamiliar language. In the frank "narcissistic neuroses," an understanding of the dynamics of the patient's illness through the communication of experience in terms of manifest meaning is largely an academic problem. We speak quite reasonably in these cases of "schizophrenic language," even though the phonetic and syntactic structure of the patient's speech may simulate the gross features of the communal language code. Initially, when confronted with the schizophrenic disorganization of language, the problem of understanding is similar to that of being faced with a foreigner speaking an unfamiliar language. In the case of the former, paralinguistic and kinesic behavior may suggest that, even after the code has been deciphered, communication of meaningful experience will not be easy because other problems in communication exist; while in the case of the normal foreigner, behavioral signals may reassure us that could we but speak the same language, we would find our thoughts easy to share. In neither case can we be certain of ideational congruence, until the varying code conventions are reconciled by mutual agreement or through the services of an interpreter. Both varieties of confusion—ideas disconnected from words and words disconnected from ideas—appear concurrently and serially in severe obsessional neuroses, borderline conditions, and those other syndromes which arise from deviations in ego functioning.[5] This same problem may arise as a result of the therapist's failure to realize the ambiguity of the task imposed on both the patient and the therapist when *thought*, *language*, and *speech* are not defined at the time free associations are requested.

What we intend by the "basic rule" has yet to be formulated in linguistic terms. What does the patient understand when we ask him to tell us "all the thoughts that come to his mind" and fail to distinguish between "all the thoughts in his mind" from "all the words" that come to his tongue? Fortunately this distinction is usually unnecessary, but in some cases its absence becomes a severe obstacle to progress. It is also necessary to recognize some of the regressive effects upon communication that our technique per se imposes. When we ask a patient to relate, for example, his fantasies, in response to an accidental event in the analysis (such as a session canceled at the analyst's behest), he must resort to signal reactions, i.e., stereotypic possibilities arising from a single stimulus without the opportunity for cognitive discrimination. A disturbance of the secondary process should not be inferred from the character of such responses.

Freud was greatly interested in the problems of language. His early monograph on aphasia (1891) reveals his interest in the psychopathology of language. There are several specific references in his writings to the psychopathology of reference (1891, 1910b, 1913b, 1915b). These are most succinctly summarized in the last of his metapsychological trilogy, the paper entitled "The Unconscious" (1915).

In this discussion of schizophrenic communication difficulties, Freud did not distinguish between speech and language. When he stated, "In schizophrenics we observe—especially in the initial stages, which are so instructive—a number of changes in *speech*, some of which deserve to be regarded from a particular point of view" (p. 197), he seemed to have *language* in mind. He then described a peculiar disorganization of communication and some examples of literal interpretations of metaphor in psychotics. This phenomenon he called "organ speech" or "hypochondriacal speech." Freud then suggested that in schizophrenics, words are subjected to the same process which makes dream images out of latent dream thoughts. "They undergo condensation, and . . . transfer these cathexes to one another in their entirety" (p. 199). In pointing to the fact that the word in schizophrenia is used as if it had a primitive sexual symbolic reference, Freud concluded, "If we ask ourselves what it is that gives the character of strangeness to the substitutive formation and the symptom in schizophrenia, we eventually come to realize that it is the predominance of what has to do with words over what has to do with things" (p. 200). He believed that this substitution was the result of similarities between the words themselves, rather than between the things and a sexual part or object. "Where the two—word and thing—do not coincide, the formation of substitutes in schizophrenia deviates from that in the transference neuroses" (p. 201). The next paragraph is quoted in extenso since it represents the key to Freud's idea on meaning and its disturbance in schizophrenia.

> If we now put this finding alongside the hypothesis that in schizophrenia object-cathexes are given up, we shall be obliged to modify the hypothesis by adding that the cathexis of the *word*-presentations of objects is retained. What we have permissibly called the conscious presentation of the object can now be split up into the presentation of the *word* and the presentation of the *thing*; the latter consists in the cathexis, if not of the direct memory-images of the thing, at least of remoter memory-traces derived from these. We now seem to know all at once what the difference is between a conscious and an unconscious presentation. The two are not, as we supposed, different registrations of the same content in different psychical localities, nor yet different functional states of cathexis in the same locality; but the conscious presentation comprises the presentation of the thing plus the presentation of the word belonging to it, while the unconscious presentation is the presentation of the thing alone. The system *Ucs.* contains the thing-cathexes of the objects, the first and true object-cathexes; the system *Pcs.* comes about by this thing-presentation being hypercathected through being linked with the word-presentations corresponding to it. It is these hypercathexes, we may suppose, that bring about a higher psychical organization and make it possible for the primary process to be succeeded by the secondary process which is dominant in the *Pcs.* Now, too, we are in a position to state precisely what it is that repression denies to the rejected presentation in the transference neuroses: what it denies to the presentation is translation into words which shall remain attached to the object. A presentation which is not put into

> words, or a psychical act which is not hypercathected, remains thereafter in the *Ucs.* in a state of repression. [Freud further states:] Probably, however, thought proceeds in systems so far remote from the original perceptual residues that they have no longer retained anything of the qualities of those residues, and, in order to become conscious, need to be reinforced by new qualities. Moreover, by being linked with words, cathexes can be provided with quality even when they represent only *relations* between presentations of objects and are thus unable to derive any quality from perceptions. Such relations, which become comprehensible only through words, form a major part of our thought processes [pp. 201-202].

Freud also suggests that it is the restitutive attempt in schizophrenia which brings about this state in which the word presentation alone is cathected. In an attempt to regain the lost object, the ego begins by cathecting the verbal part of it (the object) but then finds itself obliged to be content with the word instead of the thing.

These formulations of the essential features of the disorganization of the process of communication in schizophrenia have shed new light on the meaning of psychotic utterances. In several respects, however, Freud's hypotheses are ambiguous and too highly condensed to be applicable to other aspects of normal, neurotic, and psychotic communication. There are four major ambiguities in Freud's formulations: (1) he failed to distinguish between speech and language; (2) "unconscious thing presentation" was never clearly defined; (3) he did not relate the process of linkage of "word" and "thing presentation" to the ontogenesis of language; (4) he did not note the preintellectual speech processes or the preverbal thought processes and the part they play in the development of language.

The first ambiguity has been studied extensively by the structural linguists. They emphasize that both the intrinsic structure of language as well as the mental processes that deal with it must be considered in any attempt to explain disturbances of communication. Modern linguists distinguish carefully between speech and language. *Speech* refers mainly to the acoustical forms of words and the vocal-articulatory processes. *Language* is the mental representation of a complex learned code for communication. There are methods of communication that do not employ speech, such as writing, Morse code, etc. These depend, however, upon the same language structure for their comprehension. Speech and language can, within certain limits, be independently disturbed, either by organic or functional processes. For example, language may be quite intact in stuttering, while speech can remain relatively intact in aphasia.

It is probable that Freud was using the term *speech* to mean *language* in his topographic formulation of "organ speech" in schizophrenia. There are, however, other problems unclarified by this distinction. In schizophrenia, for example, the relatively autonomous processes of speech and language might remain intact, and the communication difficulty might be the result of disturbance in their integration rather than in their intrinsic structure.

With regard to the "unconscious thing presentation," modern studies find little evidence that the conventional shared meaning of words in ordinary communications requires an image or thing presentation. They depend rather upon concepts or referential categories. These meanings are based upon the identifying attributive features of classificatory schemata rather than upon images. In topographic terms, these schemata seem to have almost exclusively preconscious rather than conscious representations. It is probable that only some proper names of individuals or specific places have a "representation" as distinct from a "reference" which is attached to the acoustical image of the word. In schizophrenics who use many words divorced from their lexical meanings, it would *seem* to be the referential category rather than the thing presentation that loses its connection with the word; or the structure of the categories themselves is disturbed, perhaps as a result of a deviation in ego structure.

The third and fourth points raised with regard to Freud's formulation are intimately related. To postulate the presence of an unconscious thing presentation suggests that thought develops before language. Psychoanalytic constructions concerning early preoedipal phases refer regularly to preverbal thinking but rarely to preintellectual speaking. The work of some developmental psychologists presents fairly compelling reasons for considering both phenomena (Werner and Kaplan, 1963b). Vygotsky (1934), for example, believes that thought and speech may have different roots.

He adduces phylogenetic and ontogenetic reasons. The anthropoid apes display an intellect like man's in certain respects; for example, they employ tools in an embryonic fashion and have the beginning of a social organization. They are capable of emitting a wide variety of phonetic sound variations which they employ in a way similar to the expressive function of man. The close correspondence between thought and speech which has been defined as language is, however, absent. Vygotsky (1934) says, "In the phylogeny of thought and speech, a prelinguistic phase in the development of thought and a preintellectual phase in the development of speech are clearly discernible" (p. 41). Some observations of infant speech also suggest the existence of a prelinguistic phase of thinking and a prethought phase in the material of vocal and articulatory sound making. The child's activities at certain stages of development indicate an ability to conceptualize (as seen in the way in which he manipulates objects), but without the ability to describe the concept in words. At the same time the child may imitate words and even use sentences without communally valid referential implications.

During the phase of questioning, the child feels a need for meaning and tries actively to learn the signs attached to objects (Jakobson, 1941, 1960; Piaget, 1923; Ranken, 1963; Székely, 1962). As Vygotsky (1934) put it: "He seems to have discovered the symbolic function of words" (p. 43). Speech at this stage enters its intellectual phase and thought begins to acquire its linguistic aspects. "At this point the knot is tied for the problem of thought and language" (p. 43), and from this point on "thought becomes verbal and speech rational" (p. 44). Vygotsky (1934), Piaget (1923), and others (Werner and Kaplan, 1963) have suggested that this convergence in concept formation has successive nodal points, each one of which initiates a new and higher level of abstraction. The intrinsic structure of language may be expected to reflect concomitant ego functions.

Semantics is usually considered a subdivision of the field of semiotics or the theory of signs. It has two complementary models, much like the structural and topographic models of our own metapsychology. Both models are necessary for the investigation of meaning in language. The *referential* point of view is based upon the well-known "Ogden-Richards Triangle" (1923). The second, called the *operational* or *contextual* model, is less easily diagramed.

In the referential model of meaning, (1) the word symbol, (2) the concept or reference, and (3) the referent (thing, object, etc.) are schematized as the three apices of a triangle. The side of the triangle which indicates the relationship between the word symbol and the reference (or concept category) is often in classic semantics called the *name-sense complex*. It is a learned, culturally determined relationship. The causal connections are the result of arbitrary convention and are shared by the members of the whole language community. Most linguists consider it the central issue in the question of manifest meaning. The line connecting the referent (thing) and its reference is also considered a causal one. Unlike the first, it is largely determined by individual psychological events and the development, especially, of perception and cognition. The link between the word symbol and the referent is usually portrayed as a dotted line to indicate that the relationship is imputed rather than causal (see Ullman, 1962).

Freud's model of the relationship of the conscious word with the thing presentation and the relationship depicted by the semantic triangle differ in the origin assigned to meaning. Freud believed meaning was determined by the link between the word symbol and its referent, while in the semantic model, a reciprocal relationship existing between the word symbol and its reference is called meaning. This complex has its own relationship with the thing or referent. In the reciprocal relationship between word and sense, the experience of meaning is evoked by their mutual availability. Thus, a word symbol evokes a reference and a reference (sense) evokes a word symbol. From this union, the basic semantic unit is born. Other reasons exist for assuming that the phonetic shape of the word is attached to a concept category rather than to a thing presentation. Such categories are partially determined by word networks established in most languages through synonym-homonym-antonym complexes (Ullman, 1962).

How are the reference categories formed which bring name and sense together in meaning? This is the meeting ground of structural linguistics and developmental psychology. Brown (1958) describes a hierarchical order of reference categories built upon the "criterial attributes" of the referent classes that are named. The semantic unit can be identified as (1) the linkage between the invariant distinctive features which constitute the acoustic form of a word with (2) certain references in certain contexts. Brown describes four general classes of such semantic categories.

1. *Simple categories:* These are words that are defined by a single criterial attribute, usually of sensory immediacy as in the experience of a primary color.
2. *Conjunctive categories:* Most nouns fall into this category. Here two or more criterial attributes, when conjoined, define a thing.
3. *Disjunctive categories:* These are words that refer to events that have different attributes but are linked in some way by their context, such as the rules of a game; then these categories are defined by the same word and have the same meaning despite their referential differences. An example given by Brown is a "strike" in baseball. Sometimes the batter does nothing and it is called a "strike." Sometimes he swings and misses the ball and it is called a "strike." Sometimes he swings and his bat connects with the ball, and it is still called a "strike." The categorization of these disjunctive events in this case is determined by, and can be known only through, the rules of the game of baseball. Certain terms in analysis, such as *acting out,* should be similarly considered as disjunctive categories.
4. *Relational categories:* This group consists of the terms which define the special relationship of one object to another in a "family" constellation. Unlike the disjunctive category, in which arbitrary features are grouped under a common name, in relational categories the names of the objects are arbitrary but the context is determined by a natural order rather than arbitrary rules. This natural order, for example, would define the referents in the words *mother, father,* and *son* as members of a biologically determined family group.

In the second model of meaning, the operational or contextual, the true meaning of words is sought in what language does with them in ordinary operations. Wittgenstein (1953), for example, states that the meaning of a word is its use in language. He likens the word to a tool or a piece in a game of chess. Equivalences are determined by word substitutions. Thus it can be shown that the verb *to be* is not a single semantic unit but has several meanings. For example, in the two sentences: "the violet *is* blue" and "twice three *is* six," the word *equals* can be substituted for *is* in the second sentence, but not in the first. The "operationalist" asserts that the contextual meanings, discovered by this method, would remain obscure to those using the referential method. In the contextual model words are categorized like "lexical substitution counters" by the slot into which they fit. In practice, dictionaries employ both referential and contextual methods for defining words.

These investigations of the intrinsic structure of language and of the development of thought, speech, and meaning require some revision of our psychoanalytic model (of meaning). Such a revision might facilitate the construction of more precise schemata for the identification of the borderline or intermediate stages of disorders of reference. It is thought that secondary-process thinking emerges as delays in instinctual gratification lead to hallucinatory wish fulfillment in the form of images. The ability to distinguish between hallucinatory wish fulfillment and real gratification arises interdependently with the separation of the self from the object, and thus is related to the formation of self and object representations within the ego. In this formulation, words are seen as later forms of images (here, acoustical ones). They become. through association with the primary love object, linked in Freud's terms to the visual thing presentation (see also Werner and Kaplan, 1963b). An alternative model conceptualizes a parallel development of primitive thought in the form of images and of speech sounds which have no referential connections. Piaget and Vygotsky suggest that language as a symbolic system does not arise until the two are joined by a crucial conceptual act at a certain stage in ego development. This is the model which postulates the progressive episodic convergence of more and more abstract categorical references (thought) with speech development. This concept seems to me to be better suited to explain some of our clinical observations.

The two forms of semantic disturbance—ideas without suitable words and words without formulated ideas—may be the result of a regression both to preverbal thought in the former and to preintellectual speech in the latter. A most extreme form occurs as an alternating phenomenon in some cases of catatonia (mutism and echolalia).

If language is a synthesis of thought and speech, a *theory* of language disturbance must also involve the synthetic function. In any dialogue, the speaker must simultaneously cathect and synthesize the following functions or objects: (1) the coding process of translating thought into language; (2) the self representation; (3) the representation of the object; (4) time, place, and purpose, or the environmental and social context. For the listener it is the decoding process or the translation of language into thought that is cathected, while 2, 3, and 4 are analogous to the same functions in the speaker. It is the synthetic function which organizes and integrates these various systems. In other words, in order to engage in a meaningful dialogue, the speaker and listener each need a common linguistic code, a sense of time, place and person, for the self and the other, along with an awareness of the phenomena about them.

The following is an attempt to extend the features of the apices of the Ogden-Richards semantic triangle to include these aspects of the communication process. It is intended heuristically rather than definitively.

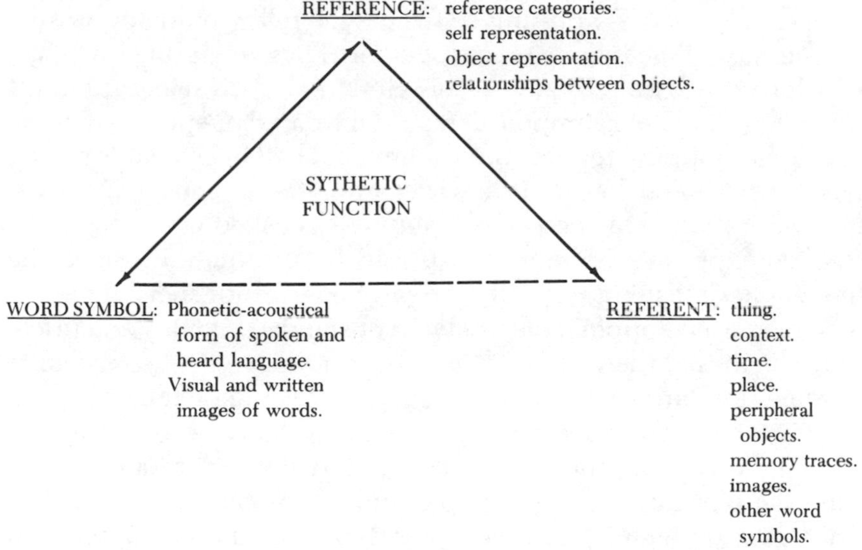

In this expanded semantic triangle, meaning is determined by the reciprocal evocation of word symbol and reference. Included in the reference are the lexical and syntactic features of conceptual categories, the personal identities of the speaker and listener, contextual awareness, and reciprocal interaction with the referent (thing presentation).

The failure to integrate any of the items in the word, reference, referent, or representation, with the rest of the process will result in a semantic dislocation. The structure of several such confusions can be illustrated in terms of the psycholinguistic diagram. In each instance the ambiguity derives from a different aspect of the meaning complex and is related to the major unconscious conflict or to a distortion of ego function.

1. *Faulty word-reference integration in a disjunctive category in the service of ambivalence.* A wealthy middle-aged borderline woman was involved in an affair with an indigent, uneducated young man in a kind of Lady Chatterley relationship. Having to support him and to buy his clothes made her uncertain of the sincerity of his feelings for her. She was, however, ashamed to be seen with him in public in his unkempt clothing and wanted him to have an "ivy league" appearance which, she felt, would obscure the incongruity of their appearance together. Thus, against her will, she was forced not only to pay for his clothing but to select it herself since she could not rely upon his taste. One day she reported that she had been shopping for neckties for him, but had been unable to find what she wanted because they were all "too expensive." As she rarely questioned the cost of her purchases I asked what she meant by "too expensive." She was surprised by my question since she thought her meaning was self-evident. She was not short of money when she was shopping, the ties were of standard quality and price. I explained that the word expensive was usually employed relative to some standard such as one's budget, the average retail price, etc. To this, the patient remarked that she had suddenly become angry at what she was doing and did not *want* to buy ties for him any longer. Thus the word *expensive* acquired an idiosyncratic meaning. The price was too high in relation to her desire for the young man. In order to disguise her ambivalence toward her lover she employed a semantic shift. Referring to the ties as "too expensive" implied that although her desire for the ties remained unchanged, her feelings for her lover had undergone a reversal.

In such patients, when there is a repetitive tendency to such ambiguous unreflective utterances, it is sometimes helpful to make a suggestion that may sound like the antithesis of the basic rule. The patient may be urged not to speak immediately but to organize the words in which he expresses his thoughts so that he is reasonably sure that they make his "meaning" clear.

2. *The affective connotations of a proper name in the service of confusion in identity.* The adolescent son of wealthy, first-generation Mediterranean parents had been sent to an aristocratic Eastern preparatory school. His parents' contradictory attitudes toward their cultural background and their own inability to decide whether to adhere to Old World or American customs had produced great confusion in the boy. There were two friends in his class whose favor and esteem he valued. One, L., a Jewish boy, was the ranking scholar of the class and admired by the patient for his intellect. The second, R., fair haired, of old American family, and captain of the football team, was admired for his athletic ability and his social standing. On the patient's return from a winter vacation in Florida, a deep tan was superimposed upon his usual swarthy complexion. As he was standing at a school dance with his friend L. and their girl friends, he was approached by R. who said in the hearing of the rest, "Hello, Rastus, how is you all?" The patient replied, "I'se fine, massah." At this point his friend L. said in a low tone to the patient, "You disguest me," and walked away with his girl. The patient could not understand what had happened. L. was even more disgusted by the patient's failure to sense the nuances of the interchange than by the event itself. The patient became depressed and developed the following obsessional fantasy, "I wish I were a New England Yankee, a Jew or a Negro" The meaning of the fantasy became evident in treatment. Because of the patient's underlying sadomasochistic identity confusion and his uncertainty as to his place in the social strata of the school, he had not known whether the reference to "Rastus" was meant as the good-natured ribbing of an equal or as an insult flung at a denigrated inferior. The fantasy suggested that, if his identity could have been clarified, he would have understood the various implications of the incident. It was not until years later that he understood L.'s reaction as the response that is often elicited by one "victim" when another "victim" identifies himself with the "aggressor."

3. *Allusion in the service of faulty reality testing.* During consultation, a borderline patient referred to relatives and friends by various locutions such as "a close relative of mine" when she meant her husband. "A business acquaintance of long standing" was

a reference to her employer. Later, as the result of a casual question of the patient, it became clear that she had misidentified a covered typewriter as a tape recorder. These allusive references were the result of misdirected discretion that fostered and served to rationalize her underlying paranoid tendencies, and perpetuated her poor discrimination of reality together with her inadequate object relations.

4. *Word-finding difficulties (pseudoanomia).* The inability to find an appropriate word occurs often during free association. The following incident demonstrates the role of empathic problems in a patient with a severe compulsive character disorder and a disturbance of object relations. The patient was an intelligent young graduate student who did very well scholastically in those disciplines which did not place a premium on verbal skills. In spite of an excellent education, his verbal style had the "tough" quality of a teen-age gangster. His "toughness" was a defense against early castration anxieties and it precluded any sentimental, tender, or sympathetic references. On one occasion, he had great difficulty in finding the appropriate adjective to describe the quality of an article on addiction in a popular magazine. He derided his girl friend for reading the magazine piece and then turned his scorn on the narcotic addicts portrayed in it. Finally admitting that his attack was neither against his girl friend nor against the subjects of the article, he attempted to find an adjective that would convey his criticism of the writing itself. After much searching on his part, I offered the word "sensational" which the patient had been trying to evoke. The analysis of this small linguistic event indicated that some sympathy for the subjects of the article as "sick people" was a necessary prerequisite for finding the critical adjective for the magazine article. It was necessary to view them sympathetically as inappropriate objects for a side-show display to evoke the "criterial attributes" of the word *sensational.* This admission of a "soft" attitude was prohibited by the patient's defense and thus inhibited his word-finding abilities.

In other patients in whom affect blocks, disturbances in orientation and confusion in self and object representations are found, similar disturbances of reference can be illustrated. The transference neurosis is particularly likely to evoke these latent tendencies. Disturbances of identity, ambivalence toward the object, and marginal defects in the testing of reality implicit in the psychoanalytic situation disturb the synthetic balance upon which the integrity of the semantic function depends. A regressive redistribution of cathectic energy between self representation, the representation of the object, and the "presentations" of the external world may become manifest in a semantic disturbance before other ego functions are recognizably involved. This disturbance of semantic function may in turn engender further regression with increasing language disorganization and subsequent involvement of other ego functions as the process extends in scope.

Most attempts to describe ego defects, to classify them, or to provide diagnostic criteria for their identification have dealt with functional disturbances of one or more of the elementary "ego functions." Beres (1956), for example, designates the functions of the ego under seven headings: (1) the testing of reality; (2) the regulation and control of the drives; (3) the mediation of the relationship of the self to objects; (4) thinking; (5) the defensive activities; (6) the autonomous processes; (7) the synthetic function. Most authors concur in general with this classification. Beres gives examples of disturbances in each of these functions which he considers to be symptomatic of ego deviation. As a diagnostic tool, this traditional procedure is often unsatisfactory. Except for gross disturbances of function which are obviously outside the range of "normal" behavior, it is difficult to establish sufficiently precise quantitative norms for such activities as reality testing, drive regulation, or object relationships to serve as reliable indicators of "ego disturbances" as distinct from neurotic symptoms. Thus such standards are impressionistic, vulnerable to subjective distortion and the influence of social value judgments which may substitute for the careful delineation of psychological norms. Nor can the clinician feel confident with these tests that his observations are primary rather than post hoc assumptions based upon a diagnosis already established from other signs. In many cases discussed in the literature, one wonders whether a given "borderline" phenomenon would be considered pathognomonic in the absence of obvious signs of severe psychopathology.

A delineation of specific types of language disturbances should provide less ambiguous signs of ego-deviational states. Reasons for the usefulness of such a tool may be summarized briefly:

1. The appearance of the ego as a psychic structure and the beginning of language development seem to be more or less simultaneous in the infant. There are undoubtedly important reciprocal relations between the two, making it likely that a disturbance in one during early developmental phases will be reflected in the other.

2. All the *functions* of the ego (as distinct from its apparatuses) (Hartmann, 1950a, b, c, 1951, 1952, 1953) must be investigated via the language function. Thus even the accuracy of our picture of the other functions of the ego is called into question when language itself is involved in the ego deviation. Furthermore, when one considers such ego functions as thinking, memory, reality testing, etc., it is difficult to separate them from their linguistic substrate.

3. Since the major function of language is communication, it has become the most carefully conventionalized and coded of all human activities. This results in a high degree of systematization of its form and a relative intolerance for idiosyncratic alteration in its internal structure. Thus, language retains invariant characteristics for the average members of a language community. Since, with language, the rules upon which the system is based and which govern its use may be formulated, a more objective assessment of impairment and a more microscopic measure of degrees of deviation from a known *external* standard is possible than in the study of impairment of other ego functions.

4. Object relations, whose disturbance is one of the key indicators of ego deviation, depend so much upon communication and therefore language that it is difficult to imagine how the one can be imapired without concomitant disturbance in the other. While there is a considerable body of experience correlating ego deviations and grossly observable disturbances of language, the more microanalytic relationships between psychopathological states and various distortions of language in communication remain to be studied.

Greenson suggested the following characteristics of borderline psychopathology: (1) impulsivity; (2) confusions in identity and role; (3) severe affective disturbances; (4) disturbances of reality testing; (5) confusion between past and present; (6) reactions to part objects; (7) disturbed synthetic function; (8) exaggerated sexual and aggressive fantasies; (9) disturbed autonomous functions (see Rangell, 1955). In any patient, these characteristic borderline features may exist alone or in combination. Some linguistic correlates of these disturbances are the following. Impulsive patients frequently react to words as signs or signals rather than to the referential meanings of words (Michaels, 1959). Individuals with identity confusions may reveal their disturbance by pronoun transpositions, affectations of speech due to their propensity for imitation and role playing, and phonetic and stylistic peculiarities due to failure of the imitative process. Often these patients produce incomplete sentences or sentences with such syntactic errors as to make them all but incomprehensible. In such patients the confusion in identity results in a failure to maintain a clear separation between addressor and addressee. The speaker verbalizes his inner thought process without consideration for the addressee's confusion when he is called upon to decode the message. In instances where the choice of words or of word order to ensure clairty of reference depends upon an accurate appraisal of the context of the auditor, patients who distort reality or use massive denial may reveal their psychopathology (Stein, 1958). Patients with disturbed object relationships, especially those who react to a part object as if it were the whole, may have difficulty in using metaphor (Sharpe, 1940). Where empathy is required, these patients (see case 4) have difficulty in finding the correct modifiers for nouns and verbs. Disturbances of the synthetic function (Chapters 2 and 12) may reveal themselves in a variety of ways. Usually the larger units, such as the sentence or the paragraph, are involved. Written language may be involved more than speech. Often it is difficult to know whether the confusions between past and present, revealed in consistent distortions of tense, are the result of a disturbance primarily in thinking or in language. Finally, disturbed autonomies (such as memory or perceptual defects) may reveal themselves in functional aphasias, word-finding difficulties, and parapraxes of pronunciation, spelling, and grammar.

The formulations previously discussed and the clinical examples suggest that a revision of Freud's topographical model of language disturbance (particularly in the narcissistic disorders) would be of value. In such a revision along "structural" lines the terms *manifest meaning* or *linguistic reference* could replace what Freud called the "word-thing presentation" in consciousness. Reference in normal language function is a synthetic product. It includes mnemic acoustical patterns of speech, syntactic structure, and conceptual categories of meaning, none of which are completely independent of the complex of self, object, and environmental representations in the ego. In this integrated structure, a disturbance of any one of the linguistic buttresses is felt in all other parts of the representation-reference system, and not only in the referential use of words whether in speaking or in understanding. Less crippling ego deviations than frank schizophrenic disorders give rise to language disturbances as a result of the simultaneous and reciprocal development of ego structures and of language (Glauber, 1944; Greenson, 1950; Kubie, 1934; Laffal, 1965; Lidz, 1963; Szekely, 1962). Often such language disturbances are the presenting signs and the most sensitive indicators of the ego deviations themselves. Semantic shifts have diagnostic implications and can be an important technical aid to therapy when they are analyzed.

Notes

1. The term *ego deviation* (Beres, 1956) is used here instead of *defect* since it implies any departure from average expectations in ego functions, whether in the direction of decreased or increased effectiveness. Hyperfunctions of various kinds in one area may produce concomitant distortions in other sectors (see Chapters 2 and 3).

2. Roman Jakobson (1941, 1964), who studied linguistic aspects of aphasia, states that many different styles of discourse fall into two major categories. He says, "the development of a discourse may take place along two different semantic lines: one topic may lead to another either through their similarity or through their contiguity. The 'metaphoric' way would be the most appropriate term for the first case and the 'metonymic' way for the second, since they find their most condensed expression in metaphor and metonymy respectively. In aphasia one or the other of these two processes is restricted or totally blocked—an effect which makes the study of aphasia particularly illuminating for the linguist. In normal verbal behavior both processes are continually operative but careful observation will reveal that under the influence of cultural pattern, personality and verbal style, preference is given to one of the two processes over the other" (Jakobson and Halle, 1956, p. 76).

3. The word "mean" in this context may have several connotations. "I mean what I say" is usually construed as a statement of intention; i.e., you can count on my being reliable, rather than the more absurd implication that I speak before I think and then assume that what I have said is what I "really" think. Even in the more usual context, however, an individual who places a higher value on the spoken word for its own sake than on the semantic will sometimes carry out or defend an unintended statement simply because it "passed his lips."

4. See Jakobson and Halle (1956) with regard to the six primary functions of language. "Ordinary dialogue" in this context would correspond to a dialogue that is devoted to a "referential" interchange in his terminology. These remarks would have to be radically

qualified in the case of "poetic," "phatic," "conative," and "expressive" modes of communication. The sixth or "metalinguistic" category is also "referential" in that its reference is language itself.

5. Both of these forms of semantic disturbance have been exploited as literary devices. In the "theater of the absurd," for example, Samuel Beckett's Winnie in *Happy Days* (1961) makes her "point" by a stream of verbigeration which appears to precede reflection, while Jonathan Rosepettle in Kopit's *Dad, Poor Dad* (1960) conveys the oppressive influence on a boy's development of an overpowering and devouring mother through his inarticulate stammering and uncompleted sentences.

CHAPTER FIVE

Disorders of Communication in Psychoanalysis

Despite the extraordinary adaptability of human language as a means for communicating ideas, its limitations under certain conditions are as impressive as its efficacy under others. It is not surprising that misunderstanding, so often regarded as part of the human condition, should occur during psychoanalysis. Recent literary forms and preoccupations reflect this view of misunderstanding. I shall concern myself here not with the general philosophical problems of thought communication (Pierce, 1961), but with certain specific difficulties in verbalizing ideas encountered during the course of analysis. Strictly speaking, the term *communication disturbance* implies an interference in the transmission or the reception of a message. I shall discuss mainly the disorders resulting from the patient's faulty transmission rather than the comprehension disturbances which may exist in the analysis. I am concerned particularly with those disorders that are made manifest by the technique of free association itself.

I am indebted to the members of a graduate study group in linguistics and psychoanalysis which has been meeting for several years in the New York Psychoanalytic Institute for the exchange of ideas that have led to this paper. I am also indebted to Dr. Elise Wechsler Snyder for editoral revision and valuable suggestions concerning the organization of the manuscript.

In the analytic situation, we encourage a form of communication in which the usual conventions of meaningful dialogue are suspended. It might therefore be thought that difficulties in the communication disorders become manifest,[1] especially those subtle symptomatic disturbances of language which, under ordinary conditions, do not interfere with the exchange of ideas.
communication disorders become manifest, especially those subtle symptomatic disturbances of language which, under ordinary conditions, do not interfere with the exchange of ideas.

We usually try to distinguish between the defensive operations of the ego which suppress, repress, or distort information and the grossly disturbed language of the psychotic process which itself renders information incomprehensible. These gross disturbances of communication are most often manifestations of thought disorders which may be reflected in nonverbal as well as verbal behavior. The difficulties which I shall describe are neither in the realm of thinking itself nor of speech. They arise in situations where certain ideas have to be encoded into words in such a way as to be fully comprehensible to a listener (Balkanyi, 1964; Glauber, 1958; Jakobson, 1935, 1964; Rosen, I., 1955; Chapter 13; Shands, 1960; Teitelbaum, 1958; Werner and Kaplan, 1963b). Although these disturbances may appear in patients whose behavior, abstract, concrete, and imaginative thinking are relatively unimpaired, I believe that they are the result of an ego deviation or early developmental conflict (Crocker, 1963; Ekstein, 1964; Nagera, 1966). Outside of the analytic situation, these disorders are either not apparent or are seen merely as idiosyncrasies in mode of expression or as peculiarities of verbal style. One of my hopes is that this presentation will evoke an interest in the systematic observation of these phenomena so that they may be more thoroughly classified and investigated.

Before proceeding, it might be well to define the sense in which the words *information* and *communication* are being used. It is of interest in this connection that the word *inform* has antithetical properties. As an adjective it denotes shapelessness or the absence of regular structure, while as a verb it implies a process of organization, an arranging or composing of facts as a necessary prerequisite to the imparting of knowledge. Whether "informing" has the purpose of confusing or enlightening a listener, the emphasis is on a message and especially upon the verbal composition of the message.

The dictionary definition of communication is: "Any act of giving to another as a recipient." The word implies some transmission from one individual to another of substances or signals. Only a secondary meaning of the term applies to the transmission of information by means of the spoken or written word. Thus information may be knowledge acquired or possessed without the involvement of another individual, while communication implies a process of sharing, not necessarily of information, among individuals. For this reason, it is theoretically possible for information to be transmitted without verbal communication and for verbal communication to take place without the transmission of information. For practical purposes, however, communication and the sharing of information seem to be inseparable.

One of Freud's paramount interests, well documented in his writings, was in the disturbances of language. While he was a neurologist, he arrived at an original approach to the problem of aphasia (Freud, 1888), which was, in some ways, a precursor of his brilliant analysis of the essential disturbance of verbal communication in schizophrenia (Freud, 1915b). Such scholarly, incisive contributions as "The Antithetical Meaning of Primal Words" (Freud, 1910b), "The Dynamics of Speech Parapraxes" (Freud, 1901,) and some less well-known annotational excursions into philological problems, seem almost to be digressions from the mainstream of his work (see, for example, Freud, 1913b). These works reveal, however, that throughout his life he retained a concern for problems of language. They demonstrate the originality and impetus that his psychoanalytic discoveries can give to an understanding of linguistic phenomena. One of the most impressive of Freud's creations was the development of the technique of free association for the exploration of psychic processes. Free association depends upon the verbalization of thought. It is necessary that the language function of both patient and analyst be relatively intact for this method of exploring psychic processes to be utilized. Free association can therefore be regarded as a special mode of communication. Freud's mastery of precise exposition may have been one of the factors that gave him the security to experiment with unconventional modes of communication.

Freud first conceived of free association as an alternative to hypnosis; another way of evading the limits imposed by the internal censor on the transmission of information. He thought that free association would provide access to pathogenic fantasies, memories, and affects without the drawbacks of hypnosis. In ordinary discourse, such fantasies, even when they are conscious, are denied verbal expression. In Freud's early writings, dominated as they were by the topographic model, the censor was seen mainly as a conscious monitoring agent. Later sophistication suggested that many of the operations of the "censor" were more subtle, unconscious, and autonomous than had previously been considered. The concept of ego defenses arose in part from such considerations. Thus far, psychoanalytic theory has explored those limitations imposed upon the communication of information in free association by the conscious and unconscious operations of the censor. There has been a relative neglect of the limitations arising from the conventions of language itself, as well as from the stylistic variations which its semantic and grammatical alternatives provide for individual expression and taste (Chapter 12; Cunningham, 1966).[2]

I think that the usual linguistic aspects of free association may enable us to study the communication process itself. Free association makes possible the investigation of two aspects of the communication process along avenues that are not open to methods which utilize conventional dialogue. Using free association we can first study the limits imposed by language itself on the transmission of information about intellectual and affective experience. Free association can also allow us to uncover the latent difficulties in any particular speaker's use of language for the encoding of his ideas. This is the use of free association as an investigative tool with which I am most concerned at this time.

In free association, not only are the judgments of the censor suspended, but so are the auxiliary devices of gesture, posture, and facial expression upon which many speakers rely to make their meanings clear. These devices, in some individuals, are so effective that they obscure the verbal deficiencies that made them necessary in the first place.

What are some of the advantages of free association over conventional dialogues in eliciting such subtle disturbances? The term "communication disorder" does not contain a judgment on whether the disturbance is in the transmitter of the message or its receiver. If the sharing of information is the desired end, it makes no difference whether the encoding of the message makes it incomprehensible or whether the listener lacks the means for understanding it. Either eventuality bars both speaker and listener from their common purpose.

Human language as used in ordinary conversation has certain "design features" (Hockett, 1960) which enhance comprehension and tend to minimize the effects of the false assumptions and ambiguities which separate the speaker's intention from the listener's registration. Paradoxically, the difference between intention and comprehension may be wider during friendly agreement than during altercations about facts or interpretations: during most conversations, people assume that the referents of the words, phrases, or metaphors employed are understood in common. The listener either implicitly or explicitly provides the missing links in the verbalized ideas of the speaker. Both speaker and listener often assume that the background information necessary for correctly identifying the subject, object, or predicate of a statement is mutually available. The probability that this assumption of congruence is valid is only fair. In friendly discourse, there is less likelihood that such assumptions will be tested than in adversary dialogues. The punctiliousness of legal phraseology in friendly contracts occurs in recognition of these tendencies. Ambiguities, which result from incorrect phonetic or grammatical construction, semantic differences, or intonational and mimetic peculiarities, are often resolved by the listener without recourse to the speaker's validation. In many ways we rely upon commonly held conventions to fill in the missing details of ordinary verbal interchange. When the roles of speaker and listener are exchanged, the erstwhile speaker performs the same revisions upon the erstwhile listener's reaction to the original message.

As a result of these automatic operations during ordinary dialogue, what is idiosyncratic, unverbalizable, or simply nonverbalized, is neglected and seems almost to be nonexistent. If both participants in a dialogue rely upon the relatively intact capacities of one member to overcome the results of the disabilities of the other in verbalizing his thought, an illusory appearance of information sharing is fostered. This appearance is not the result of defensive operations or the conscious suppression of information. For example, the psychiatric resident who asserts that the patient cannot have a thought disorder since he (the doctor) understands what the patient means is himself supplying the connecting links which the patient has omitted. It may be that group dialogues increase this masking of misinterpretation in direct proportion to the number of participants involved.

If, during free association, we are as interested in the patient's ability to verbalize his manifest thought as we are in its latent content, we can use the technique as a means for observing defects in the communicative function of language which might otherwise remain hidden. With some patients one has the impression that the interpretation of latent content is not so much a discovery of the common denominator of a series of statements as it is the gradual clarification of the hidden assumptions, contradicitions, and ambiguities in a particular utterance. Mental contents can also be transmitted by signal systems other than spoken language, such as gesture, posture, facial expression, intonation, pictograms, writing, and notational symbols such as those employed by mathematics or music. Although these do not involve language events, they may be partly translated into, replace, reinforce, or substantially modify linguistic phenomena. One of the tenets of analytic technique is that our results will be enhanced to the extent that the patient can transform all paraverbal messages into verbal communications. It may be that, for many individuals, deficiencies in verbal ability are compensated by nonverbal talents or are masked by the judicious use of auxiliary signals. In these cases the inhibition of these supplementary signal systems may also help to uncover defects in verbal communication, rather than enhancing the flow of associations.

There are many syndromes of communication disorder which result from defects in function rather than from ego defenses. Their systematic description and classification remains a task for the future. We may be in the unique position of observing certain kinds of verbal communication events that do not come to light in any other context, and increasing our therapeutic effectiveness by broadening our access to the range of conscious experience. The reconstructive data related to and derived from such phenomena will also extend our knowledge of the ontogenesis of language and communication.

I would like to describe four examples of disturbances which interfere with the analyst's understanding of the manifest content of the patient's verbal associations. It will be apparent that these phenomena overlap the area of mannerism and personal style (Chapter 12). I shall also attempt to identify the origins of these related syndromes in early language development.

The first is a phenomenon that has been called "paraphonia" (Spoerri, 1966). It consists of an incongruity between the tonal features of speech and the content of the verbal message. The second, which by analogy might be termed "paramimesis," is a similar incongruity between the content of the message and the facial expression and gestures which accompany it. The two other syndromes are related to the two predominant ways in which the formal connections between undirected conscious ideas take place. Roman Jakobson (1935, 1964), in the context of aphasia, suggested that such connections are made either on the basis of simile or on the basis of contiguity. When one or the other mode of making connections is absent, the term *simile* or *contiguity deficiency* seems appropriate. Of the four language disturbances, the first two are termed *paraverbal* disorders, while the latter two I shall call *parasyntactic* disorders. In the paraverbal disturbances, the difficulty is in the integration of the message with its expressive overtones, while in the parasyntactic disturbances the defect is within the message itself.

In ordinary conversation, the mood conveyed by the tonal aspects of speech determines how a given statement should be construed when the words themselves are ambiguous. Paraphonic disturbances can be more subtle than a trivial complaint conveyed in an angry voice or a fear of impending disaster voiced in a tone of lighthearted complacency. Frequently, while listening to a patient on the couch, we are aware of a growing sense of bewilderment. Although the message seems clear, something is awry. An assertive or propositional statement may be accompanied by an interrogative inflection, or, in a series of concessive remarks, an imperative overtone may be present. These are more subtle paraphonias. When such incongruities occur in everyday dialogue, they convey the impression of peculiarity. Their more blatant forms are suspicious of more serious psychopathology. In fact, the diagnosis of schizophrenia in a clinical interview is often based upon such paraverbal disorders rather than upon the content of the patient's speech.

The extent to which latent tendencies to paraverbal disorders become manifest during free association is striking. The patient, for example, who has shown no particular discrepancy between tone and content in the ordinary speech of the initial interviews (Chapter 12), suddenly develops a strange and inappropriate tone, facial expression, or posture on the couch. Sometimes the expressive accompaniments of speech seem to disappear altogether so that the patient's tone becomes flat and mimesis disappears. He conveys the impression that all statements are equally significant and that no information is to be considered more emotionally charged than any other. Sometimes the patient's tone, pitch, volume, rate of speech, or other mood indicators seem excessive for, or incongruous with, the content. In some instances this phenomenon disappears when the patient is made aware of it and can give his associations to the manifestation itself so that its meaning can be analyzed. In other cases it is a more intractable development and a concomitant of free association. In Chapter 12, I give several clinical examples of this phenomenon.

Parasyntactic disturbances are more apt to be overlooked than *paraverbal* ones. In most patients whose capacity to convey information verbally is intact, there is a balance between ideas whose sequence is determined by some element of likeness or simile and ideas whose connections result from temporal and spatial proximity or contiguity. In some patients this balance seems to be disturbed in one or the other direction.

It is my impression that such paraphonic distortions as overstatement and understatement often accompany simile and contiguity association styles. Whether the two types of disturbance are combined in any characteristic pattern would make an interesting project for clinical investigation. The following are examples of each type of disorder:

A young woman with severe object choice difficulties had been given a handwritten bill at the end of the previous session. She had been charged for some sessions that she had been unable to attend. She began the next session with the question, "Do you believe in handwriting analysis?" She continued, "I know that I will not get an answer to this question so I will tell you why I ask. I had the thought last night that I would submit my handwriting to a handwriting analyst to find out what it would show. Then I would have an independent check on your interpretations. Perhaps it would also be helpful to you. It might shorten my analysis. I wonder whether you take notes? If you do, when would you have time to look at them? Don't bother to answer. I imagine that you look at them just before I come into the office. The patient who just left was smiling as if *she* had a good session. If you take notes, I do not see how you have enough time to write about the last patient and read about the next one with the small amount of time you take between patients. Perhaps you have total recall. Now I am thinking about the books on your shelves. The light in here is bad. I can't see how you read by it. . . ." The libidinal and aggressive aspects of her associations seem to refer to her resentment over being charged for the sessions she missed, but what is so striking is that the connections between the ideas are determined almost exclusively by contiguities of persons, things, places, and time. These cluster aound the ambience of the patient, the analyst, and the analytic process. There are obvious temporal and spatial connections between note taking, reading, and memory. The implied comparison between herself and the previous patient, the various references to office appurtenances and to the analytic process all limit the geographic and temporal range of her associations to the here and now. The ambivalent content is strongly suggestive of a transference fantasy. The failure to mention the bill may seem merely the result of defensive operations. This, however, was not so. The communication of thought by contiguity of references was so thoroughly a part of this patient's linguistic habits that when I suggested that she saw some *similarity* between my handwriting on the bill and her own or that of someone close to her, she did not deny it but stated that she thought she had already made that clear in her associations. This patient's omission of information was a built-in characteristic of her communication style, rather than defensive. The latent transference derivative (as I shall explain later) was to be found in the simile deficiency rather than in the specific content of her associations.

A patient whose style was very different from this lady's was a young man with sadomasochistic character difficulties. One day, he arrived late for his session and appeared agitated. He said that he had overslept because that previous night had been distressing. Before telling me about the distressing event of the previous evening, he wanted to speak of an event in his childhood that the evening had brought to mind. He had done something to make his mother very angry. She had threatened to leave and never return. He had run out of the house in his pajamas looking for her. Actually she was home all the time and had not made good her threat. This reminded him of his first girl friend. He had been her "patsy." He let her walk all over him because he was afraid that she whould give him the gate if he argued with her. Her name was A. He associated the name with another girl who married a friend of his and then ran away with a former lover. A. is also his mother-in-law's name. He hated his mother-in-law from the very first. He should have known that his wife would turn out like her mother and that he would be kicked around as her father was, etc. The connections between this man's statements, whatever their other determinants, are between similarities of affects, situations, names, and personality attributes. It was characteristic of this patient to give only fragmentary accounts of events. Narrative sequences require an attention to temporal and spatial contiguities. The similes used as the connecting links between ideas seemed to lead his associations further and further away from the original episode. Thus the connection of ideas by simile seemed to serve as a series of distractions rather than connections. In the present example they interfered with the communication of information concerning his lateness and the events of the preceding evening. As a result of this typical manner of expressing himself (if left uninterrupted by direct questioning), the sadomasochistic enactments within his marriage would not have come to light. Actually, following a violent scene with his wife he had slept in another room where there was no alarm clock. I discovered this only by reminding the patient that he had not told me why the previous evening had been distressing.

Episodic narrative cannot exist when links are based solely upon similarity. The patient thought I understood that an argument with his wife had taken place from the *implications* of his associations. He was surprised when I mentioned the omission and likened me to one of his teachers whom he called a pedant. This teacher had commented that the patient expected him to read his mind rather than his writing.

One of the most promising suggestions for the understanding of these communication peculiarities comes from Roman Jakobson (1935, 1964). He stated that the two most fundamental operations underlying verbal behavior were word selection and word combination. Selection is based upon similarity and combination upon contiguity. In normal conversation, the speaker selects that word which both closely approximates the sense of his idea and is a symbol which the listener shares with him as part of their common verbal code. Thus, the encoding of the speaker's thoughts into words is based primarily upon simile. The listener, on the other hand, decodes the message by matching words with meanings on the basis of context and contiguities.

Thus, simile corresponds primarily to the speaker's act of encoding thoughts into words; and contiguity, to the listener's act of decoding words into thoughts. The actual processes are, of course, vastly more complex. The speaker begins with an analytic operation, the selection of words from his preconscious store. This is followed by a synthesis (the ordering of the words in accord with the grammatical rules of his language). The number of words available to the speaker is large. Once he has made his choice, the synthetic (i.e., syntactic) alternatives for sentence structure are relatively limited. The listener receives the synthesized data and proceeds to their analysis. The alternatives are at first numerous. The context of the speaker's references gradually narrows the possible alternatives. Frequently, the act of verbalizing makes an initially vague idea clearer to the speaker for whom the listening feedback aids the encoding process.[3] Normal individuals vary in their ability to encode and decode. Some are articulate speakers, while others are good listeners. A talent for speaking is easily recognized. Less obvious are the decoding talents of the listener. These entail much more than mere silence and a willing ear.

Different literary forms encourage or at least invite one or the other of these communication styles. Jakobson (1964) suggested that simile was the inherent trope in lyric poetry, while contiguity tropes were the leading metaphors in epic verse. The correspondence to speaker and listener also obtains in this context. The lyric poet endeavors to present himself as the original speaker, whereas the epic poet takes on the role of listener who is merely transmitting legends and deeds learned by hearsay.

Most patients, when presented with the task of free association, assume either a preponderantly lyric or epic style. The loss of the usual social feedback engendered by the analyst's silence causes a disintegration of usual patterns of dialogue. The result is sometimes a pseudocommunication, a caricature which excludes large quantities of information. In such cases, the analyst must confront the disorder in the construction of the message, before elisions resulting from defense or transference resistance can become manifest. This concept of the intimate connection between language and thought can also be summarized in somewhat different terms. In listening to our patient's productions, it may be important to distinguish language structured by an idea from an idea that has been given its form by language.[4]

Other aspects of the technical implications of these observations are suggested by some genetic speculations and some experiences with language development in early childhood.[5] Most observers agree that the symbolic use of words is the most crucial step in the process of individuation in the infant (Crocker, 1963; Ekstein, 1964; Greenson, 1950; Irwin, 1960; Jakobson, 1960; Leopold, 1952; Lewis, 1951, 1959; Peller, 1964; Piaget, 1923; Werner and Kaplan, 1963b). Since individuation seems itself to be a prerequisite for the development of language, it is clear that these processes are reciprocal. The prestages (Peller, 1964) of language are seen in the development of a system of signals between parent and infant. These signals convey needs and diffuse organismic states. The meanings of the infant's signals, while ambiguous to others in the environment, may be highly specific to the mother. The transition from signals to words is the ontogenetic recapitulation of the phylogenetic leap from anthropoid to human intellect (Vygotsky, 1934). The use of language symbols rather than signal sounds and gestures permits a prodigious increase in the range and precision of information that can be communicated, as well as an increase in the number of individuals who will be able to comprehend it. Although the stages in this crucial evolution from signals to symbols seem to follow a regular pattern, the earliest stages are difficult to record and even more difficult to interpret (Irwin, 1960; Leopold, 1952). The nature of the communication event leads to difficulty in separating the observational data from their interpretation. The following account is schematic and highly condensed: between the hunger cry of the neonate and the first truly linguistic event there appear to be two stages. In the first stage are crude vocalization and mimesis. The hunger cry and the smiling response are typical examples of this period. In the second stage, the articulatory efforts of the tongue and lips begin to modify the cries of purely laryngeal origin and result in "babbling." At this time the extremities, particularly the arms, join in a mimetic-gestural system in which more complex schemas for signaling finally become integrated with vocal ones. In this gestural system, the development of forefinger pointing is said to be a milestone in prelanguage evolution (Werner and Kaplan, 1963b). Some observers think that the first true linguistic event occurs when the intonational pattern of babbling takes on the characteristics of the paraverbal intonations of the parents' language. It has been asserted (Pittenger, 1966) that before the first recognizable word is learned, there is a detectable difference in the babbling of, for example, English and French babies. The metric and tonal characteristics of the babbling anticipates that of the future language. If paraverbal intonation is the first occurrence in language development, it lays the foundation for the phonetic auditory-vocal imitation that produces the child's first words. Other aspects of infant behavior at this stage also suggest that there is a particular sensitivity to the tonal qualities of adult speech. Even later, when young children are quite articulate, they remain more responsive to how the adult sounds than to what he says. Many parents are intuitively aware of the importance of establishing a congruence between tone and message, not only in what they say to the child but also in what they permit the child to say to them. The demand, for example, that a child speak softly when making a request not only is training in social etiquette but has important linguistic implications as well. Even adults, as we can all testify, are often more sensitive to the tone of a statement than to its content. This is especially true during periods of regression. A hypochondriacal patient once explained to me why he could never recall what his internist said. He said, "I was so busy watching my doctor's expression and listening to see if he was angry at me for coming to see him too late for treatment, that I never heard the words themselves."

Some studies of language development (Werner and Kaplan, 1963b) have suggested the extent to which mother-child separation and language development are interdependent (Ekstein, 1964). The naming of objects begins as a game between the parent and child. The name probably does not take on the characteristics of a referential noun until the child experiences his saying the name as an act which can elicit the desired object from the environment, especially in the absence of the mother. This may be one of the major reasons for defective language development in symbiotic children.

Naming and word acquisition belong in general to a period of adult-child play in which the antitheses between simile and contiguity are first established. The child is taught or discovers quite early that certain phonetic symbols designate an object (or an activity) in the environment that has certain sensory attributes. Soon thereafter he discovers that the word designates not a single object but a class of objects with similar features. The name and the class are constant, whether the objects are in the field of perception, near or distant, or entirely absent (Peller, 1964; Werner and Kaplan, 1963b). After name-object connections have been established for one specific object, the referent of the word is enlarged to include the class, and the formation of conceptual categories is begun. When this symbol constancy has been achieved, things can be designated by their names. "This one (here) is a dog" establishes an ostensive contiguity. "That one (over there) is also a dog like the one in the picture book" indicates the ability to use simile and demonstrates that the symbolic process has evolved to the stage in which it can designate a class of objects regardless of their distribution in time or space. The concept of the class of similar objects is not established until *pointing* (which establishes contiguity) is no longer necessary. The stage is now set for the more complicated processes. The speaker in any dialogue must select from his vocabulary the terms that most resemble the referents of his ideas. The analysis of the word-thing correspondence is the major decoding process of the listener and is based upon the contiguities of the referents in the speaker's sentences. The noun-conscious child, for example, now asks for an object that he has learned to name. The child's inadequate phonetic development or his misconception of the word make it necessary for the adult to play a guessing game. The ostensive process is reversed. The child may be asked to repeat the word or point to the object. If the game is successful, the adult can deduce what the object is either from the contextual contiguities in the child's request, or from the object's position in space. If an absent object is being designated, the successful game may be based upon a vacancy, such a daddy's chair after he has gone to work. The listener's analytic deduction, that the child is asking for the father by the designation of his empty chair, is an example of decoding by contiguity. The space left by the familiar object designates it by its erstwhile proximity to the object, rather than by any attributive similarity. The ability to designate an absent object in this manner, when the specific word is not available, is a crucial stage in symbol formation. This form of metaphor based on contiguity is known as *metonymy*. The basic processes of reference by simile and metonymy repeat themselves in more elaborate form at various levels of language development. Metonymy can be especially obscure. For example, "The agile precincts of the Lark's return" is a metonymy which has the lilt of poetry but derives meaning only through a simile when we know that the poet thought of bridge cables as swinging places where birds alight (Cunningham, 1966).

It is my impression that certain patients undergo at least a partial regression to such early stages of communication when faced with the task of free association. The recumbent position has many regressive effects. Some need not be discussed here. It does, however, deprive the patient of the usual visual, mimetic, and gestural clues from the listener which tend to correct projective distortion. Other more subtle stimuli to regression exist in the recumbent position. Thinking and speaking are, for most adults, autonomous processes. Like the *bourgeois gentilhomme* who was surprised to discover that he was talking prose, our novitiate patients are astonished to learn that not only are they supposed to have "thoughts" and "associations," but also that verbal symbols exist which will make these thoughts communicable to another. It is likely that one ubiquitous transference stems from the primitive relation to the first language teacher of infancy (Greenson, 1950; Peller, 1964). Such transferences probably vary with each unique linguistic developmental experience. The patient who says that his mind is a "blank" may at one level mean that "a thought" as a noun is a new concept. Are some patients saying in effect, "Show me an example of this thing that you have given a name to so that I may recognize one when I experience it"? Or, corresponding to a more advanced level of development, "I have lots of thoughts, but I do not know what 'information' is, i.e., what data an analyst needs for the successful treatment of a patient." In this unstructured situation a conflict rapidly develops between the anxious patient's immediate need for specific clues and the analyst's need for diverse exploration. This situation is reminiscent of early problems in the communication process and early language learning. The analyst may respond to the patient's confusion in a manner similar to that of the bewildered language teacher of the patient's early childhood. Unable to empathize with the patient's encoding problems, the analyst seeks to decode the patient's ambiguous communication according to his own sophisticated linguistic devices. The success of the analysis may depend upon the degree to which the analyst avoids a repetition of early patterns of misunderstanding and mutual frustration in the verbal interchange of parent and child. With "borderline" patients, so-called classical technique (Stone, 1961) may produce a stalemate when the analyst (like some mothers) makes the expression of ideas for which no word symbols have yet been assimilated a prerequisite for his own verbal response. In these instances, it is as though the patient were saying, "I cannot tell you what I mean until you tell me what I have to know," and the analyst were saying, "I cannot tell you what you need to know until you tell me what you mean" (Chapter 13).

All of the communication styles or disturbances I have discussed seem to stem from preoedipal influences. Although they may be transient defensive phenomena, components, for example, of pseudonaiveté, they are more frequently rigid patterns indicative of early fixations or "developmental conflicts" which occurred during individuation struggles. Thus one may expect to find these disturbances combined with identity problems. In treatment their appearance is probably indicative of a confusion of the speaker and listener roles. The patient described above, whose associations were dominated by similes, was a twin. Like the child in the early stages of language learning, the patient seeks clues for the understanding of the therapist's meaning from his facial expression or tone of voice rather than from the content of his message. It is my impression that simile and contiguity deficiencies occur during periods of identity confusion when via the transference (or for some other reasons), the patient has become uncertain of the boundaries between his ideas, feelings, and wishes and those of the analyst.

If the finding of similes is the major part of the encoding task for the speaker, while the finding of contiguities is the paramount aspect of the decoding process in the listener, the patient's conception of his role as speaker or listener may determine the dominance of the kinds of connecting links that he uses in verbalizing his thoughts. The analytic situation is fraught with ambiguity. The analyst, like the child, often finds himself in the position of assimilating new information which the patient (like the verbal adult) imparts to him. The patient, one moment a teacher imparting information, must also be prepared like the child to revise old concepts and to form new ones from the analyst's interpretations. Thus the patient must be able to accept passive aspects of the active task of imparting information. He must abdicate the activity of selecting the information that he imparts. He must also realize that the listening of the passive analyst has active components. The analyst must decide on how to order and to integrate the information that he passively receives from the patient. This bivalent potential of speaker and listener with regard to activity and passivity characterizes one aspect of the analytic situation (see Stone, 1961). This duality is easily exploited by the transference neurosis and/or the repetition compulsion.

Let us consider the communication distortions previously discussed in this light. What of the patient with a simile deficiency whose associations were determined preponderantly by contiguities? One might speculate that such a patient is a speaker who is functioning as a listener. He is more intent on decoding the meaning of his own utterances than on imparting information to someone else. Rather than being the passive transmitter of information he is apparently identified with the analyst's active need to understand. In my experience, such patients are monitoring their associations and making their own interpretations. When they ask the meaning of their associations, they are more concerned that the analyst's interpretation agree with their own than they are in receiving new concepts. Such patients often seem fixed in this active role. They find it difficult to deal with their own interpretations as merely additional data in the stream of ideas contained in the associative process. Although they may be introspective and psychologically oriented, for them learning is likely to be in the service of active mastery rather than self-awareness. Many individuals whose career choices are the behavioral sciences may be expected to show these tendencies. I suspect that this type of distortion will often be found in association with the fantasy of becoming a therapist, as it was in the patient previously described.

Those patients whose associations are rigidly determined by simile also seem to have fixations in an early undifferentiated phase. They are unable to identify with the active aspects of the analyst's function and almost caricature the most passive elements of the patient's task. They appear to be overidentified with that aspect of the patient's role in which judgment about the relevancy of information must be suspended. By giving up *all* monitoring activities, they become oblivious to the listener's needs. The suspension of critical judgment about the selection of the kind of information given is extended to the lexical and grammatical forms in which the information is transmitted. But what are some of the very early determinants of these conditions? In the woman whose associations were determined primarily by contiguities, the communication difficulty had its origin in the effects of her mother's deafness on her early development. The mother's hearing difficulty began during her pregnancy with the patient and was gradually progressive. The patient felt both responsible and unfairly blamed for her mother's disability. As so often happens with such disabilities, the mother used it in the service of her own emotional needs. At times she pretended to be able to hear when she could not and at other times she pretended not to be able to hear when the volume of sound was well within the compass of her auditory capacity. When the patient was a child, battles about whether she or her mother had or had not made certain statements, and whether the statement had or had not been misinterpreted, were frequent. It was evident that they came to play an important part in the pattern of the patient's oedipal phase and in her future relationships, especially with members of her own sex. What is important for our purposes is their relationship to her "simile defect." Several aspects of the characteristic dialogue with her mother stand out in this respect. The attention to listening was given a special emphasis. The patient noted not only the gist of an utterance, but like a court stenographer she appeared able to give a verbatim transcript of all statements made in a dialogue. The attention to objects in a room and their arrangement also had an important genetic relationship to this problem. Memory based upon contiguity was often considered decisive evidence in her arguments with her mother over what had been said and who had said it. For example, one or the other would say, "I remember when I told you such and such that I was sitting right over there in that chair before we changed the reading lamp and I was reading that book by so and so." The importance of handwriting was also an outgrowth of the inhibiting effect of the mother's deafness upon spoken dialogue. When either one wished to avoid their interminable sadomasochistic battles, they would leave each other written notes. When separated they wrote copious letters to each other which were invariably warm, informative, and free of rancor, unlike their spoken messages. One can attempt to reconstruct the language development of this patient in the preoedipal period from some of these later patterns. For example, it is likely that the mother's deafness prolonged the stage of pointing to objects and thus enhanced the tendency toward relating things by contiguity rather than simile. There was probably an additional effect of the mother's deafness. The child, in identifying the strained attention of the mother, probably developed a hypercathexis of the listening or self-monitoring aspect of speaking, which is such an outstanding characteristic of patients with "simile defects.[6]

Although time does not permit me to give the background data on the other patient, there are reasons to suspect that an overemphasis on words for their own sake and a neglect of the listener's needs played a part in both the patient's "contiguity deficiency" and his apparent failure to give the minimum monitoring attention to his own verbal productions. Patients such as this one speak as though they assumed that they would be understood, no matter how recondite the subject of their thoughts. It is characteristic of these individuals to mention a new person or event without giving the analyst the information necessary to comprehend what they are talking about. These are the patients in whom a pseudocompliance with the rules of free association is often overlooked.

Some of the complicated events in the early development of language have engaged the attention of psychologists, linguists, and educators for a long time. Their focus has been mainly on the process by which phonetic, semantic, and grammatical forms are acquired. Some of the larger patterns of communication between parent and child, when the latter is beginning to emerge from the stage of babbling, have not been so well elucidated. The babbling child can be described as a passive talker, while the parent is the active listener intent upon catching the first indications of meaningful phonetic combinations. Later the child begins to talk actively and to initiate requests. The parent must now play the role of passive listener and ascertain the child's real meaning before responding. With the further development of communication, the interchange of the bivalent roles of speaking and listening become more autonomous, both intrapersonally and interpersonally.

There is no more complex interaction between parent and child than language learning. Passive repetition, active selection, and synthesis through simile of idea and word in the child learning to talk find their counterpart in the active analysis, passive decoding, and resynthesis through contiguity on the part of the parent. Not only experience in his own role, but identification with the listening parent play a part in the child's learning both to speak and to comprehend another speaker. Problems in verbal expression or comprehension on the part of the parent will be reflected in the child (Lidz, 1963). Some authors (Nagera, 1966) have suggested that we consider "developmental conflict" as another source of disturbed function. This comes about, for example, when there is a marked discrepancy in the rate of development of certain ego functions or when the training of some ability is attempted before the ego apparatuses necessary for the task have reached a requisite state of maturity. It may also occur, conversely, when the precocious child is held back by the environment. Such conflicts may result in symptom formation just as a trauma and ego defect in the more usual sense in which these are understood. It is possible that, of all the ego functions, language is the most vulnerable to conflicting developmental phases.

Thus, I have suggested that the study of communication in the analytic process may reveal special types of disorders. To uncover them requires more than the interpretation of resistance and defense, the reconstruction of childhood traumas, and the analysis of transference. All analyses seem to some extent to partake of the characteristics of early experiences in the development of verbal communication.

When a patient is asked to free-associate and left to his own devices, disturbances in the way in which ideas are expressed are sometimes encountered. Four examples have been described as paraverbal, paramimetic, simile, and contiguity (parasyntactic) disorders. These are probably but a few of many similar subtle disturbances in the encoding of the thought process which emerge during free association. These disturbances are reminiscent in some ways of the multiplicity of phenomena encountered in aphasia, although there is no evidence that they stem from organic brain damage. In some ways the term "paraphasic" disorders may be appropriate for these conditions. In other respects, however, these disorders seem to be muted variations of the more regressive disorganized communication patterns of schizophrenia. Some of the early stages of language development may be re-enacted or merely uncovered by the process of free association. The distortions in the verbalization of thought when communications are not corrected by the feedback in ordinary dialogues are uncovered by free-associating. During psychoanalysis, the process of verbalization can become an object of scrutiny in its own right as it is during childhood. Much communication between parent and child concerns language itself.

The therapeutic process may benefit from the study and classification of such disturbances. We might, for example, be better able to reconstruct some of the special conditions of the parent-child relationship as they affect the acquisition of language. Some of the patterns of so-called developmental conflict may become clearer and allow greater access to the analysis of the preoedipal period. Finally, some aspects of language learning in early childhood which cannot be investigated by direct observation may become comprehensible by analytic reconstruction in the same way that the analysis of adult symptom formation has shed light upon early instinctual organization and ego development.

Notes

1. Meerloo (1964) has made a similar suggestion which he has developed along different lines. Shands (1960) comments on some of the unexploited linguistic research possibilities in the psychoanalytic situation. Loewenstein (1956) has also discussed free association in terms of linguistic theory. See also Teitelbaum (1958).

2. Whorf (1956), a linguist, suggested that speakers of specific languages might, unknown to themselves, have certain attitudes toward their internal or external environment which are determined by the conventions of their mother tongues rather than by thought and reality. In association with Edward Sapir (1921), he developed a theory of linguistic relativity. If it is true that the conventions of specific languages limit the way in which a speaker can conceptualize the world around him, theories of psychic structure conceived in a given language may also require reexamination in terms of linguistic relativity. See also Carroll (1958).

3. The converse is also possible. A clear concept may be difficult to verbalize. At such times the speaker may become aware of his inadequate verbal ability or the deficiencies of language itself.

4. Whorf (1956) and Sapir (1921) give examples, from exotic languages whose structure is very different from standard Indo-European, of the way in which grammatical forms determine transitivity. If in Shawnee (Whorf, 1956) the cleaning of a rifle bore can be expressed only as a movement of the tube over the ramrod, it would be incorrect to assume that an individual from this culture using this syntax was expressing a primal-scene fantasy of male passivity and female activity.

5. For an excellent review of the psychoanalytic literature on this subject, see Paulson (1966).

6. Language development in the child of deaf mutes shows some of these characteristics. See also Goldfarb and Braunstein (1956) on vocal auditory feedback phenomena in schizophrenic children.

CHAPTER SIX

Schizophrenic Language Disturbance

One of the most fascinating of Freud's metapsychological propositions is his theory of the language disturbances that usually accompany schizophrenic psychoses. The present discussion is a limited reexamination of some of these concepts in terms of certain linguistic theories of meaning.

There is general agreement that Freud's neurological orientation had a lasting effect upon his later clinical interests and theories. His interest in language became manifest while he was a neurologist. His monograph "On Aphasia" (1888) met with little interest in the

In 1939 and 1940 the present writer was a resident in neurology at Montefiore Hospital. Sidney Tarachow, who had completed both his neurological and psychiatric residency training, was at that time an attending psychiatrist to the neurological service of Montefiore Hospital. This paper, which was begun before his death, seemed to me to be especially appropriate to the recollections of my own early associations with and indebtedness to him. Already imbued with Freud's contributions, Sidney Tarachow was an inspiring mentor for a newcomer who accompanied him when requests had been made for psychiatric consultation on the neurological or other services of the hospital. Language disturbances due to organic brain disease or acute psychotic episodes were frequently the reasons for these consultative requests. Even in those days Sidney Tarachow was an independent thinker, a talented teacher and diligent physician. Time and the "synthetic function" often obscure the sources and derivations of what one claims as a proprietary interest in an idea. I cannot document at this time what I may have borrowed from Sidney Tarachow then or in the intervening years on this particular subject. Here the specific may be less important than the general. At the very least I owe him a debt of gratitude as an early source of information, influence, and learning, and an even greater debt in subsequent years for his friendship and confidence.

German-speaking medical world. Hughlings-Jackson (1958), however, the great English innovator in neurophysiology, quickly appreciated it. It is likely that part of Jackson's response was the recognition of the stimulating effect that his own ideas had had on the evolution of Freud's theories on aphasia. In his monograph "On Aphasia" there are the precursors of some of Freud's ideas on psychogenic language disturbances and on psychic structure itself.

There are some interesting correlations between Freud's neurological theories of aphasia and his psychological theories of word-thing relationships (as presented in his 1915 paper, "The Unconscious") and some of the semantic theories of modern linguists (Ogden and Richards, 1923).

Freud's theory of aphasia was the first to replace the classical anatomical localization theories with a functional concept. In his functional theory he recognized that the motor, sensory, and mnemic aspects of language, while dependent upon the integrity of certain cerebral areas were nonetheless integral aspects of a global function. The performance of the global function depended upon the integrity of each of its parts and the part functions in turn were always impaired to some extent by any disturbance of the supraordinate global function. Such a reciprocity suggested that careful examination would always reveal some disturbance of language as a whole regardless of the predominant disturbance or the site of the cerebral damage which was responsible for it.

Freud's functional concepts helped to explain the difficulty in finding pure examples of any of the postulated varieties of aphasia. The existence of such pure examples had been predicated on anatomical grounds in patients with single circumscribed lesions of the brain. The functional approach also helped to clarify the contradictions inherent in explanations of any given aphasic syndrome on the basis of predictable combinations of lesions as demanded by localization theories.

The concept of levels of control of total and part functions was the aspect of Freud's theory that most appealed to Hughlings-Jackson (1958). It was relevant to Jackson's own concept of "disinhibition" by which he sought to explain the release of primitive patterns of central nervous system activity as a result of impairment of more highly differentiated neural structures. Disinhibition, described in more appropriate psychological terms, became in turn a central feature of Freud's model for regression in psychic functioning in his later metapsychology.

Freud's aphasia studies are also important for the anticipatory schema contained therein of his theory of word-thing relationships and the language distortion of schizophrenia (Freud, 1915b). In fact Freud's most extended detour into the field of psycholinguistics occurs in this context.

Finally, it should be noted that, in the aphasia monograph, the concept of cathexis, which plays such an important role in later psychoanalytic metapsychology, is anticipated. The suggestion that "word presentations" bring sensory qualities to abstractions which have no concrete external "thing" counterpart is the seminal idea. Freud states that in this way thought has access to concepts such as spatial and temporal relationships which otherwise could not be manipulated as part of directed conscious thinking. It is interesting to compare the diagram of word-thing relationships which summarizes his views on aphasia (Freud, 1888) with the implicit diagram of word-thing relationships in "The Unconscious" (Freud, 1915) and the semantic triangle of later linguistic theory (Ogden and Richards, 1923).

When Freud abandoned the attempt to derive psychological phenomena from neurophysiological models, he was able to make a highly original contribution to the understanding of schizophrenic language. Theories of schizophrenic language disturbance prior to Freud were unable to give a satisfactory explanation of the frequent coexistence of normal language and communication with disorganized, idiosyncratic, noncommunicative language in the same individual at the same time. Neither the neurophysiological theories nor the psychological hypotheses then extant could deal with the bewildering variety and inconsistencies of schizophrenic language disorders. His most illuminating contribution to the subject appears in the last paper of his metapsychological trilogy, "The Unconscious" (Freud, 1915b). Here he says: "In schizophrenics we observe—especially in the initial stages which are so instructive—a number of changes in speech, some of which deserve to be regarded from a particular point of view." He then described the psychotic patient's tendency to interpret metaphor literally with its consequent disorganization of communication. This phenomenon he called "organ" or "hypochondriacal" speech. He suggests that in schizophrenics words are subjected to the same process which transforms latent dream thoughts into dream images. In pointing out that the schizophrenic uses the word as if it had a primitive sexual symbolic reference, Freud concluded, "If we ask ourselves what it is that gives the character of strangeness to the substitutive formations and the symptom in schizophrenia, we eventually come to realize that it is *the predominance of what has to do with words over what has to do with things*." He believed that this substitution was the result of similarities between the words themselves, rather than between the things they referred to and a sexual part or object. "Where the two—word and thing—do not coincide," he said, "the formation of substitutes in schizophrenia deviates from that in the transference neurosis." The following paragraph is worth quoting in extenso since it represents the key to Freud's ideas on the nature of the semantic disturbance of language in schizophrenia.

> If we now put this finding alongside the hypothesis that in schizophrenia object cathexes are given up, we shall be obliged to modify the hypothesis by adding that the cathexis of the *word*-presentations of objects is retained. What we have permissibly called the conscious presentation of the object can now be split up into the presentation of the *word* and the presentation of the *thing*: the latter consists in the cathexis, if not the direct memory images of the thing, at least the remoter memory-traces derived from these. We now seem to know all at once what the difference is between a conscious and an unconscious presentation. The two are not, as we supposed, different registrations of the same content in different physical localities, nor yet different functional states of cathexis in the same locality; but the conscious presentation comprises the presentation of the thing plus the presentation of the word belonging to it, while the unconscious presentation is the presentation of the thing alone. The system Ucs. contains the thing cathexes of objects, the first and true object cathexes; the system Pcs. comes about by this thing-presentation being hypercathected through being linked with the word presentation corresponding to it. It is these hypercathexes, we may

> suppose, that bring about a higher psychical organization and make it possible for the primary process to be succeeded by the secondary process which is dominant in the Pcs. Now too we are in a position to state precisely what it is that repression denies to the rejected presentation in the transference neurosis; what it denies to the presentation is translation into words which shall remain attached to the object. A presentation which is not put into words, or a psychical act which is not hypercathected, remains thereafter in the Ucs. in a state of repression. [Freud states further,] Probably, however, thought proceeds in systems so far remote from the original perceptual residues that they have not retained anything of the qualities of these thing residues, and in order to become conscious, need to be reinforced by new qualities. Moreover, by being linked with words *cathexes can be provided with qualities even when they represent only relations between presentations of objects and are thus unable to derive any quality from perceptions.*

Such relations, which become comprehensible only through words, form a major part of our thought processes. Freud suggested that it was the restitutive attempt in schizophrenia which brought about the state in which the word presentation alone is cathected. "In an attempt to regain the lost object, the ego begins by cathecting the verbal part of it (the object) but then finds itself obliged to be content with the word instead of the thing."

There are anthropological and cultural counterparts of this aspect of the schizophrenic process. For example, in animistic cultures, taboos against uttering the name of a person are common. In these instances, the name is treated as though it were the tabooed person himself. Even in modern civilized societies, phobic euphemisms are current for words that connote dreaded or forbidden things or conditions, e.g., "growth" for "cancer"; "passed away" for "dead," etc. It is as though the forbidden word might conjure up the thing by its close proximity to it. In English not even a polite euphemism is available employing a transitive verb for the most pleasurable activity in which men and women can engage. Euphemisms, by virtue of their ambiguity and generality, can be made to seem separate from their referents. Unlike the idiosyncratic euphemisms of schizophrenic language however, social euphemisms regain their connections with things by the common agreement that *certain things* in certain *social contexts* will be denoted by circumlocutions. This conspiracy of silence, so to speak, makes the euphemism part of the language code rather than an idiosyncrasy of one or a few individuals.

It is interesting to examine the complementary aspects of Freud's aphasia studies and his essay on the unconscious. In the former, different kinds of language disturbances produced by structural defects in the nervous system are categorized by those special features which deviate from normal modes of communication. An analysis of those features and of the interrelationships of the language defects led Freud to a revised concept of the structure and function of that part of the cerebral apparatus concerned with language. In the essay, "The Unconscious," an analysis of the patterns of disturbance in schizophrenia (as well as other phenomena) led Freud to perhaps the most crucial evidence for a revised model of the psychic apparatus.

Some of the difficulty in following Freud's highly condensed formulation may be reduced by closer examination. For example, certain ambiguities in his formulation pose great difficulties. Let me attempt an elucidation of some of these problems before discussing what may be learned about schizophrenia from Freud's analysis of schizophrenic language and what may be learned about language from his theory of schizophrenia.

What do we mean when we talk about "meaning?" To what do we refer when we say that a statement is "meaningful" or "meaningless?" The problem is as old as philosophy and a central one for the science of psychology. In modern semantics, *meaning* is defined as the mutual evocability of a word symbol and the thing to which it refers as a result of evolution or common convention in the encoding and decoding processes of communication (Brown, 1958). In this context the word *thing* is better translated by the word *referent*, which is less likely to connote a tangible object. *Referent* suggests any object or relationship in the external world, any sensory or affective experience whose identity has more or less been agreed upon by the community and given, by mutual convention, a symbolic designation. In this sense, a *word* under normal conditions can also be a thing or referent, as when, in the metalinguistic function of communication, we use words to talk about words, e.g., dictionary definitions. Freud did not have this use of "the word" in mind when he spoke of schizophrenics using words as though they were things. With this extension of the notion of "thing" in mind, it may be helpful to review Freud's formulation of the meaning of meaning.

In the normal state, the continuous cathexis of things in the external world maintains their psychic presentations and their connection in the preconscious word pool with their *references* (the word symbol which designates the referent). As long as this cathexis of external things is active, the primordial "unconscious thing" which had once existed as the precursor of both the word and the "conscious thing presentation" is kept in repression and does not interfere with conventional meaning. In states of psychotic regression there is an interruption of the cathexis of the external thing according to Freud's topographic hypothesis with a consequent disruption of the link between the conscious thing presentation and its conventional word presentation. As a consequence of this changed equilibrium the barrier of repression is disturbed and the word and thing presentations reestablish their respective connections with the unconscious thing presentation. The word symbol is thus cut off from its external referents and becomes subject to the processes of condensation, displacement, etc., which govern the presentations of unconscious mental life.

At this point let me suggest some areas of ambiguity in Freud's formulation. I believe that there are four major ones: (1) he failed to distinguish between speech and language; (2) the "unconscious thing presentation" was never fully defined and is discussed as if the conscious, and unconscious representations of the object were identical except for the word *symbol*, which is attached to the former and absent in the latter; (3) he did not tell us how he thought words and things came to be linked; and (4) at this stage of his exposition of theory he had neither distinguished sufficiently between language and thought nor suggested the ways in which preverbal thought and preintellectual speech play a part in language development. (See for example Crocker, 1963; Ekstein, 1964; Kubie, 1934; Peller, 1964; Piaget, 1923, 1954; Reiss, 1963; Vygotsky, 1934; and Werner and Kaplan, 1963b.)

Here I would like to suggest how some of the ambiguities in Freud's concept of the psychological structure of referential language can be clarified by the contributions of linguistic and developmental psychology.

In modern linguistic theory, speech and language are carefully distinguished in a way that is often neglected in our clinical literature. Such neglect, I believe, has led to a great deal of conceptual confusion. The word *language* should be reserved for the representational system of certain symbolic forms which are organized according to acoustical, syntactic, and semantic schemata and which together define the shared habits and codes for the communication of thought in what the social scientists call a "language community." Just as the community has evolved the code that defines its language, the language in turn has come to define certain aspects of the community and its weltanschauung (Whorf, 1956). Language and speech are both defined by a multiplicity of attributes some of which overlap and are interdependent. Other attributes however are distinct. Language, for example, can be reproduced independent of speech as in writing or Morse code. If speech is defined as the vocal-articulatory aspect of language it cannot be independent of the formal "design features of language," at least as they apply to phonetic, semantic, and syntactic rules. Speech however can be relatively independent of meaning or the communication aspects of language as for example in echolalia or sleep talking.

The most difficult step in Freud's formulation appears to become clearer once the distinction between speech and language has been defined, i.e., when we have distinguished between an instrument for communication with other individuals through the vocal-auditory pathway and the mnemic representational system that serves as one of the elements and vehicles of thought. This has to do with the schizophrenic withdrawal of cathexis from objects, by which we mean persons and things in the external world. It is not immediately evident why the withdrawal of cathexes should disrupt the link in consciousness between word presentations and thing presentations. Why should it not be possible for the link between a word symbol and its referent, the product of a lengthy period of learning and utilization, to remain intact in spite of the withdrawal of interest from the actual referent? There is evidence that the link does indeed remain intact. During remissions, the schizophrenic patient does not have to relearn the language code as an aphasic might. Even during psychotic episodes the same word used in a contextually nonsensical way in one sentence may be used in accordance with its usual meaning in the next. For example, a young man in an acute psychotic state who had torn up his money and identification cards said, when asked for an explanation: "I am identified with God, I do not need any other identification." The abstract concept of identification with another in this statement is confused with the more concrete meaning of personal identity which in turn is treated as if it were a material entity, the card. Yet the reference to the card as a means for identification indicates that the word can be used in its usual lexical sense. It is possible that in schizophrenia there is a retention of interest in thought and speech but a decathexis of the language code as a shared entity (in this sense as an external thing). Some of the conceptual difficulties in the original formulation may be minimized by such a revision. We now assume that the link between the conscious thing presentation and the word presentation that belongs to it is a function of the language code, i.e., of the degree of interest that the speaker has in sharing his experience (conscious thing presentations) and in sharing in the conscious thing presentations of others. This interest in the sharing of ideas provides the most important cement for the meaning link between a word and its referent. If the language code is decathected, if the schizophrenic loses the wish *to share* his experiences with others and to share in theirs, it is probable that both thing presentations (object categories [Brown, 1958]) and word presentations (the purely verbal lexicon) remain intact but unrelated.

Why should the word in this case assume the characteristics of a thing presentation? In losing its function as a coded symbol, why does the word take on the features of a personal or sexual symbol which is what Freud meant by "hypochondriacal speech." It is in this instance that the ambiguity of the term *unconscious thing presentation* offers conceptual difficulty. The unconscious thing presentation is said to remain attached to the word when the word becomes disconnected from its conscious thing presentation. An understanding of the ontogenesis of language may help to provide the solution for this problem. Modern linguists have found little evidence that the conventional shared meaning of words in ordinary communication requires an image or thing presentation. Meaning depends rather upon concepts or referential categories. These meanings are based upon the identifying attributive features of classificatory schemata rather than upon images (Brown, 1958; Ogden and Richards, 1923; Piaget, 1923, 1954; Ullman, 1962; Werner and Kaplan, 1963b). In topographic terms these schemata seem to have almost exclusively preconscious, rather than conscious, representations. It is probable that only some proper names, either as applied to individuals or specific places, have a representation that accompanies the word as distinct from a reference (i.e., a category) which is attached to the acoustical image of the word. When a schizophrenic uses a word divorced from its lexical meaning, it is the referential category rather than the thing presentation that loses its connection with the word.

As I will suggest later in more detail, the thinglike quality of words in schizophrenic language is the result of regression to an early stage in the development of language. In this stage before the individual has formed categories, words were used as though they had an independent existence as things. To postulate an unconscious thing presentation is to suggest that thought develops before language. Psychoanalytic reconstructions of early stages of development frequently contain references to preverbal thought but rarely to preintellectual speech (a phase of vocal-articulatory development that is distinct from babbling). The work of some developmental psychologists presents fairly compelling reasons for considering both phenomena. Vygotsky (1934), for example, believes that thought and speech have different roots. He adduces both phylogenetic and ontogenetic reasons. The intellect of the anthropoid apes is like man's in certain respects—for example, apes employ these sounds in a way similar to the expressive function of social organization. They are capable of emitting a wide variety of sounds which resemble the phonemes of human speech. They employ these sounds in a way similar to the expressive function of man. The close correspondence between thought and speech, the essence of language, is, however, absent. Vygotsky (1934) says: ". . . in the phylogeny of thought and speech a prelinguistic phase in the development of thought and a preintellectual phase in the development of speech are clearly discernible."

Observations of infant speech (Crocker, 1963; Ekstein, 1964; Peller, 1964; Piaget, 1923, 1954) suggest the existence of a prelinguistic phase of thinking and a prethought phase of vocal-articulatory sound making. The child's activities at certain stages of development indicate an ability to conceptualize (as seen in the way in which he manipulates objects) but without the ability to describe the concept in words. During this phase of development he may be able to imitate words and even use sentences without any communally valid referential implications. During the phase in which curiosity and interrogatory utterances predominate, the child feels a need for a clearer comprehension of meanings and tries actively to learn the signs attached to objects. "He seems suddenly to discover the symbolic function of words." Speech at this stage enters its intellectual phase, and thought begins to acquire its linguistic aspects. "The knot is tied for the problem of thought and language." From this point on most thought is verbal and most speech is rational. Piaget (1923, 1954), Kasanin (1944b), and Werner and Kaplan (1963b) have suggested that this convergence in concept formation has successive nodal points, each one of which initiates a new and higher level of abstraction for both thought and language.

In their studies of language symbol formation, Werner and Kaplan (1963b) suggest that the earliest word symbols are fused not only with the object that is the ostensible referent, but also with the mother herself who taught the word. Before the word symbol can become attached to a category, it must first be detached, not only from its specific referent but also from the personal object, the mother, who first proposed the word. Their work is confirmation of psychoanalytic studies which suggest that the child's differentiation of self and object is a prerequisite to cognitive development. For example: a 20-month-old child who was taught to recognize the letter "A" on billboards and in children's books went around for several days calling all letters of the alphabet, paper, pencils, crayons, her own act of drawing, and her mother in the act of writing, an "A" or "making A's." One may ask at this point why sophisticated words, the late accretions in an individual's vocabulary, should also succumb to the regressive process, as well as those simple words acquired in early childhood. Here too Werner and Kaplan (1963b) have made some interesting observations. They show that all new terms when they are first acquired and before they become an autonomous part of the individual's lexicon, pass through a stage of idiosyncratic assimilation which they call "symbol rotation." This process is a recapitulation, however brief, of the characteristics of the earlier stages of vocabulary development.

We can learn a great deal about the schizophrenic process in general as well as the dynamics of a particular case from the language of a schizophrenic. The central feature of the schizophrenic process are said to be related to withdrawal from the external world, thinking disorders and regression of various kinds and severity (Kasanin, 1955b; Lorenz, 1961). We do not really know whether one process is the primary defect or whether there is a regularity in causal sequence. Regression may be a consequence of the decathexis of objects or it may be the cause. Likewise disturbances of thinking may be primary or secondary to the other two. Whichever is a consequence of the other, each condition is a regular feature of the schizophrenic syndrome.

At the time he wrote "The Unconscious," Freud was more concerned with establishing the necessity for his topographic assumptions than he was with elucidating the dynamics of psychotic states. He first stated the reasons for postulating three topographic systems: the conscious, preconscious, and unconscious. (These had already been described as a consequence of his observations on hysteria, dreams, and the psychopathology of daily life.) After describing the general features of the topographic system, he attempted to apply this construct to a variety of dissimilar psychological phenomena as a test of its general validity. His formulation of the relationship between conscious word and thing presentations and unconscious thing presentations in schizophrenia appears, in some ways, to be more a *tour de force* demonstrating the power of a theory than further validation of the theory by induction from additional data. For other views of Freud's linguistic theories see Laffal (1964) and Peller (1967). Thus Freud at that time was more concerned with the schema that would explain the disturbance of referential language in schizophrenia in terms of topographic rearrangements following "the decathexis of external things" than he was in schizophrenic language per se. His construction was ingenious and provided the first satisfactory clue to the puzzle of schizophrenic concreteness and literalness in the use of words. His observation that the word is used by the schizophrenic as though it were a thing rather than a linguistic symbol has been extremely useful. The topographic schema, however, does not aid in understanding other schizophrenic language phenomena (see

Arlow and Brenner, 1964). For example, schizophrenics whose speech reveal marked disturbances of reference and syntax may have no difficulty in asking for things by their correct names, in defining concrete or abstract nouns, or in coherently describing past events. Schizophrenics may be able to do this even when they are grossly delusional about the here and now. If a cathexis of the external thing were necessary for the preservation of the tie between the conscious thing presentation and the word presentation, then the ability to use referential language would not coexist with schizophrenic verbigeration as it so often does.

It may be useful to place the language disturbance of the schizophrenic into another perspective and reverse some of the causal chains suggested by the topographic model. Such a change is in greater accord with Freud's later model of the psychic apparatus, the "structural theory," and in conformity with some of his later formulations on psychosis and with ego psychology in general (Chapter 4).

In what follows I will postulate the primacy of the ego regression in the schizophrenic process. It is not relevant here whether this regression is a consequence of drive disorder or structural defect. Social withdrawal is seen as a consequence of this regression rather than its cause. In this alienation from the group we may postulate a decathexis of a process rather than of *things*. The process decathected is the usually autonomous encoding and decoding of the shared representational language symbols which make it possible for one human being to have access to the conscious experiences of another. In other words withdrawal from the language community means both word and object decathexis. Such an explanation of schizophrenic disintegration has several advantages over the topographic object withdrawal schema. It is better able to deal with the fluctuations between apparent thought and language disturbance on the one hand and their coexistence with normal or even extraordinary feats of mentation on the other. The ability of some gifted individuals who succumb to psychosis to carry on side by side highly creative and delusional activities is frequent enought to require that a theory of schizophrenic dynamics take this phenomenon into account. Nietzsche, Newton, and Van Gogh are historic examples of individuals with so-called gross disorders of thought and language who were able to engage in the highly intellectual processes of mathematical, philosophical, scientific, or artistic creation with distinction and apparent lucidity. Especially in fields like mathematics and the plastic arts which do not require much inner verbalization, the disturbance of the communicative function of language may leave many areas of thinking in both verbal and nonverbal terms intact.

Schizophrenia is frequently diagnosed, described, and understood in terms of a thought disorder, that is, if thought is here defined as the intellectual function of manipulating object relationships, logical relations, problem solving and the creation of new syntheses of ideas. Thought employs the contents of consciousness, images, affects, words, etc. It is difficult to understand how thought can be scrutinized without reference to language or language evaluated without reference to thought. For the normal adult engaged in usual activities, language and thought are inextricably bound. It is the untying of this knot, the regression to preintellectual language and preverbal thought which is the schizophrenic process. Just such a regression, it should however be noted, when controlled, is at the root of creativity, since it allows for new and unusual recombinations of words and ideas in science and in art, as well as in our dreams.

One may consider in a phylogenetic sense what the relationship of the language code must have been to the range of conscious human experience. If the primary function of the language code is the communication of thought, the development and facilities of the code must favor the more usual contents of human thoughts and experience while neglecting, in the interest of clarity, the development of conventions for the communication of the more idiosyncratic and isolated aspects of human experience. In both acute and chronic organic states it can usually be shown by indirect methods that thought and language are reciprocally but separately involved. In deleria thought disorders are primary. The evidence for this is the rapidity with which the language disturbances disappear when daylight, the removal of eye bandages, etc., restore perception and orientation in space and time. In organic aphasias however it is the language disturbances which are primary. For example, many motor aphasics can perform complicated intellectual tasks without being able to utter the words which describe what is going on in their thoughts. It is doubtful whether any of our indirect methods of investigating mental processes during acute or chronic schizophrenic states can reveal to the observer with any degree of certainty, whether the patient can think but cannot find the verbal means to communicate the results of his thought process to us, or whether he is unable to think in ways which overlap sufficiently with average thought to find communally acceptable language symbols to describe his thoughts.

There is, however, another possibility which must be considered. Suppose that in the condition we call schizophrenia, both the ability to think and the representational preconscious mnemic system called language are intact. And that, as a result of regression, the Vigotsky knot, which produced verbal thought and intellectual speech, has become untied. Would this schema explain some of the language phenomena of schizophrenia more satisfactorily? I refer to those states in which bizarre thinking, which we infer from bizarre language locutions, goes hand in hand with unusual intellectual accomplishments and linguistic abilitites. Such a schema has several advantages over one in which the withdrawal from objects in the "real world" results in the disturbance of thought and language seen in schizophrenics. As I see it, such a regression does not presuppose a return of all thinking to its preverbal forms, nor of all language to preintellectual phases. I suggest that the first step in schizophrenic disorder is a return to earlier phases of ego development, phases in which the social motivations for turning ideas into language and language into ideas are weak and primitive. Under such circumstances, especially when the regression has a fluctuating character, the following mutually inclusive phenomena can be observed: the patient who can perform complex feats of thought without desiring or being able to find the verbal forms in which to communicate them; the patient whose speech retains the characteristics of his adult linguistic capacities but is not connected with his adult intellectual functions, his speech being organized instead around its early preintellectual or primitive intellectual connections. And, finally, the patient in whom fluctuations of the drive and/or ego disturbances which produced the initial regression, allow for periodic reverbalization of thought and reintellectualization of speech in accordance with changing internal and external conditions.

Since Freud's theory of the disturbance of word-thing connections is a theory of dislocation of meaning, it applies to what the modern linguists call the semantic level of language organization. It is interesting to compare Freud's model of semantic relationships briefly with one from structural linguistics.

Semantics is usually considered a subdivision of the field of semiotics or the theory of signs. It has two complementary models, much like the structural and topographic models of our own metapsychology. Both models are necessary for the investigation of meaning in language. The referential point of view is based upon the well-known "Ogden-Richards Triangle" (1923). The second, called the operational or contextual model, is less easily diagrammed.

In the referential model of meaning (1) the word symbol, (2) the concept or *reference*, and (3) the *referent* (thing, object, etc.) are schematized as the three apices of a triangle. The side of the triangle which indicates the relationship between the word symbol and the reference (or concept category) is often in classic semantics called the *name-sense complex*. It is a learned, culturally determined relationship. The causal connections are the result of arbitrary convention and are shared by the members of the whole language community. Most linguists consider it the central issue in the question of manifest meaning. The line connecting the referent (thing) and its reference is also considered a causal one. Unlike the first, it is largely determined by individual psychological events and the development, especially, of perception and cognition. The link between the word symbol and the referent is usually portrayed as a dotted line to indicate that the relationship is an imputed rather than a causal one (see Ullman, 1962).

Freud's model of the relationship of the conscious word with the thing presentation and the relationship depicted by the semantic triangle differ in the origin assigned to meaning. Freud believed meaning was determined by the link between the word symbol and its referent, while in the semantic model, a reciprocal relationship existing between the word symbol and its reference is called meaning. This complex has its own relationship with the thing or referent. In the reciprocal relationship between word and sense, the experience of meaning is evoked by their mutual availability. Thus, a word symbol evokes a reference and a reference (sense) evokes a word symbol. From this union, the basic semantic unit is born. Other reasons exist for assuming that the phonetic shape of the word is attached to a concept category rather than a thing presentation. Such categories are partially determined by word networks established in most languages through synonym-homonym-antonym complexes (Chapter 4; Ullman, 1962; see also Brown, 1958).

In this presentation I have attempted to demonstrate in schematic terms, the relationship between Freud's topographic model of the psychic apparatus and his hypothesis on the nature of schizophrenic language. Freud observed and then succinctly summarized his explanation of schizophrenic literalness with the statement that patients with this psychosis use words as though they were the equivalent of things. Other aspects of schizophrenic phenomenology, recent contributions of developmental psychology, and some linguistic considerations have suggested some objections to and revisions of this schema which would also bring it into greater concordance with the structural model of the psychic apparatus. According to this revision the psychotic individual does not suffer a "decathexis of things." It is suggested that as a result of regression and withdrawal from social relationships, which both necessitate and facilitate verbal communication, language code connections are disrupted. That part of the mental life of the individual which is concerned with the encoding and decoding process of socialized verbal communication returns to its primitive state before the word had referential significance and before "things" had symbolic representations.

CHAPTER SEVEN

Sign Phenomena and Unconscious Meaning

The meaning of meaning (Ogden and Richards, 1923; Sebeok et al., 1964; Ullman, 1962) has preoccupied scholars for many centuries. Plato's *Cratylus* (Hayden and Alworth, 1965) is said to be the first comprehensive statement of the major semantic problems. Since his time, epistemologists, philologists, and psychologists have grappled with the intricacies of the questions raised. Recently semantics has become one of the major subdivisions of linguistics and the major focus of two other recent disciplines, information theory and communication theory. The latter two disciplines lie athwart the boundaries of linguistics, psychology, and mathematics. The interest in semantic problems has also given rise to the hybrid but fertile field of psycholinguistics.

I will not address this discussion primarily to the general problem of meaning. Rather, I will try to consider what psychoanalysts mean when they talk about "latent" or "unconscious" meaning (see also Beres, 1962). I will reexamine two examples of parapraxes given by Freud (1901) as models of the investigation of unconscious meaning. Some ideas from the field of semiotics[1] (the theory of signs) will be helpful because of the overlap between that discipline and our own.

The existence of an unconscious mental apparatus, capable of a wide variety of mental operations, is one of the central hypotheses of psychoanalytic theory. One can infer from this hypothesis that symbolic processes exist in the human mind outside of conscious awareness. This hypothesis, and the evidence that he marshaled in support of it, was one of Freud's major contributions to psychology. Unlike the philosophical and psychological investigations that preceded it, psychoanalysis did not begin with an investigation of what the scientific minds of its day considered to be "significant" problems. Parapraxes, dreams, and neurotic symptoms were considered "meaningless" phenomena or at best minor examples of physiological dysfunction. Thus, in a certain sense, Freud's original clinical investigations were an attempt to find meaning in the meaningless.

I believe that one of the keys to the present endeavor will lie in a comparison of the dynamics of the cognitive experience of significance with the experience of meaninglessness as it occurs in the analyst during the analytic process. It is here that I think the theory of signs will complement psychoanalytic formulations. In the ensuing discussion I will use the word *sign* in a generic sense to mean any one of three entities: a "signal," a "sign," or a "symbol."

A preliminary discussion of relevant aspects of the definition of meaning is necessary. *Meaning* is one of the most ambiguous words in our language. In ordinary parlance it is understood as a cognitive phenomenon and then described in a variety of ways. Most of these descriptions turn out to be circular statements. Examples of such ambiguous definitions would be: "meaning is an experience of significance" or "meaning is the cognition of representational relationships." The ambiguity can be reduced, but by no means resolved, if one narrows one's attention to "sign" phenomena (Greenberg, 1957; Ullman, 1962). (We will consider *sign* in its generic sense for the moment, as denoting a thing by which some other thing is known or represented.) The ambiguity can be even further reduced by considering only the problem of verbal meaning. For the purpose of this discussion I will consider the usual semantic definition of meaning as sufficient. Meaning consists of the reciprocal relationship between the symbol and the symbolized, or in simpler terms (when words are the symbols) the mutual evocability of name and sense (Chapter 4; Ogden and Richards, 1923; Shapiro, 1967; Ullman, 1962).

Whether we follow a narrow or a broad definition of meaning, the experience of significance (by definition) is not possible unless something can be seen as representing something else. This is a minimal level of behavior or experience that can be termed *cognitive*. Anything less is primitive perception, the mere registration, so to speak, of figure and ground. Thus the process of mental representation and the ability to react to signs are fundamental to the experience of meaning. The experience of meaning results then from the proposition that A stands for B and that B is designated by A. It occurs whether the relationship between A and B is the result of a veridical relationship of natural order, of arbitrary convention, or of the subject's misinterpretation or idiosyncratic interpretation of the relationship between A and B. The subjective experience of significance (or should we say *signification*?) is the same even when the subject perceives that the connection between A and B is incorrect. He knows what the speaker means even when he knows it to be untrue. We can infer from these propositions what we mean when we say that something is "meaningless." A statement need not be untrue to be nonsense. It need only be lacking in any sign value. In other words, to be truly meaningless or nonsensical a thing must be seen as standing only for itself. In linguistic terms the correct concept of nonsense would be a word without a referent or a referent without a name. If one says that the proposition that A signifies B is false, it does not follow that the proposition is nonsense. It may merely mean that A is recognized as a sign but that it does not signify B. The statement that a proposition is nonsense may also be true only for the speaker, i.e., it may be a statement of nonsignificance or of ignorance.

If we understood the word *meaning* as the experience which occurs when the signified is recognized by its sign, unconscious meaning (if such an entity exists) can be understood as the use of or reaction to signs without the conscious experience of significance. In the discipline of semiotics (the theory of signs) the literature reveals a lack of agreement and (from the point of view of psychology) a lack of consistency in the use of certain terms. In the ensuing discussion I will use the term *sign function* to designate signals, signs, and symbols and will distinguish between them when necessary. Let us consider my previous statement that the experience of nonsense is the assertion that a thing or event has no sign function. It would be more correct to say that something is nonsense when it is lacking in *relevant* signal, sign, or symbolic functions for the individual who is experiencing it. According to the semiotician (who is not interested in the *psychological processes of signification* as such), signals, signs, and symbols form a continuum and cannot be strictly delimited since the same event which functions as a signal in one context may function as a symbol in another (Greenberg, 1957; Pierce, 1961; Rycroft, 1958; Ullman, 1962). For example, the utterance "look out there" may be a nonspecific signal of impending danger, or a conative suggestion for a specific action in linguistic symbols. To the psychologist, however, for whom relevance within a context is a central issue, qualitative distinctions between signals, signs, and symbols are not only possible but essential. For example, the gestures which accompany spoken language are part of a sign system which in itself has limited semanticity. When these gestures are organized as in the communication code of deaf mutes, the semiotician still describes them as a "sign language." When normals become aphasic, there is usually an augmentation of the range and expressiveness of their paraverbal gestures. Aphasia in deaf mutes, however, produces a profound interference in their use of gestures. We must assume, therefore, that the difference between the gestures of a vocalizing speaker and those of a deaf mute is not just quantitative, but qualitative as well, as far as the central nervous system is concerned.

The differences between the psychologist and the semiotician can be illustrated in another way. A player in a game of anagrams finds himself confronted with a set of random letters which cannot within the rules of the game be combined into a word of three letters or more. To say that all the combinations are nonsensical and that there are no meaningful symbols relevant in the context would be a correct psychological statement. The semiotician would agree, but would suggest that we eradicate the context or change the rules. Now we see that each letter in itself is a phonetic *sign*. Three of them, let us say S.O.S., are a well-known signal of distress, and one of the letters, let us say *c*, is a mathematical symbol for a physical constant. It would appear, as I will try to demonstrate later, that the semiotic method of dealing with sign analysis in a random set of apparently nonsignificant events is closer to the psychoanalytic process than is the psychologist's strictly contextual investigation of the same phenomena.

What are the differences between signals, signs, and symbols from the point of view of the experience of significance? Let us begin with signal phenomena. Whatever its form, an event A is a signal when it gives rise to the cognitive expectation of the materialization of event B. From this point of view nimbus clouds signalize rain, an epileptic aura is a signal of a seizure, and the whistle of a locomotive is a signal because it anticipates the arrival of the train. Signals may or may not have a cause and effect relationship with what they signalize; they may be simple or complex events; they may belong to any sensory modality; they may have a natural association with the event signalized, as with clouds and rain, or a conventional one, as in the case of train whistles and trains. They may also be personal, idiosyncratic, systematized, or random. The one feature that signals seem to share in common is *a close temporal or spatial contiguity between the signal and the event signalized*. A *sign* in its specific meaning denotes *an event A that indicates the existence of an event B*. A sign does not imply the materialization of event B, nor is it necessarily based upon any temporal or spatial relationship to the event it signifies. Thus an arrow on a street post signifies a one-way street for vehicular traffic, and footprints in the sand of an uncharted island are a sign of human habitation. In other respects signs may have all of the same sensory, causal, personal, natural, or conventional relationships with the signified that a signal has with the signalized. The one essential attribute shared by signs is *the similarity between some feature of the sign and some feature of the thing signified*. This relationship is also called iconic or pictographic. Thus the arrow of the directional sign gains its status from its similarity to the pointing finger, the footprints theirs, from their resemblance to the human foot. Evolutionary transmutations of a sign may obscure its iconicity with the thing signified. Sometimes historical reconstruction is necessary to find the original iconic relationships.

What I shall call a symbol differs from a signal or a sign in one important respect. The relationship between the symbol and its referent or the thing symbolized is arbitrary and assigned by convention. It is probable that contiguity or similarity to their referents played some role in the origins of symbols, but these aspects of the symbol are no longer reconstructible, and for all practical purposes one can say that the relationship of symbol A to referent B has the algebraic characteristic "let A refer to B." Thus the nouns for common objects have no apparent contiguous or pictographic relationship to the objects they denote (a frequent exception noted by the linguists is onomatopoeic words). Phonetic and notational symbols are arbitrary abstractions. They may be used as signals or signs, but a symbol as such does not necessarily arouse the expectation of the materialization of its referent nor even avow its existence in the "real" world. The referent of a symbol may be purely imaginary, like the square root of minus one. There is no way to signalize or signify a "Jabberwock" except by name. Verbal or notational symbols have one other feature in common besides their arbitrariness, and that is the rules which govern their permissible combinations. In language this is called syntax. Most symbols are designed for the communication of thought. Their evolution is toward maximum explicitness of reference and away from ambiguity. Ambiguity is a necessary consequence of representation by contiguity or similarity. Thus symbolic systems must have syntactic rules to ensure a congruence between encoding and decoding processes. Within the semantic and syntactic rules which prescribe their utilization, symbols have an infinite combinatorial potential in contrast to the relatively limited possibilities for permutation of signals and signs. The use of symbols in contrast to signals and signs results in an economy of energy expenditure in representation and communication—for example, the reduction of the number of signs in phonetic alphabets as compared with pictographic ones. The paradigm of symbolic systems is the communal language code, but it is not the only one used in mental operations.

At this point I would like to suggest the possibility that what we call *primary process* is largely a signalizing and signifying activity, while *secondary process* is characterized by the predominant use of symbols. I will also try to show in the discussion that follows that the primary process uses conventional symbols only by converting them into signals or signs and that, conversely, the use of signals and signs by the secondary process depends upon their acquisition of arbitrary conventional referents. Other characteristics of the primary and secondary processes are probably consequences of their utilization of signal-sign phenomena or of symbols (Chapters 4 and 5; Edelheit, 1967). For example, the difference in so-called speed of discharge of the primary process or the relative delay in discharge which characterizes the secondary process may be a consequence of the difference in time necessary for the simple decoding operation in the case of signals and the relatively complex one necessary in the case of symbolic systems. Results of primary-process activity are usually unconscious, while those of secondary-process activity are usually conscious or easily accessible to consciousness. I will also try to demonstrate that the analytic process attempts to decipher unconscious meaning in two ways: (1) by reducing personal events described in secondary-process symbols, to signal and sign events; and (2) by interpreting idiosyncratic signal and sign events in terms of conventional language symbols (see also Rycroft, 1958; Shapiro, 1967).

The relationship between the signal and signalized is one of contiguity and the relationship between the sign and the signified is one of simile; they are thus important components of two forms of metaphor: metonymy and simile, respectively. Metonymy is that form of metaphor which utilizes the familiar mechanism of *pars pro toto* or a contiguous object as a means of reference. Thus the crown comes to stand for the king and a directive is said to come from the White House rather than from the President. Metonymies are often signal words. Thus the cry of "Fire" is a warning of danger, i.e., something is on fire and there is danger of its spreading to other things and causing a conflagration. The fire is only a contiguous part of something that is burning. Pointing is often another feature of metonymy which has signal characteristics. The statement "a sail" on the high seas, with pointing, indicates a vessel on the horizon.

On the other hand, simile is a verbal form of iconic representation. A simile may be simple and descriptive; the phrase *lemon yellow* conveys a particular shade of the yellow part of the spectrum as it appears to one viewer's eyes through its similarity to the color of a common citrus fruit. A simile may be complex and creative, as in the case of T.S. Eliot's Mr. Prufrock, who sees "the evening spread out against the sky like a patient etherized upon a table" (1917). The invitation to share an idiosyncratic view of the twilight sky and the anaesthetized patient in the imagination of the poet may or may not be illuminating to the reader. It will certainly not evoke the kind of overlapping common experiences that are implicit in the phrase *lemon yellow,* but it may evoke a new imaginative one. Yet both utilize that essential feature of simile in which one whole object is compared with another to elicit a mental representation of something unfamiliar to the listener in terms of the familiar. In simile the familiar object used for representational evocation need have no temporal or spatial contiguity with the objective counterpart of the image that it seeks to evoke. The representation of the unfamiliar in terms of the familiar in simile, particularly in poetic forms, resembles global rather than selective identification. Preoccupied with the likenesses that present themselves to him in his trope, the poet seems to be unconcerned with the inappropriate attributes of the things that he has been comparing. As metonymies are frequently used as signals, so are similes often used as signs—for example, the Dove of Peace in the U.N. emblem, or the Scales of Justice of the Federal Judiciary. In fact, emblematic devices are some of the most felicitous examples of the utilization of simile for sign purposes. Let me mention several other outstanding attributes of metonymy and simile (Jakobson, 1964; Jakobson and Halle, 1956):

1. Condensation, especially in simile: *lemon yellow*, for example, fuses two objects, the citrus fruit and the object to whose color I am comparing it.
2. Displacement: when "the Crown" stands for the king the attributes of the whole object are displaced onto the part. The Crown is said to speak, take note of, etc.
3. Plastic representation: especially in simile an abstraction or a collective noun is compared to another object which has greater discreteness and representability. Thus "the evening," a diffuse entity, obtains plastic representation as a more discrete one, "a patient etherized upon a table."
4. Generalization: in simile especially, the usual result of portraying the unfamiliar in terms of the familiar is to replace a particular unfamiliar thing with a category of familiar things. The simile *lemon yellow* conjures up not only the whole class of lemons but a large variety of things that have a similar yellow shade.
5. Rapidity of response: in both metonymy and simile (as with signals and signs) the metaphor strives for instantaneous recognition. The part object is more easily evoked than the

whole. The familiar comes to mind more quickly than the unfamiliar. In word-association tests the shortest reaction times are seen in responses by contiguity or simile; delays accompany responses that deviate from this pattern.

6. Omission of tense: the proximity of the part to the whole in metonymy does not allow the development of the concept of elapsed time. A metonymy, like a signal, is synchronous with what it stands for. In simile as well the mental presentations to be compared are simultaneous even though they come from widely separated places or eras. These are the characteristics that we also assign to the primary process. Conversely, specificity, discreteness, abstract representation, categorization and delay of stimulus response are characteristic of conventional symbols[2] and of the secondary process.

Finally, I would like to point out that the concepts of sign and signal, of simile and metonymy are relevant to the cultural manifestations that we call totem and taboo. In taboos both the *mana* of special virtues and the noxious influences of evil forces are acquired or warded off by "distancing operations" in temporal or spatial terms. The amulet which is a metonymous stand-in for a powerful protector is also a signal to the spirits of evil that they may suffer if they approach the wearer. Totems, like signs and similes, are iconic representations, drawn from the animal world, of the myths of the clan. Like emblems and trade marks they also serve as signs of identity and of kinship ties. In totem and taboo phenomena, as well as in the whole animistic magical phase of primitive culture, there is an intimate intermingling of signal and sign phenomena.

In many of his early writings, Freud was at least implicitly aware of the importance of signals and signs and of metonymy and simile in the mechanisms of neurotic symptoms, of dreams and in the psychopathology of everyday life. I would like to reexamine some of his examples, particularly those contained in *The Psychopathology of Everyday Life* (1901), from the semiotic point of view. I would also like to call attention to some of his general statements in this context.[3] For example, following his diagram of the substitutions and displacements which determine the paramnesias around the name "Signorelli" (1901, p. 5), Freud says: "Thus the names have been treated in this process like the pictograms in a sentence which has had to be converted into a picture puzzle (or rebus)." The role of simile in the prefixes and suffixes of the substituted names is clearly indicated in the diagram. In a footnote on the same page he says of the "Bosnia-Herzogovina" links in the chain of his reconstruction: "These two portions of the Austro-Hungarian Monarchy used to be habitually spoken of together almost as though they formed a single word." One might add that their spatial proximity is a contiguous determinant of this compound designation. Indeed the larger area within which these provinces existed was a similarly hyphenated entity, the Austro-Hungarian Empire itself. On the next page one finds the following remarkable passage:

> The conditions necessary for forgetting a name, when forgetting it is accompanied by paramnesia, may then be summarized as follows: (1) a certain disposition for forgetting the name; (2) *a process of suppression carried out shortly before*; (3) the possibility of establishing an external association between the name in question and the elements previously suppressed. The difficulty of fulfilling the last condition need probably not be rated very high since *considering the low standards expected of an association of this kind, one could be established in the great majority of cases*. There is, however, the profounder question whether an external association like this can really be a sufficient condition for the repressed elements disturbing the reproduction of the lost name—whether some more intimate connection between the two topics is not required. On a superficial consideration one would be inclined to reject the latter demand, and accept as sufficient a *temporal contiguity* between the two, even if the contents are completely different. On close inquiry, however, one finds more and more frequently that the two elements which are joined by an external association (the repressed elements and the new one) possess in addition *some connection of content*; and such a connection is in fact demonstrable in the "Signorelli" example.

By the "low standards expected of associations of this kind" I think that Freud means that the connection of ideas by mere contiguity or simile requires no problem-solving effort nor any particularly advanced level of intelligence or sophistication. I think that he also implies the necessity for concurrent signal and sign linkages in the personal content for the production of a paramnesia. Finally, he says (1901, p. 13):

> The chief importance of the "aliquis" example lies in another of the ways in which it differs from the "Signorelli" specimen. In the latter, the reproducing of a name was disturbed by the after-effect of a train of thought begun just before and then broken off, whose content, however, had no clear connection with the new topic containing the name "Signorelli". *Contiguity in time* furnished the only relation between the repressed topic and the topic of the forgotten name; but this was enough to enable the two topics to find a connection in an external association. Nothing on the other hand can be seen in the "aliquis" example of an independent repressed topic of this sort, which had engaged conscious thinking directly before and then left its echoes in disturbance. The disturbance in reproduction occurred in this instance from the very nature of the topic hit upon in the quotation, since opposition unconsciously arose to the wishful idea expressed in it.

I think that here Freud is saying that either the suppression of an idea occurs first and removes some element from consciousness to which it is connected by simile (a "connection of content") or by temporal contiguity. Alternatively, he says, a series of ideas may abut suddenly upon a previously suppressed thought (to which they are associated by simile or contiguity) with a resulting disturbance in the evocation of some conscious word (symbol).

In Chapter 5 I suggest that a simile or contiguity encoding disorder could produce a disturbance in communication. Thus a series of statements connected by some spatial or temporal contiguity requires a simile to convey information to a listener. For example, two people who are strangers might arrange by letter to meet in some public place. Confusion with other bypassers might result from an agreement that specified only time and location. If one or the other describes his appearance, a simile is added which markedly reduces the likelihood of missing their rendezvous. Conversely, a series of ideas linked by similes precludes narrative. A story requires some kind of temporal ordering of events to make a "happening" comprehensible to a listener. Associations based solely upon simile result in a series of digressions which seem to lead the speaker farther and farther from his original topic. Ultimately, the impatient listener may demand to know the relevance of the speaker's statements. In a communication style where ideas are associated predominantly by simile, the ambiguities can often be resolved by the insertion of place, time, or person, which explains the context of the speaker's digression. Thus, inferential probabilities, if not precise reference, depend upon the conjunction of simile and metonymy (see also Spence, 1968, on the role of redundancy).

I believe that in the reconstruction of unconscious meaning a similar process is involved. Signs are sought for the elucidation of signals and vice versa. The "pictographic sentence or rebus" (of "substitutive displacements" described by Freud) is meaningless until we discover its contiguity to a suppressed thought. The "motive" for the suppression of an idea, on the other hand, remains obscure until we find the common features (similes) of the elements of the rebus and the unconscious thought. It is these common features which enable the substitutions and displacements to occur and which lead to our understanding of hitherto incomprehensible behavior.

Let me review some of the steps in the "Signorelli" example by way of illustration. While riding on a train from Dalmatia to Herzogovina, Freud was speaking with a stranger about travel. The conversational topic was most likely determined by simile to their immediate activity. He inquired whether his companion had "ever been to Orvieto and seen the famous frescoes painted by—." The amnesia occurred at this point and only the substitute names "Botticelli" and "Boltraffio" came to his mind. Freud's investigation of the associative connections of these substitute names led him to the realization that the topic preceding this question had concerned the customs of the Turks living in Herzogovina. Freud's companion had commended these Turks for showing unusual stoicism in the face of incurable illness. This had reminded Freud of another anecdote about this same community which he had suppressed. In contrast to their resignation in the face of imminent death was their despair when suffering from a sexual disorder. Freud thought that these Turks placed a higher value on sexual enjoyment than they did on life itself. This suppression was partly motivated by Freud's shyness about discussing sexual matters with a stranger. However, the suppression also helped to divert Freud's mind from a recent bit of bad news. A patient of his suffering from an "*incurable sexual disorder*" had committed suicide while Freud was away on vacation. The anecdote about the Herzogovinian Turks functioned as a sign related by simile to a painful episode which Freud preferred to put out of his mind. I think that we may infer the simile from Freud's use of the word *incurable* in connection with *his* patient. This must have been a period (1901) when Freud was sorely beset by medical criticism which charged him with charlatanism. Like the "incurable" Turks who reassured their doctors that they were dying in the belief that "all that could be done had been done for them," Freud must have wished that his patient too could have lived in resignation rather than adding another "blemish" to his (Freud's) questionable reputation as a therapist at that time. If one reexamines the diagram of associative links in this example they also consist of a series of similes and metonymies. This associative chain does not lead back to the forgotten word, but it does remind the parapractic speaker of the suppressed idea immediately preceding the lapse of memory. Since it was a suppressed simile that gave rise to the paramnesia, it may be of interest to note that the name of the *place*, "Orvieto," where Signorelli worked, a contiguity so to speak, was clearly recalled. What then is the unconscious meaning of the "Signorelli" paramnesia? In terms of its sign function we would have to say that "Signorelli" stands for the inevitability of death and the ultimate impotence of the physician to do more than defer it for a small fragment of time. Freud at first disavows this connection and sees the name as an accidental and "external" one. (His resistance to his own method is familiar in our patients.) He suggests that the same fate might have befallen any other proper name at this juncture. In a later footnote (1900, p. 13), he revises his opinion and states:

> I am not entirely convinced of the absence of any internal connection (i.e. simile) between the two groups of thoughts in the "Signorelli" case. After all, if the repressed thoughts on the

> topic of death and sexual life are carefully followed up, one will be brought face to face with an idea that is by no means remote from the topic of the frescoes at "Orvieto".

The editor of the Standard Edition suggests another contiguous determinant when he says, parenthetically, that "Dr. Richard Karpe has suggested that there may be a connection here with the visit to an Etruscan tomb near Orvieto, mentioned in *The Interpretation of Dreams*" (1900, pp. 454-5).

The "aliquis" example which follows reveals the same process in reverse. An academic friend of Freud's ends an impassioned speech about the unfortunate status of the Jews in his social world with a quotation from Virgil: "Exoriare aliquis nostris ex ossibus ultor" (Let someone arise from my bones as an avenger), but with the omission of the word *aliquis* (someone). Freud, at his colleague's request, supplies the missing word and his friend persuades him to help in the reconstruction of the dynamics of the lapse through Freud's method of free association. Here again the associative links proceed through a series first of phonetic similes and then historical-religious contiguities to the miracle of St. Januarius, a phial of whose preserved blood is said to liquefy miraculously on a particular holy day. St. Januarius, also a calendar saint, is thus a striking metaphor for the menstrual period. It might also be pointed out that religious miracles are "signs" of the existence of divinely inspired (usually healing) powers in certain chosen individuals. At this point the sanguine trail of simile leads to an idea that was barely saved from suppression. The idea is a contiguity which reveals the context of the similes and, by inference, the motive for the amnesia. The speaker admitted that he was waiting anxiously to hear from a lady, with whom he had enjoyed a recent contiguity, about whether her menses had begun. Insofar as it was the "liquis," "liquid," "liquefy," liquefied blood (associated with the word *aliquis*) which led to the suppressed thought, we are dealing with a series of similes. To the patient it referred to a materialization and in this sense the word served as a signal. The materialization could be confidently expected in one of two forms: if not the lady's menstrual period then a fetus ("exoriare nostris ex ossibus").

Why should sign phenomena be so important in establishing unconscious meaning? It seems likely that in early childhood signal systems are the chief type of communication between parent and child. The neonatal hunger cry and the later smiling response are pertinent examples of this early stage. The materialization of the breast is soon linked to the hunger cry and one of the earliest signals is established. In a later phase with more complex combinations of mimetic, gestural, and babbling behavior which are increasingly *imitative* (iconic), signs are added to the signal system. It should be noted that it is imitation which is the vehicle for sign formation and simile through primitive identification. It is also likely that sign formation can proceed when maturation has reached a stage of motor independence in which the mere existence of the need-satisfying object is sufficient to allay anxiety without the actual appearance of need-satisfying substances. With the advent of language, a new system for the expression of meaning supersedes but does not replace the signal-sign systems. What kind of relationship can we infer between this new superordinate schema and the more primitive communication system from which it arose? Are they parallel independent or reciprocal interdependent processes? It is difficult to conceive of a vast bin of word symbols punch-carded for easy retrieval, as some naive assumptions would imply. It is more likely that what we call the preconscious verbal system is a relay station for a system of mnemonic signals and signs which can be translated into verbal symbols under the influence of propitious internal and external influences. Werner and Kaplan's (1963b) detailed studies of symbol formation give an account of the developmental processes by which signals and signs become transmuted into language symbols. They show that in the process of acquiring conventional symbolic codes, especially language, each individual goes through idiosyncratic processes of associating tactile, auditory, and other sensory stimuli (signals), childhood theories, fantasies, and experiences (signs) to the conventional word symbol. These idiosyncratic influences are interwoven with other processes that help the language symbol acquire its standard meaning. It is this evolution that gives each word a denotative and a connotative meaning. Clinical experience (see also Chapters 4 and 5; Meerloo, 1964; Rycroft, 1958; Shapiro, 1967; Weich, 1968) indicates that, as a result of regression, these archaic signal-sign associations can become reattached to the word. If the meaning of meaning is taken as the mutual evocability of words and things, a more sophisticated definition of meaning would be the reciprocity of the encoding-decoding process. Encoding is basically the evocation of the word symbol by the sign or signal of its referent, while decoding is essentially the evocation of signal and sign phenomena by word symbols. This reciprocal process is interpersonal when it takes place between speakers, and intrapsychic when it takes the form of "inner speech." In this schema the autonomous functioning of a word-evocation system of almost limitless possibilities (when one considers combinatorial permutations) depends upon the undisturbed operation of a scrambling and recombining process of a relatively limited number of signal-sign entities.

Various accounts of language learning in childhood (Leopold, 1952; Lewis, 1951; Werner and Kaplan, 1963b) indicate the importance of signals and signs in presymbolic communication. The phonetic signals of the period of babbling and crying become signs as previously indicated when they are phonemically organized in imitation of the adult. These imitative words are signs as long as the imitation for its own sake takes precedence over any consistent use of the word for reference, i.e., they are iconic with the sounds of the language teacher (like parrot language) rather than conventional symbols used in the communication of ideas. The word can be said to achieve initial symbolic status when it becomes detached from the imitative stimulus and is consistently applied to a referent (even if the referent is misidentified). This is the stage of personal or idiosyncratic meaning. When invariance and category formation are added to the child's cognitive repertoire, the word becomes further detached from its idiosyncratic referent and attains its conventional lexical character.

It has been postulated that the autonomous functioning of the subordinate signal-sign system is necessary for the evocation of words in the superordinate language system. The converse is apparently also true, as I will elaborate later. Unless the intended word reaches consciousness, it disturbs the autonomy of the subordinate signal-sign system. In other words, we might speculate that we have here mutually activating systems which can be disturbed in either direction. Highly charged personal signal-sign combinations evoked by "neutral" words or phrases might interfere with the subordinate signal-sign system, while "neutral" signal-sign stimuli may evoke a highly charged word for the individual involved. Thus in the "aliquis" example I would suspect that the neutral word *exoriare* had already touched off the metonymy of "someone arising from the speaker's bones" with the resulting elision of the signal word *aliquis*, which threatened to join the speaker's bones and his mistress's ovulatory cycle in an anxiety-fraught possibility. In the "Signorelli" example, a series of unpleasant signs referring to death interrupted the autonomy of word evocation in the subsequent shift of context from the highly charged topic of sick Turks in Herzogovina to the "neutral" name of an Italian Renaissance painter.

Actually the process by which we arrive at what we call the unconscious meaning of the meaningless parapraxis is a reversal of the process by which the slip occurred in the first place. By the process of free association we retrace a series of seemingly nonsensically connected similes and contiguities to the point where the autonomous process of symbol evocation went astray. It is like tracing an electric circuit until we find the break in the line. Sometimes the retrograde process causes another disruption so that it is impossible to find the first one. We call this resistance but it may be a similar interference to the one produced by a displacement of the affective charge to new elements of the superordinate or subordinate system. In other cases, such as those cited by Freud, it is possible to elicit the unverbalized conscious thought which preceded the "power failure."

What then is the latent meaning of a parapraxis? I think that we can say that there are two meanings: a general and a specific one. In general, the parapraxis is itself a sign—a sign of the elision in consciousness of a relevant idea—one that has disturbed the autonomous activity of the encoding process. Most examples lead to such a conclusion. The specific meaning of a parapraxis revolves around the motives for the suppression of the idea that interfered with the autonomy of evocation in the first place. The motive (or motives) can be "read" by solving the rebus of similes and metonymies provided by the displacements and substitutions of the process of free association. We call this solution of the rebus an interpretation.

It is my impression that finding the meaning of a parapraxis is the paradigm of the process by which we arrive at most interpretations in the analytic process. One of the problems of the meaning of unconscious meaning hinges upon what we mean by a correct interpretation. Many criteria have been suggested for judging the validity of an interpretation by its sequelae. Among these may be mentioned: (1) the sense of conviction that it produces in the patient; (2) the sense of conviction felt by the analyst; (3) confirmatory associations, affects, and other reactions which follow the interpretation; (4) the degree to which predictive inferences can be drawn from the interpretation and subsequently validated; (5) the productivity of the interpretation in producing new information, especially new childhood memories, dreams, or fantasies; (6) the appearance of new symptoms; (7) the disappearance of old symptoms; (8) the undoing of one or more defenses; (9) the resolution of a resistance, especially one which seemed to have produced an *impasse* in the analysis; (10) *the revelation by the patient of some consciously withheld thought, dream, experience, etc*. Although all of these criteria are suggestive, none of them singly or in combination can be called conclusive.[4]

I have italicized number (10) in the list of sequelae, since in my experience this eventuality is highly illuminating, whether or not it constitutes veridical proof according to the postulates of scientific method. In the unraveling of the various forms of the psychopathology of everyday life, the conscious suppression of an idea in the course of an exposition or narrative is consistently found. The consciously suppressed thought is found in two frequent types of analytic sessions which are analogous to the "Signorelli" and "aliquis" examples. In one kind of session, an interpretation brings to light a buried piece of information by way of the confession of a withheld idea. For example, a medical student with school problems was told that he seemed to be "dosing" the information that he gave me about certain events by providing bits and pieces of them from session to session. I said that I thought that this was part of a tendency to usurp the role of doctor rather than remaining the patient, by prejudging the relevance of what he told me. He responded by saying that he had been feeling nauseated during this session from its very beginning. He had not mentioned this because he knew that it was due to a gastrointestinal virus that had been "making the rounds" and that it had no psychological importance. This, however, reminded him of something that he had never told me during two years of analysis, namely that in the first and second grades he had had a severe school phobia which was accompanied by nausea following breakfast on school days, but not at weekends. One of his associations to beginning medical school was that it "felt like being back in the first grade."

In the second type, the revelation that a thought has been withheld is a clue to the meaning of the previous associations. This often occurs at the end of the hour. For example, a young woman during a session expressed obsessional fears about her treatment and about the possibility that "the price of cure" in terms of "sacrifice of her self-determination" was too great. She was unable to explain why this had suddenly begun to worry her when everything had been going well. Turning, as she was about to leave the office, she said: "I know that I should have mentioned this; it has been on my mind all during the session, but I will not be able to come tomorrow. I will explain it next time." The "signal" reduction of the thought was that I (like her father) would interfere with any plans made on impulse and insist that she discuss them first. Hcr depressive character and impulsive tendencies were strongly centered about this transference residual.

Summary

If meaning is an ambiguous concept, unconscious meaning is doubly fraught with ambiguity. In this discussion conscious meaning has been defined as the reciprocal evocability of words and things, or, in a more general sense, of symbols and their referents. Freud's concept of word-thing relationships as described in his paper, "The Unconscious" (1915b), is in essential agreement with this concept of meaning borrowed from general semantics. One revision of Freud's formulation has been suggested. Instead of a wordless thing presentation, residing in a topographical unconscious, it is proposed that a primary process which uses signal and sign phenomena exists as a subordinate system within the superordinate symbol utilizing secondary process. These primary process signal and sign phenomena are not thing presentations but stand for them—the former by contiguity and the latter by simile. The relationship of signals to the things signalized by contiguity, and the iconic character of signs, make them appear to be representations of so-called things in themselves. Furthermore, it is postulated that this subordinate system operates as a mnemonic resonating device for the evocation of symbolic forms in the superordinate secondary process, especially the evocation of the phonetic, semantic, and syntactic aspects of language symbols. This reciprocity likewise includes an influence of the superordinate system on the signalizing and signifying events in the subordinate system (primary process). When the interaction of the two systems proceeds autonomously, all meaning is felt as if it derived from the word-thing relationships in the secondary process alone, which usually concides with the topographic Conscious system. Clinically we are aware that there are a large number of manifestations of interference in this autonomy which appear to be nonsensical if attempts are made to decode them according to the rules of symbolic systems. A parapraxis, the paradigm of such a disturbance, can occur when there is a voluntary interruption of encoding in the superordinate system which interferes with the functioning of the subordinate one. Alternatively, the same effect may occur when the signal-sign combinations do not find a corresponding representable symbol in the superordinate system.[5] The analyst listening to the process of free association temporarily disregards the semantic and syntactic rules for decoding linguistic symbols and utilizes their simile and metonymy characteristics to decipher the signals and signs from which they arise. An interpretation is a translation and resynthesis in referential language of the signal-sign operations that he infers in the subordinate system, which is produced by a disruption of encoding autonomy. This replication is an attempt to find out, under relatively controlled conditions, how the sign-symbol encoding and decoding functions went astray in the first place. The inferences that we draw from this replication are what we call "unconscious meaning."

Notes

1. It is interesting that the term *semiotics* (Sebeok et al., 1964) was confined in its earliest usage to the medical theory of symptoms and their interpretation. The term was first introduced into philosophy at the end of the seventeenth century by John Locke to denote the study of signs in general. If semiotic concepts are indeed useful in the extension of the understanding of some manifestations of psychopathology, its alterations in meaning will have made a full cycle.

2. I will not include here a discussion of the discrepancy between the psychoanalytic and the semiotic use of the term *symbol,* except to say that in semiotic terms the sexual symbols of the dream, of hysterical symptoms, etc., would more properly be classified as signals or signs. They resemble similes and metonymies and are recognized by contiguities or by iconic representations and not by any conventional covenants.

3. For the purpose of this discussion I will assume the reader's familiarity with the details of the "Signorelli" and "aliquis" examples. I will only recapitulate those aspects of the two examples that are relevant to the immediate issue.

4. I wish to defer discussion at this point of the question of hierarchies of relevant interpretations for any particular constellation of associations. I will be content for the time being with the original proposition that we can say that something has meaning when we know (or think that we know) what it stands for.

5. Diffuse affects, such as so-called free-floating anxiety, may be such disturbances emanating from the signal system. It is possible that they are free floating because the signals do not find any corresponding symbols to evoke.

CHAPTER EIGHT

Language and Psychoanalysis

Ferdinand de Saussure (1916), who is called the father of modern linguistics, is also the father of a distinguished psychoanalyst, Dr. Raymond de Saussure, but there are other important ties between the two disciplines. Psychoanalysis cannot do without language, and the study of language cannot dispense with psychology. Psychoanalysis has contributed important insights into the psychopathology of language (for an excellent account of this and a good bibliography on the subject see Laffal, 1965). The study of the structure of language, on the other hand, promises to provide us with some important glimpses into basic patterns of the organization of the ego (Chomsky, 1957; Edelheit, 1968; Freud, 1888, 1895; Luria, 1961; Miller and Isard, 1963; Vernon, 1967; Vygotsky, 1934; Werner and Kaplan, 1963b; Whorf, 1956).

Linguistics and psychoanalysis also share several methodological similarities. Both are based upon deterministic assumptions. They place a similar emphasis on historical development and both depend heavily upon the reconstruction of the past as an important tool. Both fields are analytic in their approach. Clinical theory and the study of the structure of specific languages afford interesting similarities, while even more striking in their analogous relationship are the metapsychology of psychoanalysis and the "metalinguistic" systems for the study of language (e.g., the transformational grammar of Chomsky, 1957).

The relationship of language to thought is central to both disciplines and continues to preoccupy linguists directly and psychoanalysts by implication in all of their activities.

Both linguists and psychoanalysts have significant overlapping interests in the communicative function of gesture and mimesis and the complex field of paralinguistic phenomena in all of their varied ramifications (Chapter 5; Kubie, 1934; Loewenstein, 1956; Mahl, 1968; Mahl and Schulz, 1964; Rycroft, 1958).

Scarcely any modern linguist needs to be persuaded of the importance of psychology as an auxiliary discipline, while increasing numbers of analysts in recent years have become interested in the internal structure of language for the light that it may shed on many aspects of psychic functioning. The development of Freud's structural theory had its forerunners in his monograph *On Aphasia* (1888) and in *The Project* (1895). In these monographs he first stressed the unique potentiality of the auditory modality for the development of language. He was aware that only in the auditory sphere is there a simultaneous communication with the object and feedback of the centrifugal stimuli to the self, so that interpersonal and intrapsychic communication become important mirrors of each other. In the early stages of its development the ego has no mechanism for the reproduction of visual or other sensory modalities comparable to the auditory-vocal self-reproducing mechanism that makes possible the development of speech. Only sound images are "self-reporting" and capable at the same time of being brought into congruence with images coming from external objects. No sensory modality, with the possible exception of touch, is such an early and fateful source of interchange between the infant and its mother as vocalization and hearing (Lidz, 1963; Peller, 1964, 1966).

There have been recent speculations on the exceptional relationship of the auditory sphere to the development of psychic structure, e.g., Isakower (1939) and Edelheit (1968). Freud (1915) also suggested that consciousness might be intimately connected with words, both in terms of the self-awareness that language affords through the encoding of thought and the sensory "trace" that words provide for abstract concepts. In modern psychology this concept of the relationship of words to ideas has come more and more into question (Luria, 1961; Vernon, 1967; Vygotsky, 1934).

In the analytic situation the couch position (Loewenstein, 1956) interrupts the usual signal sending and receiving systems. It not only places an almost total emphasis on the vocal-auditory interchange, but through the technique of free association, channels mental activity that might otherwise be expressed in action, or other modes of behavior, into spoken language. Thus while it encourages fantasy it asks for the most articulate account of it of which the individual is capable. It is as if the most developed as well as the most regressive aspects of human object relations were condensed into a single controlled situation. The alteration of the structure of the ego through language is one of the goals envisaged by the psychoanalytic process.

I do not have to remind you that one of Freud's earliest and most fruitful findings was that neurotic symptoms had symbolic meanings or, to put it in another way, they could be understood as part of a regressive communication system with its own conventions. Freud (1915) called this symbolic code "body" or "organ" language and saw it as one of the ubiquitous phenomena of the various categories of psychopathology. A major endeavor of psychoanalysis ever since has been to work out the significance of symptoms and to find out how to translate the idiolect of body language into the dialect of everyday speech. In my opinion this requires methods that are more analogous to those of linguistics than to those of any other discipline.

As psychoanalysis has developed we have found that the question of meaning is essential to all of our hypotheses, even those that appear to have the form of causal statements. For example, we recall that Freud first proposed a causal theory of hysteria in citing sexual seduction in childhood as a specific determinant of the adult neurosis. The story of his initial disappointment and later revision of this hypothesis is an important one in psychoanalytic history. The important theoretical revision was the rediscovery that *the meaning* of certain childhood events in terms of antecedent fantasies was more important in understanding symptom formation than any direct effect of the events themselves. When the effect of a pharmacological agent is studied in general psychiatry an attempt is made, by double-blind studies and other experimental controls, to exclude the meaning of the event to the patient or the investigator in order to test causal hypotheses. In psychoanalysis we never assume that an identical intervention has the same meaning for all patients; our assumption is rather the reverse. Thus in psychoanalytic clinical theory we deal with entailment hypotheses rather than causal ones. This has its counterpart in the study of the grammatical transformations of a language, where the general principles underlying the transformational rules are also derived from the entailment relationships of sentences used by native speakers.

It seems to me that there are three seminal areas in which the problems of modern linguistics and psychoanalysis intersect. These might afford a focus for a discussion of language and psychoanalysis from both a clinical and theoretical point of view and lead to other questions which have not been raised in this cursory introduction.

The first has to do with rule-directed behavior which, beginning with language, dominates such a large segment of the development of psychic structure. Balkányi (1964, 1967), expanding on Isakower's (1939) formulations, emphasizes the possible genetic importance of the rules derived from the language code for the development of the superego. Ballanyi's phrase "a sense of the rules" suggests that a cognitive schema first grasps the principles upon which language is organized and then becomes the nucleus of the structure upon which the superego is built. This formulation suggests that we might look for defects in the superego derived from early disturbances in language development. The same may be inferred for certain aspects of ego development (Chapter 4; Edelheit, 1968; Freud, 1915; Lidz, 1963; Miller and Isard, 1963). What does it mean to follow a rule? The most characteristic thing about rule-directed behavior is that the person who has acquired the rules knows intuitively, and prior to analysis, whether he is proceeding correctly or incorrectly even when he is unable to formulate the rules themselves. One might say in other words that he knows what it is to make a mistake. Observations of the ontogenesis of language suggest that, by the age of three to five years, normal children have incorporated the basic rules of the syntax of their mother tongue. These rules are a set of organizing principles. It is an inherent disposition of the human ego to develop such complex cognitive schemata prior to the adaptational demands of the environment. It is these cognitive schemata which make the early acquisition of language possible. For the mature individual, other rule-governed activities, such as manners, taste, laws, etc., afford a flexible guide to human relationships within a similarly invariant structure of numerous combinatorial possibilities. One may thus suspect that one set of rules is derived from the other, or that both come from similar precursors in early childhood. One might point to the smiling response as an example of one of these early inherent schemata. The smiling response is not elicited by like stimuli but by equivalent ones. Equivalence refers to the invariant configurations or patterns of relationship between stimuli rather than to their particular nature. The same ability in somewhat later development will make it possible for the child to register and recognize invariant linguistic patterns as, for example, the acoustical structure of words. So we may ask how early language deprivation affects ego development, in the same way that we ask the reverse question.

The relationship of language to the thought process has long been a matter of preoccupation for both linguists and psychologists. The answer to the question concerning the nature of the relationship of the early origins of language and thought has important consequences for clinical theory. The traditional views on this subject are that thought and language have a simultaneous origin and a completely interdependent development. Freud's account of the development of the secondary process lends itself to this interpretation. His theory of schizophrenic language (Freud, 1915), on the other hand, seems to suggest the possibility of separate origins with interdependent evolutionary phases. If this is so, why is it that in the psychoanalytic literature we find numerous references to preverbal thought (Bion, 1962; Székely, 1962) but few, if any, to preintellectual speech. Besides the convincing arguments of many theorists on the subject (e.g., Vygotsky, 1934), there is interesting evidence for the relative independence of the two processes from other sources, such as the studies of intelligence in prelingual deaf mutes (Vernon, 1967).

For most clinicians schizophrenia is conceived as primarily a thought disorder with secondary effects on language. Is there greater explanatory power in dealing with some of the disparate phenomena of schizophrenia by dividing the observed cases into two predominant groups: one where thought is primarily disturbed with secondary effects on language and the other a disturbance primarily of language with secondary effects upon thought?

One of the serious shortcomings of psychoanalytic theory has been the terminological confusion caused by its idiosyncratic concept of the symbol. Here I think that linguistic formulations can foster conceptual clarity. What psychoanalysts have traditionally been describing as symbols (Kubie, 1934; Silberer, 1951) in the dream process for example, linguists would describe as signals or signs (Ullman, 1962; Werner and Kaplan, 1963b). Linguistic theory reserves the term *symbol for conventional and arbitrary signs which are* in the service of the intentional communication of meaning, such as words. In psychoanalysis we use the term indiscriminately for both varieties of phenomena. The capacity to symbolize in the linguistic sense of the term is thus quite different from such an ability in our psychoanalytic lexicon.

Finally it seems to me that a central issue presented to psychoanalysts comes from the proponents of the theory of linguistic relativity, the so-called Sapir-Whorf hypothesis (Carroll, 1958; Whorf, 1956). This hypothesis suggests that important aspects of the shape of our ideas are determined by language itself and also by the particular language that we speak. Although this theory has received little confirmation from a study of the cognitive differences of speakers of different languages, it may well be an important factor in determining some aspects of unconscious mental processes that only psychoanalysis is equipped to study. The theory of linguistic relativity poses another question for us. If language is an important determinant of the formal qualities of thought, to what extent do we ascribe the latent content of our patients' productions to intrinsic factors such as intentions or fantasies when they belong to extrinsic ones such as the inflexibility of some grammatical locutions in certain languages (Carroll, 1958; Isakower, 1939; Miller and Isard, 1963; Whorf, 1956).

I have not attempted an exhaustive catalogue of the many issues that might be included in a topic of this magnitude. If we direct some of the questions posed herein to a reexamination of the process of free association from the point of view of language theory as well as psychoanalysis, we may find that our patients communicate more than we are aware of and less than we often think that we discover.

CHAPTER NINE

The Metapsychology of Therapeutic Interpretation

The relevance of the metapsychological formulations of psychoanalytic theory to clinical practice has always been moot. In the case of Freud's theory of the death instinct, the overwhelming verdict has been conspicuously against its applicability to the exigencies of everyday practice. There seems to be an increasing tendency in some quarters to emphasize Freud's clinical contributions and to treat his metapsychological constructs as if they had greater historical than practical importance.

Two recent contributions (Klein, 1969; Needles, 1969) by eminent psychoanalytic theoreticians are illustrative. One (Needles, 1969) emphasizes the irrelevance of some of the economic aspects of drive theory to the understanding of the phenomenology of pleasure, while the other (Klein, 1969) asserts that drive-discharge theory reduces the cognitive phenomena of pleasure and unpleasure to a quasi-physiological model. Both papers are representative of the objections raised in other contexts in less organized and closely reasoned form.

Having had the opportunity to discuss both of these stimulating contributions at their initial presentation, I have been encouraged to elaborate those comments for whatever heuristic value they may contain. My disagreement with the views of these two authors, stated briefly, is that metapsychology is not only an abstraction of clinical theory, but explicitly or implicitly determines many of the interventions that occur in the course of psychoanalytic treatment.

I will comment separately on these two papers, which have different approaches to the problems, before discussing the features that they share in common.

Klein's (1969) presentation is entitled "Discussion of Freud's Two Theories of Sexuality." His major premise is that the psychoanalytic conception of sexuality exists in two versions. The first he calls the "clinical theory" because it is the one that tacitly guides actual clinical work. Of this theory he says, "It centers upon the distinctive properties of human sexuality, upon the values and meanings associated with sensual experiences in the motivational history of the person from birth to adulthood, upon how nonsexual motives and activities are altered when they acquire a 'sensual' aspect and vice versa" (p. 137). The "second theory," Klein says, "translates these causal connections into quasi-physiological terms of a model of an energic force that seeks discharge. This drive-discharge model is the basis of the rest of Freud's metapsychological theory which stands in a parallel relationship to the first theory without any necessary interconnection between the two" (p. 137).

My main disagreement with this statement, which is derived from clinical experience rather than theory, is concerned with Klein's (1969) implicit equation of "sensual" and "sexual" (an equation that is very common in clinical and theoretical literature). By making these terms interchangeable I think that he commits the converse of the error that he calls our attention to in examples that he gives of the misuse of the drive-discharge model. It is true that Freud's early work with hysterical patients emphasized the ubiquitous character of the repression of erotic sensual experiences in both the genetic and dynamic aspects of symptom formation. In "Instincts and Their Vicissitudes" (Freud, 1915a) however, where he was more explicit about his concept of "drive" than in any of his previous writings, he speaks of drives as having a "source," an "aim," and an "object." He thought that the drives had psychic representations and could be represented in psychological terms. It was only the question of source which seemed to cause him some confusion and for which he sought physiological explanations. Thus, a full description of the libidinal drive at a particular stage in its development, let us say the oedipal period in the male, consists, according to drive theory, of not only an unknown "force" but also of a particular aim, phallic penetration, of a particular object, the maternal one. Furthermore, the broad spectrum of clinical phenomena that have been investigated since the days of "The Studies" has given rise to revisions of such concepts as defense, narcissism, and conflict. The terms *libidinization, sexualization, instinctualization,* or Hartmann's (1950b) concept of deneutralization as applied to activities or functions is purely deductive and does not imply that a conscious erotic sensual experience has ever been associated by the patient with the disturbed activity or function. In such instances it is possible that it is drive-discharge theory (whatever its ultimate validity) that more accurately than so-called clinical theory suggests the clinical connections of diverse observations. (This is not meant to contradict Klein's assertion that a naive use of metapsychological concepts can be misleading.)

Let me present a clinical example of an instance where drive theory may be more illuminating than a theory derived solely from the phenomenology of sensual experience. A seventeen-year-old male is being treated for a learning problem in school. In spite of a very high intellectual capacity he finds it difficult to study and does poorly in certain subjects. He is a product of "progressive schools" and parents who are "psychologically sophisticated." There has been great freedom in discussing sex in the family and an emphasis on avoiding any inculcation of shame or guilt about sexual matters in the patient. From the beginning of his therapy the patient speaks freely about his frequent but not compulsive masturbation and about his masturbatory fantasies and the sensual experiences that accompany them. His fantasies are active, heterosexual, and not unusual. Although his casualness is impressive, it does not appear to be peculiar or pathological. Sometime later in his treatment, with great difficulty the patient admits to the habit of nail biting, which is accompanied by considerable guilt in the doing and shame in the telling. Why would most analysts agree that this activity should be explored as a masturbatory equivalent—that it is most likely a sexualized activity, in spite of the absence of sensual pleasure associated with it and the lack of full erotic sensual experience obtained in the seemingly unrelated masturbatory activity? In my opinion this clinical deduction (which incidentally could be validated in this patient) follows from drive theory. I think that the general direction of inference on the part of most psychoanalytically trained clinicians would go as follows: The patient's environment has redirected his conflict. Guilt and shame have been largely removed from the conscious, erotic sensual experience but not from the drive as a whole. The patient is not conscious of the oedipal aim and object of his apparent sexual activity so that this part of the drive has been displaced to another activity where, despite the fact that it is unaccompanied by any conscious sensual pleasure, it becomes involved in the same conflicts as one that has such accompaniments. In this instance *sexualization* is not synonymous with *sensualization*. Thus what Klein (1966) has described as "clinical theory" would not be sufficient to lead us to a therapeutically useful hypothesis, as in this case. There is therefore in my opinion, a use for both "clinical" phenomenological theory and an economic (metapsychological) one in the development of the interpretations that are the day-to-day stuff of clinical practice.

Leaving these objections aside, I think that Klein has raised some fascinating questions and has made some astute observations and suggestions. On the basis of one of these suggestions I can see the possibility of a revision of drive theory that would make it more consistent and perhaps increase its range of application to clinical phenomena. I think that Klein is quite right in pointing to the great clinical importance of the varieties of sensual cognitive schemata. He is also correct, in my opinion, in his statement that psychoanalysts have not been as interested as they should be in exploring the conditions, the development, and the meanings of sensual experience, and he is correct in his criticism of a tendency to confuse phenomenology in this area with theory. The neglect in the exploration of the varieties of erotic sensual experience extends to other forms of sensuality as well. I think that Klein also points out correctly that we have not even consistently assigned the cognitive aspects of sensuality, i.e., pleasure, to a special class of mental events as we have in the case of other mental phenomena. Klein's most interesting suggestion in this paper is that the consummatory aspect of the experience of pleasure may become its own "drive." Rather than replacing drive theory as he suggests, Klein offers an ingenious opportunity for making the drive-discharge model a completely psychological theory unencumbered by any appeal to physiology for its explanatory power.

Some of Freud's uncertainities about his own drive theory are recounted in Klein's paper. The most outspoken statement of his difficulties in relating the concept of drive "source" with the qualitative aspects of experience appears in "Instincts and Their Vicissitudes" (1915a). After describing drives as having a source, an aim, and an object, Freud says:

> By the source of an instinct is meant the somatic process which occurs in an organ or part of the body and whose stimulus is represented in mental life by an instinct. We do not know whether this process is invariably of a chemical nature or whether it may also correspond to the release of other, e.g., mechanical forces. The study of the sources of instincts lies outside the scope of psychology. Although the instincts are wholly determined by their origin in a somatic source, in mental life we know them only by their aims. An exact knowledge of the sources of an instinct is not invariably necessary for purposes of psychological investigation; sometimes its source may be inferred from its aim [p. 123].

Freud then goes on to make the following statement (which seems to justify at least part of Klein's complaint that economic theory is ambiguous or equivocal):

> Are we to suppose that the different instincts which originate in the body and operate on the mind are also distinguished by different *qualities*, and that that is why they behave in qualitatively different ways in mental life? This supposition does not seem to be justified; we are much more likely to find the simpler assumption sufficient—that the instincts are all qualitatively alike and owe the effect they make only to the amount of excitation they carry, or perhaps, in addition, to certain functions of that quantity. What distinguishes from one another the mental effects produced by the various instincts may be traced to the difference in their sources. In any event it is only in a later connection that we shall be able to make plain what the problem of the quality of instincts signifies [p. 123].

The editor of the Standard Edition says in a footnote at this point that it is not clear what "later connection" Freud had in mind. It seems doubtful that he ever returned to the issue. But since Freud was also uncertain as to whether the source and the aim of a drive can really be distinguished, Klein may offer a way out of the dilemma. He implies, if I understand him correctly, that once the cognitive schema for the sensual pleasure involved has been stimulated and experienced, the internalization of the circular process becomes the source of the drive much like the electrically wired rat who presses the lever to stimulate his own hypothalamic centers for sensual experience. Consummatory reinforcement of such a circular process may account for many such features of drives as their "preemptoriness" (Klein's term), rhythmicity, and invariance. If we also assume that the internalization of this circular process can become unconscious and secondarily autonomous, we have returned to a drive concept without invoking any mysterious forces that operate outside of the mind. It is important in this connection to recall that we have body image representations (i.e., psychic representations) of the organs connected with the leading erogenous zones, which are probably part of what Klein calls the "cognitive schemata for sensual pleasure." This would also clarify Freud's observation that sometimes the source of the drive may be inferred from its aim.

There is another dilemma posed by Freud's drive theory which may find a more consistent solution if these hypotheses are correct. In regard to the object of an instinct, Freud (1915a) says that it "is the thing in regard to which or through which the instinct is able to achieve its aim" (p. 122). "It is," he says, "what is most variable about an instinct and is not originally connected with it, but becomes assigned to it only in consequence of being peculiarly fitted to make satisfaction possible" (p. 122). This somewhat ambiguous statement, which asserts that the object is both a facultative and an obligatory part of the instinctual organization, is also implicitly clarified by the theory of internalization of a process of consummatory reinforcement of sensual gratification. The maternal object, it can be conjectured, would in this case be both the source and the object of the drive, in its inception at any rate, since in most instances it is she who sets the consummatory process of sensual experience and reinforcement into being in the first place. In *Three Essays on the Theory of Sexuality* Freud (1905a) had already alluded to a similar possibility albeit somewhat tangentially. He says, "A mother would probably be horrified if she were made aware that all her marks of affection were rousing her child's sexual instinct and preparing for its later intensity. Moreover if the mother understood more of the high importance of the part played by instincts in mental life as a whole . . . she would spare herself any self reproaches. She is only fulfilling her task in teaching the child to love (p. 223). In Klein's formulation there is thus another possible revision of classical notions about psychic structural development. According to such a revised view it would be the species-specific sensual cognitive schemata, ready for stimulation and consummatory reinforcement by the mother's nurturing care, which are the inborn mechanisms, rather than "drive forces." In this sense the child could be said to come into the world as an ego anlage. The id and later superego organization could be said to be determined in their inception by the degree and manner in which maternal stimulation of built-in ego schemata takes place. Far from making drive theory parallel to clinical theory, such a view of the origin of the drives places them at the center of interpretable genetic phenomena. This hypothesis, incidentally, also seems to be more fruitful as an explanation of the syndrome of maternal deprivation in the first year of life than the one based upon depression due to object loss; i.e., what looks like depression is really drive deficiency. I think that it may also offer some interesting addenda to an understanding of the sensual aspects of the perversions.

Needles (1969) in his presentation, "The Pleasure Principle, the Constancy Principle and the Primary Autonomous Ego" suggests that neither the pursuit of pleasure nor the avoidance of pain is dependent upon drive-discharge phenomena. Unlike Klein, he does not suggest that all economic considerations be abandoned, but he does feel that the "constancy principle" (a corollary of the drive-discharge theory) is inaccurate and unsatisfactory for the explanation of the empirical data of the experiences of pleasure and pain. A major argument for this conclusion is that pleasurable stimuli are still perceived as such after satiation. Needles thereby infers that excitation followed by the discharge of energy is not the only avenue to pleasure.

Before confronting the main issue raised by Needles, I would like to comment on the terms *stimulation* and *excitation*, which Needles uses interchangeably in his paper. He says for example, "the ego plays a significant role in the experience [of pleasure] as well through its perceptual apparatus; visual, auditory, tactile, olfactory stimuli impinge upon it with great intensity and this excitation provides a preponderant pleasurable component of no mean proportion" (p. 813). In common speech the terms *stimulation* and *excitation* have overlapping meanings. It should be recalled however that Freud had an electrical model in mind when he proposed his theory of drive discharge to explain the pleasure principle. According to the Oxford English Dictionary the electrical meaning of *excitation* refers to the induction of a charge in any instrument capable of discharging electrical energy, as for example, a Leyden Jar. In the same context, a *stimulus* is that which imparts the "excitation" to the apparatus which may store or discharge the energy thus induced. Hence the reaction of chemicals in food upon the taste buds is a stimulus, while the pleasure of the perceived flavors is the excitation.

The psychic model differs from the electrical in that psychic stimuli may arise within as well as outside the apparatus. If we define the concepts as I have outlined, then the processes of stimulation and excitation, although often interdependent, may at times be relatively independent of each other. For example, there may be stimulation without excitation if the apparatus is for some reason in a refractory state. Or there may be excitation and discharge of energy without prior stimulation if, for example, the capacity of the apparatus to store its charge is lowered. The possibility for this relative independence of stimulation and excitation is not included in the examples given by Needles (1969), examples which presumably refute the constancy principle. Thus he says,

> It seems to me that the acceptance of a functioning ego at birth renders more admissible the concept of a psychic apparatus that seeks excitation because it is pleasurable; and that this in turn necessitates the modification of the constancy principle which does not include seeking for excitation. Basic to this conclusion is the view that from the Id there can only be satisfaction from discharge but in the ego there can be pleasure from excitation of a certain type [p. 817].

If stimulation and excitation are different processes, this objection does not necessarily hold true. It is still possible to conjecture that the ego seeks stimulation rather than excitation (although I would prefer the passive verb *receives* rather than the active connotation of *seeks*) and that the excitation produced as the consequence of this stimulation must be discharged in the interest of a homeostatic equilibrium that is necessary for optimal ego functioning. It is also conceivable under these conditions to postulate that the cognitive experience of pleasure derives from the discharge of excitation rather than from the sensory stimulation. The same reservation holds for Needle's objection to Schur's (1966) formulation. Needles says,

> It is rather puzzling that Schur retains the terms "pleasure" and "unpleasure" to designate principles that he claims have nothing to do with pleasure and unpleasure but only with energy levels. But does Schur really succeed in dispensing with feelings of pleasure and unpleasure in his formulation? Does the organism, for example, in avoiding the blistering heat of the sun react to the quantity of excitation or to the discomfort? [p. 820]

In my opinion this is a pseudoquestion. If the processes of stimulation and excitation are clearly differentiated there is no contradiction in Schur's formulation. One must specify whether the discomfort experienced in this hypothetical case arises primarily from psychological or physiological causes. One can imagine certain conditions under which the individual does not perceive discomfort, in spite of a powerful noxious stimulus, and others where there is intolerable discomfort from stimuli which are minimal in physiological terms.

As I have just indicated, these questions of definition are related to what I consider to be the main issue. I think that we often forget that drive-discharge theory applies to the pleasure principle as a psychological phenomenon. It was not intended to elucidate the neurophysiology of sensual pleasure. Thus to test the validity of the constancy principle it is necessary to be sure that we are dealing with psychic and not with physiological data. As Needles alluded to in his paper, it is possible that there is a tendency to equate the two which results in confusion. The problem, as in the case of Klein (1969), may arise from an indiscriminate use of the term *cognitive.* To speak of the "cognitive" experience of pleasure may imply to some that only the phenomena of the peripheral organs belong to physiology and that anything which occurs in the central nervous system belongs to the realm of psychology. I think that we must consider brain psychology and mental events as different phenomena. To my way of thinking, psychology deals with mental representations. I do not think that the mental representations of pleasure and/or pain are the same thing as the ability to perceive pleasurable or painful stimuli, as for example, in a neurological examination. Freud was always quite explicit in defining the id as a psychic structure although he noted its physiological roots. If we are to be consistent, we must test Freud's formulations in terms of psychic pleasure. Nowhere is this distinction more clear and yet more likely to be confused, as Needles suggests, than in the phenomena of orgasm. How else, for example, can we account for the intensity of orgasm in dreams where there is little or no peripheral stimulation, or the orgastic phenomena of perversions where aberrant stimulation is utilized. Would it not be safer to assume that it is the meaning of the stimuli rather than the stimuli themselves that produces the difference in the cognitive experiences of orgastic pleasure?

Keeping the distinction between physiological and psychological events in the forefront, it seems to me that the same examples employed by Needles (1969) and others who have offered similar arguments, can be used to support the constancy principle. Needles cites, for example, the pleasure that an individual may derive from a liqueur following a meal which has amply satisfied his hunger. Why is this phenomenon different from that of the infant whose need for sucking pleasure continues after he has been adequately fed? Freud, it may be recalled, insisted that hunger and the oral drive for pleasure were anaclitically related and not identical; i.e., hunger is a physiological need while the oral pleasure is a psychological one. It may be argued that the pleasure of the liqueur after a full meal can be used as evidence for a residual undischarged oral excitation which can only manifest itself in undisguised form when it is no longer in the service of predominantly nutritional needs. Indeed the character trait of greed would have no referent making it discernible if it were not for the implicit concept of the constancy principle. We do not interpret behavioral phenomena as "greedy" unless the acquisitive need continues past the point of satisfaction of all the reasonable requirements of the individual.

It is generally agreed that the investigation of the phenomena of sensory physiology requires a research design that excludes psychological events as concurrent variables. Conversely we must also exclude the physiological effects of sensory phenomena before we can study their psychological effects. The same rules should apply to the "normal" psychology of what we call "cognitive" experience. I am not sure that Needles's interesting data or some of the findings of experimental psychologists deal consistently with the *psychology* of pleasure rather than its physiology. Since the economic theories of drive discharge have been derived from psychic phenomena, their validity should be tested only in terms of their ability to predict and to explain the phenomenology of the psychological aspects of pleasure and pain. On the basis of the evidence so far presented, I do not think that we are ready to discard either the constancy principle or the drive-discharge theory.

The question of the relevance of metapsychological theory to clinical interpretation cannot be separated from our view of the overall purpose of interpretation. In my opinion, both authors referred to above neglect the relationship between metapsychology and the central task of interpretation, which is to infer the *unconscious meaning* of the clinical phenomena observed and to transmit this inference to the patient in a linguistic message (Chapter 7). Thus in the example of the adolescent nail biter previously mentioned, we would not infer that this activity could have the meaning of a masturbatory substitute without the concept of a displaceable libidinal drive seeking alternate avenues of discharge when its usual mode of expression is blocked. Likewise, if we accepted Needles's argument that the continued seeking for pleasure-producing stimuli following satiation was a refutation of the constancy principle and Klein's concept of the irrelevance of metapsychology to clinical theory, we would probably fail to recognize the *meaning* of a variety of clinical phenomena that fall into this paradoxical category of behavioral events, including symptoms which represent sexualization without sensual pleasure.

Notes

1. A careful reading of these papers (see Klein, 1969, and Needles, 1969) will make the ensuing remarks more intelligible and will also be of interest to the reader in their own right.

CHAPTER TEN

The Nature of Verbal Interventions In Psychoanalysis

This chapter was Victor Rosen's last effort in psychoanalytic writing before his death. The manuscript was given to me as a revised second draft, and in rather polished form characteristic of Rosen's clear and logically rational style. Because I did not wish to disrupt the flow of his ideas and the mark of its author I have made only the most minor editorial changes.

The paper is in many ways a modest legacy of its author's intellect, but taken in the context of his other writings it contains many of the recurrent themes and concerns of his efforts. The exposition of a question, the narrowing of the discursive field, the application of clinical vignettes, and the concern with integration of language theory with psychoanalysis are all hallmarks of Rosen's work.

Having pursued a path along with him in his later years, I can pinpoint the origin of some of the logical philosophical discussion in the later part of the paper for our readers, for they are new in his writing. They grew out of a discussion Rosen gave of a paper by Benjamin Rubinstein, "On the Inference and Confirmation of Clinical Interpretations," given at the New York Psychoanalytic Society Meeting on May 28, 1968, and pursued further at a joint meeting of Rubinstein's seminar on Psychoanalysis and Philosophy of Science and the Psycholinguistic Study Group. In a large sense these integrative study groups of the New York Psychoanalytic Institute were the breeding ground for this integrative annual.

Of no less importance than Rosen's quest for Cartesian "clear and distinct ideas" was his "humane" view of clinical analysis. The chapter is an exquisite melding of these two features of his work.

—Theodore Shapiro, M.D.

There are many contradictory concepts concerning the nature of verbal interventions in psychoanalytic treatment. They require extensive reexamination, sorting, and organizing. I do not expect in this discussion to contribute more than a gloss on some of the issues. I will not discuss problems of validation, timing, or finding the correct level in therapeutic interventions except insofar as these questions are relevant to the clarification of conceptual problems.

I have the impression that there is not only a lack of agreement concerning various aspects of technique of interpretive interventions in psychoanalysis, but also a variety of implicit disagreements about what constitutes the range of permissible verbal interventions and what kinds of statements should be called interpretations. From many discussions of technique in psychoanalysis one would infer that only interpretive interventions have any therapeutic effect and that all others, if permissible at all, need be considered only insofar as they evoke reactions which lend themselves to the furthering of the interpretive process, or to preparation for it. Finally, there is considerable ambiguity concerning the term *interpretation* itself and the form that such an intervention must take to be properly regarded as "interpretive."

Since it is not possible to resolve all of these difficulties at a stroke of the pen, I will limit myself to a preliminary discussion of only those varieties of verbal statement, occurring more or less routinely in treatment, that can be described and classified. I will try to indicate their importance for the therapeutic process and will also discuss the kind of "truth statement" that is inherent in the way we use interpretations in psychoanalysis.

Since Freud first described psychoanalytic technique, "interpretation" has occupied a central position in the method. Even those

The proceedings of the discussion group "On the Nature of Interpretation," chaired by Dr. Charles Brenner at the 1971 Mid-Winter Meeting of the American Psychoanalytic Association, were an important stimulus for this paper.

therapies that differ from psychoanalysis on many grounds make extensive use of interpretive techniques. At times the term has been applied to a very specific type of verbal intervention and at times to almost any verbal statement made in the course of therapy. I have chosen the term *intervention* as a more neutral description of any utterance on the part of the therapist during the analytic session in order to avoid confusion in usage.

Ideally, interventions should include grunts, sighs, coughs, pen scratching, borborygmi, striking of matches, and furniture squeaking, among others. I will not, however, include these important adventitious phenomena since they are neither coded, rationalized, nor apparently intentional as are verbal interjections. For the present I will use the term *interpretation* to cover both those interventions that aim at clarification and translation and those that attempt constructions or reconstructions of external events or psychic activity. In so doing I am conforming to current psychoanalytic usage, although, as I will explain later on, I do not think that clarification and translation are equivalent.

Some of this ambiguity in the meaning of interpretation is foreshadowed in Freud's introduction to *The Interpretation of Dreams* (1900). He says:

> In the pages that follow I shall bring forth proof that there is a psychological technique which makes it possible to interpret dreams and that if that procedure is employed every dream reveals itself as a psychical structure which has meaning and which can be interpreted at an assignable point in the mental activities of waking life. I shall further endeavour to elucidate the process to which the strangeness and obscurity of dreams are due and to deduce from those processes the nature of the psychical forces by whose concurrent or mutually opposing action dreams are generated [p. 1].

Thus Freud states that in this context he uses interpretation to mean one of two distinct activities: (1) the translation of terms from one symbolic system to another (a decoding or translating operation), and (2) the depiction of a model of an apparatus that generates dreams (a process of construction).

In accordance with standard lexical usage, *intepretation* refers to clarification, exposition, the representation of one person's work by another, or the act of translating from one language or symbolic system to another. It is only by our own technical conventions that interpretation has come to include inferential deduction leading to construct formation. In "translation" it is assumed that what is rendered in one language is transcribed into another so as to keep the original idea or statement unchanged. In deductive or inductive reasoning, the interpreter, if indeed we can call him such, is adding a concept of his own, be it only the pattern of arrangement or the configuration that he sees in the data he is observing.

Others have noted and commented upon this discrepancy in usage: Stone (1961), for example, says "our entire interpretative method involves the analyst's own mental activity, which leads to a subjective transformation of what the patient has shown into something manifestly different albeit latent or implicit in what was shown." In its most frequent usage in general parlance, interpretation is defined as a correct exegesis of ideas that are not immediately self-evident (for example, parables). Or it is a frankly subjective rendering of one person's creative product by a second person where veridicality is irrelevant, for example, a conductor's interpretation of a composer's symphony. Such an interpretation is creative rather than exegetical. There is no suggestion on Freud's part, however, that a therapeutic intervention in the form of an interpretation can be a completely subjective creation of the therapist's and still be therapeutically effective. For him, constructions were either correct or incorrect.

He did, however, make a distinction between interpretation and construction in his paper on "Constructions in Analysis" (1937), written 37 years after *The Interpretation of Dreams*. In this context he says, "If in accounts of analytic technique so little is said about 'construction', it is because 'interpretations' and their effects are spoken of instead. But I think that 'construction' is by far the more appropriate description. 'Interpretation' applies to something that one does to some single element of the material, such as an association or a parapraxis, but it is a 'construction' when one lays before the subject of the analysis a piece of his early history that he has forgotten."[1] Essentially, then, as Freud goes on to explain, interpretation is applied to small items of behavior, while constructions are used in elucidating a large gestalt linking genetic, dynamic, and economic aspects of a patient's psychic life. However, Freud is talking about two different kinds of construction here, and the essential ambiguity of the term which he introduced in the earlier context is not confronted by these addenda.

From the rather extensive literature on the theory and technique of interventions, I will outline the views of a few authors who have attempted to classify or define the varieties of verbal interventions in the course of the discussion of general problems of psychoanalytic technique. Since there is considerable overlap and redundancy, this review of the literature is necessarily sketchy and incomplete.

In a rather comprehensive discussion of the nature of interpretation in treatment, Ekstein (1959) points out the ambiguity that the term *interpretation* has developed. German has two synonyms for this word, the German cognate of the English, *Interpretation,* and *Deutung,* which adds the notion of prophesy, fortunetelling, and prediction to the usual meanings of the English cognate. Ekstein points out that Freud always used *Deutung* and never *Interpretation* in his writing. In commenting on the magical connotations of the word *Deutung* he wonders whether any and/or how much of this usage is reflected in psychoanalytic writings, explicitly or implicitly. He goes on to say that "Freud's introduction of this prescientific word into his scientific work has deep psychological meaning and hints at logical and methodological difficulties." In the case of dreams Ekstein suggests that Freud equates interpretation with deciphering cryptic meaning. Here it is essentially a translation through the substitution of dream elements by associations. Ekstein also distinguishes interpretation as explanation and interpretation as therapeutic intervention. "Correct explanations," he says, "do not necessarily cure, and effective interpretations do not necessarily describe the decisive determinants of an illness."[2] In this very fine discussion, however, Ekstein does not sufficiently distinguish between the validation of an interpretation (and/or construction) as such from the validation of the psychoanalytic process as a whole.

Greenson (1960) says that "to interpret means to make an unconscious phenomenon conscious. More precisely it means to make conscious the unconscious meaning, source, history, mode or cause of a given psychic event." He further notes, "The procedures of clarification and interpretation are intimately interwoven. Very often clarification leads to an interpretation which leads back to a further clarification." In several places he equates interpretation with confrontation. Bibring (1954), on the other hand, uses the terms *clarification* and *interpretation*, the former applying to conscious material and the latter to the elucidation of unconscious processes. Brenner (1955) speaks of interpretations as "conjectures" that the analyst forms about his patient. He presents this conjecture to the patient as an interpretation at the technically appropriate time and looks for either confirmation or refutation in the patient's response. Brenner says that the conjecture is usually formed in an intuitive way but that the steps should be retraceable consciously. Brenner's essential distinction between a conjecture (which corresponds more or less to what others have called a construction) and an interpretation is the distinction between an unspoken hypothesis and its verbal communication to the patient. Loewald (1960, p. 26), like Stone (1961), implies that interpretation is more than the translation of unconscious into conscious meanings. He sees interpretation as a synthesis of the data provided by the patient with an imaginative elaboration by the analyst which is not meant to be a complete and veridical explanation of all that it encompasses. He says: "Language, in its most specific function in analysis, as interpretation, is thus a creative act *similar to that in poetry* [italics mine], where language is found for phenomena, contexts, connexions, experiences not previously known and speakable. New phenomena and new experience are made available as a result of reorganization of material according to hitherto unknown principles, contexts, and connexions."

Loewenstein (1951, 1957) begins his discussion of interpretation in psychoanalytic therapy by asserting that a variety of other kinds of verbal interventions are a legitimate and necessary part of psychoanalytic technique. These, he says, "create the conditions without which analytic procedure would be impossible." He suggests (1972) that, as part of the rule of abstinence, the therapeutic silence or nonresponse should also be considered an intervention, albeit a passive one. He defines interpretation as "those explanations given by the analyst which add to [the patient's] knowledge about himself." Loewenstein states that he defines interpretation in such general terms because he does not think that "it should be defined rigidly." Kris (1947) says that "careful description, i.e. exposition of the patient's manifest patterns of reaction," should be considered part of interpretation. "Exploratory description," he says, "is aimed mainly at uncovering defense mechanisms and not at an id content." Presumably the uncovering of "id contents" is for Kris another kind of interpretation for which I suspect he would have accepted the term *construction.* Hartmann (1951) suggests that an "interpretation" operates on the principle of "multiple appeal." This may be the most important characteristic of therapeutic interpretations.

Shapiro (1970) has considered the process of interpretation from a linguistic (primarily semantic) frame of reference. He speaks of interpretation as "naming" with increasing precision of designation as its goal, "realized ultimately in the naming of an unconscious fantasy." He uses linguistic theories of reference and naming to construct a complementary view of psychic processes. Six paradigmatic patient responses to the therapist's interpretive interventions are described in the light of this model. Shapiro uses "naming" in a wider sense than categorizing with a single symbol. He agrees with Stone and Loewald that an interpretation is more a synthetic than an analytic event.

In addition to ambiguous referents for the term *interpretation,* there is also a general impression among many psychoanalytically oriented therapists that interpretation is, if not the only permissible intervention in the therapeutic process, certainly the most essential and potent one. Those who distinguish clarifying from constructive interpretations usually believe that the best therapeutic effect comes from the latter. During the proceedings of the Colloquium on the Nature of Interpretation (Mid-Winter Meetings of the American Psychoanalytic Association, 1971) it appeared that some analysts were firmly convinced that only interpretations were legitimate interventions in psychoanalytic therapy, while others, who recognized the necessity or at least the inevitability of other kinds of utterances on the part of the therapist, referred to these as *parameters.* It seems to me that "parameters" in psychoanalytic treatment, described very well by Eissler (1953), refer to verbal interventions that are necessary in the treatment of patients who for reasons of diagnosis or other exceptional conditions cannot utilize interpretive interventions. The noninterpretive interventions that I will mention here are usual modes of responding in what I would call "standard" analytic procedure with "standard" analytic patients, and by no stretch of the imagination to be considered parameters. Before discussing the validity of such constraints in the therapeutic process and the possibility that other kinds of interventions are also necessary, I would like to present a schema of the varieties of interventions, both verbal and nonverbal, that occur as a matter of average expectation in most analytic treatments.

A Proposed Schema of Interventions that May Occur In Psychoanalytic Therapy

1. FORMAL INTERVENTIONS
   - A. Salutations.
   - B. Congratulations.
   - C. Condolences.
   - D. Miscellaneous.

2. INFORMATIONAL INTERVENTIONS
   - A. Practical. Details of schedule, etc.
   - B. Corrective. A factual correction of patient's statement to clarify some matter of timing, sequence, or occurrence.
   - C. Educative. A patient's lack of some kinds of information may require a pedagogical intervention to prepare him for an interpretation.
   - D. Personal. E.g., in order to analyze a projection it may be necessary to give a patient some information about the therapist.

3. INTERLOCUTORY INTERVENTIONS
   - A. For clarification. E.g., Please explain. Please remind me who X is.
   - B. Educative. For educational hiatus in therapist. E.g., What is a palimpsest?
   - C. For evocation. What are you thinking? How do you feel about that?
   - D. For confirmation. Do you agree?
   - E. For specification. Please give me an example.
   - F. For comprehension. Is that clear?

4. NONINTERVENTIONS
    - A. Silence. (Usually signifying I am waiting, listening, etc.)
    - B. Explicit statements of uncertainty or inability to interpret or need for more information.

5. ADVISORY INTERVENTIONS
    - A. Introduction to patient's role in therapy.
    - B. Incidental advice in critical life situations. (Commonsense priorities are the indications here.)
    - C. Suggestion. Preliminary to interpretation of resistances. E.g., interdiction of smoking on the couch.

6. CONFRONTATIONAL INTERVENTIONS
    - A. Confrontation of a contradiction in fact or logic.
    - B. Confrontation of behavior, attitude, repetitive pattern, etc.
    - C. Confrontation of unacknowledged symptom. (Frequently phobic symptoms or affects.)
    - D. Confrontation with conscious withholding. Unusual delay between a dramatic event, experience, etc., and an account of it in therapy.
    - E. Confrontation of a cognitive lapse. Parapraxis of speech, memory, etc.
    - F. Criticism. (A rare necessity.)

7. INTERPRETIVE INTERVENTIONS
    - A. Clarifying interventions:
        1. Paraphrasing to ensure congruence of meaning.
        2. Lexical. E.g., help in word finding, correction of misuse of term.
        3. Resolution of ambiguity in phrasing. E.g., "It was a small boys school."
    - B. Translational interventions:
        1. Naming. Giving an organizing concept that brings together a large number of seemingly disparate items. E.g., "All of this suggests that you are depressed or lonely, angry, anxious," etc. Sometimes a "spade" term undoes a defense and makes some behavior accessible to investigation. E.g., "That is stealing." "You mean you are addicted, alcoholic," etc.

2. Deciphering and decoding, E.g., puns in dreams, evidence of cryptomnesic observations. Obvious meanings of slips and parapraxes.

C. Parabolic interventions (as a rule not highly regarded):
1. Wit.
2. Irony.
3. Analogy.
4. Anecdote.

8. CONSTRUCTIONS
A. Current dynamic, adaptive, economic, and/or topographic, structural inferences.
B. Reconstructions. A genetic inference with or without other considerations listed in 8A.

9. PARAVERBAL INTERVENTIONS: advertent or inadvertent:
A. Grunts, groans, laughs, coughs, sighs, flatus, borborygmi, etc.
B. Joint or furniture crackles or squeaks, pen scratching, paper rustling, striking of matches, etc. (These might better be called adventitious rather than paraverbal interventions.)

I will discuss three aspects of interventions in psychoanalytic psychotherapy: (1) some of the effects of nonconstructive (or noninterpretive, if you wish) interventions; (2) some reasons for distinguishing interpretation as explication and/or translation from interpretation as construction and reconstruction; (3) some comments on constructions as "truth statements."

Quite aside from the question of optimal therapeutic efficacy from one kind of intervention compared with another, one must consider the atmosphere of a therapy in which one participant's contributions to a dialogue are strictly limited to "metaresponses." By *metaresponse* I mean to a statement that addresses itself to the latent meaning of the speaker's utterance, or to its form rather than its content. Some of the dialogue of modern dramatists has this character.

The following imaginary dialogue is an attempt to illustrate the ambience produced by a therapist who limits his remarks to metaresponses. It is a caricature for heuristic purposes. The patient in this exchange wants to tell his therapist about a scene in a movie which produced a special emotional impact on him and one which he considers to be important for his therapy:

P: Before I tell you about this film, I would like to know if you have seen it.
A: We should try to discover what it means to you to know whether I have seen the movie.
P: I only want to know in order to save time. If you have seen it, I will not have to fill you in on all that went before.
A: By avoiding the details, you are resorting to your usual device of ambiguous reference which enables you to pretend that you have no emotional reactions.
P: Yes, that is true, but this time I wanted to tell you how I really felt about one scene without having to develop the whole story for you.
A: This is such a reasonable statement that it disguises the adversary intent within it. It is an example of your defense against recognizing your feelings of anger toward me.
P: (petulantly) Sometimes I wonder if you are for real.
A: You see?

Analysis carried on exclusively in this fashion probably produces in both participants a feeling of alienation and artificiality—an artificiality that is difficult to discuss in the therapy because it quickly becomes built into the process. Thus informal queries, informational and advisory interventions have, as well as their specific purposes, the nonspecific goal of establishing a more humane and credible therapeutic atmosphere. I have the strong impression that such an easing of rigorous constraints not only reduces tension in the patient but makes the therapist's work less fatiguing for himself as well. Some nonconstructive interventions are also necessary on purely practical grounds. I have heard it said that an advisory comment is never necessary in a well-conducted analysis. Certainly this overlooks those advisory statements that are necessary to institute and maintain the patient's candid nonselective communication that makes interpretation and construction possible in the first place. How can one deal with the patient's role in treatment without advising him on how best to carry it out? Often this advice must be repeated during the course of treatment. What of the patient who seems to need medical investigation but does not know it, or whose symptoms cannot be approached psychologically until organic factors are excluded? Unless we advise him directly and sometimes even peremptorily, how can we expect him to do what is necessary for his immediate welfare as well as for the future of his treatment?

Some interlocutory statements are clearly advisory and should be acknowledged as such. When a therapist, in response to a patient's generalization, says "For example?," he implies that although the patient has reached a conclusion concerning some general proposition which covers the data, it would be more productive for him to relate the specific events upon which his conclusion rests in order to allow the therapist to exercise his own judgment in the matter. Interlocutory interventions aimed at reminding the therapist of forgotten facts or aimed at clarifying ambiguities and inconsistencies in a patient's statements seem to be necessary for self-evident reasons, yet Olinick (1954), a psychoanalyst, says, "Questioning is to be resorted to only under very special conditions." He names five that should be fulfilled (reminiscent of the conditions that Eissler proposes for parameters) before a question is asked during an analytic session (p. 64).

Less obvious than the need for questions is the therapist's felicitous use of what I would like to call tactless confrontations. Examples of these would be avowals, *in certain circumstances*, of fatigue, boredom, or, more often, simple noncomprehension. These avowals may be most effective in reducing a patient's unrealistic fantasies of the analyst's omniscience (an undoing of the frequent image of the analyst as a man who pretends that he does not know everything), thus making such fantasies more amenable to reconstructive explanation. Such avowals may lead to the uncovering of fantasies of a special relationship between patient and therapist or of a hostile intent in the way information is communicated. There seem to be some patients who are not intrinsically dull but who unconsciously go out of their way to be boring and pedestrian. Sometimes this kind of confrontation is more effective than a careful construction in dealing with some problems, as, for example, when a masochistic patient apologizes because the therapist has nothing to say about the material of a given session. It can be quite revealing to some patients in such circumstances to be told that the difficulty has nothing to do with his productions but is rather the therapist's inability to "put it all together." Time does not permit an item-by-item examination of this catalogue of noninterpretive comments.

One example may illustrate the frequent disparity between the analyst's and the patient's conception of what interventions have been most important in the treatment. A depressive patient whom I had been treating for some time told me one autumn that things had changed radically in his life since the previous summer. He was more energetic than he recalled ever having been and was deriving more pleasure from his daily activities than before. He ascribed this to one remark I had made to him just before the summer vacation. He described it as "the most telling thing" I had ever said to him. I asked him what this remark had been. He said, "When you shook hands with me and said goodbye you also said, 'try to enjoy yourself this summer.'" Discounting the hyperbole and the ambivalence in his assessment of this "turning point" in his therapy, I am disposed to take some of it at face value. He reacted of course partly to an authoritarian image of a medical prescription to go forth and enjoy himself, but also, I hope, to a genuine wish of mine and to an informal way of conveying it.

Why is it important to distinguish the several meanings of *interpretation* from each other and from the process of construction? I think that there are three. The first has to do with referential clarity. Only confusion can result from a dialogue in which two participants use the same word in different senses, thinking that they are talking about the same thing. A separation of the term into its several meanings will help us to be more precise in designating the character of the therapeutic intervention under investigation. Second, when we talk about the validation of an interpretation, we are obviously referring to constructions or reconstructions. A clarification has a self-evident validity, while a translation needs only to be verified rather than validated. Finally, and even more important than correct denotations of the term, are its connotations. The science of interpretation in general is called hermeneutics. The word derives from the Hermeneuts, of early Christianity, who were the interpreters of Holy Scripture. Theirs was not just a personal rendering of obscure meanings in Biblical texts but a "true" interpretation of the revealed word. The infallibility of the Hermeneuts derived from God himself, or so they averred. Others honored their avowals, probably on the grounds that no one would make such an outrageous claim unless it were justified. By calling a construction an interpretation I fear that we may foster similar claims and attitudes in ourselves. This hubris, leading to a belief in the ultimate truth value of a construction, is sometimes found among therapists both old and young. These personal proclivities to the arrogation of omniscience may be fostered by the hermeneutic implications of so-called interpretive activities. Thus interpretation is an antithetical word denoting both an objective and subjective meaning of meanings.

Nowhere is greater humility needed and less to be found than in the interpretation of so-called unconscious fantasies, for these are actually inferential formulations which are at best approximations. Clinical phenomena are one of the categories of sign phenomena. The generic term *sign* stands for signals, signs, and symbols, all of which have to do with different levels of meaning. The inferences in the construction of unconscious meaning translate signal-sign phenomena into symbolic language. The correctness of the construction derived from this translation depends upon many factors: the validity and universality of the coded "symbols" of psychoanalysis, the cooperativeness of the patient, and the education, skill, and intuition of the therapist. A construction is therefore not only an inference, it is an inference expressed according to a systematic encoding procedure. Information theorists tell us that no encoding procedure will lead to completed unambiguous decoding transformations. Repeatability, which is our major criterion of validity, is not sufficient evidence of veridicality. In psychoanalysis we often confuse the repeatability of a construction by a number of similarly trained judges with an ultimate test of truth value, whereas repeatability is only a first stage in such a test rather than its final confirmation. For this reason as well as others, it would be well for us to treat constructions as more or less congruent models of unconscious meaning in which the style and psychology of the therapist, as well as of the patient, are on display.

Finally, I would like to discuss some of the logical implications of constructions in psychoanalysis. Where in a schema of truth statements should we classify psychoanalystic interpretations?

Most analysts seem to assume that a psychoanalytic construction is analogous to a proposition in one of the natural sciences, differing in the degree to which dependent variables can be controlled, but subject to the usual experimental methods of validation for scientific hypotheses. Thus most psychoanalysts would agree that the logic of scientific method would demand extrinsic tests of clinical propositions to move them from being plausible to being probable. They would probably also agree that the major obstacle to such testing is the feasibility of an experimental design to deal with the complexity of the data. But the problem seems to me to be more fundamental than this. "Truth statements" in science, such as those that characterize physics, for example, are invariably causal propositions. Most psychoanalytic propositions, whether they are of limited generality, such as an interpretation in the treatment of a patient, or of wider generality, as in metapsychological constructs, fall into another large class of "truth statements" known to logicians as "entailment propositions." These are usually statements about symbolic or historical events. By and large, they are statements about meaning or statements whose truth or falsity can be tested by the rules of classification or definition. Entailment propositions which use the words *because, due to,* or *caused by* are frequently mistaken for causal propositions. Thus it is acceptable English usage to say that an anesthesia of a limb is "caused by hysteria." This is, however, an entirely different kind of truth statement from one which asserts that an anesthesia is caused by a peripheral neuritis. In the first case we are dealing with a nosological entity which is defined by the existence of certain symptoms (among which simulation of neurological disease is frequent). In the second we are dealing with a causal statement. It asserts that certain events (such as anesthesia) follow from the inflammation of a nerve. In this case the emphasis is on a sequence of events whose regularity can be demonstrated both clinically and experimentally.

With entailment propositions, what may be stated as if it referred to a causal sequence actually refers to phenomena which exist simultaneously, in this case hysteria and anesthesia. *In entailment propositions we can also reverse the subject and predicate of the proposition without changing the "truth value" of the statement.* For example, the statement that the patient is hysterical because he has symptoms that simulate neurological disease is as logical as the reverse statement that he has symptoms simulating neurological disease because he is hysterical. In a truly causal proposition such a reversal completely changes the meaning and truth value of the statement: for example, the patient's peripheral neuropathy is caused by the anesthesia of his limb. The truth value of causal propositions is amenable, at least in form, to experimental-statistical methods of validation. The truth value of entailment propositions requires a different method of validation. The experimental method applied to an entailment proposition leads to a tautology rather than a proof. I suspect that this is one of the reasons that psychoanalytic clinical and metapsychological propositions strike many people trained in scientific method as being irrefutable as well as untestable. For example, the statement that "John is a nephew" depends upon the existence of siblings of one or the other of his parents. If it can be demonstrated that there are such siblings then the statement is true, but only by virtue of the definition of terms concerning categories based upon events of natural order. Mathematical propositions are entailment statements. For more complex entailment propositions, such as those which arise from the rules of a game or a legal code, logical analysis is the only method of validation that is applicable.

Psychoanalytic interpretations are largely entailment statements (whether or not we call them "constructs"). This is true even for the majority of psychoanalytic propositions that use the words *because* or *caused by*. When analysts treat such statements as causal propositions they foster the syncretism that we sometimes ascribe to our critics when they ask for experimental validation of our hypotheses. I will elaborate on this point later.

One distinction between psychoanalytic and many psychiatric propositions is, I believe, the difference between entailment and causal statements. When the psychiatrist tests the clinical hypothesis that ECT produces a remission in cases of involutional melancholia, he does not, as a rule, investigate the unconscious meanings of the procedure to the patient. Conversely, the psychoanalyst attempts to exclude as far as possible physical or pharmaceutical interventions during psychoanalytic treatment in order to be able to study *the meaning* of clinical phenomena. It is the difference between an interest in meanings and an interest in effects. *Meaning* is the answer to the question "What does that stand for?" The observation of effect is the answer to the question "What does that do?" In the case of ECT in involutional depression, the significance of the procedure to the patient may or may not have anything to do with its symptomatic effects. If we do discover the meaning of the procedure for a particular patient, it will be entailed in his statements about the procedure and not in its effect upon his illness. Conversely we do not really study the effects of interpretations during psychoanalytic treatment; we examine their meaning to the patient.

Like the problem of indeterminacy in physics, our technical tenets (for example, the substitution of verbalization for action) entail the conclusion that we cannot study meaning and causality at the same time. It is doubtful to me that in so-called psychoanalytic research we can investigate the same phenomena that we investigate through free association, which is contrived to explore meanings rather than effects. I am sure that the reader need not be reminded that one of Freud's earliest and most fruitful findings was that neurotic symptoms had *symbolic meanings*, or, to put it another way, they could be understood as part of a regressive communication system with its own conventions. Freud called this symbolic code "body" or "organ" language. He saw organ language as one of the ubiquitous phenomena in hysterias, phobias, obsessional neuroses, and the psychoses. A major endeavor of psychoanalysts since Freud made these observations has been to work out the significance of symptoms and to find out how to "translate" the idiolect of body language into the dialect of everyday language. In my opinion this requires methods which are more analogous to those of linguistics than to those of natural science.

As psychoanalysis has developed we have found that the question of meaning is essential to all of our hypotheses, even those that appear to have the form of causal statements. For example, Freud first proposed a causal theory of hysteria in citing sexual seduction in childhood as a ubiquitous antecedent event in all cases of hysteria. His initial disappointment and later revision of his hypothesis stemmed from the finding that many of these so-called seductions in childhood had taken place in fantasy. The revision of this hypothesis is an important chapter in the evolution of psychoanalytic theorym Jones and later Kris describe this revision as the rediscovery that the meaning of events and of the fantasies woven around them was more important in understanding symptom formation than the events themselves. When we study the effect of a drug in psychiatric treatment, on the other hand, we attempt by double-blind studies and other experimental controls to *exclude the meaning* of the event to the patient and the investigator, thus ensuring that we are dealing exclusively with causal relationships. Furthermore, in psychoanalytic treatment we do not assume that an identical intervention will have the same meaning for all patients or even the same meaning for the same patient at different timesm Our assumption is rather the reverse. If we look for the meaning of a given stimulus for the patient, we cannot speak of the "input" and "output" events of a causal sequence; we can speak only of "psychic events."

What do we mean by "unconscious meaning" when we make an interpretive formulation in the course of treatment? Meaning is conveyed by signals, signs, and/or symbols. A very elementary definition of meaning is that it is the relationship between a sign or symbol and the mental representation of the signified or symbolized to which it is attachedm This relationship is such that the sign/symbol A can evoke the representation A or the representation A can evoke the sign/symbol Am In essence, meaning is the reciprocal capacity that each has in evoking the other (Chapter 7). Most symbols are established by convention as part of a communication system. Others are invented by individual fiat. Man is said to be pre-eminently a symbol-forming animal with a highly developed communication system. When his most advanced symbolic system is disorganized or inadequate to the expressive demands of internal psychic events, he resorts to more primitive or more idiosyncratic modes of expression. Psychoanalytic technique is designed to investigate the meanings of these more primitive and idiosyncratic expressive modes. One of the technical injunctions of psychoanalysis is the exclusion of information which circumvents the patient, no matter how disinterested and reliable the source of the information may be. This injunction does more than protect the privacy of the patient. Even more basically it protects the psychoanalytic process from the intrusion of attempts to validate causal sequences. It emphasizes the search for the intrinsic meaning of events to the patient.

Consider the following clinical example: Asked for his associations to something, a young male patient becomes silent. In the previous session he had been given a bill. The analyst knows that the patient feels that free association on the couch is a kind of coercion. He feels that he is forced to say everything that he thinks or he will be punished in some manner for his disobedience. The patient was reminded of this feeling and was told that his silence might be a test of the fantasy that things like ideas or money would be taken away from him by force. The patient responded with a recollection. When he was a small child he had a strict nurse who used to make him sit on the "potty" at a certain time each day. She would threaten to go away and leave him to take care of himself if he did not have a bowel movement. On subsequent occasions when the patient arrived late for a series of sessions and still later when he began to delay the payment of his bill, the same meaning was suggested for his behavior. As a result of working through a large number of incidents, dreams, and fantasies, the transference situation that followed in the analysis could be interpreted as his withholding something of value to test my intentions of forcibly taking something from him. The relationship of this behavior to anal withholding and to events in his early life was also suggested.

There are no causal propositions in this formulation. It states that the meaning for the patient of the fundamental rule was a coercive attempt to extract information from him. It does not say that withholding is a response caused by another event, i.e., the request that he say everything that came to his mind. As in the decoding of an exotic language with the help of a native speaker, the analyst has inferred that silence for his patient is a verb with the general meaning "you are trying to coerce me into talking against my will." A contextual analysis of this inference which consists of inserting this translation of the meaning of silence in the various contexts in which it appears confirms, denies, or modifies the meaning of silence for this patient. This formulation does not assert that the withholding tendency was "caused" by early toilet training at the hands of a strict nurse. Rather, as I see it, the childhood memory is one of the confirmations of the correctness of the meaning of silence for this patient. Further, the interpretation implies that in retrospect there is a childhood memory of a prototypic event which had the meaning "a strict nurse was forcing me to have B.M. and I thought she would punish me if I did not perform." We do not need to know if the nurse was actually strict and punitive, or even whether the event actually occurred or was the residue of a childhood fantasy, since its meaning is what we are concerned with.

Finally, what should be said about metapsychological propositions if the clinical hypotheses from which they are derived are entailment statements? The question is beyond the scope of the present discussion, except for the suggestion that metapsychological propositions may be analgous to general transformational rules for the interpretation of the "organ language" of symptom formation—something like the generalized grammatical rules that apply to all Indo-European languages rather than to any specific one. Seen in this light, metapsychological propositions will stand or fall in terms of the consistency with which they serve as "master keys" for the decoding of the special cryptograms of symptom formation, dreams, and the psychopathology of everyday life.

Summary

I have indicated some of the ambiguities inherent in the concept of interpretation in psychoanalysis and have summarized some of the literature on this subject. Besides formal interpretations, other categories of verbal intervention have been described. On occasion some of these noninterpretive interventions may have more significant therapeutic effects than interpretive ones. It is suggested that the term *interpretation* should be differentiated into several component categories, such as clarifying interventions, translational interventions, constructions, and reconstructions. Some of the advantages of this terminological revision are suggested. The relativism, inferential character, and synthetic nature of constructions and/or interpretations are discussed. Psychoanalytic constructions concerning individual dynamics, clinical theories, or metapsychological propositions are entailment rather than causal statements. Since the psychoanalyst searches for meanings rather than causes, the validation of a construction requires a different method than the testing of the truth value of a scientific hypothesis. Unconscious meaning is an inferential construction, on the part of the analyst, of signals and signs communicated by the patient which the analyst reformulates in conventional linguistic terms.

Notes

1. Although *construction* may apply to recent or remote events, *reconstruction* is the term usually applied to the latter. Loewenstein, however, speaks of "reconstruction of the present" (1951).

2. See also Glover (1931). However, Glover's use of the expression *inexact interpretations* implies that there are exact ones. This may be misleading in regard to the relativism of clinical knowledge.

PART II

STYLE AND CHARACTER

Introduction

by MILTON E. JUCOVY, M.D.

Psychoanalysis lost one of its most gifted, imaginative and charismatic practitioners and theoreticians with the untimely death at the age of sixty-one of Dr. Victor H. Rosen on February 5, 1973. His warmth, gentleness and exceptional intellectual talents all contributed to his outstanding career as a clinician and teacher, to his innovative impact on the science of psychoanalysis, and to his unusual ability to stimulate so many of his students and colleagues.

Victor Rosen's personal manner and style was truly unique. At first glance he seemed shy, diffident, and self-effacing. Sometimes he would appear hesitant and even uncertain, qualities which belied the closely reasoned and tough-minded nature of his thinking. When he addressed himself to some subtle clinical or theoretical question, one could note an almost imperceptible and seemingly apologetic nod of his head, which was thoroughly disarming, and as one came to know him, one recognized that this stylistic quality was an integral part of his rapierlike wit and incredible charm. His wry humor punctuated both his verbal and written communications; it was composed of occasional modest self-mockery and an iconoclastic teasing of people and institutions he regarded as pompous and overbearing. It was this wit, this charm, this ability always to avoid the obvious and banal which made Victor Rosen, with all his modesty and lack of pretension, one of the most exciting and appealing of companions. His very presence at a professional or social gathering created a golden aura of infectious exhilaration, which, once experienced, was unforgettable.

Victor Rosen was born on November 21, 1911, the son of Alex and Molly Rosen. He had one sister, Norma, two and a half years his junior. Both his parents were school teachers and active socialists. His father had been a serious student of Greek and Latin but he was denied a license to teach these subjects because he had run for office on the Socialist Party ticket. It would not be altogether presumptuous to speculate that enduring identifications with both parents fostered Victor Rosen's later pedagogic, linguistic, and humanitarian interests. An episode characteristic of that uncertain and repressive period of his childhood occurred when Victor was six, and he always recalled it as quite traumatic. His father was delivering a speech for a Socialist Party rally and young Victor was in the audience when the police suddenly descended, arrested his father, and carried him away to a temporary incarceration.

Victor Rosen's mother was one of the first in the United States to be psychoanalyzed and she remained very much intrigued with psychoanalysis. His father, on the other hand, was considerably less sanguine about its value. Perhaps one may sense here also the identifications which emerged as a blending of Victor Rosen's deep and abiding commitment to psychoanalytic ideas and to his continued searching and quest for a better, clearer, and more comprehensive understanding of human psychological processes. It was because of his mother's interests that Victor and his sister were sent to the Walden School for their early education, for it had a distinctly Freudian orientation in the early 1920s. On admission, Victor's test scores were so high that he received a full scholarship to Walden; his sister was also admitted on full scholarship, sight unseen, on the strength of *his* apparent genius. The predictive perceptiveness of the school was clearly vindicated when years later Victor Rosen was honored at a special dinner as one of its outstanding and distinguished alumni.

While attending Walden, Victor, ever energetic and enterprising, began working as a delivery boy at the age of ten. He used most of his earnings to buy expensive bird books and binoculars and became an avid bird watcher. A poignant reminder that the social scene then was not so totally different from today's was that the young amateur ornithologist's binoculars were stolen from him in Central Park one day by some ruffians. Victor Rosen joined the American Ornithological Society at twelve and remained an enthusiast all his life. In addition to watching birds, he bred white mice, rabbits, and canaries in the small railroad flat in Manhattan where the family lived. He remained always a great lover of animals.

Victor Rosen continued his early education at the Walden School. His mother was primarily responsible for keeping him there despite pressure from other mothers, who were transferring their children out of fear that they would not be admitted to college from such a "revolutionary" institution. Her faith was rewarded when he was admitted to Columbia University. Although he majored in the sciences and was a committed premedical student, his scholastic record in mathematics and the humanities was outstanding, so much so that he was asked by Irwin Edman, the distinguished philosopher, to join his special seminar. While at Columbia he helped pay his tuition by tutoring other students. His family was aware that he had wanted to become a physician from the time he was a very small boy, and he knew definitely from the age of fourteen that he wanted to become a psychoanalyst.

After his graduation from Columbia University he was admitted to the College of Physicians and Surgeons at Columbia, graduating in 1936 and receiving his M.D. degree. He then served as an extern in Pathology at Mt. Sinai Hospital in New York from 1936 to 1937 and as an intern at the Brooklyn Jewish Hospital from 1937 to 1938. He then became a resident in Neurology at Montefiore Hospital in New York until 1940. An episode from that period of service reveals his intense curiosity in the pursuit of truth and his reluctance to be satisfied with facile answers to perplexing medical questions. A middle-aged woman on his service was believed to be suffering from a neoplasm of the brain. She had been losing her eyesight and there appeared to be other confirmatory signs of an intracranial tumor. Dr. Rosen had some doubts about the validity of this diagnosis, and in working the patient up further he noted that her hair was dyed an unusual color. He discovered that the onset of her visual disturbance followed the dying of her hair and was caused by a response to the dye. This observation led to the publication of his first paper, "Optic Neuritis Caused by a Coal Tar Hair Dye," coauthored with Dr. Moses Keschner and published in the *Archives of Ophthalmology* (Rosen and Keschner, 1941). Leaving Montefiore, Dr. Rosen became a Fellow in Psychiatry at the Henry Phipps Psychiatric Clinic of the Johns Hopkins Hospital in Baltimore from

1940 to 1941. There, his interest in language and thought, which had begun in college, was further stimulated by the opportunity to work under Dr. Adolph Meyer.

Victor Rosen had married Elizabeth Ruskay upon his graduation from medical school in 1936. Two daughters were born of this marriage, Barbara in 1941 and Winifred in 1943. The marriage was later dissolved and in 1965 he married Dr. Elise Wechsler Snyder, a psychiatrist.

After finishing his fellowship at the Phipps Clinic, Rosen entered military service during World War II. For the greater part of his military career he was stationed in England, attaining the rank of Major and becoming Chief of the Neuropsychiatric Service of the 98th General Hospital. He served in the army for five years, from 1941 to 1946 and upon his return to civilian life at the conclusion of the war he began his psychoanalytic training at The New York Psychoanalytic Institute. After receiving his certification he became successively a member of the New York Psychoanalytic Society and the American Psychoanalytic Association. The years immediately following the end of World War II represented a period of intense and exciting growth in the psychoanalytic movement, and many gifted and talented young candidates were being trained at institutes all over the country. Even among these, Rosen's exceptional qualities were soon recognized, and he was asked to become the Assistant Director of the Treatment Center of The New York Psychoanalytic Institute, serving under Dr. Leo Stone in this vital treatment arm of the Institute's training program. When Dr. Stone retired from his position in 1957, Dr. Rosen became Director of the Treatment Center. In the same year he was appointed Training and Supervising Analyst and member of the Faculty of the Institute, assuming responsibilities for conducting didactic analyses and supervising candidates during their period of training.

As Medical Director of the Treatment Center, he served as an ex officio member of the Educational Committee, participating actively and creatively in its deliberations. Following his resignation as Medical Director, he again served on the Educational Committee and in 1964 was elected Chairman of this committee, a recognition by his colleagues of his superb abilities to assume this most prestigious position as leader and coordinator of the Institute's training program.

In addition to his many activities and responsibilities at his own Institute, Victor Rosen had been active on the national as well as on the local scene and had played an active and seminal role in the growth and development of the American Psychoanalytic Association. An indication of the respect and esteem in which he was held by his colleagues across the country was his nomination and election as president of the association, a position he held in 1965-66. Subsequently he was invited to join the faculty of the Albert Einstein College of Medicine in New York as Clinical Professor of Psychiatry, in which capacity he served from 1967 until 1972, when he joined the faculty of Yale University College of Medicine with the same title. His death only a year later brought to a premature conclusion a brilliant career which had already more than fulfilled his early promise and potential. An entire generation of his teachers, colleagues, students, and patients whose lives were enriched by his scholarship, erudition, and luminous personality will continue with his family to mourn their collective loss.

From an early point in his developing career, during college and medical school, and later, when he served his internships and residency, Victor Rosen showed a serious and keen interest in social issues and causes, an interest which existed side by side with his commitment to classical psychoanalysis and the study of individual human psychology. He was always actively engaged, often in the vanguard, in any movement which was devoted to the improvement of the human condition, whether it was concerned with academic freedom, the betterment of the lot of struggling young interns, or the protests which mounted in the 1960s against our country's involvement in Viet Nam. Despite his firm anchoring in psychoanalytic discipline, he never believed in blind conformity or in a narrow and strictured parochialism. He had a large and comprehensive grasp of issues which extended to his hopes and aspirations for the future of psychoanalysis. He deplored the isolation of psychoanalysts and, in a delightfully witty and charming conclusion to an essay on the relationship of a psychoanalytic institute to the community, wrote:

> A careful review of the literature on the subject of Institute-community relationships sheds very little light on either the metapsychology or the sociology of the subject. Most analysts

seem to have regarded the community as a collective myth of archaic origin which is retained in the deepest layers of the unconscious. In most instances we do not try to analyze the fantasy but feel best advised to leave it undisturbed. The anarchist political philosophers, such as Proudhon and Kropotkin, seem to have dealt more forthrightly with the subject than the analysts. In *The Philosophy of Poverty* Proudhon, for example, predicts the ultimate disappearance of the community. Thus one solution to the problems inherent in this relationship is to remain quietly indoors until it disappears. In this way one day we can become a series of Institute outposts across the nation with no surrounding communities to disturb us with relationships.

On the basis of further investigation I would like to report the following tentative conclusions on this curious cultural interaction: There is a community that surrounds the Institute. Our relationship with the animals and plants leaves much to be desired. We are on somewhat better terms with the people of the community since we get brief glimpses of them not only on our couches, but as we ride from our offices to various celebrations in quick-moving vehicles. Occasional members of this populace wave to us from the streets and we often wave back to them in little mutual outbursts of relatedness. Travelers report that we speak a similar tongue to the surrounding natives but subtle changes in the meaning of words often require complex verbal transactions for mutual understanding. Only the common verbs and nouns retain their original significance in our vocabularies.

The members of this community are, on the whole, a friendly and industrious people who spend much of their time engaged in the simple arts and manufacturing crafts. One of their greatest skills is described as the making of money. A discussion of this community activity would, for the present, take us too far afield. Suffice it to say that at times these gentle folk try to give some of this money that they have made to the people of the Institute. Sometimes this is a shy method of asking for a relationship. According to our proud and ancient tradition, however, these offerings are always politely refused.

> Otherwise the danger exists that they would ply us with this money in ever-increasing amounts, sapping our moral fiber and causing us to become soft and irresolute like the Greeks and Romans before us. Of course there are times when one part of our community, the Treatment Center, requires the replenishment of certain articles of manufacture like paper cups or instant coffee, which are only obtainable for money in the larger community. In this instance it is necessary to acquire small amounts of the native medium of exchange. Experience has shown that the direct barter of our own commodity for these supplies is rarely practical. On such occasions we do not touch the money ourselves but send our womenfolk, known as the Auxiliary, to negotiate with the inhabitants for this purpose.
>
> This concludes the relevant part of the study. If I have given an oversimplified account of these two cultures and the relationship between them it has been out of desire to deal with the most basic aspects of this largely unexplored field. If I have conveyed the impression that there could be more relating between the analytic and the nonanalytic community than now exists, I will have achieved my purpose [Rosen, 1962, pp. 53-54].

It was therefore most natural and appropriate that Victor Rosen, almost at the outset of his psychoanalytic career, should have become associated with the Treatment Center of The New York Psychoanalytic Institute, where his energies and talents contributed so much to its manifold activities and where his personal impact was felt on the therapeutic, educational, and community service aspects of its functions. The opportunity to serve a clinic where low-cost psychoanalytic treatment could be offered to potential analysands in low or marginal income groups was a project eminently suited to his emerging analytic gifts and to his personal philosophy. During his administration, both as Assistant Director and Director, the procedure for interviewing and assessing applicants was refined and consolidated. He played an important role in the organization of an Affiliated Staff of graduate analysts who could treat many deserving patients who might otherwise have been considered unsuitable for treatment by Institute candidates. During his tenure semimonthly staff meetings featuring the presentation of clinical material from ongoing analyses and prepared discussions by staff members and members of the Institute faculty became a regular feature of the postgraduate program of the Institute. He played a role in the organization of a child analysis division of the Affiliated Staff and was also active in the initiation of a referral service for those patients who were unable to be accepted in the Treatment Center program. Statistical figures have indicated the scope of the Treatment Center's activities and provide powerful evidence of the extent of the low-cost analytic treatment provided. They are even more impressive when one considers the enormous amount of time spent in the intake process by the medical directors, social worker, and the various members of the intake committee in evaluation and selection procedures. In answer to some who seemed to have taken a pessimistic view of the possibilities of a prospective applicant being accepted into the program, Dr. Rosen commented:

> Many of our colleagues think that it is simpler to get a man into space than a patient into the Treatment Center; but this is not so. Psychoanalytic patients are admitted, and at least in this respect we lead the Russians [Rosen, 1962, p. 48].

Foreshadowing his already developing interests in questions of "style," he noted the individual stamp and character imparted to the Treatment Center by its several directors:

> Dr. Heinz Hartmann, its first medical director, fostered its autonomous functions and suffused it with neutralized energy. Dr. Leo Stone, its next custodian, taught the written word, the importance of records, and respect for the law [Rosen, 1962, p. 48].

What he did not of course describe, with characteristic modesty, was the direction and style of the Treatment Center under his own aegis as Director. It was typified by his very special elegance in the writing of interview reports, the stimulation it provided for others to try to emulate his rich and meticulous observations and his vivid and imaginative formulations. In retrospect one can see how his interests in style and language permeated his evaluations. His inspiring direction as discussion leader helped diagnostic interviewing become an additionally refined tool in the selection of patients suitable for supervised analysis by students in training. He urged that careful attention be paid not only to selection of cases on the basis of their conformity with standard diagnostic categories, but also to the assessment of other, more subtle elements such as motivation for treatment, integrity of ego structure, unusual character defenses, and the potential for susceptibility to regressive trends. His own masterly and often intuitive grasp of these issues was an invaluable aid to the intake committee in choosing patients who would provide a student with the optimum probability of a sustained analytic experience free of insurmountable difficulties. The *esprit de corps* of the committee and the lively and interesting discussions during Dr. Rosen's tenure were memorable and intoxicating experiences.

In his strong and continued sense of identification with the Treatment Center, Victor Rosen hoped and felt that it would respond with growth and change to the continued examination of the field of psychoanalytic education and play an important role in the years to come. He believed that the direction of this growth could be discussed under several rubrics: the part played by case selection in facilitating or interfering with the supervision of student analyses; the area of postgraduate development; and the important area of research in psychoanalysis. He was ever aware of the problems remaining to be solved in the teaching of analytic techniques and of the subtle problems involved in case selection. He was also very much aware of the need to integrate answers to questions involved in the goals of supervision, in the selection of patients for the realization of these goals, and in the blending of educational aims with patients' therapeutic needs, which were then at best arrived at mainly by intuitive guesswork. His belief that the gathering of archival experience might make it possible to formulate procedures of greater certainty and predictive power has in some degree been substantiated. A recent survey performed by his successors has indicated that, in spite of some lapses, the patient selection from Treatment Center sources has been more successful than that provided from private and individual referrals. Some significant studies involving issues of follow-up of patient analyses were begun while Dr. Rosen directed the activities of the Treatment Center and he provided the impetus and stimulation for them.

The leadership that Dr. Rosen and his assistant director, Dr. Leo

Loomie, exercised at the regular Affiliated Staff conferences provided an important contribution to postgraduate education at the Institute. They provided a forum at which analysts of varying levels of experience were able to meet for the mutual discussion of theoretical and technical problems. Dr. Rosen recognized the importance of these study groups, as they might overlap with the development of psychoanalytic research, and he was ever mindful of the opportunities presented by the case material of the Treatment Center for investigation by colleagues whose private clinical material was of necessity limited. He was also aware of the role of the Treatment Center as a training ground for a cadre of future faculty members. It is not accidental that a large number of future training and supervising analysts emerged from the group that worked with Victor Rosen at the Treatment Center and were inspired by him.

The impetus given to postgraduate education by the organization of the Affiliated Staff and the group conferences sponsored by the Treatment Center led to the evolution of smaller groups. One such model group, the Gifted Adolescent Project, served as the birthplace and testing ground for Dr. Rosen's developing and expanding interests in problems of creativity, style, and linguistics in relation to psychoanalysis. This project, led at the onset by Ernst Kris, was eagerly embraced by Victor Rosen, and he was one of its most enthusiastic and productive members. A number of his later papers germinated in the stimulating atmosphere of this group. Several years later he organized and chaired another study group, dealing specifically with linguistics and undoubtedly the definitive forum for the crystallization of his own ideas. The work held much promise for further clarification of psychoanalytic concepts and provided much stimulation and inspiration for his colleagues in this dynamic and productive group.

Dr. Rosen's participation in the work of the Gifted Adolescent Project was a crucial part of his life and scientific development. This group project was perhaps the first organized group effort devoted to the investigation of the creative process, and the influence of Ernst Kris, its leader, and of the other members is important to note if one is to understand and appreciate how Victor Rosen's later work developed in this stimulating crucible.

In an essay on the study of creative persons, Donald W. Mackinnon (1967) points out that the psychologist who tries to study creative people faces the problem which confronts every student of human behavior and character: he must decide whether his enterprise is a humanistic study or a science and, if a science, what kind it is. The dilemma between the concept that the outstanding characteristic of man is his individuality and the dictum that the single individual is not the concern of science would seem to create an impasse.

One camp has it that individuality cannot be an object of scientific study. Mackinnon quotes Max Meyer, the pre-Watsonian behaviorist who said, "A description of one individual without reference to others may be a piece of literature, a biography, a novel. But science? No." In contrast are those who maintain that if science is not able to deal with the fact of individuality then a new science equal to this task must be created. The German philosopher, Windelband, brought the conflict between description and analysis and between understanding and explanation into sharp focus. He urged the recognition of two types of science: the nomothetic and the idiographic. The former includes the natural sciences that seek to establish causal laws of the greatest generality, while the latter includes social and cultural disciplines, uses the methods of history in its investigations, and has the same right to be called "scientific." He pointed out that an idiographic psychology would have as its object the study of human individuality. Other psychologists, such as Allport and Lewin, have sought to reconcile these views and have indicated that the study of the individual can proceed to a general law and that the two approaches are not necessarily mutually exclusive.

The Gifted Adolescent Project, which grew out of Treatment Center study groups and used the Treatment Center facilities for case selection (as reported by Dr. Rosen with Drs. Leo Loomie and Martin Stein [Loomie, Rosen, and Stein, 1958]), was indeed a pioneer study in this field, utilizing the psychoanalytic method for a study of problems of creativity and the creative process. The deep convictions about psychoanalytic theory and practice which were held by the members of the group permitted no tampering with the methodology of psychoanalysis. The fundamental thesis which guided their work involved forgoing the wish to understand the special gifts of the patient and focusing instead on what was wrong with him, how his neurosis developed, what the conflicts and defenses were, and how the work of interpretation should proceed. The decision was made that generalizations would be allowed to follow at the proper time and in the proper place as the analyses continued in their particular and exquisite details.

The explorations of the study group focused on a number of issues concerned with the creative process, object relations, special gifts, and certain technical considerations. Rosen and his collaborators were naturally much influenced by the previous work of Ernst Kris dealing with problems of sublimation and neutralization. Kris's clinical experience had shown that success or failure in a number of professions depended substantially on the extent to which the activity itself has become autonomous, that is, detached from the original conflict which may have turned the person's interest and talent in a specific direction. Kris had pointed out that paradoxically there is a high degree of proximity of the highest mental processes to instinctual gratification. It might have been supposed that in certain very gifted people the distance from the conflict would be very great and that a high degree of skillxulness implied that an activity was least impeded by closeness to instinctual sources. Clinically, however, it can be shown that conflicts do exist and may hamper the level of performance significantly. Kris had suggested that the ordinary use of the term sublimation or desexualization involves a statement about the result of a transformation of psychic energy and that the speed of the process is generally neglected. He felt it might be possible to study these phenomena by using an alternate hypothesis in which the rapidity of the transformation would be the central issue. A gifted person might then have the characteristic of being able to effect a greatly accelerated transformation of energy discharge from primary to secondary process. Further discussion of clinical material by the group impressed Kris, Rosen, and their collaborators with the omnipresence of instinctual gratification in the sublimated act and how defensive and gratifying aspects are constantly interwoven in the sublimation.

Rosen was very much impressed by another theme highlighted by Kris. Although he favored the view than an original core of endowment is a prerequisite to the development of any talent, he also stressed the reciprocal effects of the gift and the surrounding environment. He emphasized how such endowments may influence life experience and the role it may play in facilitating the detachment of certain ego functions from conflict and in establishing autonomy in certain activities, views which might be useful in organizing clinical impressions and in observations of child development.

The discussions of the study group also focused on the role played by complex vicissitudes of processes of identification in gifted people. Kris had pointed out that he had never seen any concrete material on a gift in which identification did not play a part. He reminded his colleagues that the first item on sublimation in the analytic literature is a story of identification. When little Hans got well, he became interested in music, which was his father's profession, and later in life became a musician. A clinical experience of our own (MEJ) seems to substantiate this observation. A young woman who was especially gifted in language entered analysis for a variety of problems which included conflicts involving object choice. She was then doing more or less routine secretarial work for a nonprofit organization. Her mother was a writer and her father had been a brilliant public official who was vilified and literally hounded to death during the dark and fearful days of the McCarthy era for his progressive political views. Although she consciously idealized her father, the analysis indicated that she had unconsciously identified with the aggressor and blamed her father for his ultimate fate. For many years she loudly proclaimed that she was totally disinterested in political questions and hardly ever read the newspapers. Her attitude was: "A plague on both your houses." When she achieved an understanding of her conflicts she became a gifted translator of progressive political literature, thus combining the talents of both parents.

Characteristically, Victor Rosen was very much interested in certain special technical considerations which arose in this group investigation. There was general agreement that presenting case material to a seminar did not significantly interfere with the analytic process, as it can in the training situation, in which different motivations are at play. There appeared to occur here a sharpening of observation, a greater keenness of perception and understanding, and there was a beneficial effect from the contributions of the group. Other technical questions were considered as well, such as the effect on an analysis of the multiple interview technique, which many of these patients had undergone as part of the Treatment Center procedure before they were accepted for analysis. The general consensus was that this did not lead to distortions but contributed to the unfolding character of the analytic process.

Victor Rosen and the members of the project were very much aware of the problem of how one might develop a scientific method of evaluation which might be applied to psychoanalysis. Statistical methods, successful in other fields, present problems when applied to psychoanalysis. Analysts cannot accumulate a significant series of cases during their lifetimes, and some material cannot be presented because of its confidential nature. The characteristics of the discipline of psychoanalysis also involve values which are difficult to define or express quantitatively. The members of the study group clearly indicated how they hoped to sharpen the power of analytic observation beyond the point to which one man could develop it. The group experience could then lead to methods for more adequate validation of analytic hypotheses and formulation of new ones. Returning to the question posed by those who are critical of methods other than those utilized by the natural and physical sciences, Victor Rosen and the others believed that the procedures employed by their group could be instrumental in elucidating and validating psychoanalytic questions in a convincing fashion and could convey to a broad audience a sense of proof without the introduction of nonanalytic contaminants.

The work of the study group on gifted adolescents has been stressed because many of Victor Rosen's later papers were based largely on clinical material presented there. These papers, covering the period from 1958 to 1964, were devoted to such questions as abstract thinking, imagination, originality, and character style. They were firmly rooted in meticulous clinical observations and ranged from a clarification of theoretical concepts involving psychic energy and instinctual discharge to discussions of principles of mental functioning and defensive formations.

Perhaps their most fertile additions to our knowledge were the refinements they contributed to psychoanalytic diagnosis and technical questions. A few examples from this most impressive array might be cited. In "Abstract Thinking and Object Relations"

(Chapter 3), he studied the way in which abstraction can be used as a regressive defense in highly gifted individuals. Against the background of Piaget's studies of the development of cognitive processes, he showed how abstract thought could be used in the service of the ego and reality testing or in the service of the primary process, where it can represent simply another aspect of the use of regression. He felt, however, that regressive defenses require more specific characterization in terms of their secondary-process content than is ordinarily afforded them. His clinical material demonstrated how individuals who have an unusual capacity for abstract thinking can use such "perversions" of abstraction more frequently than others for defensive purposes and how it leaves a special mark on their personalities and object relationships. His formulations in this paper have an important usefulness for the analytic practitioner in terms of refinements of analytic techniques.

A paper titled "Originality and the Adolescent Group" (Rosen, 1959) written for *Child Study*, has a more popular appeal. It begins by describing vividly the massive contradictions and antithetical attitudes and behavior which exist in the turbulent period of adolescent life. In reviewing the processes of identification which take place at this time, he proposes that a minority of gifted individuals, who are capable of making "selective identifications" are able on the one hand to conform to the group in certain traditional ways and are indeed deeply identified with the culture and institutions of their society, but that on the other hand they are able to make departures and original leaps based on the evidence of their own senses. He makes the very important point that the work of some highly creative people was not originally motivated by considerations of personal revolt against their society. It was only after they had to endure ostracism because of the unpopularity of their new ideas that their capacity to tolerate it became an important trait. In deploring the prevailing tendency to look upon childhood and adolescence as intermediate phases of "becoming," without importance and stature of their own, Rosen raises some important educational questions. He suggests that we might ask the adolescent to help us understand our world, in addition to our helping him to understand and cope with his turmoil and uncertainty.

In a more scholarly and complex work which might be coupled with the paper mentioned above, Rosen further develops some ideas about the characteristics of artistically gifted individuals who offer resistance to group judgments, particularly in the area of aesthetic values. He notes in his paper, "Some Effects of Artistic Talent on Character Style" (Chapter 14), that in these people questions of illusion and standardization of subjective choice and preference produce a special tension between the cognitive experience derived from cultural pressures and the perceptual experience of the individual. He suggests that there is a spectrum of cognitive styles, ranging from the artist who sees illusory possibilities in phenomena not consonant with conventional interpretations to the literal-minded and practical "realist." This disparity may contribute to the trait, found in so many talented people, of considering oneself an "exception"; apparently based on principle, it is actually an obligatory trait covered by rationalization. Rosen postulates that some roots of this obligatory behavior lie in constitutional differences originating in sensitivities to perceptual stimuli and that this tendency may develop further during early childhood when separation from the mother and attachments to playthings are important problems. The unusual attachment to playthings seen in highly gifted children may influence aspects of the parent-child relationship and foster defenses against parental influence in value judgments, which in turn would result in resistance to cultural conformity. This feature of the artistic predisposition can become an asset for the implementation of creative talent as well as an element in the artist's object relations and conflicts. This chain of developmental events can contribute to success in artistic endeavor as well as to certain social problems due to the subject's "exceptional" nature. Rosen also suggests that more detailed observations of the relationship of children to their playthings in the transitional-object stage could perhaps be revealing if the studies were correlated with estimates of precocious perceptual development and capacity for controlled illusion.

Continuing his investigation of problems connected with creativity and giftedness, Rosen in 1960 published "Some Aspects of the Role of Imagination in the Analytic Process" (Chapter 11). There he defines imagination as an important synthetic process of the ego based on early experience with the disappearance and reappearance of objects. A later development than image formation, imagination serves to master object loss so that the object can remain under the control of the ego and be manipulated as a psychic reality even when no longer available in the field of immediate perception. The later development of imagination requires the concomitant development of "object constancy." Further development of mature psychic processes requires a synthesis of projected mental contents with an introjection of percepts of external objects, a capacity for "controlled illusion," and a special method for handling ambiguity. The importance of this paper lies in its careful attention to the psychopathology of imagination as it might be encountered in a variety of analytic resistances. In discussing these technical considerations, Rosen stresses how an analyst must be alert to and interested in the external and internal factors which interfere with the patient's ability to maintain an equal distance between illusion and reality. He must also be concerned with the variety of interferences with the mutual contract between the analyst and the patient to exclude the contradictions implied by treating both the idea and the object as both real and illusory at the same time.

These, then, are some of the examples of the elegant and aesthetically conceived work devoted to thinking and creativity which developed out of Victor Rosen's work in the study group on gifted adolescents. These studies stimulated later and further studies of cognition and language, which he felt had so far been relatively neglected in a field where the interaction between patient and therapist depended so basically on verbal communication. His increasing familiarity with the field of linguistics and his mastery of its intricacies were applied to psychoanalytic theory and technique with fruitful results.

The advent of studies in ego psychology encouraged analysts to pay increasing attention to the major defenses of the patient involved in the analytic process, albeit in a relatively gross way. The contributions this added to psychoanalytic technique are well known and carefully documented in many major papers. Victor Rosen's studies of creativity, imagination, abstract thinking, and style form a natural bridge to his later studies of language and symbolism. The link they forged from somewhat different points of view enables the analytic practitioner to focus in a more refined and even microscopic way on subtle defenses which might otherwise be relatively neglected by even a most careful observer. The tools these studies provided are invaluable for a spectrum of analytic patients, but are particularly important for an understanding of those with even minimal borderline pathology.

A clinical example demonstrates the use of Rosen's formulations concerning style and linguistic disturbances in illuminating a difficult analytic problem and highlights as well some of the exquisite additions to technique which comprise an important part of his legacy. The patient was a young woman whose life was scarred by a stark and central feature: frequent hospitalizations for a chronic renal illness from the age of two. In her analysis she quickly revealed difficult and frustrating behavior patterns. She found it difficult to use the couch and to associate freely. She also showed a mumbling type of speech which made it very hard to understand her communications, and when she was not mumbling she whispered. Rosen's description of the linguistic correlates of borderline disturbances seemed particularly applicable to this patient. He pointed to a tendency to react to words as signs or signals rather than to the referential meaning of words. Often such patients produce incomplete sentences or sentences with such syntactic errors as to make them all but incomprehensible. Confusion in identity results in a failure to maintain a clear separation between addressor and addressee. The speaker verbalizes his inner thought processes without consideration for the addressee's confusion when he is called upon to decode the message. Patients who distort reality or use massive denial reveal their pathology in instances where the choice of words or word order to insure clarity of reference depends upon an accurate appraisal of the context of the auditor. Rosen further pointed out how disturbed object relationships, lack of empathy, and disturbance of the synthetic function are revealed in a variety of language disturbances. In normal language function, "reference" is a synthetic product. A disturbance of any of the linguistic buttresses is felt in other parts of the representation-reference system. Ego deviations less obvious than frank schizophrenic disorders give rise to language disturbances as a result of the simultaneous and reciprocal development of ego structures and of language. Various hypotheses about the meaning at the level of content of this patient's mumbling and whispering seemed inadequate, while Rosen's formulations were of marked help in understanding the difficulties and resistances she displayed; this success attests to the enduring validity of the investigations and writings of Victor Rosen.

CHAPTER ELEVEN

Imagination in the Analytic Process

Imagination is a word that is used rather loosely in the English language. It is, however, capable of definition and seems to describe a psychological process that we are aware of intuitively whether or not its precise boundaries have been semantically delimited. This discussion is an attempt to offer one definition of this activity and to explore the usefulness of reexamining certain aspects of psychic functioning in the light of a process so defined.

A survey of the psychopathology of imagination, which may be implied by the title of this presentation, would be a most ambitious project and would, in the end, become a clinical treatise on the organic and functional disturbances of the mental apparatus. I propose here, to discuss a limited and rather discrete area of the disturbance of this mental function as it relates to analytic resistance and the analytic process, and to suggest some alternative formulations on the dynamics of the transference as it is ordinarily encountered in the analytic procedure.

The ensuing discussion is based upon the assumption that imagination is a thought process with special characteristics. It is proposed that the prototype of the capacity for imagination in early ego development is connected with the development of "object constancy" and the behavior toward vanished objects. As in later ego development, similar mechanisms are utilized to extend the process of concept formation. The discussion will also develop the thesis that disturbances of the capacity for imagination, while present in a variety of clinical conditions, have as common factors: a relative inability to relinquish or vary images and concepts once formed, an inability to retain the elements of a decomposed image through a series of transformations, a disturbance of the synthetic function, and an incapacity for "controlled illusion" or "make believe" with difficulties in coping with perceptual ambiguity. Finally, it is intended to discuss the role of imagination in the analytic process and in the analytic transference as a variant of the usual ways in which these phenomena are viewed.

In its simplest terms *imagination* denotes a mental act which attempts to replace by an image, word, concept, or construct, something which is thought to exist but which cannot be perceived by sensory means at the time. According to Webster (1953), "our simple apprehension of corporeal objects, if present, is perception and if absent, is imagination." In many discussions eidetic imagery is described as the most primitive form of imagination (see Jaensch, 1923; and the "Marburg School," Allport, 1924, Schilder, 1942 and Griffith, 1945). The subject is complicated, however, by the application of the term to mental events that are much more complex and more extended in time than the formation of images. According to a late edition of Webster's *Unabridged Dictionary* (1953), imagination is "the formation of mental images of objects not present to the senses, especially of new ideas or ideas from elements experienced separately. . . ." In *A Midsummer Night's Dream*, Theseus says, "And as imagination bodies forth the forms of things unknown, the poet's pen turns them to shapes, and gives to airy nothing a local habitation and a name." Finally, it is defined by Webster as "the power of the mind to decompose its conceptions and to recombine the elements of them *at its pleasure*."

Ruth Griffith (1945), who has published a comprehensive study of certain types of imagination in childhood, says, "There seems to be a good deal of confusion between the terms 'imagination' and 'imagery.' Some writers," she says, "treat these as if they had the same meaning. Throughout the present work [Griffith], imagination is regarded as a type of thought. . . . Images themselves may or may not accompany imagination. A child may create for himself the idea of an imaginary companion and may deliberately pretend that such a person is present, but it does not necessarily follow that he sees the companion or has images or hallucinations accompanying this experience." If viewed genetically and developmentally, I would not agree that such a sharp distinction can be made and would prefer to view the relationship between image and imagination as stages in a common development. In (Chapter 3) this was outlined as follows:

> In Freud's formulation regarding two principles in mental functioning, the thesis that the secondary process develops its special characteristics as a result of the reality-testing activities of the individual, and is thus in large part a reflection of the external world of objects (although drive motivated) is first clearly indicated. The first stage of the development of the secondary process must therefore be conceived as consisting of images which are representations of the percepts of the animate and inanimate object world. In the later phase of language development, the gradual substitution of word symbols for images requires the withdrawal of some cathectic energy from the mental image, as the development of the image in the first place, required the withdrawal of certain quantities of libido from the external objects as "things in themselves." Abstract thought is, at least developmentally, the most advanced stage of the secondary process. It is made up of many elements . . . [such as those] that deal with *class, quantity,* and *spatial relationships* (Piaget, 1954). The formation of these ideas requires an additional decathexis of the image-word representation of the external object. The economy of psychic energy expenditure appears to be one of the striking progressive gains for each stage in this process, and most particularly this final one. . . . In so far as this development requires the withdrawal of a certain quantity of libidinal cathexis from the object world, it would appear to be the antithesis of the mechanism by which reality testing and object relations were established in the first place. Thus it is necessary to conceive of two concurrent processes in this development which are in a sense the antitheses of each other. The process of reality testing implies the successive releasing of quantities of libido, formerly narcissistically directed, for the investment of external objects. The formation of certain aspects of the

> secondary process, on the other hand, seems to require the concurrent withdrawal of object libido for the cathexis successively of images, words, and finally concepts. This could be described as essentially a process of narcissistic reinvestment. The delicate balance of this interchange has many implications for psychoanalytic theory and practice that have not yet been fully explored. One of these is the observation that for many creative activities of thought, which utilize certain aspects of the primary process in the service of the ego (Chapter 1; Kris, 1952), there are to be found analogous invasions of the secondary process which utilize certain aspects of its function in the service of the id.

An example of this is the use of abstract ideas as an intellectualizing defense in analysis. A patient described in Chapter 3 in this context was able to program involved problems in physics for an electronic computer but could not keep her checking account in balance. But even her arithmetical lapses, when scrutinized closely, revealed the evidence of her mathematical sophistication within her stupidity.

Before Piaget had fully developed his imaginative work in *The Construction of Reality in the Child* (1954), Freud had already perceived the importance of the child's experience with vanishing objects in the development of crucial aspects of ego functioning. In *Beyond the Pleasure Principle* (Freud, 1923), he reports the observation of a child of eighteen months who has mastered his separation anxiety by means of a game with an object on a string. The passively experienced, anxious displeasure, which emanates from an object that vanishes and returns at its own pleasure, is turned into the active satisfaction of making the passive object vanish and reappear at the subject's will. The analogy to the passive experience of image formation, when an object is presented to the senses, and the active experience of imagining it when it is absent from the field of perception, is inescapable.

Piaget (1954) has demonstrated the stages of the formation of "object constancy" in the maturation of perception in the child. I would like to reemphasize the three decisive stages in this process that have a special importance in the discussion of imagination. The first is the separation of the percept from the current activity of the subject so that it becomes an attribute of the object rather than of the self, the stage described by Piaget as the "objective" one. This stage is really the precursor of the capacity for image formation. The second is that in which an active search for the object is initiated after its disappearance and is described as "permanent objectification." Its achievement indicates that the child has the capacity to retain an image of the vanished object and it is analogous to the most primitive form of imagination, i.e., the capacity to retain the image when the object has been removed from the immediate field of perception. The third and most crucial phase is described as the "representational" stage in which the child can retain both the image of the vanished object and the probable course of its displacements. This final stage is also described by Piaget as the beginning of the apprehension of "invariance." It indicates the capacity not only to retain, but to recreate the image of the lost object. Put in other terms, the child first realizes at this level of development that in a series of transformations of the object certain of its attributes which appear to undergo change remain constant, while others which appear to remain constant undergo a change. This treatment of the object would seem to be the early prototype for the more complex imaginative processes of later life such as the syntheses of new ideas. Analogous stages to those involved in the formation of the "constant object" are shown to repeat themselves in an upward spiral in the growth of logical thinking, and the stages of concept formation at higher levels of cognition (Inhelder and Piaget, 1958; Piaget, 1952, 1956).

Let me clarify at this point what is meant in the present discussion by "imagination in the service of the ego" and thus distinguish it from fantasy in general and from other mental processes. Purely mental events without any immediate discharge in action or behavior must initially be described phenomenologically, from the point of view of introspection. This reveals a series of thought processes with varying degrees of organization or haphazardness in the sequence of images, affects, words, or abstract ideas that follow one upon the other. Thus the series would seem to extend (see Kris, 1950, and a recent elaboration of the subject by Joseph, 1959) from dream, hallucination, and hypnagogic phenomena, at one end of the scale, through various forms of fantasy and daydreams to classifying, planning, and problem-solving logical thought processes at the other. The degree of organization on a causal basis, in the sequential arrangement of the mental contents, is the sole criterion for classification in such a scheme. The ego, the larger part of whose activities is engaged in the testing, fitting into, and mastering of the environment, seems to find those processes in which there is a high degree of causal organization most useful for this purpose. Clinical experience has made it clear, however, that we cannot ascribe a strict correspondence to the degree of organization of a mental process and its usefulness for ego mastery, adaptational, or reality-testing activities. For example, in paranoia, problem-solving thought, with a high degree of inner logical consistency, can be utilized in the service of the id, while examples of the solution of difficult problems in dreams or in freely wandering reveries can be documented by numerous observations (Chapter 1; Hadamard, 1945; Poincaré, 1952). We need, it would seem, to use another coordinate to make the distinction between fantasy, imagination, and logical thinking meaningful.

The ego, as suggested by Hartmann (1939), does not deal with means alone but is also concerned with ends. He says, "The world of thought and the world of perception—both of which are among the ego's regulating factors and are elements of that adaptation process which consists of withdrawal for the purpose of mastery—need not always coincide. Perception and imagination orient us by means of spatial-temporal images. Thinking frees us from the immediate perceptual situation." And in another place, "The inner world and its functions make possible an adaptation process which consists of two steps: withdrawal from the external world and return to it with improved mastery. The fact that goals are not directly approached but reached by interpolated detours (means) is a decisive step in this evolution." These ego ends differ from those of the id in ways that are fundamental to all of our psychoanalytic concepts. By and large the ego ends of reality testing and adaptation are best served by organized thought, which we usually assign to the secondary process. These thought processes are characterized by their initial relationship to certain axiomatic postulates. They are accompanied by a subjective sense of being directed, *the direction being determined by the rule of exclusion of contradiction in causal sequences*. Imagination, on the other hand, while beginning with an axiom, is ready to abandon it for a trial period in order to examine the consequences of its antithesis or its negation. It also seems to differ from typical problem-solving thought in its readiness to admit "undirected" mental contents of a lower order of organization in which contradiction is not necessarily excluded, thus resembling fantasy in many of its characteristics. Its ends, however, are the extension of cognition rather than instinctual discharge. It appears to be better suited to the achievement of certain kinds of ego ends, where the data of experience are insufficient for typical problem-solving thought, or where speed in the handling of the data is of special importance.[1] If one prefers to call this "fantasy in the service of the ego" rather than "imagination," I can see no objection.[2] It is currently quite fashionable in the fields of both mathematics and modern physics to recognize the importance of this process in the advance of scientific theory. Bronowski (1958), for example, an eminent mathematician writing about creativity and scientific method, says,

> The man who proposes a theory makes a choice—an imaginative choice which outstrips the facts. The creative activity of science lies here in the process of induction. For induction imagines more than there is ground for and creates relations which, at bottom, can never be verified. Every induction is a speculation and it guesses at a unity which the facts present but do not strictly imply. To put the matter more formally; a scientific theory cannot be constructed from the facts by any procedure that can be laid down in advance, as if for a machine. To the man who makes the theory it may seem as inevitable as the ending of Othello must have seemed to Shakespeare. But the theory is inevitable only to him; it is his choice as a mind and as a person, among the many alternatives that are open to everyone.

An act of imagination is an important part of the psychoanalytic process both in the analyst and in the patient. It may be useful to examine some of the difficulties that may arise in the analytic process in terms of disturbances in the capacity for imagination, as special instances of those disorders that are grouped under the heading *ego defect*.

To a certain extent the role of imagination seems to be implicitly minimized in the teaching of analytic technique in order to emphasize not only the "scientific" aspects of analysis but also what is reproducible and transmissible. Respectability in the social sciences seems to demand the fiction of the strictly rational as well as a standardized pedagogical curriculum. One wonders if in this respect, as well as others, the social sciences lag behind the natural ones?

Some interpretations in the course of an analysis may be derived by the process of deductive logic. Most typically, however, they seem to be examples of an inductive or an imaginative process. Freud's emphasis on the attitude of "freely hovering attention" (Freud, 1912) in the analyst seems implicitly directed toward providing the optimal conditions for such a development.

The role of the patient's imagination in the analytic procedure has been more extensively studied than that of the analyst. Kris (1952), and later Beres (1951, 1957), for example, have indicated in several communications how a study of the psychodynamics of the artist's relationship with his audience can extend the understanding of the analytic process. The ideal interpretation for the patient is one that contains both the aesthetic immediacy of art and the insightful grasp of a scientific theory.

Among the great variety of nonverbal as well as verbal transactions between the analyst and the patient, imagination must play a large role. It is obviously never possible for either one to communicate more than a relatively small fraction of the total information that might be useful for the work of reconstruction. Many omissions must be filled in by an act of imagination on the part of one or the other. Kris (1951) says in this connection, "The infinite number of steps left to new decisions [i.e., in the process of interpretation] position between the familiar and the unexplored, the analyst can only trust the integrative capacities of his ego to guide his way." Although the optimal interpretation is often communicated with an economy of words, the patient's response in this fortunate circumstance indicates that an imaginative synthesis has gone on which likewise transcends his verbal acknowledgment of comprehension.

Thus imagination can be viewed as an ego function or constellation of ego functions in its own right. It is designed to fill the void of ambiguity with a new conceptual structure that can become the basis for further exploration of the inner or outer world. It must do this by being able to retain an equidistant position between external reality and illusion or psychic reality. The apprehension of object "invariance" permits this important state which is described below as "controlled illusion" and which is an important condition of analysis for both the patient and therapist. The following examples are some of the ways in which disturbances of the function of imagination may be encountered in the course of analysis. I have chosen a few familiar ones, most often seen in the more severe conditions of current psychoanalytic practice (see Stone, 1954). For ready, although rather crude, purposes of classification, they can be grouped under the headings of: (1) exaggerated concreteness or the literal attitude; (2) excessive generalization or the figurative attitude; and (3) alternations between the two. All three have as a common denominator an inability to deal constructively with ambiguity. A fourth less frequent source of resistance due to another variation in imaginative capacity is seen in unusually gifted individuals (Loomie, Rosen, and Stein, 1958) where the specialized quality of the patient's ideas may exclude the analyst from full participation in them. In this group of patients, a further source of resistance is often the result of the speed of the preconscious process which yields its end result to conscious awareness but not its intermediate steps. In the Univac operator referred to above, for example, one source of an inhibition in completing her thesis was the ability to comprehend the problem and arrive at the solution in almost a single operation. She had a recurrent fear, however, that someone would ask her to reproduce the intermediate steps which she would be unable to explain (Chapter 3).

Case 1

A young man with rather severe social anxiety understands the process of free association but cannot reconcile himself on one point. When he wants to know whether the analyst has read a certain book, or is in possession of certain other first-hand information, he must reject the counterquestion, "Why do you ask?" This, he claims, is not due to an unwillingness to proceed with his associations nor to a desire for economy in the expenditure of the energy involved in description. But rather a completely rational anxiety produced by his inability to know whether the analyst understands him from first-hand experience or must fill in the gaps produced by the failure of mutual overlapping experience through an act of his (the analyst's) imagination. On this point, he needs concrete information and cannot proceed *as if* the analyst did not have first-hand data. Further exploration of the problem reveals that this seemingly constructive desire to promote the analyst's understanding of all the nuances of his communication through a similar first-hand experience covers an irrational fear of the "unstructured" from which he has always sought to protect himself. During the administration of a Rorschach test some years before analysis, he had become so anxious that the testing procedure had to be discontinued. In overlapping first-hand impressions of people or things, the analyst might discover that something had escaped the patient's attention or had been subjectively distorted by him. This young man lived in a great dread of appearing naive. This had an important bearing on his social anxiety. As an adolescent, he had found it very difficult to "catch on" to jokes, particularly those that referred to something sexual. He was ashamed of this defect as he was of his lack of sexual experience and would cover up his failure to comprehend the joke in a similar fashion. On one occasion, after a particularly trying session characterized by repeated attempts to engage the therapist in a question-answering dialogue, the patient admitted that he had been summoning up the courage to ask the meaning of a cartoon that he had seen in a magazine in his dentist's waiting room. This depicted two nurses leaving a hospital operating room. The caption indicated that one of the nurses was saying (apparently referring to their patient who had just undergone an operation), "I would have sworn that she was a natural blond." This made no sense to my patient and made him feel hopelessly lacking in some essential intellectual faculty. The subsequent explanation of the joke revealed in further associations the patient's shocklike displeasure, covered by the affect of shame, not at the discovery of his own naiveté, but in its discovery by another. Thus the patient sought to protect himself from surprise, a passive experience, in the familiar manner of first turning it into an active one. It hardly need be anticipated that subsequent reconstruction of childhood experiences relating to scoptophilia indicated a characteristic reaction to the first experience of mutual exhibiting with a little girl at an early age. The response to the genital difference had the character of denial. It retained the more primitive concept of the existence of the phallus in both sexes while displacing the evidence of the missing part to a defect in the patient's own perception. Nor could the affect of shock in any way be recaptured by the patient in the memory of this experience. It seemed from further reconstruction that this affect had undergone an additional vicissitude and had become attached to the discovery of the defect in the patient's comprehension resulting from the original defensive reaction (i.e., his naivete). This could easily be recalled in connection with an experience around puberty in which he suddenly found himself being teased by a group of his friends for inadventently revealing that he had retained the idea that babies were born through the mother's anus.

Case 2

A young woman warded off most interpretations or even attempts to engage her interest in certain curious aspects of her own behavior with the phrases "Doesn't everybody?" or "Isn't this true of most people?" What she meant to convey by this was the idea that while the analyst's formulation was correct, it should be understood as a figure of speech with a generalized applicability. She had suffered from a childhood fear that she was unique and alone in her castrated condition. By ascribing an illusory quality to the interpretation, she was able to retain her identity with the group and thus protect her illusory penis.

Case 3

A third patient with a fetishistic perversion, a seemingly rather practical, middle-aged businessman, also interested in politics, was quite derisive toward certain kinds of interpretations. For example, following several dreams in which the President of the United States played a major role, it had been suggested that the ineffectuality which he appeared to attribute to the President might be a secret criticism of the analyst. As evidence of this possible connection, he was reminded that the building in which the analysis was taking place was called "The White House." The patient was quite ready to admit that he was often secretly critical without being able to express his criticism but he could not accept such an imaginative leap from President to analyst by way of their common association with a white house. He had distrusted ideas that developed in this way. He had distrusted modern nonrepresentational art. He said, "It allows people to imagine they understand it when they do not—It is like the 'Emperor's New Clothes.'" In a subsequent dream, he was on a stage playing a part opposite a character named Ophelia. During the whole performance he seemed to be floating so that his feet never touched the ground and while doing so, the patient experienced the severe height phobia which along with the fetishistic phenomena had originally brought him into analysis. In this dream, he equated imagination with madness and expressed the fear that he might be destroyed if the analyst's feet were not planted firmly on the ground. The derision of the analyst's imagination was also a projection and represented his fear of self-destruction through the wildness of his own imagination, like Ophelia. Some of this patient's business mistakes had been partly due to his own imaginative ideas prematurely carried into action and partly due to the increasing distraction of his seeking for perverse sexual outlets. Unlike the two previous patients, this patient at first used literal arguments to counter interpretations. Once he became aware of their relevancy, however, he would see all of his behavior in terms of the latest interpretation, losing sight completely of his former objections. It was now as if the previous attitude had never existed and could no longer be recalled or reexperienced. This obliteration interfered seriously with the process of "working through."

This patient, for example, as indicated above, could not imagine that he could ever be contemptuous of the therapist. When he finally became convinced that his chronic lateness was an expression of contempt, he himself interpreted lapses of various kinds as expressions of his latent deprecatory attitude. Once, when he was late for what appeared to be entirely external reasons, he insisted that it must have been due to his hostility. He resisted the suggested possibility that external factors may have played a decisive role on this occasion, and could not recall having once argued that circumstances beyond his control excluded the possibility that negative feelings were expressed by his failure to be punctual.

Discussion

In the description of the eighteen-month-old child with the recoverable toy in *Beyond the Pleasure Principle*, Freud (1923) comments that "above all" the child "never cried when his mother went out and left him even for hours at a time." He further remarks that "the meaning of the game was then not far to seek. It was connected with the child's remarkable cultural achievement—the forgoing of the satisfaction of an instinct—as the result of which he could let his mother go away without making a fuss. He made it right with himself, so to speak, by dramatizing the same kind of disappearance and return with the objects that he had at hand." One suspects that a more reciprocal relationship between the letting go of the mother and the game would have been stressed if Freud had been interested in the details of the evolution of the game rather than the part played by the observation in the development of his larger thesis.

If the process of imagination in its more advanced forms requires the relinquishment of a concept so that it can be actively reconstituted in a revised form (cf. Klein, 1959), then we might expect that certain concepts that are invested with instinctual need would show a variety of resistances to dissolution. In certain cases, their abandonment would provoke separation anxiety which would act as an obstacle to any productive imagination, at least in this particular area of thought. The opposite instance, in which the failure of any significant instinctual investment might be expected to keep the concept at too great a distance and thus unavailable to the process of intellectual recombination, must also be considered as an impediment to imagination.

Piaget indicates the nature of the conceptual transformations that free the "subjective" thought life of the child and transform it into the so-called real categories that make possible the feats of mentation of the adult (Inhelder and Piaget, 1958; Piaget, 1954). His description of the phases of this process leaves the impression of a strictly predetermined maturational unfolding in which only innate neural structures and the immediate influence of the environment are to be reckoned with. His account gives us no basis for explaining the temporary progressions and regressions of the process in the fully developed adult as well as the child, in response to affects, changes in personal object relations, and the vicissitudes of instinctual rhythms and tensions.

At this point, I would like to suggest a distinction between a sexual fantasy and a concept that is invested with instinctual cathexis. Most of what we ordinarily speak of as infantile sexual fantasies should more properly be called sexual "theories." In speaking of the "sexual researches of children," Freud (1905a) certainly implied that theories of concepts resulted from this primitive research. To call them fantastic is a retrospective judgment of the sophisticated adult. From the child's point of view, ideas concerning oral impregnation, anal birth and the like, are concepts arrived at by his own methods and instruments of observation. They may be the point from which the elaboration of more complex ideas, daydreams, images, inventions, stories or dramatizations begin, but in themselves they represent notions concerning anatomy and physiology which are the best available to the child at a given stage of his level of experience, ego maturation, and drive organization. This implies that such concepts are invested with phase-specific libidinal and aggressive cathexes. Thus, as with the external need object, a variety of factors involving the economics of drive, ego, and environmental organization can imprison or release the concept from its drive investment. This is inherent in the notion of both conflict and fixation. A release of a particular concept from its instinctual investment may allow its reorganization either regressively or progressively depending upon the direction of the changing economy of forces. It is in the process of the recombination of the elements of the disinstinctualized concept that imagination, according to the present hypothesis, can play its maximum role. This would be true both in the low-speed transformations of the maturational changes described by Piaget and the high-speed ones seen in such mental events as inspiration, illumination, or insight (Chapter 1).

Thus the basic pathology in which imagination can be expected to be most severely affected would be more akin to fixation than to other pathogenic processes. This may account for the poverty of imagination that appears to be such a widespread characteristic of certain types of preoedipal character disorders (particularly the depressive ones) where stereotypes of thought and limitation of the range of affect and behavioral responses are so striking.[3]

Of the patients briefly described above, the first case retained a need investment in the concept of the phallic female, an infantile theory that required support from his ego in the form of pseudonaiveté and denial. The second patient's self-esteem was intimately bound up with the possession of an illusory phallus. By making all concepts illusory, she was able to keep her own illusion from being disturbed. In the third case, magical omnipotence, with a predominantly phallic motif, played an important role. This patient protected his infantile concept of invulnerability by a repetitive acting out of the play with danger, thus chaining his imagination to need satisfying "practical" objects like money, in much the same way as the compulsive gambler. In all three cases, various levels of castration and separation anxiety were compounded to keep their imaginative capacities more or less anchored to rigid infantile theories that were treated as external need objects.

Where does the capacity to deal with object invariance fit into this dynamic view where imagination functions normally? The theory of play in its relationship to imagination is most important in this connection (Waelder, 1933; Greenacre, 1959). If Coleridge's "willing suspension of disbelief" is a necessary attitude for the artist's audience, one must go one step further to the active attitude of "let's make believe" for imaginative activity to proceed whether in its creative or more mundane forms. In imaginative play, a mobile cathectic energy is necessary which can shift back and forth between concept and process and between the representational and the illusory. It must keep simultaneous contact with reality and fantasy.[4] In the game situation (Peller, 1955), as in other forms of play, there is an implicit contract between the participants. This contract also has its analogue in the analytic situation and in a variety of other contexts in which imagination is required. It has been described for wit and humor (Freud, 1928; Wolfenstein, 1951) and for the artist and his public particularly in the form of "the dramatic illusion" and "aesthetic ambiguity" (Kris, 1952). This contract is basically the abandonment of the axiom of the exclusion of contradiction and the agreement to treat the game as simultaneously illusory and real until its denouement. If either party deviates from the contract, the game cannot proceed. Thus, the opponents in a chess game can unfold an infinite variety of permutations and combinations of the pieces as long as one participant or the other does not suddenly decide either that he is protecting a real king with real weapons (see Jones, 1931, on "The Problem of Paul Morphy") or, alternatively, that the royal symbol is only a piece of wood and need not be protected at all.[5]

The same agreement to suspend the rule of the exclusion of contradiction, thus remaining equidistant from reality and illusion, applies to the individual engaged in a purely personal act of imagination. This is seen, for example, in the development of new systems of mathematics such as the non-Euclidean geometries which begin with the "let's pretend" assumption that parallel lines can meet.

A prosaic example from the field of perception is the line drawing of a transparent cube in perspective on a plane surface. Such a figure requires an act of imagination of which we are largely unaware, in order to be seen as a three-dimensional abstraction and a three-dimensional representation is excluded by an act of make-believe. For a fairly large group of individuals, the loss of the "as if" aspect of this imaginative act and the disturbance of the controlled illusion can be demonstrated by an inability to transpose the position of the near and far surfaces at will. This should be possible if the contract to treat the figure as simultaneously really planar and illusorily solid is consistently maintained.

The discussion thus far has attempted to describe certain aspects of the process character of imagination, and some of the conditions that are unfavorable to its full development as a function of the ego. There has been an allusion to the role of anxiety in the active mastery of the passive experience of object loss. The ego's capacity for controlled illusion as an outgrowth of childhood play activities has been mentioned. No attempt has been made to discuss the drive contributions to the normal process of imagination. A final closing comment on the relationship of the ego to perceptual ambiguity and its role in the normal development of imagination, as well as in its inhibition, is indicated. This contribution comes not only from the controlled regression to archaic ego states, but also from the world of external objects and might be designated *metareality testing,* a special aspect of the development of cognition. One of the important aspects of the child's relationship to vanishing objects may be the idea of an extrasensory world. The maturation of the apparatuses of perception with increasing capacity for differentiation brings with it the discovery of objects, their attributes and relationships, where formerly there had been a void. This probably prepares the adult for the discovery of the physiologically "built-in" limitations of his sensory organs—"the more things in Heaven and on Earth" than Horatio's philosophy had ever apprehended. It portends a more sophisticated body image, as well as concept of space, time, matter, and energy than "practical" reality testing had initially achieved. It has given rise to and received its final confirmation from the development of science and the instruments which transform extrasensory stimuli into those that can be registered within the ordinary range. The process of reality testing in this ultimate sense must include an expectation of a reality beyond the space-time horizons of current cognition. (*Cognition* is used here as a term distinct from *perception* with the implications of "knowing" in the former as distinguished from something more akin to "registering" in the latter.) It would seem likely that in the controlled illusion of the audience in the theater, or the art gallery, or of the patient on the couch, there is not only the opportunity to recathect, in relative safety, the unconscious object representations of his childhood in the external world, but also the expectation of finding another dimension of reality behind the illusion that holds his attention.[6] It is in this aspect of the process of reality testing that imagination receives a significant impetus and often fulfills an important promise.

This suggests another genetic factor in the etiology of disturbances of imagination. One might conceive that in the genesis of the reality-testing activities of the ego, there would be room for a wide variety of patterns of discovery and treatment of ambiguous percepts (i.e., of objects in the process of appearing or disappearing). This would be due partly to the influence of the environment as well as to variations in innate ego structure and in the strength of the scoptophilic drives. Sully (1910) says, in this connection, "I have treated the myths of children as a product of pure imagination, of the impulse to realize in vivid images what lies away from and above the world of sense." In assessing the role of imagination in cognition, it is not without some importance that Jonathan Swift, for example, writing in 1710, has the Houyhnhms discover that Mars has two moons, thus anticipating the astronomers by almost a century, nor that Jules Verne's Nautilus with a limitless source of power preceded the atomic submarine of the same name by a like interval of time. I would not suggest the operation of any mystical premonition in such works of science fiction, but merely the increased opportunity for anticipating an important discovery that comes with imaginative transcending of immediate space-time boundaries.

It is of considerable importance for the analytic process to consider whether there is such a thing as "pure imagination" in the sense of the projection of an inner psychic process free from an immediate perceptual input. Certainly, the so-called projective psychological tests do not elicit a pure projection. The figures in these tests consist of a hierarchy of graphic objects ranging from the fully representational to the amorphous. The Rorschach ink blots, which have special status in this field, are not a blank screen but rather ambiguous figures, as if in the process of emerging or vanishing. They offer the possibility for the subject to add certain elements from his own reservoir of images for the synthesis of a new image which is partly project and partly introject. Their special utility is that they invite neither reality testing nor hallucinosis, but rather the condition of controlled illusion. Fisher and Paul (1959) (using Poetzl's technique) have shown that the same effects can be achieved by reducing the time factor tachistoscopically in perception. The patient's imaginative reconstruction of what he sees under these conditions of ambiguity is related *both* to the stimulus and to his own individuality. It is a transformed image and not a completely new one. Fisher and Paul (1959) have convincingly shown that the invariant elements of the subliminal percept along with the invariant features of the patient's unconscious conflicts are demonstrable in the new image that emerges either in the subsequent dream or as a product of creative imagination in his drawings of what he imagines that he has perceived.

The analytic transference is a process that must be seriously reviewed in this same context. We are prone to write and think of the anonymous analyst as a transference "screen." It has been traditional to speak of the analyst as the screen upon which the patient projects his transference fantasies. This concept, it seems, needs considerable modification and refinement. The analyst, through his anonymity, provides a relatively ambiguous figure, but not a blank screen. He has gender, clothing, speech, appearance on greeting and leave-taking, mannerisms, and aesthetic preferences which his surroundings reveal in varying degree. Unless the patient is psychotic, it is likely that he elaborates upon an ambiguous percept when he refers to the analyst. It would seem that this belongs more properly to the process of imagination than to pure fantasy. It is noteworthy that most speculations concerning the analyst contain varying degrees of projection of attributes of infantile objects combined with undistorted observations of the analyst's characteristics. It is often a matter of nice judgment whether to begin with the former or the latter for the more telling interpretation. Transference fantasies are thus really controlled illusions in which the participants enter into the same contract as in play. They are simultaneously real and illusory in varying degree. Another source of disturbance of imagination in the analytic patient that must be continuously reexamined is the iatrogenic one. This would result from the propensity of the analyst to treat the imaginings of the patient, when they refer to him, as if they were pure projections. In the same way they can often be blocked in the opposite manner by too much personal extra-analytic contact between patient and analyst such as may occur in some didactic analyses or in the common practice of certain "deviationist" schools. In the latter instance, with the shift from illusion to reality, there is a loss of the necessary degree of ambiguity for the optimal operation of the imaginative process. It may be useful to view the resistance produced by "acting out" on either the patient's or the analyst's part from this point of view, i.e., to consider that it is not only a substitution of action for verbalization but an abrogation of the "controlled illusion contract" in so far as it denies the illusion by making it happen in the real world. An opposing variation to this form of breach of contract occurs in the patient who produces only stories and anecdotes on the couch instead of associations. This is an invitation for both patient and analyst to live vicariously in the patient's illusory account of reality, thus implicitly denying that it also has an existence in the real world in its own right. The subject is a large one and deserves a more thorough consideration. Beres (1957) has suggested, in his review of the role of imagination in psychoanalytic theory, that many problems of psychic functioning can be better understood when viewed in terms of this process; problems of psychoanalytic technique should also be included in this category. Finally, the amazing reflexivity of imagination and its capacity for intuitive understanding of even its own devices must be recognized. The astronomer Johannes Kepler, several centuries ago, wrote: "The roads by which men arrive at their insights into celestial matters seem to me almost as worthy of wonder as those matters themselves" (Kepler, 1958).

To summarize: imagination is an important synthetic process of the ego based upon its early experience with the disappearance and reappearance of objects. Image formation is a device which serves, among other purposes, the active mastering of object loss so that the object and the "course of its displacements" (Piaget) remain under the control of the ego and can be manipulated as a psychic reality even when they are no longer available to the field of immediate perception. The later development of imagination in which concepts and their transformations replace images cannot take place without the development of object constancy and the notion of invariance. Since the progression from earlier stages of image formation to later stages of concept formation requires a synthesis of projected mental contents (fantasy) with an introjection of percepts of external objects, the capacity for controlled illusion and a special method for handling ambiguity are necessary ingredients of the mature process. In the psychopathology of imagination, especially as it is encountered in a variety of analytic resistances, the analyst's interest is in those external and internal factors which interfere with the patient's equidistance from illusion and reality. He is also concerned with the variety of abrogations of the mutual contract between analyst and patient (as in children's games) to exclude the contradictions implied by treating both the idea and the object as simultaneously real and illusory.

Notes

1. An analogue to this aspect of imagination's function can be drawn from the problem of weather prediction. In former times, although the data for an accurate twenty-four-hour weather prediction was available to meteorologists, it was necessary to solve a system of nonlinear partial differential equations to accomplish this. With ordinary digital computers this was a seven- to fourteen-day task which made the solution obsolete when it was finally obtained. With the newer computers the same results can be obtained in two hours, thus making it possible to put the data to practical use.

2. I am indebted to Dr. David Beres for calling the following passage from one of Keats's letters to my attention: ". . . what quality went to form a man of achievement especially in literature, and which Shakespeare possesses so enormously—I mean *negative capability*, that

is, when a man is capable of being in uncertainties, mysteries, doubts, without any irritable reaching after fact and reason."

3. This formulation does not account for those gifted and imaginative individuals who show varying degrees of borderline psychopathology. In Chapter 3 it is suggested that unlike the stereotypes of primitive "object-bound" characters, the "preoedipal" phenomena in these individuals represent a regressive use of their talents, thus placing them in a category which should be viewed in a different diagnostic framework.

4. See Winnicott's (1953) discussion of "transitional objects" and "transitional phenomena."

5. Peller's (1955) distinction between "play" and "games" should be noted in this connection.

6. It is of considerable interest in this connection that there is convincing experimental evidence indicating that an individual may be able to describe many details of a stimulus from an image that he was unable to describe in a direct report upon the stimulus from its percept (see Klein, 1959, and Fisher and Paul, 1959).

CHAPTER TWELVE

The Psychology of Style

"Le style est l'homme même"—Buffon, 1855

Although the literature of art history, criticism, and aesthetics deals extensively with problems of style in many forms and contexts, psychoanalysis has yet to concern itself with a "psychology of style" (Kris, 1952).

The present study has no expectation of filling this gap in the understanding of style or of dealing with the enigmatic multidisciplinary problem of artistic style, except in so far as some aspects of it are relevant to the current issue. This is rather a preliminary attempt to define the general problem of style, to explore it as a feature of personality for psychoanalytic study, and to suggest some areas in which psychoanalysis may make a contribution to this theme and reap some benefit, both practical and theoretical, from so doing.

An attempt will be made to show that style is best defined as a progressing synthesis of form and content in an individually typical

Many stimuli for this chapter have come from participation in the work of the Gifted Adolescent Project of the Treatment Center of the New York Psychoanalytic Institute. This project was originally organized by Ernst Kris with the aid of a grant from the Arthur Davison Ficke Foundation. Numerous discussions with other colleagues who participated in this work (Loomie, Rosen, and Stein, 1958) have had much to do both with the urge to define the problem and with many of the ideas contained herein. It is hoped that a more extended and evolved statement on style and special talents may ultimately emerge from the combined efforts of those who have engaged in this project.

manner and according to the individual's sense of "appropriateness." Style is conceived as an expression of the organizing function[1] of the ego, which may display itself in this process in an unusually accessible form. Each individual style has an invariant aspect which may largely be determined by characteristic uses of ambiguity. The suggestion that a study of style may help in the elucidation of some technical problems in the analysis of certain obscure resistances is also discussed. The way in which such a study may be useful in understanding the largely unsystematized "cues" that are utilized in the diagnosis of borderline states is also suggested. This is not an attempt to formulate any new concepts, but merely a view of some well-known clinical phenomena offered from a different vantage point.

If *style* is not a primal word in the English language, it does at least partake of the antithetical properties which Freud (1910b) ascribes to such words in root languages. Derived as it is from the Latin *stylus,* with one end sharpened to cut into wax and the other blunt for erasing, its fusion of opposites, as well as the origin of its major connotation in the area of writing and linguistic expression, becomes apparent. Thus a composite dictionary definition of style is "the mode of expressing thought in language, oral or written, especially such use of language as exhibits the spirit and faculty of the writer." Only secondarily is it defined as "the distinctive or characteristic mode of presentation, construction, or execution in any art, employment, or product." Those aspects of the word that refer to the unique or individual are summed up as "the quality which gives distinctive excellence to expression, *consisting especially in the appropriateness and choiceness of relation between subject matter, medium, and form and individualized by the temperamental characteristics of the creator.*" But *style,* particularly in its use as a verb, has a directly opposite connotation. Here it means to entitle, term, name, denominate, or characterize. This aspect of the word merges with the notion of "stylized," where to conform to a style means to imitate, conventionalize, or reduce to a stereotype, thus eradicating those deviant aspects of the form or subject matter which might differentiate the specific from the generic. The two meanings of *style* are fused in certain activities of man. A style of handwriting, for example, is specific for each individual and yet utilizes the conventional "stylized" characters of the alphabet for its medium of expression. It is through such activities that personal style in its most ubiquitous sense can best be observed. It is in this sense, i.e., the individual's use of a conventional form for the expression of his own thoughts or feelings to a recipient who participates in the completing of the message, that the term is used in the ensuing discussion.

Since Plato, the theory of art has included various doctrines which have implied a correspondence between some aspect of the personality of the artist and the nature of his product. Even a brief digest of this vast literature would be quite beyond the scope of this paper.[2] The literary mind seems to have been particularly stimulated by this problem. The romantic period of art theory and criticism has been intrigued by the "style is the man" thesis, but has usually sought to identify style exclusively with form, or at other times with content alone. The oversimplified equations produced by the separation of the component parts made the thesis offensive to its critics. Thus a rather naive dissertation read to the Royal Irish Academy in 1793 by the Rev. Robert Burrowes bore the ornate title "On Style in Writing Considered with Respect to Thoughts and Sentiments as Well as Words and Indicating the Writer's Peculiar and Characteristic Disposition, Habits and Powers of Mind" (Abrams, 1958). Samuel Johnson gives an instance of the acerbity produced in a man of letters by the naive equating of an author's manifest life with his works. This practice reminded him of having heard of a lady who remarked that she could gather from a certain author's poetry three parts of his character, namely, that he was a great lover, a great swimmer, and rigorously abstinent. Johnson found the observation "ill timed." He could state on reliable authority that the man in question "knew not any love but that of sex; had never been in cold water in his life; and indulged himself in all luxury that came within his reach" (Abrams, 1958).

In psychoanalytic writing, the suggestion that style can best be studied by "reversing the separation of the unique from the conventional" has been made by Kris (1952). He says, "Instead of accepting the division of form and content, maintained in many areas of the history and criticism of art, psychoanalytic orientation suggests the value of establishing their interrelationship." Concerning Freud's study of Leonardo da Vinci (1910a) he says, for example, that Freud

> had been able to enter deeply into the secrets of a man of genius. Determinants of Leonardo's scientific interest, his obsessional and frequently self-defeating working habits could be plausibly traced to infantile imprints. The child raised by two mothers, the peasant mother and the wife of his father in whose house he grew up, was stimulated to unite, almost for the first time in Italian painting, the Virgin and Saint Anne with the infant Christ. Unity between the three was established not only by gesture; they seem to merge into each other since they are inscribed into a pyramidal configuration. By similar devices, Leonardo created in several of his paintings compositions which exercised considerable influence on the development of the art of his time. The phenomenon investigated has thus been approached from two sides, the life history of the artist and the solution of the artistic problem: one can demonstrate the interaction of an incentive in the individual's life history with the stringencies of an artistic problem, determined in Leonardo's case by the development of Italian painting.

The fusion of such opposing features as a consequence of the synthetic function of the ego is also discussed by Nunberg (1931), Hartmann (1939) and as part of Waelder's (1936) concept of the "principle of multiple function." Hartmann describes artistic creation as "the prototype of a synthetic solution" (1939). Psychoanalytic literature, however, is singularly lacking in a unified definition of the organizing function, its genesis, development, and the effects of disturbances in its activity. Sharp distinctions are not always made between developmental and maturational forces, on the one hand, which promote the organization of the ego's apparatuses into new structures and systems on a more or less stable basis and, on the other, those active processes of the ego (at whatever stage in its development) which form combinations and recombinations of various psychic elements into new images, ideas, or affects, for more or less temporary purposes. Nor, in this latter sense of the term, do we differentiate the singular or episodic manifestations of the organizing function, as in inspirational phenomena for example, from its continuing, more stable, and repetitive manifestations, such as, for instance, a style of thinking. One such episodic mental event is fantasy. "Fantasy—not just in the sense of a talent for making new combinations, but also in the sense of symbolic pictorial thought—can be fruitful even in scientific thinking. . . . Fantasy may (also) fulfill a synthetic function by provisionally connecting our needs and goals with possible ways of realizing them" (Hartmann, 1939). Dreaming, memory, problem-solving activities, and many complex affective experiences are also psychic events in which various elements are selectively sorted and combined according to unique personal propensities. The function of differentiation and synthesis is thus ubiquitous in all of them. Such mental phenomena are, however, often transitory and frequently nonreproducible. They are often themselves found in nebulous states of higher molar organization. Although the analytic process is largely concerned with mental events of such transitory character, it requires preparation and an alertness for unusually propitious moments to observe the organizing process in action through them. More often it is necessary to reduce such mental contents retrospectively into their original components. Style, although it may manifest itself in transitory as well as in continuous phenomena, is by definition one of the most constant aspects of the expressive activity of the individual. Here the organizing function may be kept under more or less constant scrutiny with temporal comparisons of its variations and evolution. Furthermore, since volition and external stimuli are less involved in the style of expression than in either its form or subject matter, it is more likely to betray the autonomous and unconscious features of the synthetic function than other aspects of the individual's communication. This emphasis upon the organizing function should not suggest any notion of exclusiveness of agency. The participation of an audience in the final product as an essential feature of the process will be discussed presently.

Implicit in the present definition of style is the characteristic of invariance (Chapter 11). This consists in the peculiar recognizable or identifiable feature of a particular style that is so difficult to denote. It is the feature that remains a constant part of the activity or its product throughout a series of transformations that may otherwise affect the continuity of either its form or its subject matter. Even when styles undergo evolutionary development or involution, the invariant aspect[3] remains, so that the individuality or hallmark of its origin is retained. The detection of forgery or imitation in works of art, for example, depends to a large extent for its reliability upon this phenomenon. Discontinuities and disintegrations of style are typified by the abrupt disappearance of the invariant feature, although apparent similarities of form and content may remain in the subsequent activity. Kris (1952) and Pappenheim, for example, studied the productions of a schizophrenic artist who had been an accomplished architectural designer and sculptor. During the patient's psychosis his drawings continued to suggest the draughtsman's skill, and the content remained largely architectural but with a highly personal meaning. The patient referred to them as "written drawings" in contrast to his previous work. His interest was directed exclusively to their content. One gains the impression from the reproductions of these sketches that he retained a continuity of subject matter with his prepsychotic state in his "sphera" columns and sculptor's figures, but that the regressive withdrawal had produced a complete change in the manner of their synthesis with the formal features of his draftsmanship, and a consequent discontinuity of his style.

The development of a manageable notational system is one of the problems that confronts a study of individual invariance in style. Until such a system is available within the framework of psychological discourse it will be difficult to know whether this feature can be described in terms of the vernacular of current characterology or whether style in expressive activity reveals fundamental aspects of human personality in the manner postulated, for example, by the students of graphology. Nor will it be possible to determine whether the expressive activities of the individual in all media have a style which is consistent throughout or unique for each one. Many interesting problems await psychoanalytic investigation in this area, in which guidance and aid should be sought from the humanities, from clinical psychology, and from other ancillary disciplines in our own field.

In the analytic process itself, stylistic phenomena are most frequently observable in the individual variations of speech, mimetic expression, manners, dress, and less frequently in writing. On relatively rare occasions artistic or manufactured products of the patient's creative activities are available. Unfortunately the direction of the analyst's interests, the usual focus of his attention, and notational inadequacies hamper adequate communication of analytic observations and investigations of these matters. Most important, however, in the relative neglect of style as an object of study in the individual patient, are some of the demands of psychoanalytic technique itself. The analyst listens to his patient with the ultimate hope of being able to understand those aspects of the patient's unconscious mental contents which produce his symptoms. For this purpose he alternately observes the content of the patient's associations or the form in which they are communicated. In the latter case form is usually treated as an alternative conveyor of content, be it in its aspect of defense or direct expression of need or wish. Thus if the patient changes languages in the course of free association, we may ask him what the change in linguistic form means to him in order to elicit further information in a personal context. The most ready response of the patient, however, is usually that the second language is more *appropriate* to the expression of the idea that is in his mind, thus serving a stylistic consideration, whatever else it may denote.

If style is the product of the synthetic fusion of content and form according to a guiding sense of the "appropriate," then it would be expected to disappear in the reductionism of the laboratory of analysis, at least as an object for scrutiny by the investigator.

The term *appropriateness* in the previous definition of style requires some elaboration. This characteristic may seem to be more relevant to the problem of artistic style. In the present discussion, however, the assumption is made that all individuals consciously or unconsciously choose certain media and forms to express the subject matter of their mental lives, and that these are more or less appropriate within a wider range of variation from an ideal than is usually permitted by art criticism or strict aesthetic value judgements. *Appropriateness* and *suitability* have different connotations in this connection. The suitability of a given formal medium for a particular subject matter is largely determined by the adaptability or "tricks of refraction" (Pater, 1905) of the medium to what the individual wishes to express. Thus prosaic language and graphic diagrams may be most suitable for the expression of involved ideas concerning, for example, the construction of a machine; paint and canvas may suit visual images, and so forth. Synaesthetic artistic experiments such as a "dance ballad" may cross the boundaries of the usual standards of suitability without being inappropriate. The standards of suitability are largely externally determined in this sense by the properties of media. *Appropriateness,* however, has affective overtones. It is concerned with control of the formal aspects of expression so that they remain within the confines of communicability and bear a relevance to a total situational context. This is largely an internally conditioned phenomenon which is a composite of many determinants, among which early object relations and later cultural influences play important roles. Cultural-historical influences determine the styles of eras, social groups, and nations, as well as of individuals. By way of incorporation and identification, these global styles may simultaneously partly determine both the form and the content of an individual style.

In the case of the artist, the "situational context" or the "reality" in which he creates a style exists, according to Kris (1952), "in the restricted sense of immediate need and material environment [and in] the extended sense of the structure of the problem which exists while the artist is creating, the historical circumstances in the development of art itself, which limit some of his work, determine in one way or another his modes of expression, and thus constitute the stuff with which he struggles in creation." In a similar but less self-conscious sense an ordinary man also struggles with immediate needs, the exigencies of a material environment, and his own historical circumstances. Within this context his limited personal acts of self-expression can be viewed as more or less stylistically appropriate even when intended as mundane interpersonal communication devoid of aesthetic considerations. These characteristic modes of combining form and content with varying degrees of appropriateness are the signatures of the ordinary man's style in a manner similar to the artist's.

Thus a sense of appropriateness implies a process of selection and combination, a process in which the synthetic function of the ego is decisively involved. It should be reemphasized that considerable confusion as well as oversimplification may result from the too ready equation of individual style in ordinary activities with creative style in the arts. In the latter one must assume not only a greater intensity of conscious awareness and mastery of stylistic considerations but a larger number of determinants which have varying degrees of influence upon it and which must be taken into consideration in understanding the end product. Thus, not only individual, cultural-historical factors and special "stringencies" for each of the arts, but also a quality best described as "economy of energy expenditure" must be considered among the many facets of this problem. In regard to the latter feature, Schiller has said that an artist may be known more by what he omits than what he includes. Although it is the intention of this discussion to maintain a distinction between artistic style and the style of the ordinary activities of an individual, it seems possible to use the results of artistic creation for illustrative examples of some of the problems of style that have a more general application. Selma Fraiberg (1957), for instance, gives an excellent example of the selection of form as an optimal vehicle for content in her paper "Kafka and the Dream." The effect of her separation of the elements of his style illustrates the loss of the invariant quality when the synthetic product is reduced to its parts so that we are no longer left with the sense of its uniqueness.

It was apparently Franz Kafka's conscious purpose to utilize his nocturnal dreams for literary creation. He kept extensive records of his dreams in notebooks, and it is easy to trace the source of many of his works as a direct borrowing from these records. In discussing Kafka's style, Fraiberg points out that there are significant problems in conveying the uncanny aspects of the dream world and its imagistic content in literary form. "Kafka," she says,

> did not trouble himself at all with the mechanical problems of entering the dream world. He found an easy solution to the problem of the language barrier. He simply walked through it. . . . Since the uncanny is not a quality of the dream itself but derives from an impairment of an ego faculty, that of reality testing, a narrative which attempts to simulate the experience of dreaming or to evoke the "uncanniness" of the dream must deceive the critical and judging faculties of the ego through a prose form which apparently sustains logic and belief at the same time that it affirms the delusion. The ideal prose for this treatment is everyday speech, a factual narration in simple declarative sentences. The narration of events and visions from

> a night world in the ordinary accustomed prose of waking life produces exactly that sense of dissolving reason which makes reality a dream and the dream a reality, the essence of the quality of uncanniness.

Can the same effect, she asks, be achieved through an experiment upon language itself? "By abandoning the patterns of everyday speech, the writer can introduce phrasing and rhythms which recall the fluidity and merging of primary-process thought. The dream can be taken as the model for bold invention and license in language." Fraiberg thinks that such experiments have rarely produced important results. It may be that she neglects the opposite cases where the everyday banality of the subject matter can safely be communicated with "experiments upon the language itself" as, say, in the case of Joyce, but this is a matter for the experts in literary criticism to resolve. In any case, although Fraiberg gives a fine analytic description of his literary technique, the unmistakable style of Franz Kafka cannot be conveyed by his use of narrative speech in "simple declarative sentences." Such a formal determinant would scarcely distinguish him from a great many others who choose or are limited by other considerations to such a medium of expression. Nor can one imagine that the recounting of a dream in simple declarative statements is necessarily uncanny or productive of a strong sense of the individuality of the narrator. Something in the fusion of the two, as accomplished by Kafka and no other writer, must be the feature which is sought for in the "style" of his work.

We are disturbed in an exactly opposite sense by the attempt of George Meredith (1888) to describe the style of Thomas Carlyle. Meredith makes no attempt to reduce Carlyle's style to its elements. The attempt is global and is characterized by the free utilization of subjective metaphorical images to achieve his purpose. He says Carlyle had

> a style resembling either early architecture or utter dilapidation, so loose and rough it seemed; a wind-in-the-orchard style, that tumbled down here and there an appreciable fruit with uncouth bluster; sentences without commencements running to abrupt endings and smoke, like waves against a sea wall, learned dictionary words giving a hand to street slang, and

> accents falling on them haphazard, like slant rays from driving clouds; all the pages in a breeze, the whole book producing a kind of electrical agitation in the mind and joints.

Here, for all its poetry, is an overemphasis on another feature of the synthesis that is alluded to by the formal definition of style when it is averred that style is the quality that gives distinctive excellence to the product. Since "distinctive excellence" is an aesthetic value judgement, it must refer to the subjective response of the observer, to the stimulus that emanates from the stylist. This may be a feature that forms a bridge between the problem of artistic style and style in the ordinary sense. Thus it is suggested that the response of the observer, so clearly implied in Meredith's description of Carlyle's style, is also fused with the synthetic product to give it its distinctive characteristics, in much the same manner that the Rorschach blot can be said to derive meaning from the patient's percept. In this sense one may anticipate the possibility that the artist and the art critic are an inseparable unity whose functions are reciprocal and interdependent rather than antagonistic. Kris (1952) implies this in his discussion of aesthetic ambiguity when he describes the aesthetic response of the audience projected into a work of art as an essential feature of the product and one which becomes fused with it and is reprojected as one of its essential components (see also Gombrich, 1960).

The indissolubility of form and content in the formation of a style is illustrated by Strunk and White (1959) in an elementary treatise for students of English literature. They cite the profound effect upon style of a small change in word sequence. Quoting the following from Thomas Wolfe, "Quick are the mouths of earth and quick the teeth that fed upon this loveliness," they propose this change in the word order: "The mouths of earth are quick and the teeth that fed upon his loveliness are quick too." "What was poetic and sensuous," they say "has now become prosy and wooden; instead of the secret sounds of beauty we are left with the simple crunch of mastication." The change, however, is not merely in form with consequent alteration in style. An insidious change is manifest in the content as well. The shift in emphasis for the reader from "loveliness" to "chewing," a result of the diminished ambiguity of the statement, no less than the change in word order, is responsible for the transmutation of poetry into a macabre prose.

It can be postulated that if all style is not necessarily "artistic," then all responses to style need not necessarily be aesthetic ones. But some response can be assumed even if it be a mere recognition of its individuality. It is possible that just as in the projected synthesis of the aesthetic response, this observing act of recognition is also an essential feature of nonartistic style—a collaboration in effect between the producer and the observer. Thus to the original suggestion that personal style is a product of individual mental contents amalgamated with the formal conventions of certain media must be added the element of meaningful collaborative response from another individual. How are these three elements related in terms of the direction of libidinal energies and object relations? Psychic events, which constitute the content of style, require a narcissistic investment of the self in terms of self-awareness and self-observation. Little formal structuring of these events is necessary if the purpose is merely to catch elements of the psychic stream as it goes by. The formal conventions of expressive media (e.g., the English language or the chromatic scale) are socially and historically determined. They are object-directed and make it possible to translate the images and "inner speech" of self-awareness into a form in which they can be communicated to others. These formal conventions also represent, particularly in recordable media, a contact with the past (and future) of the race and thus a bridge to a continuity of human experience. Walter Pater in his "Essay on Style" (1905) describes both the limits and the challenge thus imposed:

> For the material in which [the writer] works is no more a creation of his own than the sculptor's marble. Product of a myriad of various minds and contending tongues, compact of obscure and minute associations, a language has its own abundant and often recondite laws, in the habitual and summary recognition of which scholarship consists. A writer full of a matter he is before all things anxious to express, may think of those laws, the limitations of vocabulary, structure and the like, as a restriction, but if a real artist will find in them an opportunity. His punctilious observance of the proprieties of his medium will diffuse through all he writes a general air of sensibility of refined usage. . . . He will feel the obligation not of the laws only but of those affinities, avoidances, those mere

> preferences of his language which through the associations of literary history have a part of its nature, prescribing the rejection of many a neology, many a license and many a gipsy phrase. . . ."

Thus the translation from purely personal content into a conventional form imposes a challenge and an opportunity, but also a penalty. The full extent of the individual idea is to some extent tailored and curtailed by the very fact of its being made articulate; while the formal medium in accommodating the idea must also undergo some degree of distortion so that it no longer conforms with absolute rigor to the original abstract ideal. The synthesis and mutual accommodations of form and content into a style thus requires simultaneous contact with the self, the inner world of psychic events and the object or outer world of human society. This simultaneous contact between the inner and outer world must also sense the appropriate place of the one in the other. Another consideration in the appropriate selection of form for content is determined by the needs of the object of the communication. Just as ambiguity beyond certain limits disturbs the reception of meaning by offering too great a number of possible interpretations, so too an excessively explicit message limits the recipient's participation in the process to mere registration and excludes him from the creative act of the completion of meaning by the resolution of ambiguity. It is this feature that is reflected in the appropriateness of form to content, considered by the aestheticians to be the essence of stylistic distinction, and in the present context to be an integral aspect of the synthetic function of the ego.

This would suggest that a disintegration or failure of integration of a style in ordinary expressive activities may be a measure of disturbance of the synthetic function and an indicator of ego defect. From the foregoing we should expect such stylistic deficits to be evident in one of several directions. For example, what is expressed may be so personalized that it more or less overwhelms the formal aspects of the medium of expression. In such a case what is produced may be amorphous and devoid of social communicability. Rather than of style we talk in such extreme cases of eccentricity or mannerism. Extravagant examples such as hebephrenic neology and the facial grimacing and bizarre posturing of the catatonic form a continuum with the more subtle personalized productions of "borderline" individuals which merely overrun the boundaries of the permissible range of deviation in formal conventions. Or the investment in the conventional restrictions and stringencies may develop to such a degree that what is expressed loses any characteristic that would distinguish its individual origin. The cliché is an excellent example of this. Stein (1958) has described its defensive use in the analytic process. He suggests that the individual who habitually talks in clichés has a disturbance of ego function: "Such activity," says Stein, "is an indication of disturbed object relations, isolation, and hostility, as well as the use of words for magic rather than information." In other instances, where the formal characteristics of expression overwhelm the personal, we become aware of rigidity, boredom, and banality. Finally, it is possible to distinguish a deterioration in style in which both the formal elements and the personal content appear to be preserved but inappropriately combined.[4]

In regard to the evaluation of various kinds of borderline phenomena, Stone (1954) has implicitly suggested the importance of data on style. He says, "We need . . . detailed observation of the patient's thought processes and language expression, and an opportunity to observe his postural, gait, voice and mimetic reactions. Certainly in these modalities the patient may reveal to the sensitive observer psychotic fragments from a descriptive point of view."

It is not infrequent that obscure resistances in analysis are best approached by attention to the style of the patient's communication rather than through an attempt to analyze the defenses that may appear in it. Such global approaches to resistance are well-known devices and have been described as "character armour" by W. Reich (1949) and "personal myths" by E. Kris (1956). Such technical devices remain, however, largely intuitive and unsystematized. Consider from the point of view of "stylistic defenses" these phenomena might be categorized under the headings *overemphasis on content*, *overemphasis on form*, and *inappropriateness of subject matter to form.*

1. *Overemphasis on Content.* For example, a young lawyer misused the conventional requirements of speech in the analytic

process to convey his ideas in a curiously disjointed manner. He spoke rapidly with a display of rather passionate feelings about certain subjects. His tone was oratorical and better suited to slogans than to conveying personal information. Other matters were passed over quickly in muffled tones as if they were brief asides of minor dramatis personae, scarcely relevant to the main stream of the dramatic plot. The total effect was to evoke a sense of confusion in the listener similar to that produced by certain clever entertainers who are able with minor distortions of language (a species of "double talk") to raise a doubt whether the listener's powers of comprehension have failed or the speaker is talking nonsense. It was an excellent example of a highly personalized style, bordering upon the eccentric with little attention to the formal elements of syntax. It gradually became apparent that many of the significant items were usually contained in the vague asides. Confrontation with a description of the total effect of his productions brought associations from the patient to his father, who had been a clever politician in a local political machine. He had been a glib spellbinder in an era when dissenting hecklers who asked embarrassing questions of the man on the platform were forcibly ejected from the hall. A great deal of useful information lay behind the device. Its immediate purpose was to discourage the analyst from asking questions that would have led to the patient's official malfeasance, so to speak, in withholding certain facts about his financial assets.

2. *Overemphasis on Form.* Another patient, a woman of middle age, spoke for many weeks in a matter-of-fact, objective manner about singularly banal and inconsequential matters, such as the time her husband had left for the office in the morning, when he had returned the previous evening for dinner, and reports of his meetings with various business associates during the day. Once in recording a dream it became apparent that the temporal spacing of the words was at what reporters call diction speed. When it was suggested that the patient was telling "all the news that was fit to print" with the "objectivity" of an honest reporter, she agreed. When urged, however, to editorialize on the news of the day it was discovered that the patient had indeed once been interested in a newspaper career. Her objective reportorial style hid her suspicions

and deep distress over the circumstantial evidence that her husband was having an affair. The intimate subject matter of her dread was implicit in, but completely obscured by, the formality of her communication.

3. *Inappropriate Synthesis.* Overpersonalized and overformalized communications are less difficult to distinguish. The inappropriate combinations of form and content are often more difficult to perceive but no less significant in forming clinical estimates of the severity of ego distortion. Psychoanalytic technique when applied according to its established tenets provides a greater opportunity for the emergence of this kind of disturbance than other less structured psychotherapeutic methods. It provides within its context a set of formal conventions of its own, so to speak, within which content can be assimilated synthetically into a style. It may be useful to consider the familiar defense of "acting in" as an example of stylistic inappropriateness. One such patient, treated in the Gifted Adolescent Project and reported in Chapter 3, was a young man with unusual musical and mathematical gifts. His chief complaint was his shyness and inability to ask a girl for a date. The word *love* was intensely embarrassing to him and was assiduously avoided even as an indirect reference. Much of the inappropriateness of his manner consisted of various "acting in" defenses. One of these consisted of a disguised guessing game in the treatment. This was characterized by the production of a series of ideas designed to test the analyst's level of comprehension of certain abstruse subjects by his response to them. This had its counterpart in the patient's effort at one time to use his gifts for musical composition to write an encoded musical fugue which combined his mathematical and musical talents, to convey a cryptic love message to a girl who was a fellow music student. A similar inappropriateness was implied in some of his mathematical work. This patient's only sibling had been born precisely on the same day of the same month as himself; he was twelve years the patient's junior. A great deal of the patient's time which might have been spent in original mathematical investigation was occupied instead in the lengthy solution of problems involved with the occurrence probabilities of various rare coincidences. For example, he once worked for many hours on the probability that among fifty people in the same room any two would have the same birthday. He was quite unaware of the relationship of such interests

to his own biography or to the affects that were isolated by this intellectual endeavor. Isolation was his favored defense. A curious inappropriateness of manner and expression also revealed itself in the transference where he enacted a strangely gauche behavior. He rarely acknowledged a greeting or expressed gratitude for a favor. He was careless of muddy shoes and smeared the wall next to the couch with sooty hands. This had its analogue in his early relationship with his mother, from whom both his musical and mathematical endowments seemed to stem. She appeared to have been a cold, angry woman to whom he was endeared by his talents but who rarely, if ever, expressed any physical affection toward him. During a period of childhood encopresis she manifested extreme disgust at his dirtiness and left all his cleaning up to his less squeamish father. The patient used a massive isolation to defend himself against feelings or rejection. This made it difficult for him to maintain a simultaneous awareness of himself and his surrounding social environment. His defective rapport seemed to be one of the expressions of his identification with his mother's conflicting attitudes towards his talents on the one hand and his bodily functions on the other. One consequence of this was his inability to have a seminal emission in the waking stage, although nocturnal emissions were quite frequent. In contrast to the patient's behavior in the analytic situation was his model deportment at college with his professors and fellow students. He complained, however, that in class and social situations with academic acquaintances he was often "tongue-tied" and unable to "think on his feet" or to grasp simple ideas when others were talking to him.

Consistent with the suggestion that appropriateness in style depends upon a simultaneous contact with the self and the social situation or context was this patient's inability to accomplish this synthetic task. Thus in the analytic situation, which demanded introspective efforts, along with the patient's gauche behavior, the listener experienced a feeling of alienation, as when someone speaks to him seemingly coherently but in a foreign tongue, while in ordinary social situations polite formalities were maintained, but at the expense of the patient's alienation from his own powers of comprehension.

In the case of a child with austistic manifestations and both musical and artistic talents,[5] communication with his therapist during a large part of his latency years was carried out largely through drawings of the animal figures living in model cities that filled his fantasies. He would answer queries with the sounds of musical instruments or the noises of locomotive and automobile horns. This child's mother, who subsequently became psychotic, did not talk to the patient during the early period of infancy, and although this patient could read at the age of two years and hum tunes in perfect pitch, he did not begin to speak until the age of four. For many years he was also kept from contact with other children. Not only formal speech but mimetic expression, gesture, and posture showed the severe limiting effects of the absence of social stimulation. An early promise of creative musical ability seems also to have been finally submerged in his slow disintegration.

The following description of the patient in his treatment session at the age of fourteen gives a vivid impression of a communication process in which style has never developed beyond idiosyncrasy and mannerism. The therapist writes:

> His long gaunt face is rigidly set. His movements are slow, purposeful, and devoid of spontaneity. He seems much older than his almost fourteen years. He has an abstracted air as though he were involved in an all-absorbing formidable inner task which requires all of his attention and energy. He sometimes responds to my greeting with a quick nod and then walks stiffly with something of a propulsive gait to the consultation room. There he stares through me with his eyes apparently focused at the wall several feet behind me. He never says the first words and his response to a question of mine is usually a flat offhand "Fine" or "All right." Sometimes he says "Why," but this is said without a questioning intonation and without interest. He utters his monosyllabic answers with a somewhat patronizing manner. If he is pressed he becomes restless and gives evidence of a "Don't bother me with your silly questions" attitude. When asked, he will tell me that his mind is occupied with one of his various projects or with a fragment of music. On occasion, but less frequently than in the past, he will suddenly and violently beat out time to the rhythm of inner music. He pounds it out with clenched fists beating at the arm of his chair. At such times his body jerks violently.

Sometimes he accompanies this activity with a harsh unpleasant chant.

It seems evident that the early relationship of the child and the mother, with its emphasis on communication of needs through sound, gesture, facial expression, and finally speech, must be the important precursor of style in establishing the means by which subject-matter becomes adapted to the formal aspects of communication. In this relationship we can also see the possibilities for certain conditioning experiences that might favor one or the other extreme of stylistic deficiency. For example, the mother who constantly anticipates the child's needs with inadequate insistence upon their being made explicit may discourage the development of precision in formal verbalization, while a parental influence that makes premature demands upon such a development might promote a formalism that submerges the full capacity for individuality of expression.

Some interviewers of patients seem to have unusual abilities for detecting the existence of "borderline" psychopathology in its more subtle aspects. These impressions often cannot be based upon the patient's history or thought processes, but must be inferred from small details of manner, behavior, and verbal style. This suggests the residue of "art" (or better, "art criticism") in the protoscience of psychiatric diagnosis. It may be suspected that the mysterious facility which these examiners possess in diagnosis and prognosis is, in addition to other factors, based upon the observation or intuitive reaction to the patient's style. The history of the development of the arts and sciences reveals a series of progressive steps from the amorphous and indeterminate to schemata and categories and finally to the recognition of the particular. The study of the individual is still in a schematic stage. Perhaps as an extension of "ego psychology" a "self psychology" will have to develop before a study of style and the individual can come into its own. Both Trilling (1957) and Wilson (1957), from the point of view of literary criticism, see the "neurosis" as a banal aspect of the creative process. "Neurosis," being a universal state of man, in a certain sense, falls into the category of the conventional. Thus it is only in the special way in which the neurotic process itself is synthesized into his creations that it is relevant to style. These authors imply "selves" in opposition as features of literary creativity, although one of these "selves" is externalized by them in the guise of the prevailing culture (see also Greenacre, 1958b).

In summary, it has been suggested that personal style is the individual's unique method for utilizing the conventional forms of expressive media, so that his synthesis of subject matter and form allows for an appropriate degree of ambiguity, in the resolution of which, both the subject and the object can participate. Three major categories of stylistic deterioration in varying degree can be recognized in the communications of certain individuals. In one, the formal aspects of expression overwhelm the personal content and produce monotony and stereotypy. In the second, personal content is expressed without regard to the conventional rules of the formal medium producing chaos and confusion. In a third variant, inappropriate media of expression are used to convey the personal subject matter, resulting in a feeling of alienation in the listener as if the message had been directed to someone else. It is further postulated that the synthetic function of the ego is observed in the formation of a style, while a disturbance of this function is made manifest by its disintegration. Sensitive observers may derive early cues for the recognition of "borderline" conditions and other ego distortion states from stylistic eccentricities. It has often been said that the psychiatrist has a wealthy nomenclature for the designation of psychopathology but only a primitive argot for the description of normal functioning. Perhaps in the observation and classification of the wide variations of normal personal styles we may develop an equally rich nosology for a "psychophysiology." I do not think that anyone has said this better than Walter Pater in the polished stately prose of the late nineteenth century:

> In this way according to the well-known saying "The style is the man," complex or simple, in his individuality, his plenary sense of what he really has to say, his sense of the world; all cautions regarding style arising out of so many natural scruples as to the medium through which alone he can expose the inward sense of things, the purity of this medium, its laws or tricks of refraction: nothing is to be left there which might give conveyance to any matter save that. Style in all its varieties,

reserved or opulent, terse, abundant, musical, stimulant, academic, so long as each is really characteristic or expressive, finds thus its justification, the sumptuous good taste of Cicero being as truly the man himself and not another, justified, yet insured inalienable to him thereby, as would have been his portrait by Raffaelle, in full consular splendour on his ivory chair.

Notes

1. Hartmann's (1939) term for the synthetic and differentiating functions acting in concert.

2. M.H. Abrams (1958) in *The Mirror and the Lamp* gives a revealing account of the vicissitudes of this controversy through various historical periods. A section on "Style and the Man" treats the problem from the point of view of the philosophy of aesthetics. E. H. Gombrich (1954) has a similar discussion from the viewpoint of the psychology of perception.

3. It has been suggested by a mathematician (personal communication) that actually a "set of invariants" would have to be identified for a notational system that would differentiate one style from another.

4. The existence of two or more completely integrated styles existing simultaneously in a single individual is a fourth variant which will not be discussed in this presentation. It may or may not be evidence of significant psychopathology (see Greenacre, 1958, and Kris, 1952, on the writings of Baron Corvo). Stein in a personal communication has told me of a writer who has two distinct styles corresponding to the works published under hiw own name and others written under a pseudonym.

5. This patient, also part of the Gifted Adolescent Project, was first treated by the late Mrs. Christine Olden, and subsequently by Dr. Bertram Gosliner, to whom I am indebted for permission to quote from his conference report.

CHAPTER THIRTEEN

Obsessions as Comic Caricatures

In an introduction to a recent collection of parodies (Lowry, 1960), Nathaniel Benchley describes a scene in the French town of Nancy near the German border in the summer of 1938. A small man with a brief case was knocked down by an angry crowd and saved from severe bodily injury only by the timely intervention of some alert gendarmes for whom the scene was no novelty. An onlooker explained to the American visitor that the man was a local accountant who had such a strong facial resemblance to Hitler that he often felt impelled to make Hilteresque tirades at street corners or in cafes. "Usually," the informant said, "he ended these burlesques with *Vive la France* and everybody took it as a good joke, but sometimes things misfired, as they apparently had on that evening. Also there seemed to be other people who did not think that the *fuhrer* should have been derided in the first place." "All in all," Benchley comments, "the man was living dangerously no matter how you looked at it." The incident suggests the compulsive reenactment of a scene. It also contains various features of comic caricature in the form of parody, travesty, and burlesque, with at least a suggestion of tragedy as well. What Kris (1952) calls the "double-edged" quality of the comic and the "brinksmanship" with which its practitioners live are also implicit in the event. Most impressive, however, unlike other forms of humor, is its potential for misfiring and suddenly reversing the roles of aggressor, victim, and audience, without warning.

It is the general thesis of this chapter that obsessions are grotesque parodies without laughter and that compulsions are ritual travesties devoid of fun. The discussion will emphasize what can be learned of obsessional symptom formation and resolution in the transference neurosis in response to comic synthesis.

Caricature and related forms of comic derision utilize the distortion of some aspect of an individual or his creations to produce a ridiculous effect. The mighty are diminished in stature when mirth can substitute for awe. The essence of the comic, according to Freud (1905b), lies in the pleasure derived from the saving in energy expenditure when by comparison the same effect is observed to be derived from excessively large and unexpectedly small outlays of effort in movement or ideation. But even in this aspect of caricature there are two edges when parody becomes, in the words of Oscar Wilde, "the tribute that mediocrity pays to genius."

Some of the similarities and antitheses that exist in the psychodynamics of comic distortion on the one hand, and obsessive-compulsive phenomena on the other will be examined. This juxtaposition initially presents itself in psychoanalysis in its simplest form when we find that much of what a patient has said in jest turns out to have serious import, while his most serious and unbearable complaints may ultimately be the source of laughter rather than tears.

If I may be permitted a somewhat confused chemical metaphor, both comic distortion and obsessional phenomena seem to have isomeric structures in common. Comedy, however, is a polymeric form of obsessional phenomena; obsessive and compulsive symptoms are degradation products of comic distortion.

Comic caricature in its various aspects is a universal expressive activity of man which may deteriorate into compulsive ritual when divested of fun; on the other hand, the tyranny of obsessional phenomena has humorous aspects and can be significantly vitiated by the introduction of comic relief.

Some remarks on the analytic process and suggestions for special techniques in these and related clinical conditions are inevitable in the course of such a discussion since symptom formation can often be observed in *statu nascendi* during analysis, while reformulations of dynamic theory often suggest technical maneuvers whose effects in turn serve as evidence for verification or invalidation of the revised assumptions.

Freud has already suggested certain similarities between man's most serious pursuits, the methodic systems of science, philosophy, and art, and the structure of obsessional ideas with caricature as the connecting link. In the short paper "Obsessive Acts and Religious Practices" (1907) he says, "In this respect an obsessional neurosis presents a travesty, half comic and half tragic, of a private religion," and later in the same paper he asserts, "In view of these similarities and analogies one might venture to regard obsessional neurosis as a pathological counterpart of the formation of a religion, and to describe that neurosis as an individual religiosity and religion as a universal obsessional neurosis." In *Totem and Taboo* (1913a) Freud returns to this theme and in an oft-quoted paragraph suggests some further analogies. He says, "The neuroses exhibit on the one hand striking and far-reaching points of agreement with those great social institutions, art, religion, and philosophy. But on the other hand they seem like distortions of them." It might be maintained that a case of hysteria is a caricature of a work of art, that an obsessional neurosis is a caricature of a religion, and that a paranoid delusion is a caricature of a philosophical system. Later in the same work, however, Freud indicates that one does not have to look beyond the obsessional neurosis itself to find all the caricatures of methodic systems that are borrowed from serious disciplines. Concerning obsessional ideas and the omnipotence of thought he says, "In only a single field in our civilization has the omnipotence of thought been retained and that is in the field of art. Only in art does it still happen that a man who is consumed by desires performs something resembling the accomplishment of these desires and that what he does in play produces emotional effects—thanks to artistic illusion—just as though it were something real." Thus, he remarks, "The construction of caricatures of systems is seen most strikingly in delusional disorders, where it dominates the symptomatic picture; its occurrence in other forms of psychoneurosis, however, must not be overlooked."[1] I suspect that it has already been observed that the touch of method in all madness has its counterpart, therefore, in the grain of madness implicit in all methods.

Caricature, travesty, and parody are related creative forms of the comic. In aesthetics they are generally viewed as inferior to serious artistic efforts, and their creators are given grudging condescension as second-class citizens by the elite of the artistic community.

Caricature refers almost exclusively to distortions of the image of personal physiognomy, while the terms *parody* and *travesty* are applied to similar treatment of literary or dramatic productions. MacDonald, a literary critic, points out that the dictionaries cannot be relied upon to concur in the subtle distinctions of meaning in the various terms (1960). All three forms, as well as burlesque, have certain features in common. They exaggerate or minimize certain aspects of the object for the purpose of mockery while leaving the illusion of recognizability of the original object intact. Travesty usually refers to a caricature of dramatic or literary form, while parody satirizes the content of the literary production. A play by Wallach (Lowry, 1960) with the title *A Tatooed Street Car Named Desire* might serve as an illustration. A character named Mike is on stage. "As the curtain rises he tears it to shreds." The title of the play is parody, while the opening stage directions fulfill the criteria for travesty. Burlesque is considered by some to be an even more "degraded" relative of travesty.

The word *caricature* is derived from the Italian *caricare* and the French *charger*—thus literally to overcharge the object, i.e., with feeling. The *parados* of parody was one of the conventionalized parts of the liturgy of the Greek drama that reflected repetitively in vocal chorus the main events of the dramatic plot. The roots of the word *travesty* are the same as those of *transvestism,* thus suggesting that the ultimate distortion of form is one sex playing the role of the other. (The relevance of bisexuality to symptom formation should be noted as well.) According to MacDonald, travesty is the most primitive form of literary caricature. "It raises laughs from the belly rather than the head by putting high classic characters into prosaic situations." Achilles thus becomes a football hero and Helen of Troy an Atlantic City beauty queen. Burlesque (from the Italian *burla*, to ridicule) is, according to MacDonald, a more advanced form of caricature since it at least attempts to imitate the style of the original. It differs from parody in that the writer or speaker is concerned with the original not in itself but merely as a device for topical humor. Parody "concentrates on the style and thought of the original. If burlesque (or travesty) is pouring new wine into old bottles," MacDonald suggests, "parody is making a new wine that tastes like the old but has a slightly lethal effect."

Kris (1952) and Gombrich (1960), borrowing freely from Freud's contributions to the psychology of jokes and the comic, have suggested many directions in which the psychology of caricature can elucidate problems of ego functioning and the creative process (see also Tarachow, 1949, 1951; Reich, 1950; Jacobson, 1946; Grotjahn, 1957, 1961; and Reik, 1937). Kris and Gombrich also point out that while travesty and parody are as old as European literature, caricature is unknown in the history of the visual arts before the end of the sixteenth century (Hoffman, 1957). In the history of art many great creative artists have been accomplished caricaturists. In the field of literature, however, great writers have often successfully turned their pens to parody, but few, according to some critics (MacDonald, 1960), succeed as well as the mediocre ones. Great gifts in creative writing often seem to interfere with successful parody, or perhaps the matter should be put the other way around: a gift for parody interferes with serious creative writing. It has been noted, on the other hand, that talented artists and writers in the field of the comic (Greenacre, 1955) often deteriorate, become stereotyped and repetitive with time, especially when they are unusually prolific and financially successful. In this characteristic there is a hint of the potential for repetition and regression. One reviewer of the collected verse of Ogden Nash (*The Times Literary Supplement*, 1961) says, for example, "What depresses one after 500 pages is the sense of a talent too easily exploited, a feeling that having hit upon a form *sui generis* and certain favorite subjects . . . Mr. Nash rested charmingly on his laurels. Rather like those witty unknown Belloc followers composing their endless ballades."

It is also in the nature of caricature that its effect is severely circumscribed by time and that it is quickly dated by the demise of its subject matter. The same is true of parody but to a more limited extent since the original literary product survives for more ready comparison with its caricature. Without a firsthand knowledge of the "live" victim it is difficult to assess the success or failure of caricature, although the work may continue to convey other attributes of artistic achievement. Similarly the symptoms of a childhood neurosis when viewed from the vantage of their adult residuals seem less comprehensible than when they first appeared and may be serving a different purpose.

Kris (1952) suggests that within the history of art alone, the emergence of caricature cannot be explained, although several factors of a purely historical and social nature must be considered among its multiple determinants, for example, the new humanism of the Renaissance and the high development of portrait skill in the same period. The former development allowed for a sufficient distance from ritual magic to permit the distortion of the image of the object without fear of the destruction of the original, while the latter technical advance was essential to the subtle devices that are inherent in the drawing process itself. These analogues to some of the mechanisms of ego control in the individual suggest also the means by which the patient transmutes an obsession to a comic device and vice versa.

Gombrich (1960) in his treatise on the subject revises one aspect of his previous view of the development of caricature. He states that he is no longer impressed with the idea that the persistence of image magic fully accounts for the failure of the appearance of caricature as an historical development in art before the sixteenth century. He views it rather as a special case of the discovery of equivalence which also advanced the technical development of serious portraiture in the same period. Equivalence is superior to likeness in producing graphic images. Equivalence does not rest upon the similarity of elements so much as on the identity of the viewer's response to certain invariant relationships of the parts of the object, even when the parts themselves are unlike those of the original. The equivalence of relationships rather than likeness is an especially potent part of the technique of convincing portrayal of mimetic expression, and it is in the course of this observation that Gombrich believes that the secret of caricature was revealed. The substitution of "equivalence" for "likeness" is relevant to the evocation of comic pleasure and to the resolution of obsessional symptoms.

There are some important differences between obsessional symptoms and compulsive rituals on the one hand and examples of comic distortion on the other. In successful comic caricature or its literary counterparts, the object of the distortion is clearly delineated or implied. This object is one whose role or works are usually in the public domain (or are at least a group property). He is "fair game" for such attacks as one of the hazards attached to his role rather than to his person. The motive of the caricaturist stresses the aggressive component of his ambivalence or it is unambivalently aggressive, but the form of his aggression remains within the limits set by social and artistic convention. The aim of the comic distortion is to produce mirthful pleasure as well as derision in an audience. The effect upon the victim himself is secondary. In obsessive-compulsive phenomena the object of the aggressive distortion is obscured or displaced. The disguise may be an apparent attack on the victim's role but is ultimately meant as an attack upon his person or possessions. The apparent sadistic motive for the obsessional distortion often covers a masochistic aim, so that aggressor and victim frequently become confused and are no longer clearly identifiable. The form of the attack is not contained within the limits prescribed by social proprieties or the logic of causal sequence. No audience is required for the obsessional counterpart of caricature. The effects are merely provocative and the pleasure component is confined to the patient where it is largely unconscious. In both comic distortion (Tarachow, 1949, 1951) and obsessional phenomena, an array of sadomasochistic pregenital object relations are found in limitless combinations and permutations.

Although it may appear that these remarks apply to the sadomasochistic components of any symptom organization, they appear to be more specific for those that fall into the obsessional category. This is due to the overriding importance of sadomasochistic features in obsessional phenomena and the peculiar facility of obsessional symptoms and traits for obscuring this aspect of object relations (see also Bak, 1946, and Gero, 1962).

In the following account of some clinical experiences an attempt will be made to illustrate a few of these reciprocal relationships. Perhaps the best known instance of unsuccessful "travesty" in obsessional neurosis is the Rat Man's celebrated attempt to repay a small debt supposedly owed to a fellow army officer. Freud describes this as a "delirium," confessing, one suspects, by the use of this term his own initial confusion and dismay at the patient's behavior. Close inspection reveals the similarity to travesty in this charade of misdirected punctiliousness. There are two repetitive themes in the incident. The patient, in spite of having been informed of the identity of his creditor, is determined to pay the money that he owes to the wrong person, or as an alternative solution he is willing to arrange to have the money go to the right creditor but only if it is repaid as if someone other than the patient were the debtor. If his elaborate plans could have been carried to their ultimate conclusion, the objects of his gratitude would have become involved in a burgeoning web of inconvenience and misadventure as a reward for their solicitude. Add flying custard pies, and the plot would have served for an old-time Mack Sennett short preceding the main feature.

Within the analytic situation travesty is most frequently simulated by the obsessional patient in his method of dealing with the directives for free association. This usually involves a pseudocomic distortion of one or more of the elements of the original formulation of the process by the analyst at the beginning of treatment. Regardless of the various ways in which "tell me everything that comes to your mind" is elaborated, certain distortions are common experience. One patient, placing the emphasis on the word *everything*, becomes a replica of an old *New Yorker* cartoon showing a woman on an analyst's couch reciting cookbook recipes. I am indebted to Dr. R. Loewenstein for an allegorical counterpart of this example of obsessional resistance. Some years ago the French customs inspectors, frustrated in their request for higher wages and denied the right to strike by government statute, resorted to the device of meticulous observance of all the details of the government regulations covering the inspection of import and export shipments. The resulting paralysis of trade brought quick capitulation from the authorities, much as the "Good Soldier Schweik" humbled the high command of the Austrian Army by his insistence upon a literal interpretation of the "regulations." In another familiar variety of similar "travesty," the patient may choose to emphasize the "comes to your mind" phrase in the original directive sentence. This reformulation becomes the justification for the exclusion of any idea which is not literally a part of the here and now of the analytic situation. A patient, for example, reveals that he has been thinking about transmitting a bit of important information for several weeks but has decided that it would be against the rules to verbalize it because it had not originally occurred to him on the couch. Attempts to modify these misunderstandings by purely explanatory methods often produce recriminative disputes into which the unwary therapist may be insidiously drawn. The following colloquy between a young analyst and his first analytic patient is apocryphal, but its similarity to real individuals and events is not entirely accidental:

Analyst: I cannot understand what you are saying because you drop your voice, jumble the words, and leave out important connecting episodes in your account of the event.
Patient: I am only saying what comes to my mind, the way it comes to my mind, just exactly as you told me to.
Analyst: But I did not tell you to be incoherent.
Patient: I do what you ask me to do and then you say it is all wrong. I don't know what you want any longer.
Analyst: I am not saying anything critical, I am only trying to help you to describe things more clearly so that I can comprehend what you are saying and so that the treatment can go more smoothly.
Patient: If you are not criticizing me why are you grinding your teeth in a rage?
Analyst (bellowing): I am not grinding my teeth and I am not enraged.
Patient (meekly): I was only saying what comes to my mind.

Before drawing the curtain of compassion on this scene, it should be compared to a dialogue written by one of the greatest masters of travesty. This interchange takes place between Antipholous of Syracuse and Dromio, his faithful retainer, in *The Comedy of Errors*:

Dromio of Syracuse: But pray sir, why am I beaten?
Antipholus of Syracuse: Dost thou not know?
Domio: Nothing sir, but that I am beaten.
Antipholus: Shall I tell you why?
Dromio: Why sir and wherefore, for they say that every why hath a wherefore.
Antipholus: Why first for flouting me and then wherefore for urging it the second time to me.
Dromio: Was ever any man thus beaten out of season, when in the why and wherefore there is neither rhyme nor reason? Well sir I thank you.
Antipholus: Thank me sir, for what?

Dromio: Marry sir, for this something that you gave me for nothing.
Antipholus: I'll make amends next time and give you nothing for something.

As in the previous instance, the play here is upon the theme, who is the victim, who the aggressor, and what are the motives for their actions? In Shakespeare's version, no matter how confusing this may be to the characters involved, the audience at least is clear on the matter of identities and can derive pleasure from the plight of the hapless Dromio. The master is clearly the aggressor and the servant is his victim no matter how *they* try to becloud the issue. In this instance the motive is also clear. The master needs no reason to beat his servant. It is his right and he does so at his pleasure and for its own sake. It should be noted that the tendentious joke, in contradistinction to the purely comic, exposes in a sudden flash not only the nature of the roles of the participants and their motives but the primary-process technique that is being used in their logic to keep the nature of the roles ambiguous. Freud's famous caviar story in *Jokes and Their Relation to the Unconscious* (1905b) is a prime example of this. A rich man who has lent money to a poor relative finds him eating caviar. When he remonstrates with him, the poor relative says, "When I have no money I cannot eat caviar. When I borrow money I am not allowed to eat it. When am I supposed to eat caviar?" In this instance Freud points out that it is the mechanism of displacement that allows the aggressor to pass himself off as the victim. These matters are less clearly defined in the case of the young analyst and his patient who are doubly victimized by being deprived of the comic pleasure which rightfully should be theirs.

The analogues of parody are best seen in analysis by the manner in which the obsessional patient reacts to an interpretation. One rather commonplace variety might be described as a reduction of the analyst's statement to triviality by a distortion of its form or content (Chapters 11 and 12). This is often accomplished by ignoring the implicit invitation in the interpretation to a collaborative exploration which might resolve some of its ambiguities and thus extend its significance. In this process the obsessional patient assumes the role of victim and by parodic revision of the analyst's statement transforms his friend and servant into his master and foe. For example, a female patient seems to be convinced that her anger at her husband is in part a replica of her mother's attitude toward her father as she understood them in her childhood. It is suggested by the analyst that as part of this repetition she ignores certain events which might also reasonably incur her anger toward her husband and selects only those episodes for controversy which have as a common denominator certain kinds of disappointment. She seems to agree that this has its counterpart in the transference where her anger was also attached to incidents that gave rise to characteristic feelings of disappointment. In the next session the patient is furious. She reports that she had been thinking about the analyst's statement in the previous session. From it she understood that he had allied himself with her husband and had made it clear that he did not feel that she had any reasonable grounds for being critical of her husband. In many literary parodies the comic effect is derived from a similar device of reducing the multiple implications of the original author's theme into a single and banal statement. The serious critic who seeks to extend the meaning of life thus becomes a simpleton who reduces everything to its most prosaic elements. A parody by Riddell (Lowey, 1960) entitled "Strange Interview" takes place between a Mr. O'Neill and his inner voice and is reminiscent of this exasperating device. The scene is "A room which like life itself is all baloney; and apparently the sole occupant is aware of this. It is perfectly obvious from a glance at the furniture, that it is the room of a man who has discovered that reality is only flux and things are seldom—things being what they are—what they seem. The very tables, chairs, and draperies make no pretense of being genuine: the rich oriental tapestries by the window still display their price tags '$1.60 a yard' and a genuine antique Louis Quatorze chair is marked plainly: 'made in Grand Rapids.'"

The patient uses parody in a similar way but avoids the awareness of any comic intent by a process of isolation that separates effectively at least three essential component elements of the caricature, namely, the identities of the aggressor and victim and the motives for the attack. Unless these elements can be replaced in a composite pattern which is meaningful to an observer "the caricature," in the words of Kris, "is reduced to a riddle or a rebus." Immediate enlightenment is one of the essential components of the comic effect (Tarachow, 1949); a riddle or a rebus requires time for its comprehension, and successfully discourages laughter.

Further evidence for this tripartite isolation is also suggested by certain experiences in the analysis of obsessional patients that have to do with the evocation of laughter. Freud (1905b) first called attention to laughter as a response to interpretation. In a footnote in his monograph on jokes he writes, "Many of my neurotic patients who are under psychoanalytic treatment are regularly in the habit of confirming the fact by a laugh when I have succeeded in giving a faithful picture of their hidden unconscious to their conscious perception; and they laugh even when the content of what is unveiled would by no means justify this. This is subject of course to their having arrived close enough to the unconscious material to grasp it after the doctor has detected it and presented it to them." Less frequently, however, has it been noticed that if a patient can first be induced to laugh, the grasping of an interpretation may become possible. Jones (1912), for example, describes the humorless quality of an obsessional patient and the difficulty it poses for therapy. This patient could not join in laughter and thought that people who laughed in places of amusement did so only to convince themselves that they were getting their money's worth.

Psychoanalysis has made major contributions to the psychology of humor and laughter (Freud, 1905b, 1927) as well as to the multidetermined normal and pathological functions that laughter may serve as a tension-discharge and mimetic device (Jacobson, 1946; Kris, 1952; Reik, 1937). In brief, however, discussions of laughter as a response to the comic emphasize saving in the expenditure of psychic energy (Freud, 1905b), controlled regression (Kris, 1952), and speed of the dynamic process (Jacobson, 1946; Reik, 1937; Tarachow, 1949) as the major components of the final result. An additional possible determinant of the process seems to have been insufficiently emphasized. This has to do not so much with the mobilization of free energy in the psychic apparatus but the exchange of "bound" energy for a "free" form so that it may become available for discharge. This would be implied if the notion that obsessional phenomena exist as fragments of a larger comic unity is correct. To some extent this has already been suggested by A. Reich's (1950) description of the "grotesque-comic" as an acting-out device. Although she describes this as a "sublimation," it seems rather, in her case illustration, to have been compulsively repetitive and a device halfway between a "sublimation" and a "symptom" (see also Kanzer, 1955).

Laughter has also received a good deal of attention in group psychology (see Jacobson, 1946, and Kris, 1952, for bibliographic references). Here two interesting and revealing characteristics can be observed. This can be stated in an oversimplified form as follows. Where a group is cohesive and has strong bonds and few tensions among its members, laughter is easily evoked with minimal stimuli. Conversely, in a group in which there is considerable distance between the individual members due to unfamiliarity or hostility or tensions of other sorts, there is usually little laughter. If anxiety or hostility is introduced into the first type of group, distance increases and laughter diminishes, while in the second group anything which introduces laughter, especially a comic episode, will increase its cohesiveness and reduce the distance between the estranged individuals. That there are intrapsychic analogues to this situation has already been suggested by Freud (1905b). A precondition for comic appreciation in an audience is an optimal distance from the subject of comedy. Neither the remoteness of an unremittent hostility nor the closeness of an intense erotic interest are conducive to a comic response. A further intrapsychic analogue to the group reaction may exist between the structural elements of a comic synthesis. In other words, when they are less isolated from each other they can fuse with the release of tension in laughter, and similarly laughter may reduce the distance between the elements and allow a synthesis which otherwise might not occur. In this latter event the energy that is released would be the energy bound by isolation, by the process of keeping the elements apart from each other. Metaphorically, at least, the consequence of laughter as a precondition for grasping an interpretation might be termed a *fusion* reaction as contrasted with a *fission* reaction when laughter is a sequel to interpretation. The sources of the energy involved can be conceived as analogous to the energy relationships that exist in nuclear explosions. Nor would this be the first time that a joke has been likened to a bomb.

The characteristic disturbances of obsessional neurosis make these questions of optimal distance paramount. Such patients oscillate between a variety of detachments from affects and the objects with which they are associated to opposing extremes of overinvolvement. Jones (1912), Kris (1952), and others (Mahler-Schoenberger, 1942, see also Chapter 11) have noted how the defense of pseudonaïveté or pseudostupidity interferes with the appreciation of the joke, especially in severe compulsive character disorders, while simultaneously making the patient himself the object of comic ridicule. This concept has been condensed in the current vernacular into the notion of the "square" (i.e., a ludicrously literal-minded individual). The jesting or witty interpretation here serves two purposes. It impels through laughter a more optimal distance on the part of the patient from the subject matter or the transference. This may simultaneously allow the elements of internal conflict to be grasped in a new way with a maximum of economy. It should be emphasized, however, that even without the specific felicity of a "correct" interpretation in a witty form, laughter at certain crucial analytic moments may further the work of interpretation.

As a corollary to these ideas it should also be suggested that when comedy is used as a defense it must reveal strong and intimate bonds between the psychic elements that are fused in its structure and that are usually kept at a distance from each other under average conditions.[2]

In this model, then, a certain quantity of countercathectic energy used for isolation rather than repression had been exerted by three or more components each against the other. The energy of fusion, released by the bringing together of these elements, so that their relationship can be clearly grasped, escapes through the discharge mechanism provided by laughter. In its reduced form this formulation has been implicit in the suggestion that in comic humor the aggressor, victim, and motive must be brought into a certain optimal emotional as well as spatial proximity to a responsive audience for the full experience of the comic effect. It may also follow that certain other forms of humor such as the jest or witticism produce their more attenuated reactions on the "laugh meter" because the "fusion reaction" due to the undoing of isolation is a relatively less significant process in the energic interchange.

In speaking of fusion in the synthetic act of comic appreciation, an affinity with the creative process is also implied. Getzels and Jackson (1962), for example, indicate how the aggression in the gifted child is often inextricably bound up with a comic creative synthesis. Thus the drawing of one such child indicates a school which carries the slogan on its walls "I hate Children." Another shows "a factory being blown up by a formula for a new breakfast cereal." A gifted adolescent patient in my own practice expressed his ambivalence by designing a rocket in fantasy to place an analyst in orbit on a bagel that gained its thrust from lox and cream cheese. In so far as an interpretation is also a creative synthesis in both its construction and the response expected from it (Chapter 11), the comic *detente* may have an important synthetic function in this sense as well.

The use and misuse of the comic interpretation, and the patient's use of jokes or comical associations, can demonstrate many facets of the formation and structure of obsessional phenomena, particularly their hidden sadomasochistic components. Just as the patient may use unconscious parody as a defense against interpretations, so interpretations can be intentional or unwitting parodies upon the patient's productions. Such parodic interventions of either the "successful" or the "misfiring" brand may allow the observation of the formation or resolution of a symptom *in situ*.

A woman who was going through a severe disappointment in her treatment suffered a return of her phobic and obsessional symptoms. She became petulant and morose and reiterated during the course of several sessions that she had developed a new symptom. She was afraid that she would die in her sleep and as a result had been suffering from insomnia. She felt too fatigued during the day to come for her appointments but felt that she was being forced to come against her will by the financial stipulations. She would have been loath to miss a session for which she would be charged, but on the other hand in her state of fatigue and anxiety she felt that there was nothing to be accomplished by her attendance. She repeated many times during several of these trying encounters that she was present "in body alone and not in spirit." Her spirit she had left at home resting in her own bed. On each of such occasions she would say as she left, "I will see you tomorrow if I am still alive." In a rash moment I replied, "And if not, come in spirit and leave your body at home." It appeared that I was the only one who enjoyed the jest, and that this time I was living dangerously. At the next session the patient reported that she had been very angry at this parting quip. On entering the waiting room she had a feeling of depersonalization. She spoke of the callousness of my attempt at humor and what an indifference to human suffering it revealed. The patient had been feeling victimized for some time by the commitments she had made to the analysis. She wished to turn the tables and to remain in treatment on her own terms. We were too close to the problem at the time for wit to have any effect upon it. It was only later that I realized that the attack of depersonalization might have been a bit of counterparody, to the effect, "If you do not treat me the way I wish, I will leave both my body and my spirit at home."

A more successful example of a parodic interpretation occurred with a compulsive man who had periods, in his own words, of becoming a "cantankerous Old Scrooge." He refused stoutly to concede that these moods had anything to do with the first of the month when his bill was presented to him. On one such occasion he had a dream in which he was on trial and was being accused of "head hunting." Someone else was the guilty party, but he was having difficulty in proving his innocence. In his associations he was reminded of a newspaper report that he had read at the time of the disappearance of Michael Rockefeller off the coast of New Guinea. He was amused at the report that young Rockefeller had been buying up shrunken heads from the head hunters at inflationary prices. It had been further reported that the chief of one of the tribes, having run out of shrunken heads, had appealed to the Dutch authorities to repeal an old statute and to permit a twenty-four-hour open season on people so that the supply of shrunken heads could be replenished. "However," the patient remarked, in summation, "I am damned if I can see what this has to do with the price of lettuce." As I handed the patient his bill I remarked, "A head of lettuce is cheap, but it takes a lot of lettuce to shrink a head." He responded with the first merriment that had ever occurred during a starkly serious analysis. Subsequent sessions did produce a great deal of information about some financial problems that he had never revealed to me. The jest in this case was nonspecific in any reconstructive sense. I think that it served to reduce the tension of an ambivalent transference, in this instance by decreasing the patient's fear of retaliation. The isolation was produced not only by his anxiety about money but by an aggressive component which was linked with a fear of being victimized if he should reveal this to me. He confided after the comic relief that he had been afraid to tell me that he always felt amused rather than angry at paying for his treatment. His own comic thought was related to the idea: "What a way for a man to earn a living, listening all day to Old Scrooges like me." Anxiety related to the patient's castrative aggression through derision proved to be the more fruitful line of inquiry into his symptoms and seemed especially relevant to the inhibition of his sense of humor. In some obsessional patients, in my experience, a well-developed sense of the comic is isolated from the analytic situation by being expressed only in the social life of the patient. It is with some surprise that the analyst discovers that such serious, dour patients are regarded by their friends as "lives of the party" and unusually "funny fellows."

In discussing the psychogenesis of tendentious jokes, Freud suggests the mechanism that seems related to this problem. He says, "Let us assume that there is an urge to insult a certain person; but this is so strongly opposed by feelings of propriety or aesthetic culture that the insult cannot take place. If, for instance, it were able to break through as a result of some change of emotional condition or mood, this break-through by the insulting purpose would be felt subsequently with unpleasure. Thus the insult does not take place. Let us now suppose, however, that the possibility is presented of deriving a good joke from the material of the words and thoughts used for the insult—the possibility, that is, of releasing pleasure from other sources which are not obstructed by the same suppression. This second development of pleasure could, nevertheless, not occur unless the insult were permitted; but as soon as the latter *is* permitted the new release of pleasure is also joined to it. Experience with tendentious jokes shows that in such circumstances the suppressed purpose can, with the assistance of the pleasure from the joke, gain sufficient strength to overcome the inhibition, which would otherwise be stronger than it. The insult takes place because the joke has made it possible."

A literary critic sees similar implications in the use of successful parody from his own point of view. MacDonald (1960) says of parody, "I enjoy it as an intuitive kind of literary criticism, shorthand for what the 'serious' critic must write out at length. It is 'method acting,' since a successful parodist must live himself imaginatively in his parodee. It is jiujitsu, using the impetus of the opponent to defeat him, although 'opponent' and 'defeat' are hardly the words. Parodies are written out of admiration as well as contempt. It is hard to make the mimetic effort unless one has enough sympathy to identify with the parodee." In short, it is a process in which both parties see each other and themselves in some closer approximation to an actual scale of values in relation to surrounding objects and the forces that move them.

The relationship of caricature and parody to ritual magic has been emphasized by Kris (1952) in the history of the development of art. This may play an important role in individual as well as social psychology. Psychoanalysis has long been interested in humor as part of the psychology and "psychopathology of everyday life." It may be more than this, however. Its role in therapy and the part played by its expression and inhibition in symptom formation have as yet been insufficiently investigated. We are prone to think of reinstinctualization of a function as the precondition for symptom formation. The dialectics of probability, however, demands that we also consider the converse possibility, namely, the pathogenic effects of disinstinctualization (Chapter 12). Classical theory holds that the symptom is a compromise between an instinctual striving and a defense that attempts to thwart its discharge. It has certainly been conceded, however, that where instinct and defense have reached an adaptive compromise, a disturbance of this equilibrium can occur in a variety of ways. The instinctual forces may increase or decrease in intensity while the defenses remain constant. Or the defensive forces may vary in strength or both may undergo simultaneous but unequal quantitative changes. One can argue that in the case of the comic we are dealing with a device that includes a larger share of satisfaction of instinctual striving than of defensive activity, while obsessional and compulsive activities carry an unpleasure value because both libidinal and to a lesser extent aggressive strivings are massively overwhelmed by the defensive forces. Although most writers on the subject have stressed the pleasurable component of wit, this has been conceived as part of its energy-saving and surprise attributes. One can, however, point to the fact that certain forms of the comic remain a source of pleasure after many repetitions, when both the surprise element and the economy of energy expenditure have played themselves out. In the infantile developmental hierarchy of pleasure, play, fun, and comedy (Freud, 1905b; Kris, 1952) form an ascending series from the least to the most highly socialized of these genetically related activities (see also Peller, 1954). In this development it has been noted (Freud, 1905b, 1927; Jacobson, 1946), that it is the aims and objects that undergo the greatest degree of transmutation rather than the drives.

If "serious" is the antithesis of "fun," it may also refer to the mutual observation on the part of adults and children that adults have less fun than children under ordinary conditions. "Fun" is closer to childhood and thus to more primitive pleasure than the "delayed" gratification required by the more reality-oriented activities of so-called grown-ups. Annie Reich (1950) stresses the threat or reinstinctualization and the consequent superego disapproval as the danger that makes the "comic-grotesque" (caricature) device a labile and vulnerable one. May it be equally the threat of instinctualization and of pleasure deprivation that also threatens its equilibrium?

Summary

Obsessive-compulsive individuals are constantly engaged in relationships of varying degrees of intensity in which their roles as victims or aggressors are successfully obscured by the ambiguities imposed by disturbances of distance of the observing function. Thus they apologize when they are victimized and feel martyred when they are aggressors. The device of comic caricature when successful allows the aggressor to insult his victim without malice and the victim to feel some pride in being insulted. The by-product of pleasure for the observing function in both of them serves to reinforce the device and to give a glimmering insight into the primary-process mechanism which is distorting the critical use of judgment. The capacity for comic caricature may be a way station on the road to more mature critical abilities in which sadomasochistic needs are minimized. A disturbance of the sense of the comic may produce obsessive-compulsive symptoms through changes in the defensive equilibrium, while its restoration may make it possible for the individual to deal with his difficulties. Problems of distance of the observing function which distort the importance or lack of importance of aggression in human relationships prevent identification of the elements of a potentially comic scene and interfere with its synthesis and comprehension. Laughter is both the result of such comic synthesis and the catalyst which may be necessary under certain circumstances to make it possible. The obsessional individual seems to have to learn to insult and be insulted gracefully before his social development can proceed.

This formulation suggests that the genetic derivatives of an obsessional neurosis can be more clearly defined and their infantile sources more easily reconstructed when they have first been restored to their comic context (see also Jacobson, 1946). Some consequences for therapeutic technique have been tentatively suggested.

Notes

1. In a brief clinical note, Freud (1916) reports a visual obsession that took the form of a caricature. The patient's father's face appeared upon the father's abdomen. Terra-cotta figures unearthed at Priene in Asia Minor represent the mythological figure of Baubo. "They show the body of a woman without a head or chest and with a face drawn on the abdomen: the lifted dress frames this face like a crown of hair."

2. This notion should be compared to J.P. Richter's (Freud, 1905b) statement that "joking is the ability to bind into a unity with surprising ease, several ideas which are in fact alien to one another both in their internal content and in the nexus in which they belong."

CHAPTER FOURTEEN

Talent and Character Style

Silenus, a forest god in Greek mythology, was depicted as a shaggy old man with horse's ears, usually drunk, and often riding upon an ass or a wine vessel. Nevertheless, he was reported to be extraordinarily wise; it was rumored that, if caught, he could be made to reveal his wisdom and give answers to universal riddles. The Phrygian king, Midas, captured him on one occasion and is said to have plied him with wine and questions. It is also reported that Silenus gave him astonishing answers. Nobody learned what these were, however; all that Midas could recall, probably having imbibed some of his own beverage, was that it would have been better never to have been born (Avery, 1962).

Here juxtaposed in two figures is the allegory of the artist and his character: Midas, the man with the magic gift for transmuting base materials into a beautiful, highly valued metal, and Silenus, an elusive eccentric, a semioutcast whose gold is squandered by turning it back into cruder material. The conclusion of their meeting also suggests the inevitable pain associated with all creative effort. Atypical features of their social relationships, value systems, and behavior often set gifted individuals apart from the rest of the community and may even impel them to form their own semi-isolated "colonies" and social organizations.

The following discussion, which centers mainly upon rather narrow aspects of ego organization, is bound to give the impression that the principle of overdetermination has been neglected, especially in regard to the role of infantile sexuality and the impact of the various unconscious meanings of creativity upon structural conflict. I have no wish to exclude such phenomena nor to minimize their dynamic importance. However, I shall put them in the background in order to highlight some special consequences of the talented artist's original sensory endowment. I shall concentrate on how such endowment affects the artist's early relationship with "transitional objects" and the role of such playthings in the development of a capacity for *controlled illusion*. The capacity for controlled illusion, which will be described in more detail, may be an integral element in all artistic activity, a thread that runs through the whole fabric of the artist's personality organization.

The chapter was stimulated in large measure by the study of gifted adolescents which has been in progress for the past eight years at the Treatment Center of the New York Psychoanalytic Institute.[1] A general description of this project has been given previously (Loomie, Rosen, and Stein, 1958). In this presentation, I shall bring together some observations about these patients, referring especially to three who were addicted to infantile fetishes. Since the whole group consisted of only nine patients and does not conform to the statistician's criteria for a representative random sample, it would be invalid to draw other than impressionistic conclusions from the clinical data.

It should be emphasized at the outset that the attempt to estimate the effect of artistic talent upon the personality of its possessor differs from the attempt sometimes made to reconstruct the character of the artist from a scrutiny of his creative products. The latter aim was neatly disposed of by a young art student who once remarked that all one could know about the personality of Jackson Pollock from his paintings was the way he had played basketball. When I asked him how this was possible, he said, "You can see how he would have dribbled."

The problem of individual accommodation to a talent is discussed in a fascinating paper by Edith Jacobson (1959b). She describes first the effects of disabilities, physical and intellectual, upon character and the structure of neurotic conflict in delineating a personality variant which she calls the *exceptions*. She then continues, "not only those cursed with physical afflictions but also those blessed with extraordinary gifts, with genius, or with outstanding beauty, seem [to be vulnerable] to becoming a special variety of exception."

Greenacre (1957, 1958a, 1958b, 1959) has dealt with this problem perhaps more than anyone else. In one paper (1958b), she develops the idea that the feeling of "difference" that arises in artists as a result of their special ability leads many to think of themselves as impostors, especially at the beginning of their careers. "The possession of extraordinary gifts is apparently not easily taken for granted."

Clinicians, biographers, and writers have known this and have described it in many contexts. Only one aspect of the problem, namely, the creative individual's preoccupation with illusion, will be considered in detail here. Dealing with illusion produces a special tension between cognition and perception in artistic creation. This, in turn, may contribute to certain characteristics that are more or less peculiar to the artist.

Kris (1952) stated that the artist, by directing his artistic activity toward an audience, invites them to participate in an *aesthetic illusion* (cf. Waelder, 1963). He described this as a sharing of a common experience in the mind rather than in action. Aesthetic illusion is part of a more ubiquitous process which we shall refer to, for purposes of definition, as *controlled illusion*. This is synonymous with Coleridge's epigrammatic phrase, "the willing suspension of disbelief," in which both artist and spectator, actor and audience engage (Chapter 11; Beres, 1960). It resembles imaginative play in children. There is an implied agreement on the part of both artist and audience to abandon the axioms of logic, particularly the exclusion of contradiction, and to treat the creative product as simultaneously fantastic and real. In children's play, "make-believe" is an analogous activity. Thus, a chair may become an airplane, but no normal child will attempt to pilot it through an open window. If either the player or the audience deviates from this contract by treating the make-believe object as altogether real or altogether fantastic, the illusion is destroyed (Chapter 11). Kris (1952) also pointed out that art may contain many motifs: propagandist, religious, pedagogic, therapeutic, or erotic; but as soon as one of these becomes an end that transcends the sharing of the aesthetic illusion, the work loses its special artistic appeal and becomes a polemic, a treatise, or an aphrodisiac. In all these instances, the controlled illusion of the participants is dissipated by the transcendent purposes which aim ultimately to convince an audience that something is either real or fantastic but that it cannot be both. The far-reaching consequences for development that are inherent in the constant exposure to the process of controlled illusion constitute a problem that merits further attention.

Many authors agree that one of the essential precursors of artistic talent is a special sensory endowment which determines the perceptual organization of the individual and later becomes what Klein and his associates (Gardner, Holzman, Klein, Linton, and Spence, 1959; Gardner, Jackson and Massick, 1960; Chapter 12) have termed a *cognitive style*. This permits the handling of perceptual ambiguity from an optimal distance and with the necessary flexibility demanded by the process of controlled illusion. Greenacre (1957) also alludes to this. One aspect of genius, she says, is "an endowment [a biological core is implied by this term] of greater than average sensitivity to sensory stimulation, with a consequent intensification of experience, and also a widening of it to include not only the primary object, but more peripheral objects related in some degree or fashion to the primary one." She calls these *collective alternates*. Schachtel (1959) also speaks of the primary significance of perceptual modes in the artistically gifted, arguing that creativity is best studied through perception theory rather than depth psychology. Gombrich (1960), with the sophistication of both an art historian and a psychologist, discusses the artist's sensory equipment and its characteristics which overlap the observational aptitudes of the scientist.

Before presenting case material, I should like to make clear that the phrase *character style* was introduced into the title of this chapter to indicate that the concept of character is used here in one of its specialized meanings. The "character of the artist" is likely to conjure up the image of a bearded Bohemian, while those for whom such a stereotype has been dispelled may strongly object to any attempt at categorization. This discussion is not directed toward the usual character nosology which follows psychopathological nomenclature, nor is it concerned with specific traits or colorful peculiarities of behavior which give distinctiveness to the individual. The term *character* is meant rather to convey the sense of an overall expressive style (Chapter 12; Gardner, Jackson, and Massick, 1960; Steinberg and Weiss, 1954) which determines, in ways that frequently can be predicted, how an individual will react to situations or cope with given tasks.

One stylistic feature of the gifted artist, which often seems externalized in eccentricities or deviations from group conventions and manners, is an unusual capacity to resist the influence of majority decisions on questions of value, particularly of aesthetic value. The deviations and eccentricities produced by this tendency probably result in those characteristics which Jacobson (1959) has called the *exceptions*. This is what the present study would describe as *character style* and one which has important roots in experiments with illusion.

The patient was a nineteen-year-old boy from a well-to-do middle-class family, in his second year of college. He was highly talented in the graphic arts. He began treatment with the statement that his problem was "a question of values." He no longer felt able to make decisions concerning what was important or unimportant, essential or irrelevant. He had become very tense with his parents and complained that they devalued what was important to him. His own devaluation of all that was important to them became apparent subsequently but did not seem to be a debatable issue for the patient. He wanted to leave college, live in Greenwich Village, and lead the Bohemian life he considered essential to artistic development. His parents were alarmed by his friends, whose experimentations with narcotics and bizarre living arrangements they considered "sick." The patient, on the other hand, regarded his parents as "squares," and he went to great pains to point out to them (and to me) that the nosology of psychopathology lends itself to misuse as a tyrannical method for imposing traditional values on those whose ideas and tastes one disapproves. He commented that Freud might become the theoretician of a new dictatorship of the Philistines. Not altogether sure of his own artistic talent despite the encouragement of some experts, he was quite willing to investigate his motives before following in the footsteps of van Gogh and Gauguin. Incidentally, he also decided, from some furtive observations of my taste in art, that I was not beyond intellectual and aesthetic salvation.

He thought that his influence on me might be healthy for the development of psychoanalysis, and this was an added incentive for undertaking therapy.

Against his mother's desperate opposition, the patient had always expressed his individuality by wearing disreputable clothes and by neglecting to bathe and shave. In high school, he had won a scholarship prize which he refused to accept on the grounds that scholarship should be an end it itself; thus, scholarship and prizes were mutually exclusive. Only with difficulty had his teachers persuaded him to limit his action to returning the award and to refrain from enclosing a letter denouncing the Scholarship Prize Committee for attempting to corrupt his ideals.

Until the age of five, he had had a blanket fetish which he was finally induced to renounce "of his own free will" after prolonged nagging by his mother. Voyeuristic activities at a bathing beach occurred between the ages of nine and twelve. On one occasion, he was caught and severely punished by a stranger who had found him peeping through the transom of a woman's dressing room. His parents had viewed such behavior with ambivalent tolerance. At fifteen, he began a polymorphous perverse relationship with a female classmate. This was discovered and he was forced by his mother to renounce the association, again of his "own free will." Part of the pressure she exerted was the threat that continuing his activities might cause her to have a nervous breakdown. The renunciation was followed shortly by masturbation with the fetishistic use of pornographic pictures, a secret practice that he did not reveal in treatment for a long time. Subsequently, with even more embarrassment, he told of an obsessional symptom that had begun about the time he first came to see me. This was a fear that, while walking in the street, he would step into dog feces and then track them into my office.

I shall not try to give the patient's history in detail. At first, he was a rather shy, usually mild-mannered, unshaven, and unkempt young man who exuded a strong body odor from prolonged avoidance of soap and water. For a considerable time his sessions were characterized by stormy episodes. Although he had agreed to make no radical changes in his plans without first discussing them with me, this agreement seemed subject to change without notice on his part. Periodically, he would announce that on the following day he was resigning from college and moving into a loft studio in the Village.

This was his preferred living environment since it would afford him contact with other artists and provide proximity to the Bowery where he could find his favorite subjects for sketching: derelicts, drunkards, and heroin addicts.

Two characteristic behavior patterns became evident in his sessions. In one mood, he would angrily denounce a person, usually his mother, or a social evil such as capital punishment or segregation. In these soliloquies, he would appear as the antagonist with the clear implication that the therapist was the protagonist in the debate. When it was suggested that he seemed to be contending with a straw man and that the debate might be internal, the patient would shift ground. The following session would generally be characterized by strange, pseudonaïve submissiveness, a caricature of free association, in which the confusion of syntax, the reversal of predicates and objects, and the use of pronouns without clearly defined antecedents left the listener in a state of bewilderment. The obsession with dog feces persisted during these sessions.

Two discoveries helped prevent the impasse threatened by these seemingly impenetrable resistances. The first produced a fortuitous intervention. As I was deodorizing the office following one of his sessions, I realized that his fear of tracking in feces was no mere metaphor but a reference to an equivalent reality. Shortly afterward, I told him that I conceded no greater admiration for libertarian ideals than my own and would, if the occasion arose, seize a paintbrush and join him on the barricades to defend the right of every painter to mix his pigments according to his own conscience. However, I continued, in our group of two he was dictating aesthetic values for both of us when he came ragged and unwashed to his session. Granting his right to smell any way he wished in his own digs, I reserved the right to be the arbiter of olfactory style in my own establishment. The patient brightened up, applauded my sentiments, and talked calmly and coherently for the first time. He conceded that he had been losing respect for me because of my apparent indifference to the odor. Even he was finding himself disagreeable. He had only been waiting to learn which of us would break down first. Now he would be able to take a hot shower which he enjoyed very much and of which he had been depriving himself. It subsequently turned out that this solved not merely a conventional problem in setting limits for an overindulged child but also had an intrinsic side effect involving the integrity of perception. It should also be noted that, concurrent with his first bath, the fecal obsession disappeared.

The second discovery was that both these incomprehensible dialogue styles had their origin in doubts about some trivial detail of fact—for example, over the exact time of an appointment or the deadline for a term paper. Ordinarily, the facts in such instances were easily ascertainable. They had become ambiguous because of the patient's inattention (although this is a typical characteristic of obsessional neurotics, an additional contribution to this process is suggested in the present context). His confusion was usually suppressed until a mounting tension, with increasing incoherence of speech and personal neglect, became familiar signals of this peculiar difficulty.

Some time after the beginning of therapy, on one occasion the hour of his regular appointment was changed for our mutual convenience. The previous time had been ten minutes after the hour in the morning; the new time was ten minutes before the hour in the afternoon. Owing to the exigencies of an analytic schedule, I was often somewhat late for the new appointment. One series of alternating debating and pseudoconfusional sessions could be correlated with the fact that on some occasions the patient arrived ten minutes before the stipulated time and on others ten minutes after. When kept waiting, he usually began the session by strongly espousing a new social issue which he had discovered in the newspaper. When he was late and found me waiting for him, his pseudostupidity dominated the session. I finally asked him whether he was uncertain about the precise time that we had agreed upon. He shamefacedly admitted that this was the fact: he could not recall whether the time had been set for ten minutes before or ten minutes after the hour. Rather than set matters straight by asking me, he had tried to divine the answer by clocking the departure time of the previous patient. This proved to be an inconstant reference point and not amenable to any logical analysis. In his debating moods, he was allegorically asserting the correctness of his recollection, while in his pseudoconfusional state, he admitted the opposite possibility. It did not occur to him to ask for the information directly. On many other occasions, similar issues of fact were displaced onto questions of aesthetic value and social ethics. The patient also abjured dictionaries and encyclopedias.

His struggle over remaining in school had a similar background. Flights from scholarship were rebellions against required subjects such as languages or science. Courses in philosophy, creative writing, or the fine arts, on the other hand, gave him great pleasure, especially when the prevailing atmosphere was one in which generalization was encouraged and specific information was not essential. Although he contended that he was opposed to required courses as a matter of principle, it became clear that he was afraid of being influenced by a conventional viewpoint and thus robbed of his originality. The struggle to assimilate factual information fatigued and discouraged him.

Several childhood memories elucidated the role of illusion in the problem. The following is prototypic and is chosen from among many because its banal content was at such variance with the affect engendered in the patient. A precocious child, he had learned to read at an early age. One day, when he was five or six, he called his mother to look at the page he was reading and asked her whether the printing did not seem brown in color. She replied that it might look brown because of the light, but that the printing was black. With mounting irritation, he forced her to look again, repeating that it was brown. Again she agreed that it looked brown but that it really was black. The nascent young painter was deeply offended by this interchange and had a tantrum. He recalls feeling thereafter that he could never again trust his mother's statements about facts.

His derision of his mother's power of observation continues to the present. The meaning of the whole episode, though quite obscure, was somewhat clarified with the aid of a dream. In the dream, he showed his mother a sepia print of a woodcut he had made. It was a figure of a Bowery character, entitled *Rosenbaum*. The dream had followed a session missed because he had failed to read the signs and got on the wrong subway train. It also followed a discussion of his avoidance of technical training because, he alleged, it would teach him representational skills which might interfere with his individual style—a style, incidentally, that covered his deficiencies in draftsmanship and limited his scope. "Rosenbaum," he thought, might mean "Rosen-the-bum." This ambivalent disparagement was a punishment meted out to me for disillusioning him by having "middle-class values" and for making him feel that his failure to take the correct subway train had "psychological significance." He said he did not like to show his art work to his mother because she committed the unpardonable sin of finding a representational figure in an abstraction, assuming that this is what the artist intended. In the same way, he did not like to submit his "disreputable" friends to parental scrutiny.

Now the childhood dispute with his mother became clearer. His mother's rejoinder concerning the illusion of the brown print revealed her enslavement to conventional ideas. He knew that, in typically unimaginative adult terms, she was trying to say that in ordinary light the type would appear black and that its apparent brown color was an illusion produced by the peculiarities of the refracted light in which it was being viewed. None of this language, of course, would have been natural for either of them. The child was trying to demonstrate to his mother a discovery in artistic illusion, one that had been made by many generations of painters before him. Since the print is seen only in one kind of reflected light or another, he was demanding to know how one could be certain that one shade was "true" and the other "illusory." could they not both be "true" or both "illusory" if one were free of any preconceptions? Little did he know that he was dealing with questions of local color and tonal gradations such as Constable had struggled with (Gombrich, 1960). Literal-minded, middle-class, practical mothers have long delegated such distinctions to designers and interior decorators.

At this point I feel we must refine the view that the character of the exception found so frequently in the talented artist comes mainly from feeling set apart by virtue of an asset. In much of a child's education, cognitive correctives for illusory percepts are inculcated to forewarn him against common sources of misconception. The greater the training in any profession or craft, the more a particular body of phenomena is divested of illusion by detailed and controlled inspection. Today there is increasing distrust of illusion and more specialization in various disciplines to keep the cognitive-perceptual field as free as possible of illusory experience. Written records, laws, statutes, standards of weights and measures, etc., serve a similar purpose. This selective abstention from the interpretation of phenomena outside the field of one's special competence does not exist for the artist. It may apply to the medium with which he decides to work, although there is a tendency to disregard the boundaries of the medium of a given art as well as the boundaries of the arts themselves.

Webster defines *illusion*, first, as an unreal or misleading percept presented to the senses, a state of being deceived, or a misconception. Secondarily, it is defined as a perception which fails to give the true character of an object. "Normal illusions" are thus contingent upon ordinary sense perception. It is in this latter sense, as well as in projected fantasy, that the process interests us especially.

Most persons are capable of so-called normal illusions. As a prosaic example, when we look at a line drawing of a transparent cube in perspective on a plane surface, we are generally unaware that any active process is required to see the two-dimensional abstraction as a three-dimensional figure. Not everyone has the same ability to transpose this illusion. Many are defective in the capacity for controlled illusion and are unable to change the positions of the near and far surfaces of the transparent figure at will. This should be possible if the actual planar and illusory solid attributes of the figure can be simultaneously perceived.

Gombrich (1960) gives an illuminating account of the nineteenth-century controversy over the role of sensory experience in art. The inductivist ideal, whose chief proponent was Ruskin, advocated a process of divesting the objects of the external world of all meaning so that they could be seen in their pristine state. This was the tradition of the so-called "innocent eye." Only by making every observation without expectations based on previous experience, Ruskin argued, would it be possible for the painter to see nature as it is seen by the untutored child, undistorted by subsequent sophistication. According to the opposite, deductivist approach, as maintained by Karl Popper, every observation is a question we ask of nature, and every question implies a tentative hypothesis. Popper thought that the description of the way science works was eminently applicable to art. The formula of schema and correction illustrates the procedure. "There is a starting point, a standard of comparison to begin the process of making and matching and remaking which finally becomes embodied in the finished artistic image." Yet the ideals of the innocent eye and of deductive observation are not mutually exclusive. The temporary regression from a constricting preconception of apparently proven validity may allow new subtleties in the marginalia of sensory impressions to impinge upon the visual consciousness (Chapter 3 and 11; Beres, 1960). Once this has been permitted, however, it may be necessary to revert to sophisticated perception in order to match the equivalent relationships of the attributes of objects (the normal illusions) by which we know the natural world.

The work of experimental psychologists in the field of perception has shown that the proponents neither of the innocent eye nor of the experienced eye can explain the variability of illusion. Perception cannot be separated from cognition nor vice versa. Each imposes itself on and is a necessary component of the other. In normal illusions of perspective, texture, solidity, and other formal aspects of the perceived image, cognitive expectation must be superimposed on the percept to make it complete. This cognitive expectation can be reversed or resuspended, so to speak, by a process of disengagement—a reversal of "the willing suspension of disbelief." This is a function of a *supraordinate* rather than of a *subordinate* cognitive process as conceived by the nineteenth-century proponents of the innocent eye. Oscar Wilde's epigram, "There was no fog in London until Whistler painted it," had greater validity than he knew.

Ambiguous forms (Chapter 11; Gardner, Holzman, Klein, Linton and Spence, 1959; Gardner, Jackson and Massick, 1960) allow the play of illusion more freely than discrete ones, by permitting a switching from one cognitive reading to another in a polyvalent figure. Gombrich (1960) says that we will find it hard to describe and analyze this, for—though we may be intellectually aware that any given experience must be illusory—strictly speaking, we cannot watch ourselves having an illusion.

The artist, whether he deals with color or form, linguistic metaphor or musical sound, must continually probe his perceptions, trying alternate interpretations of their ambiguities in the process of matching them within his working medium. The effect of this constant mental operation must have widespread effects upon other aspects of his functioning. One such area of displacement, perhaps better described as concomitant developmental effect, is found in superego functioning. Here the discrete cognitive interpretation of conventional mores and value systems is exchanged for an ambiguous treatment of them. It may be this aspect of the artist's psychic structure that produces the individual not bound by the rules, the character of the exception in his social relationships as described by Jacobson (1959b).

The other aspects of ego functioning in which one can observe the effects of attaching varying cognitive elements to the perception of objects in the play of illusion are the artist's self-representation, human object choices, and his problems of identity. I know of no statistical validation of the widespread impression that there is a higher incidence of overt homosexuality among the artistically talented than among the rest of the population. Certainly analytic experience would indicate that the ubiquitous unconscious bisexuality of all human beings is more frequently utilized and expressed by artists in creative work than by others (Freud, 1910a; Greenacre, 1953, 1957; Kris, 1952).

It has been stated frequently that the special character attributes of the artist allow the creative urge to be expressed against the restrictive anxieties inherent in the molding of media. The authors of another recent study of creative adolescents have stated this as follows: "The creative person's resistance, in the face of opposition to his creative idea, is not the resistance to an id drive or its sublimation, but of the conviction of the truth of the idea, in the face of opposition, by shared autocentricity of conventional perception and thought" (Getzels and Jackson, 1962). This has become a standard notion of the personality of the potential innovator, especially in academic circles. Much has been made of it as an epic quality in the literary biographies of great men of art and science. In this stereotype, as in any other, there is probably an oversimplification. Is there not rather a reciprocal relationship, one in which the character is determined by the capacity for controlled illusion and, in turn, influences and augments the capacity itself?

What are the steps by which the original sensory endowment of the gifted becomes translated into special superego and self-representative structures other than those familiar in ordinary human development? Kris (1952) has described one initial phase in his discussions of the Gifted Adolescent Project, namely, "the crucial discovery" by the child that he has some faculty (i.e., his special sensory endowment) which neither his parents nor others in his environment possess. This is especially true of those children who have absolute pitch and show themselves musically gifted at an early age. (A patient with such a gift recalls lying awake at night as a child, listening restlessly to the whirr of an electric clock with a C-sharp pitch and the drone of a mosquito in E-flat. It was not the mosquito but the dissonance that he could not tolerate.) But there seems to be a second and more crucial stage in the childhood determinants of these attributes. This is the period in which playthings as "transitional objects" assume a special role in ego development. Our clinical data suggest that children with unusual sensory endowment have a peculiar kind of relationship with playthings and that this, in turn, has an important effect on the development of the capacity for controlled illusion.

We are indebted to Winnicott (1953) for calling our attention to the importance of playthings in the development of the intellectual life of the child. In spite of being discrete objects, playthings have sufficient ambiguity to serve a variety of illusory purposes as the content of the fantasy being enacted in play changes. Thus, a plaything, or "transitional object" in Winnicott's terms, is one of the few objects in the individual's life which is "unchallenged in respect to its belonging to inner or external (shared) reality." It constitutes a great part of the infant's experience with the inanimate world. Winnicott suggests that throughout life this capacity for re-representing the malleable object in the excitement of play "is retained in the intense experiencing that belongs to the arts and religion, to imaginative living, and to creative scientific work." A plaything that changes its character from a valued possession to an obligatory companion is called an *infantile fetish* (cf. Muensterberger, 1951; Stevenson, 1954; Wulff, 1946). This is an important feature of the childhood development of the patient just described.[2]

In two other gifted patients, reported in Chapters 3 and 12, we observed infantile fetishes that played crucial roles in their development. One such patient,seen at the age of twenty, confided in the first interview that since the age of two she had been sleeping constantly with a large teddy bear, a gift from her father some time before his death. This girl, a lonely, highly gifted mathematician, remarked pathetically on one occasion: "I live very happily alone, with my teddy bear and with my problems in variables as real functions." She was also greatly interested in the illusory aspects of experience.

I do not mean to suggest that it has been established that infantile fetishes are a regular part of the childhood experience of the artistically gifted. It seems likely, however, that in their childhood, certain factors may shift the balance of forces which determine whether a plaything will be a valued or an obligatory possession. In the gifted child, experimentation with illusion may be one of the forces which have a determining effect and which shift the balance in the direction of fetishistic overvaluation of the transitional object. Nor do I wish to suggest that every child with an infantile fetish is destined, by virtue of this token, to become artistically successful. A closer inspection of the role of playthings in the development of gifted individuals, however, might indicate that they have greater developmental importance than has been assigned them previously.

One feature deserving special attention is the attitude of the environment to any demonstration of overinvestment in such objects. An overt or covert hostility toward the fetish on the part of the parent is quite common. This is often revealed by the compensatory devaluation of the fetish in an attempt to divest it of its illusory qualities and thereby loosen the child's attachment to it. The adult's rationalization for this may range from mere matters of housekeeping convenience to pseudosophisticated fears concerning the psychological consequences of such addictions. In this way the prized possession usually becomes ambivalantly involved in a set of sharply contrasting value judgments.

In the case of our young art student, the childhood relationship with his "bah" (the blanket fetish) helped to elucidate many of the peculiar aspects of his choices and preferences and to clarify several obscure features of the transference. It explained the emphasis on the negative features of objects and activities that he prized and the need to find a parent surrogate so that the struggle of value judgments and the testing of illusion could be repeated. The patient's seemingly perverse preference for just those negative features that made the object disagreeable to the observer had its reflexive counterpart in the neglect of his personal appearance. The positive aspects of his relationship with the therapist had been paradoxically expressed by turning himself into a "bah" so that he, too, would be retained as a prized possession. His choice of friends, his preference for derelicts as artistic subjects, and for girl friends of ill repute were all part of the same pattern. Mention of the anal background of such characterological traits and the metaphorical equivalence to the child's treatment of his fecal product is necessary only to forestall the objection that it was overlooked. It seems less illuminating in its contribution to an understanding of these object-relational patterns than is the patient's struggle with his mother over the possession of his notorious "bah."

This struggle also apparently provides the prototypic object relationship for understanding other conflictual situations. The "bah" (as the ultimate in prized inanimate possessions) is a polyvalent object. Like the Rorschach blot, a waterfall, or the flickering flames of the fireplace, it allows the fascinated gazer to play with illusions—that special conjunction of fantasy and perception which almost all human beings can appreciate. Aesthetic experience can be attached to formal notions of ugliness no less than to beauty. About half a century before Picasso and other experimenters in the aesthetics of deformity, an important philosopher named Humpty Dumpty made the following observations:

> "I shouldn't know you again if we did meet," Humpty Dumpty replied in a discontented tone, giving Alice one of his fingers to shake. "You are so exactly like other people."
>
> "The face is what one generally goes by," Alice remarked in a thoughtful tone.
>
> "That is just what I complain of," said Humpty Dumpty, "your face is the same as everybody's. It has two eyes, a nose in the middle, and a mouth under it—it's always the same. Now, if you had the two eyes on the same side of the nose, for instance, or the mouth at the top, that would be some help."
>
> "It wouldn't look nice," Alice objected.
>
> But Humpty Dumpty only closed his eyes and said, "Wait till you've tried" [Lewis Carroll, *Through the Looking Glass*].

When the "bah" became a soiled, unpleasant, malodorous remnant as far as the mother was concerned, it still retained its softness of texture and acquiescent malleability of form for the patient. How better could one present one's case for the preservation of this memento than to condense the two aesthetic value judgments in typical primary-process fashion? The idea might be paraphrased thus: My "bah" is a magic possession; it is the touchstone of the omnipotence of fantasy; it can be all things to me—comfort for my lonely hours, an ally in my battles, and an enemy with which to contend when I am surfeited with allies. Besides, it is practical; it is a blanket for cold nights. My mother says that it is ugly, dirty, and smells bad. This only goes to show that what is ugly, dirty, and smells bad is what I want most in the world. Therefore it must be beautiful.

The neurotic counterpart of the innocent eye and the artist's need to probe his perceptual interpretations by remaining free of the "brainwashing" potential of standardized representations is illustrated by a waggish canard which alleges that a recent Secretary of State had a sign made for his desk which read: "Do not confuse me with facts; my mind is already made up."

Another patient (see Chapter 12) treated in the Gifted Adolescent Project revealed both the assets and the liabilities of this mode of operation. A gifted musician and mathematician, his mathematical talents were characterized by a highly individual approach to the solution of problems. His aptitude was protected by a stubborn unwillingness to investigate any previous methods of solution until he was sure he had exhausted his own store of illuminations. He suffered from severe social inhibitions and sexual difficulties. Like the young artist, he was addicted to "girlie magazines." The patient also had gone through a childhood struggle with his mother over the relinquishment of an infantile fetish—a special pillow that was necessary to his falling asleep. In his current work he often used a "pillow image" which was compressed or pushed into various shapes as a means of conceptualizing problems in the mathematical field of topology. This very quiet and unassuming young man also had an unusual capacity for making himself objectionable. He was careless with the possessions of others and had to be reminded to bathe and to change his clothes. In schedule or appointment conflicts with me, he never tried to ascertain the facts that might relate to problems of mutual convenience. Instead, he would act as if he were having an obsessional indecision over two choices that were his alone to make. Like the previous patient, he treated such conflicts as attempts to find an internal validity for an aesthetic preference rather than a practical compromise involving two people. The process followed the artistic pattern of maintaining an external ambiguity in order to foster the potential play of illusion.

The connection between fetishism and the problem of illusion is a complex and fascinating study in itself. Several authors, notably Bak (1953) and Greenacre (1953), have indicated the relationship of adult fetishism to the maintenance of an illusion of a female phallus. Anthropologists have long considered the religious fetishes of primitive man as phylogenetic precursors of civilized art. A recent study by Muensterberger (1951, 1961) relates the anthropological data to artistic creativity. The magical fetishes of primitive man were greatly prized, often highly sculptured and painted objects. The similarity in the way they are treated and in their ultimate purpose to the fetishes of childhood produces some stimulating conjectures. Muensterberger says, for example, that from "the role given the fetish, or any other magically potent object in preliterate cultures, it is possible to surmise that these devices have the task of completing what otherwise would be impossible. They provide the means of *creating an illusion*, characterized not only by the wish for omnipotence but also the denial of dependence." The same study points out what the adult fetishist (cf. Wulff, 1946) and the artist have in common. Muensterberger says that both are usually male and need an external object to sustain illusion, the one to retain genitality and the other to sustain a belief in his creative capacity.

The hypothesis concerning the role of illusion and the relationship of transitional objects to the development of the character style of artists would not be complete without also pointing out its antithesis. Two authors have written about "doll phobias" in different contexts. The doll is undoubtedly a paradigm for a plaything with transitional object potentialities.[3] Although the childhood fetish is a well-observed clinical entity, childhood phobias that refer particularly to potentially fetishistic objects have not been classified, so far as I know, as an entity. Rangell (1952) describes a male patient with a doll phobia. The phobia went beyond the specific object, however, and included "any kind of three-dimensional figure, of dolls with which children play, of manikins, of window dummies, puppets, pieces of sculpture, of figurines, of an ash tray or lamp base that might be carved as a figure, etc."—in fact anything that might produce an illusion, artistic or otherwise. Rangell's patient was not only fearful of illusion but was also a stickler for following the advice of authority and adhering to the letter, if not the spirit, of all advice given him. He was also a statistical analyst: a statistician, it should be noted, considers himself the great dispeller of illusion. Stewart (1961) also describes a doll phobia in a borderline patient whose clinical history shows that a tendency to conventionality and stereotyped ideas which interfered with the therapeutic alliance are implicit in the character of this patient. In both cases, apparently, the fear of the plaything is connected with its illusory possibilities and the disturbance of the patient's capacities for "controlling" such illusions. An inhibition of imagination and originality, with a consequent dependence upon "safe" external standards established by majority fiat, seems to be the characterological accompaniment of this symptom.

Summary

The following statement may help to solidify some of the loosely coupled ideas that have gone before: a ubiquitous characteristic of artistically talented individuals, which may be more or less shared by others who are lacking in specific gifts, is a resistance to certain kinds of group judgments. This is largely in the area of values, particularly aesthetic values, where questions of illusion and the standardization of subjective choice and preference produce a special tension between the cognitive experience derived from cultural pressures and the perceptual experience of the individual. In resolving these problems, there is a spectrum of cognitive styles forming a continuum from the artist, who prefers to see polyvalent illusory possibilities in the phenomena that are at variance with conventional interpretations, to the literal-minded, practical "realist." The artist insists upon seeing conventional standards as the illusion of the majority. This characteristic also contributes to the quality of exceptionalism found in so so many talented individuals. Though appearing to be based on principle, this may well be a rationalization that conceals its obligatory aspects. The stand against the influence of conventional illusions often needs to be sustained by resistance to seeking or registering factual details of the environment.

I suggest that some roots of the obligatory behavior lie in initial constitutional differences which originate in particular kinds of sensitivity to perceptual stimuli. This propensity may develop further during early childhood when separation from the mother and attachments to playthings are paramount problems. Playthings tend to assume a particular importance for highly gifted children, and their value as illusion-sustaining external objects increases the likelihood that transitional objects will become infantile fetishes. This unusual attachment to certain playthings in turn influences many aspects of the parent-child relationship. It may also foster particularly early and sturdy defenses against parental influence in value judgments and, ultimately, similar resistance to cultural conformity. In its turn, this feature of the artistic predisposition becomes an asset for the implementation of creative talent as well as an element in the artist's object relations and internal conflicts. In its final outcome, such a chain of developmental events contributes both to the talented individual's success as an original artist and to his social liabilities as an exception.

More detailed observations of the relationship of children to their playthings in the transitional-object stage might be revealing, particularly if such studies were correlated with estimates of precocious perceptual development and capacities for controlled illusion. Predictive testing of such studies against future creative achievements of the individual, while posing a formidable research task, might reward us richly by increasing our understanding of this important aspect of psychic functioning.

Notes

1. The study was supported by funds from the Arthur Davison Ficke Foundation and through the generosity of Mrs. Gladys Ficke. The late Dr. Ernst Kris was the organizer and chairman; Dr. Marianne Kris has served in a similar capacity since her husband's death. The following have also been associated with the project: Drs. Phyllis Greenacre, Mary O'Neil Hawkins, Edith Jacobson, Margaret Mahler, Annie Reich, and Leo Stone. Those who analyzed gifted patients as part of the project are: Dr. Leo Loomie, the late Mrs. Christine Olden, Drs. Samuel Ritvo, Allan Roos, Victor Rosen, and Martin Stein.

2. The close connection between controlled illusion, play, and imagination should be emphasized at this point. A recent paper in *Science* (Gruber, Krug, and Link, 1963) on the moon illusion describes it as an event in "imaginary space" and the result of a conflict between perception and cognition.

3. Stevenson (1954), however, would call it a "secondary" transitional object.

Epilogue

by THEODORE SHAPIRO, M.D.

If one were to mention the Zuider Zee to a reasonably educated man he would immediately grasp the denotative significance of this area of the Netherlands which was reclaimed from the sea. If the man happened to be a psychoanalyst, he would also have a simultaneous association to the simile Freud draws between that remarkable feat of engineering and the process epitomized in the epigram "where id was, there ego shall be" (Freud, 1933). On the other hand, if one said "colorless green ideas sleep furiously" to a psychoanalyst, he would probably have a hard time decoding the proposition and would no more recognize its significance than if he were told a formula in astrophysics. Nonetheless, this latter sentence calls up as many connotations to a linguist as the reclamation of the Zuider Zee does to the psychoanalyst. The contrast is but a single example of the narrow locus of activity in which specialists work. Simple reference and regular syntax no longer guarantee adequacy of communication among scientists. The richness of reference above and beyond the general scientific competence which permits one to read *Scientific American* is lost to people in specialized fields.

Victor Rosen's roaming intellect sought to master linguistics as well as psychoanalysis; in the latter he was already a competent practitioner and theoretician. He justified his attempt with the argument that the interest of psychoanalysis would be served if he could expand the scope of his understanding to include the data and theory of this burgeoning field. He seemed to have taken seriously Whitehead's call for an integration of sciences, each of which articulates with and "prehends" the other by virtue of the fact that the subject matter of each is, after all, unified by man's powers to reason.

While this integration may seem admirable and to hold great promise, we must recall that specialists of all varieties tend to be covetous of their own specific vantage points. Otherwise we would not have as many apologists, Christian and otherwise, treating those who would explore elsewhere as something alien, as dabblers and Philistines. The conscientiousness and devotion necessary to make a "specialist" requires a single-mindedness whose corollary is that exploration elsewhere is a "hobby"; serious practitioners of an art or science have little time or *leftover cathexis* for idle enterprises. The pragmatic test of usefulness is one which psychoanalysts often apply when one of its practitioners tries to introduce into the field a new area such as linguistics. In short, it is not easy to make welcome one well-formed scientific point of view into the working arena of another without some grumbling or suspicion.

During the early 1960s, when Victor Rosen had already completed work which would have earned him a lasting place among psychoanalytic thinkers, he supervised a student at the New York Psychoanalytic Institute who formulated his treatment case using a linguistic model to account for aspects of ego organization that he had observed. The new vantage point stimulated Victor Rosen and resonated with ideas already in forme fruste in his paper on style (Chapter 12); there he had already made special mention of language behavior as a major manifestation of style. With characteristic generosity, Dr. Rosen created a medium in which his student could present some of his linguistic formulations applied to an analytic case; he invited others to listen in the hope that the work would broaden the scope of analytic modeling and theorizing. Thus Rosen shepherded a student and initiated the Language Study Group at the New York Psychoanalytic Institute. Initially the group was made up of a steady and heady membership. The list of contributors and participants includes many important names within psychoanalysis in the New York area, and the visiting speakers provided an equally prominent list of thinkers in both psychology and linguistics. Among the early visitors were Roman

Jakobson and Bernard Kaplan. In 1964 Dr. Rosen, with the assistance of Dr. Henry Edelheit, took the further step of suggesting to the curriculum committee at the New York Psychoanalytic Institute that a fourth year course in Ego Psychology and Language for candidates be included in the program. The students appreciated this new vantage point, and the readings and discussion coordinating analytic work and linguistics stimulated a number of us to pursue further the interface of linguistics and psychoanalysis. Those who had joined the study group at its inception had already mastered many basic readings and the concepts they elaborated. It was a difficult thing to begin in media res where a group of distinguihsed analysts who had begun to master another field had already trod. But one realized, soon after joining, that the very heads that had been aroused to work along with Victor Rosen in this new field were beginning to weary of this new science which demanded so much concentration and study. Stunning advances and complexities had developed, especially through the work of Chomsky and his confreres, and the data seemed more and more remote from psychoanalysis; the pursuit of sentences such as "colorless green ideas sleep furiously" seemed trivial to practitioners involved in the practical human endeavor of caring for patients. Although it was challenging to think that the surface structure and deep structure of the linguist were analogous to systems Cs and Ucs, the correlations were for most difficult to come by and even more difficult to integrate with clinical practice.

In 1969, Victor Rosen himself suggested the relevant intersections between language study and psychoanalysis. In his introduction to a panel on Language and Psychoanalysis (Chapter 8) he stated that the three seminal areas of intersection were (1) rule-directed behavior, (2) the relationship of language to thought process, and (3) linguistic relativity. It is curious that, if one looks at each of these three areas, they were not, by and large, in the main stream of concern for linguists, who seemed inextricably involved in and fascinated by syntax and what was called language *competence* as opposed to language *performance*. For clarification, a brief summary of the different paths language studies take is provided by three distinctions first proffered by Morris (1938): reference, syntax, and pragmatics. Reference pertains to the relationship between words, things, and concepts. Syntax examines the relation of words to words and the meaning accrued from structure. Pragmatics involves both the relation of words to people and the sciences lying adjacent, such as communication and information theory and kinesics. The fact was that the most popular subject matter of linguistics at that time was a sentence intuited—and placed without context on an index card—by an academic linguist who spoke a specific language. This was a world apart from the data base of a psychoanalyst. The latter was involved in studying patients in dynamic action in the transference and in the interaction of their symbolic organizations with their active lives. The bridge between the two disciplines was at best uncertain in the minds of many. Were the formalisms learned from contexless grammar transferable to psychological mapping or cognitive organization? That such psychodynamic formulations as repression and dynamic unconscious applied was considered even more unlikely.

In retrospect, I believe that the realization that the linguist's method was so different from the psychoanalyst's approach became the impetus for Victor Rosen to organize an interdisciplinary colloquium held at the Mid-Winter Meeting of the American Psychoanalytic Association in 1970. Dr. Rosen brought together a group of professionals and scholars from various disciplines (including developmental psychology, linguistics, art history, and literary criticism) to talk about their understanding of symbolism and the symbolic process. There was a rich diet of mutual nourishment from the speakers and the analysts who participated. The speakers from the areas outside analysis found themselves in a difficult discourse confounded by much specialization of language and unfamiliarity with others' frameworks. When one analyst at the end of the meeting suggested that we, in analysis, could use the skills of a philosopher-linguist to recommend to us a course of revision for psychoanalytic theory, the retort offered was, "You need us like a bridge builder needs a molecular physicist!" The analogy is well taken, because although some of the data and theorizing illuminated aspects of the substructure of language organization, the means of arriving at results satisfactory to each professional's aims were quite different. The methods of analysis used by each discipline were suited to differing requirements for excellence and different pragmatic goals. These would seem discouraging results for a colloquium organized to bring people together—if one were bound to doing or accepting as one's own that which other sciences do better. However, Dr. Rosen's aim in organizing the symposium in the first place had been to expose psychoanalysts to others' knowledge of symbolism and to bear witness that the specialized aloneness of analysts was not unique and that our approach had a life of its own and was complementary to other views.

By this time there was attrition within the study group itself. Many of the early members left and some of the younger people who had been influenced by Dr. Rosen's teaching at the Institute remained and had had more recent exposure to the data from these other sciences, even in their highly specialized form. However, contentment in studying others did not last long, because application is always a problem for specialists. The interplay between thinking and doing, between clinic and theory that Freud lived and taught pushed a number of members of the study group to intergrate what they had read into new contributions for psychoanalysts. Papers integrating psychoanalysis with linguistics were produced in a number of areas. Reviewing them, one finds that these papers were not slavishly beholden to the linguistics of the period, but rather were much more concerned with the study of language in its more general sense. Henry Edelheit wrote about ego structure in relation to language organization; Sam Atkin took a close look at the relation of thought and language. These were topics both had nurtured even prior to the formation of the study group but which afterward took a more refined form. Problems of sign phenomena and their relation to unconscious meaning with respect to reference, disturbances in representation, and a new look at Freud's view of schizophrenic thinking and language were topics approached by Victor Rosen himself. Interpretation of unconscious fantasies was reformulated by this author as a form of naming. There is no paper written at that time which approaches and integrates syntactic theory, the major thrust of Chomsky's revolution. (To some degree M. Edelson's 1975 publication relates dream interpretation to a Chomskian syntactic system. He may have been somewhat influenced by Victor Rosen's brief stay at the Yale Medical School, and he clearly refers to Rosen's work in his bibliography.) While this may seem discouraging with respect to what the new linguists themselves were doing, it should not be seen as such, because the critical distinctions made by linguists of a broader persuasion were terribly useful for analytic clarification of such basic concepts as primary and secondary process and for clarification of the symbolic process both developmentally and in its many adult forms. *Meaning* is a psychoanalyst's stock-in-trade, although its meaning is elusive. Linguistic approaches were helpful in providing distinctions in terminology and categorization which analytic theory had not provided. As Victor Rosen was fond of saying, "Freud found meaning in the meaningless." He might have extended the epigram to include his own contribution. He was now finding the distinctions which were relevant for psychoanalysis in the linguists' use of, and view of, meaning.

While the Language Study Group was studying Chomsky and his followers and was struggling to remain au courant in an alien field, a curious evolution had been taking place among linguists themselves. The exclusive concern for pure contextless grammar was being challenged from within by both linguists and philosophers, and a hybrid strain of scientists called psycholinguists came on the scene in the late sixties and early seventies. The fact was introduced by these new sectarians that when one examined the formalisms used to explore competence and to derive meaning from syntax, their application to actual language use was found to be limited. The data of language as a system (de Saussure's *langue*) and the data of language in use (*parole*) did not always coincide or, more relevantly, one system did not explain fully the data of the second (de Saussure, 1916). It had been the aim and hope of Chomskian linguists to derive a quasi-mathematical statement about the structure of sentences such that one could apply a minimal set of rules which would ultimately describe an individual speaker's capacity for, or competence with, that language, even in its limitless potential for the creation of novel sentences. This minimal set of rules consisted of a base called *deep structure*. This represents a pool of potential sentences which are then acted upon by a number of *transformational rules* which a language-competent individual applies to achieve a newly generated *surface structure* in one of a variety of forms we are accustomed to call passive voice, imperative, interrogative, etc. The specific word that could be plugged into any slot within a particular sentence could be designated as appropriate for that slot by a *feature* analysis, which is a further set of distinctions which makes a word permissible or not permissible for any position in a sentence. For example, in order for a noun as subject of a sentence to fit with a predicate, such as feeling guilt, that noun has to have specific features of animateness, and more specifically humanness, rather than inanimateness to correspond to the predicate or verb phrase. Similarly, green ideas may not sleep or, for that matter, be both green and colorless. These formalisms looked very promising for the future of a mathematics of language. However, ambiguities arose when the formalisms were applied to questions of meaning and to observations of children's speech development, and within linguistics itself today there is a split between syntagmaticists and semanticists.

The new semanticists rewrote Chomsky's formulations with semantics and reference at the base and the transformations arising at the syntactic level. Copernicus and Ptolemy revisited? Toward the end of his life, I remember Victor Rosen discovering a new volume by Chafe which espoused these viewpoints. Rosen seemed to derive new excitement from the fact that the newer grammarians had moved closer to psychoanalytic modeling, which depends more on referential than on grammatical models. Our understanding of the meaning of sentences, i.e., how they are read in action contexts, is dependent not only upon base cognitive structures and syntactic organization but also upon information lying adjacent to syntactic data. Indeed the stuff of linguistics had been closely allied to autonomous ego functions, while analysts are more excited by conflicted man—or anxious man. Thus, what was happening in linguistics itself or what had now become psycholinguistics was running a path somewhat parallel to that traveled earlier by the Language Study Group under Victor Rosen. Clinical practice simply did not seem to admit of a contextless grammar application, and every paper that came from the group seemed to be shy of the mark, leaning rather toward reference, thought, and meaning than toward grammar itself.

The current growing interest in what have been called "speech acts" and an accordant interest in intentionality come closer and closer to analytic concerns than even Victor Rosen might have thought when he began the study group. He would have welcomed the new work and thought, because its emphasis is much closer to psychoanalytic formulations. In this new formulation, meaning is embedded in the speech act, which includes not only the propositional form but also a directive or *illocutionary* device stated or inferred in the grammatical structure. Such speech acts as promising and warning require analysis of intention or missed intention, either of which is subject to the distortions psychopathology may require. Victor Rosen would surely have enjoyed exploring this new area.

The Language Study Group lasted for two more years after Rosen left New York, with three or four of us studying developmental linguistics and schizophrenic language disorders. Finally I asked that we discontinue our meetings, feeling that we all missed the spark of Victor Rosen's intellect and his ability to see concordances with psychoanalysis. At our last meeting we discussed Rosen's last paper (Chapter 10), which soon after his death I had had the privilege of editing. It is a psychoanalytic paper on interventions in analysis. At first glance, it seems very far from linguistics, but it is in fact a heavily, embedded sentence with many ellipses: its referent is ten and more years of linguistic study applied to psychoanalysis.

The Writings of Victor H. Rosen

1941 Optic Neuritis caused by a coal tar hair dye. With M. Keshner. *Archives of Ophthalmology* 25:1020-1024.

1943 Effect of metrazol convulsions on conditioned reflexes in dogs. With W. H. Gantt. *Archives of Neurology and Psychiatry* 50:8-17.

1950 The role of denial in acute postoperative affective reactions following the removal of body parts. *Psychosomatic Medicine* 12:356-361.

1952 Psychiatric problems in general surgery. In *The Psychology of Physical Illness*, edited by L. Bellak. New York: Grune and Stratton.

Short term management of a child behavior disorder. With E. Landsberg. *Pediatrics* 10:484-489.

1953 On mathematical illumination and the mathematical thought process: a contribution to the genetic development and metapsychology of abstract thinking. *Psychoanalytic Study of the Child* 8:127-154.

1955 The reconstruction of a traumatic childhood event in a case of derealization. *Journal of the American Psychoanalytic Association* 3:211-221.

Strephosymbolia: an intrasystemic disturbance of the synthetic function of the ego. *Psychoanalytic Study of the Child* 10:83-89.

1956 Changes in family equilibrium through psychoanalytic treatment. In *Neurotic Interaction in Marriage*, edited by V. Eisenstein. New York: Basic Books.

1957 Panel report: Preoedipal factors in neurosogenesis. *Journal of the American Psychoanalytic Association* 5:146-157.

1958 Abstract thinking and object relations. *Journal of the American Psychoanalytic Association* 6:653-671.

Ernst Kris and the gifted adolescent project. With L. Loomie and M. Stein. *Psychoanalytic Study of the Child* 13:44-57.

The initial psychiatric interview and the principles of psychotherapy: some recent contributions. *Journal of the American Psychoanalytic Association* 6:154-167.

1959 Chairman: Isolation. A panel. *Journal of the American Psychoanalytic Association* 7:163-172.

Originality and the adolescent group. *Child Study* 36:15-20.

1960 Discussion of: "Borderline states in childhood and adolescence." In *Recent Developments in Psychoanalytic Child Therapy*, edited by J. Weinreb. New York: International Universities Press.

Some aspects of the role of imagination in the analytic process. *Journal of the American Psychoanalytic Association* 8:229-251.

1961 Relevance of "style" to certain aspects of defence and the synthetic function of the ego. *International Journal of Psycho-Analysis* 42:447-457. Also in: *Revista Uruguaya Psicoanalisis* 12:247-272.

1962 The relationship of the Institute to the community. In *Fruition of an Idea: Fifty Years of Psychoanalysis in New York*, edited by M. Wangh. New York: International Universities Press.

1963 Variants of comic caricature and their relationship to obsessive-compulsive phenomena. *Journal of the American Psychoanalytic Association* 11:704-724.

1964 Chairman: Depersonalization. A panel. *Journal of the American Psychoanalytic Association* 12:171-186.

Some aspects of the role of imagination in the analytic process. *Journal of the American Psychoanalytic Association* 8:229-251.

Contribution to: Symposium on fantasy. *International Journal of Psycho-Analysis* 45:195-198.

1966 Disturbances of representation and reference in ego deviations. In *Psychoanalysis, a General Psychology*, edited by R. M. Loewenstein et al. New York: International Universities Press.

Comment on: "Psychodynamic aspects of defence with comments on technique in the treatment of obsessional neuroses" by F. Morgenthaler. *International Journal of Psycho-Analysis* 47:210-211.

1967 Disorders of communication in psychoanalysis. *Journal of the American Psychoanalytic Association* 15:467-490.

Discussion of: "Characterological aspects of marital interaction" by P. Giovacchini. *Psychoanalytic Forum* 2:16.

1968 A re-examination of some aspects of Freud's theory of schizophrenic language disturbance. *Journal of the Hillside Hospital* 17:242-258.

Chairman: Language and the development of the ego. A panel. *Journal of the American Psychoanalytic Association* 16:113-122.

1969 Introduction to panel on language and psychoanalysis. *International Journal of Psycho-Analysis* 50:113-116. Also in: *Revista de Psicoanalisis* 27:27-34 (1970) and *Psyche* 26:81-88 (1972).

1970 Sign phenomena and their relationship to unconscious meaning. *International Journal of Psycho-Analysis* 50:197-207. Also in: *Revista Uruguaya Psicoanalisis* 12:273-310.

Chairman: Language and psychoanalysis. A panel. *International Journal of Psycho-Analysis* 51:237-243.

1971 Is it possible to have a distinctive methodological approach to psychotherapy? *Bulletin of the New Jersey Psychoanalytical Society* 3:14-18.

The role of metapsychology in therapeutic interpretation. In *Currents in Psychoanalysis*, edited by I. Marcus. New York: International Universities Press.

1972 Chairman: The relationship of language development to problem-solving ability. A panel. *Journal of the American Psychoanalytic Association* 20:145-155.

Book Reviews

Buss, A., *The Psychology of Aggression. Psychoanalytic Quarterly* 32:106-108 (1963).

Getzels, J. W., and Jackson, P. W., *Creativity and Intelligence: Explorations with Gifted Students. Psychoanalytic Quarterly* 32:423-425 (1963).

Gombrich, E. H., *Art and Illusion. Journal of Nervous and Mental Diseases* 132:344-346 (1961).

Hallman, R. J., *The Psychology of Literature: A Study of Alienation and Tragedy. Journal of Nervous and Mental Diseases* 133:556-557 (1961).

Hayden, D. E., and Alworth, E. P., eds., *Classics in Semantics. Psychoanalytic Quarterly* 37:149-151 (1968).

Koch, S., ed., *Psychology: A Study of a Science II. Empirical Substructure and Relations with Other Sciences. Psychoanalytic Quarterly* 33:448-450 (1964).

Meerloo, J. A. M., *Unobtrusive Communication: Essays In Psycholinguistics. Psychoanalytic Quarterly* 36:615-617 (1967).

Piaget, J., *The Child's Conception of Geometry. Psychoanalytic Quarterly* 30:125-127 (1961).

Piaget, J., *The Construction of Reality in the Child. Psychoanalytic Quarterly* 24:450-453 (1955).

Roe, A., *The Making of a Scientist. Psychoanalytic Quarterly* 23:132-133 (1954).

Schur, M., *The Id and the Regulatory Principles of Mental Functioning. International Journal of Psycho-Analysis* 49:100-101 (1968).

Stein, M. T., and Heinze, S. J., *Creativity and the Individual. Psychoanalytic Quarterly* 31:271-272 (1962).

Thass-Thienemann, T., *The Subconscious Language. Psychoanalytic Quarterly* 38:661-664 (1969).

Werner, H., and Kaplan, B., *Symbol Formation: an Organismic Developmental Approach to Language and the Expression of Thought. Psychoanalytic Quarterly* 34:456-459 (1965).

White, R., *Ego and Reality In Psychoanalytic Theory. International Journal of Psycho-Analysis* 46:256-258 (1965).

Bibliography

Abrams, M. H. (1958). *The Mirror and the Lamp: Romantic Theory and the Critical Tradition.* New York: Norton.

Adler, A. (1933). Was kann die Individualpsychologie sur mathematischen "Begabung" sagen. *Int. Ztschr. f. Individualpsychol.* 11: 42-43.

Allport, G. W. (1924). Eidetic imagery. *British Journal of Psychology* 15:99-120.

Ameline, M. (1913). Psychologie et origine de certains procedes arithmetiques adoptes par les calculateurs prodiges. *J. de psychol. normale et pathologiques* 10:465-490.

Arlow, J. A., and Brenner, C. (1964). Psychoanalytic concepts and the structural theory. *Journal of the American Psychoanalytic Association* Monograph series, no. 3. New York: International Universities Press.

Atkin, S. (1969). Psychoanalytic considerations of language and thought. *Psychoanalytic Quarterly* 28:103-109.

———(1974). A borderline case: ego synthesis and cognition. *International Journal of Psycho-Analysis* 55: Part 1.

———(1975). Ego synthesis and cognition in a borderline case. *Psychoanalytic Quarterly* 44, No. 1.

Avery, C. B., ed. (1962). *The New Century Classical Handbook.* New York: Appleton-Century-Crofts.

Bahia, A. (1952). El contenido y la defensa en la creacion artistica.

Rev. de Psicoanalisis 9:311-334.

Bak, R. C. (1946). Masochism in paranoia. *Psychoanalytic Quarterly* 15:285-301.

———(1953). Fetishism. *Journal of the American Psychoanalytic Association* 1:285-298.

Baker, S. J. (1951). The mathematics of the unconscious. *Journal of Clinical and Experimental Psychopathology* 12:192-212.

Balkányi, C. (1964). On verbalization. *International Journal of Psycho-Analysis* 45:64-74.

———(1967). Verbalization and the superego: some thoughts on the development of the sense of rules. Bulletin of the New York Psychoanalytic Association 7:15-17.

Barlow, F. (1952). *Mental Prodigies.* New York: Philosophical Library.

Bates, E. S. (1937). *The Bible: Designed to be Read as Living Literature, the Old and New Testaments in the King James Version.* New York: Simon & Schuster, pp. 1006-1007.

Beckett, S. (1961). *Happy Days.* New York: Grove Press.

Beke, E. (1933). Ueber mathematische "Bebabung." *Int. Ztschr. f. Individualpsychol.* 11:33-41.

Bell, E. T. (1937). *Men of Mathematics.* New York: Simon & Schuster.

Bender, L., and Schilder, P. (1951). Graphic arts as a special ability in children with a reading disability. *Medical Women's Journal* 58:11-18.

Beres, D. (1951). A dream, a vision and a poem. *International Journal of Psycho-Analysis* 32:1-20.

———(1956). Ego deviations and the concept of schizophrenia. *Psychoanalytic Study of the Child* 11:164-235.

———(1957). Communication in psychoanalysis and in the creative process: a parallel. *Journal of the American Psychoanalytic Association* 5:408-423.

———(1960). The psychoanalytic psychology of imagination. *Journal of the American Psychoanalytic Association* 8:252-269.

———(1962). The unconscious fantasy. *Psychoanalytic Quarterly* 31:309-328.

Bergman, P., and Escalona, S. (1949). Unusual sensitivities in very young children. *Psychoanalytic Study of the Child* 3/4:333-352.

Bibring, E. (1954). Psychoanalysis and the dynamic psychotherapies. *Journal of the American Psychoanalytic Association* 2:745-770.

Bieberbach, L. (1934). Personalichkeitsstruktur und mathematisches Schaffen. *Forschungen uber die Fortschritte deutscher Wissenschaft* 10:235-237.

Binet, A. (1894). *Psychologie des grads calculateurs et joueurs d'echecs*. Paris: Hatchette.

Bion, W. A. (1962). A theory of thinking. *International Journal of Psycho-Analysis* 43:306-310.

Black, M. (1952). *The Nature of Mathematics*. New York: Humanities Press.

Blanchard, P. (1928) Reading disabilities in relation to maladjustment. *Mental Hygeine*, 12:772-788.

———(1935). Psychogenic factors in some cases of reading disability. *American Journal of Orthopsychiatry* 5:361-374.

———(1947). Psychoanalytic contributions to the problems of reading disabilities. *Psychoanalytic Study of the Child* 2:163-188.

Bolles, M., and Goldstein, K. (1938). A study of the impairment of "abstract behavior" in schizophrenic patients. *Psychiatric Quarterly* 12:733-737.

Bornstein, B. (1951). On latency. *Psychoanalytic Study of the Child* 6:279-285.

Brenner, C. (1952). Problems of symptom formation. *Bulletin of the American Psychoanalytic Association* 8:142-149.

———(1955). The validation of psychoanalytic interpretations. *Journal of the American Psychoanalytic Association* 3:496-505.

Brill, A. A. (1940). Some peculiar manifestations of memory with special references to lightning calculators. *Journal of Nervous and Mental Diseases* 92:709-726.

Bronowski, J. (1958). The creative process. *Scientific American* 199:59-65.

Brown, R. W. (1958). *Words and Things*. Glencoe: Free Press.

Buffon, G.-L. L. de (1855). *Oeuvres Choisies de Buffon*. Paris: Firmin-Didot.

Buhler, K. (1934). *Sprachtheorie*. Jena: Fischer.

Bychowski, G. (1951). From catharsis to work of art: the making of an artist. In *Psychoanalysis and Culture*, ed. G. B. Wilbur and W. Muensterberger. New York: International Universities Press.

Carroll, J. B. (1958). Some psychological effects of language structure. In *Psychopathology of Communication*, ed. P. H. Hoch and J. Zubin, pp. 49-68. New York: Grune and Stratton.

Carroll, L. (1865). *Alice's Adventures in Wonderland*. Boston: Boston Books, 1932.

Cassirer, E. (1923). *Language and Myth*. New York: Harper, 1946.

Chomsky, N. (1957). *Syntactic Structure*. New York: Humanities Press.

Cofer, C. N. (1961). Experimental studies in the role of the verbal processes in concept formation and problem solving. *Annals, Academy of Sciences*.

Cole, E. M. (1951). Specific reading disability. A problem in integration and adaptation. *American Journal of Ophthalmology* 34:226-232.

Costa, A. M. (1950). Note preliminare su un fenomeno dei geometrizzazione inimagini soggestive. Descrizione del fenomeno (effeto Gu.). *Arch. psichol. neurol psichiat.* 11:229-236.

Crisp, W. H. (1949). The psychology of the poor reader. *Rocky Mountain Medical Journal* 46:833-836.

Crocker, D. (1963). Panel report: Psychoanalytic considerations concerning the development of language in early childhood. *Journal of the American Psychoanalytic Association* 11:143-150.

Cunningham, J. V. (1966). *The Problem of Style*. Greenwich, Conn.: Fawcett.

Dale, P. W. (1957). Mathematical logic and the nature of reasoning. *Psychoanalytic Quarterly* 31:1-9.

Davidson, H. P. (1935). A study of the confusing letters B, D, P and Q. *Journal of Genetic Psychology* 40:458-468.

Dearborn, W. F. (1933). Structural factors which condition special disability in reading. *Proceedings of the American Association for Mental Deficiency* 38:266-283.

———(1938). Aniseikonia as related to disability in reading. *Journal of Experimental Psychology* 23:559-577.

Diringer, D. (1948). *The Alphabet: A Key to the History of Mankind*. New York: Philosophical Library.

Durrell, D. (1940), *Improvement of Basic Reading Abilities*. Yonkers, N.Y.: World Book.

Edelheit, H. (1967). Speech and psychic structure: the vocal-auditory organization of the ego. Paper presented to the American Psychoanalytic Association.

———(1925). Negation. *Collected Papers* 5: 181-185. London: Hogarth, 1950.

———(1968) Panel report: Language and ego development. *Journal of the American Psychoanalytic Association* 16:113-122.

———(1972). Panel report: The relationship of language development to problem-solving ability. *Journal of the American Psychoanalytic Association* 20:145-155.

Edelson, M. (1975). *Language and Interpretation in Psychoanalysis.* New Haven: Yale University Press.

Ehrensweig, A. (1953). *The Psychoanalysis of Artistic Vision and Hearing.* New York: Julian.

Eisenson, pp. 71-120. New York: Harper.

Eissler, K. R. (1953). The effect of the structure of the ego on psychoanalytic technique. *Journal of the American Psychoanalytic Association* 1:104-143.

Ekstein, R. (1959). Thoughts concerning the nature of the interpretative process. In *Readings in Psychoanalytic Psychology.* ed. M. Levitt, pp. 221-247. New York: Appleton-Century-Crofts.

———(1964). On the acquisition of speech in the autistic child. *Reiss-Davis Clinic Bulletin* 1:63-79.

Eliot, T. S. (1917). The love song of J. Alfred Prufrock. In *Complete Poems and Plays* (1909-1950). New York: Harcourt, Brace, 1952.

Ferenczi, S. (1916). Stages in the development of the sense of reality. In *Sex in Psychoanalysis.* Boston: Badger.

———(1955). Mathematics. In *Problems and Methods of Psychoanalysis.* New York: Basic Books.

Fernald, G. M., and Keller, H. B. (1921). The effect of Kinesthetic factors in the development of word recognition in the case of the non-reader. *Journal of Educational Research* 5:355-377.

Fisher, C. (1956). Dreams, images and perception; a study of unconscious-preconscious relationships. *Journal of the American Psychoanalytic Association* 4:5-48.

———(1957). Construction of dreams and images. *Journal of the American Psychoanalytic Association* 5:5-61.

———, and Paul, I. H. (1959). Subliminal visual stimulation and dreams. *Journal of the American Psychoanalytic Association* 7:35-83.

Fraiberg, S. (1957). Kafka and the dream. In *Art and Psychoanalysis,* ed. W. Phillips. New York: Stratford Press.

Freud, A. (1952). Mutual influences in the development of the ego and the id. *Journal of the American Psychoanalytic Association* 7:42-50.

Freud, S. (1888, 1891). *On Aphasia.* New York: International Universities Press, 1953.

———(1895). The project for a scientific psychology. *Standard Edition* 1:287-397.

———(1900). The interpretation of dreams. *Standard Edition* 4 and 5.

———(1901). The psychopathology of everyday life. *Standard Edition* 6.

———(1904). The psychopathology of everyday life. In *The Basic Writings of Sigmund Freud,* pp. 87-94. New York: Random House, 1938.

———(1905a). Three essays on the theory of sexuality. *Standard* Edition 7:125-248.

———(1905b). Jokes and their relation to the unconscious. *Standard Edition* 8:9-238.

———(1907). Obsessive acts and religious practices. *Standard Edition* 9:117-127.

———(1910a). Leonardo da Vinci and a memory of his childhood. *Standard Edition* 11:59-137.

———(1910b). The antithetical meaning of primal words. *Standard Edition* 11:153-161.

———(1911). Formulation regarding the two principles in mental functioning. *Collected Papers* 4:13-21. London: Hogarth, 1946.

———(1912). Recommendations for physicians on the psychoanalytic method of treatment. *Collected Papers* 2:323-333. London: Hogarth, 1950.

———(1913a). Totem and taboo. *Standard Edition* 13:1-162.

———(1913b). The philological interest of psycho-analysis. *Standard Edition* 13:176-178.

———(1915a). Instincts and their vicissitudes. *Standard Edition* 14:111-140.

———(1915b). The unconscious. *Standard Edition* 14:159-209.

———(1916). A mythological parallel to a visual obsession. *Standard Edition* 14:337-338.

———(1921). Group psychology and the analysis of the ego. *Standard Edition* 18:69-145.

———(1923). *Beyond the Pleasure Principle.* London: Hogarth, 1948.

———(1925). Negation. *Collected Papers.* 5:181-185. London: Hogarth, 1950.

———(1926). Inhibitions, symptoms and anxiety. *Standard Edition:* 20:87-172.

———(1927). Humor. *Standard Edition* 21:161-166.

———(1928). Humor. *Collected Papers* 5:215-221. London: Hogarth, 1950.

———(1936). The subtleties of a parapraxis. *Collected Papers* 5:313-315. London: Hogarth, 1950.

———(1937). Constructions in analysis. *Standard Edition* 23:255-269.

Fries, M. E., and Woolf, P. J. (1953). Some hypotheses on the role of the congenital activity type in personality development. *Psychoanalytic Study of the Child* 8:48-62.

Gardner, R. W.; Holzman, P. S.; Klein, G. S.; Linton, H. B.; and Spence, D. P. (1959). Cognitive control. A study of individual consistencies in cognitive behavior. *Psychological Issues* 6. New York: International Universities Press.

———; Jackson, D. N.; and Massick, S. J. (1960). Personality organization in cognitive controls and intellectual abilities. *Psychological Issues* 8. New York: International Universities Press.

Gates, A. I. (1941). The role of personality maladjustment in reading disability. *Journal of Genetic Psychology* 59:77-83.

———, and Bennett, C. C. (1933). *Reversal Tendencies in Reading: Causes, Diagnosis, Prevention and Correction.* New York: Bureau of Publications, Teachers College, Columbia University.

———, and Bond, G. L. (1936). Relation of handedness, eyesightedness and acuity dominance to reading. *Journal of Educational Psychology* 27:450-456.

Gero, G. (1962). Sadism, masochism and aggression: their role in symptom formation. *Psychoanalytic Quarterly* 31:31-42.

Gesell, A., and Ilg, F. L. (1946). *The Child from Five to Ten.* New York: Harper.

Getzels, J. W., and Jackson, P. W. (1962). *Creativity and Intelligence. Explorations with Gifted Students.* New York: Wiley.

Glauber, I. P. (1944). Speech characteristics of psychoneurotic patients. *Journal of Speech Disorders* 9:18-30.

———(1958). The Psychoanalysis of stuttering. In *Stuttering*, ed. J.

Glover, E. (1931). The effects of inexact interpretation. *International Journal of Psycho-Analysis* 12:397-411.

Goldfarb, W., and Braunstein, R. (1956). Reactions to delayed auditory feedback among a group of schizophrenic children. *American Journal of Orthopsychiatry* 26: 544-555.

Goldstein, K. (1925). Das Wesen der amnestischen Aphasie. *Dtsch. Ztsch. Nervenk.* 83:327-339.

———, and Scheerer, M. (1941). Abstract and concrete behavior. Psychol. Monog. 53, no. 2. Washington, D.C.: American Psychological Assn.

Gombrich, E. H. (1954). Psychoanalysis and the history of art. *International Journal of Psycho-Analysis* 35:401-411.

———(1960). *Art and Illusion. A Study in the Psychology of Pictorial Representation.* New York: Pantheon.

———, and Kris, E. (1940). *Caricature.* London: King Penguin.

Gottwald, P. F., Disorders of communication. *Proceedings of the Association of Reseach in Nervous and Mental Diseases* 5:42.

Grau, M. (5937). Empirisch-experimentelle Beitrage zur Psychologie der mathematischen und sprachlichen Begabung. *Arch. f. d. ges. Psychol.* 99:80-128.

Greenacre, P. (1953). Certain relationships between fetishism and the faulty development of the body image. *Psychoanalytic Study of the Child* 8:79-98.

———(1955). *Swift and Carroll.* New York: International Universities Press.

———(1957). The childhood of the artist. *Psychoanalytic Study of the Child* 12:47-72.

———(1958a). The family romance of the artist. *Psychoanalytic Study of the Child* 13:9-36.

———(1958b). The relation of the impostor to the artist. *Psychoanalytic Study of the Child* 13:521-540.

———(1959). Play in relation to creative imagination. *Psychoanalytic Study of the Child* 14:61-80.

Greenberg, J. H. (1957). *Language as a Sign System: Essays in Linguistics.* Chicago: University of Chicago Press.

Greenson, R. R. (1950). The mother tongue and the mother. *International Journal of Psycho-Analysis* 31:18-23.

———(1960). Problems of dosage timing and tact in interpretation. *Bulletin of the Philadelphia Association of Psychoanalysis* 10:23-24.

Griffith, R. (1945). *A Study of Imagination in Early Childhood.* London: Kegan Paul, Trench, Trubner.

Grotjahn, M. (1957). *Beyond Laughter.* New York: McGraw-Hill.

———(1961). Jewish jokes and masochism. *Journal of the Hillside Hospital* 10:183-189.

Gruber, H. E.; Krug, W. L.; and Link, S. (1963). The moon illusion: an event in imaginary space. *Science* 139: 750-751.

Hadamard, J. (1945). *The Psychology of Invention in the Mathematical Field.* Princeton, N.J.: Princeton University Press.

Hahn, R. (1927). Mathematische (Rechnen) Begabung und Persönlichkeit. *Monatsschr. f. Psychiat.* 64:229-251.

Hanfmann, E., and Kasanin, J. S. (1942). *Conceptual Thinking in Schizophrenia.* New York: Nervous and Mental Diseases Publications.

Harris, A. J. (1948). *How to Increase Reading Ability.* New York: Longmans, Green.

Harrison, M. (1030). *Reading Readiness.* Boston: Houghton Mifflin.

Hartmann, H. (1939). Ich-Psychologie und Anpassungsproblem. *Int. Ztschr. f. Psa. u. Imago* 24:62-135. Translation: *Ego Psychology and the Problem of Adaptation.* New York: International Universities Press, 1958.

———(1950a). Psychoanalysis and developmental psychology. *Psychoanalytic Study of the Child* 5:7-17. Also in *Essays on Ego Psychology*, pp. 99-112. New York: International Universities Press, 1964.

———(1950b). Comments on the psychoanalytic theory of the ego. *Psychoanalytic Study of the Child* 5:74-96. Also in *Essays*, pp. 113-141.

———(1950c) The application of psychoanalytic concepts to social science. *Essays*, pp. 90-98.

———(1951). Technical implications of ego psychology. *Psychoanalytic Quarterly* 20: 31-43. Also in *Essays*, pp. 142-154.

———(1952). The mutual influences in the development of ego and id. *Essays*, pp. 155-181.

———(1953). Contribution to the metapsychology of schizophrenia. *Essays*, pp. 182-206.

———, and Kris, E. (1945). The genetic approach in psychoanalysis. *Psychoanalytic Study of the Child* 1:11-29.

———; ———; and Loewenstein, R. M. (1946). Comments on the formation of psychic structure. *Psychoanalytic Study of the Child* 2:11-38.

———; ———; ———(1949). Notes on the theory of aggression. *Psychoanalytic Study of the Child* 3/4:9-37.

———, Hoffer, W.; Freud, A.; Klein, M.; Nacht, S. S.; Scott, W.; and van der Waals, H. (1952). Symposium: The mutual influences in the development of the ego and id. *Psychoanalytic Study of the Child* 7: 9-68.

Hayden, D. E., and Alworth, E. P., eds. (1965). *Classics in Semantics.* New York: Philosophical Library.

Hayek, F. A. (1952). *The Sensory Order.* Chicago: University of Chicago Press.

Heider, F. (1941). The description of the psychological environment in the work of Marcel Proust. *Character and Personality* 9:295-314.

Hermann, I. (1924). *Psychoanalyse und Logik.* Leipzig, Vienna, Zurich: Imago Bucker 7

———(1926). Das System Bw. *Imago* 12:203-210.

———(1929). Das Ich und das Denken. *Imago* 15:89-110, 325-348.

———(1949). Denkpsychologische Betrachtungen im Gebiet der mathematischen Mengenlehre. *Schweiz Ztschr. f. Psychol. und ihre Anwendungen* 8:189-232.

———(1950). Rapports spatiaux de quelques phenomenes psychiques. *Acta Psychol.* 7:225-246.

Hildreth, G. (1934). Reversals in reading and writing. *Journal of Educational Psychology* 25:1-20.

Hincks, E. (1926). *Disability in Reading and Its Relation to Personality.* Cambridge: Harvard University Press.

Hinshelwood, J. (1917). *Congenital Word Blindness.* London: Lewis.

Hockett, C. F. (1960). The origin of speech. *Scientific American* 203:88-96.

Hoffman, W. (1957). *Caricature from Leonardo to Picasso.* New York: Crown.

Hug-Hellmuth, H. (1915). Einige Beziehungen zwischen Erotik und Mathematik. *Imago* 4:52-68.

Hughlings-Jackson, J. (1958). *Selected Writings of John Hughlings-Jackson,* ed. J. Taylor. Vol. 2. New York: Basic Books.

Infeld, L. (1948). *Whom the Gods Love: The Story of Evariste Galois.* New York: McGraw-Hill.

Inhelder, B., and Piaget, J. (1958). *The Growth of Logical Thinking from Childhood to Adolescence.* New York: Basic Books.

Ioteyko, L. (1910). Les calculateurs prodiges', avec presentation de Mlle. Uranie Diamandi. *Rev. Psychol. Bruxelles* 3:320-328.

Irwin, O. C. (1960). Language and communication. In *Handbook of Research Methods in Child Development,* ed. P. Mussen, pp. 487-516. New York: Wiley.

Isakower, O. (1939). On the exceptional position of the auditory sphere. *International Journal of Psycho-Analysis* 20:340-348.

Jacobson, E. (1946). The child's laughter. *Psychoanalytic Study of the Child* 2:39-60. New York: International Universities Press.

———(1954). Contribution to the metapsychology of psychotic identifications. *Journal of The American Psychoanalytic Association* 2:239-262.

———(1959a). Depersonalization. *Journal of the American Psychoanalytic Association* 7:581-610.

———(1959b). The "exceptions." An elaboration of Freud's character study. *Psychoanalytic Study of the Child* 14:135-154.

———(1964). *The Self and the Object World.* New York: International Universities Press.

Jaensch, E. R. (1923). *Eidetic Imagery.* New York: Harcourt Brace, 1930.

Jakobson, R. (1935). Aphasia as a linguistic problem. In *On Expressive Language,* ed. H. Werner, pp. 69-81. Worcester, Mass.: Clark University Press, 1955.

———(1941). Kinderspache, Aphasia und allgemeine Lautgesetze. *Uppsala Universitets Orsskrift* 1-83, 1942.

———(1960). Why "Mama" and "Papa"? In *Perspectives in Psychological Theory,* ed. B. Kaplan and S. Wapner, pp. 124-134. New York: International Universities Press. Also in: *Selected Writings,* pp. 538-545. The Hague: Mouton, 1962.

———(1964). Towards a linguistic typology of aphasic impairments. In *Ciba Foundation Symposium on Disorders of Language,* ed. A.V.S. de Renck and M. O'Connor, pp. 21-42. London: Churchill.

———, and Halle, M. (1956). *Fundamentals of Language.* The Hague: Mouton.

Jakobsson, S. (1944). Report on two prodigy mental arithmeticians. *Acta Medica Scandinavica* 119:180-191.

Jones, E. (1912). An analytic study of a case of obsessional neurosis. In *Papers on Psycho-Analysis.* 4th ed. London: Bailliere, Tindall and Cox, 1938.

———(1931). The problem of Paul Morphy, a contribution to the psychology of chess. *International Journal of Psycho-Analysis* 12:1-23.

———(1956). The nature of genius. The Freud Anniversary Lecture of the New York Psychoanalytic Institute.

Jones, M. R. (1943). Effect of mental arithmetic in frequency and patterning of movements. *Journal of Genetic Psychology* 29:47-62.

Joseph, E. D. (1959). An unusual fantasy in a twin with an inquiry into the nature of fantasy. *Psychoanalytic Quarterly* 28:189-206.

Kasanin, J. S. (1944a). The disturbance of conceptual thinking in schizophrenia. In *Language and Thought in Schizophrenia,* ed. J. S. Kasanin. Berkeley, Calif.: University of California Press.

———(1944b). *Language and Thought in Schizophrenia.* New York: Norton.

Kanzer, M. (1955). Gogol: a study on wit and paranoia. *Journal of the American Psychoanalytic Association* 3:110-125.

———(1958). Image formation during free association. *Psychoanalytic Quarterly* 27:465-484.

Kepler, J. (1958). Writings translated by A. Koestler. *Encounter,* December, 1958.

Ketcham, W. A. (1951). Experimental tests of principles of developmental anatomy and neuroanatomy as applied to pedagogy of reading. *Child Development* 22:185-192.

Kirk, S. A. (1934). A study of the relation of ocular-manual preferences to mirror writing. *Journal of Genetic Psychology* 44:192-205.

Klein, G. S. (1959). Consciousness in psychoanalytic theory. *Journal of the American Psychoanalytic Association* 7:5-34.

———(1966). Freud's two theories of sexuality. In *Clinical-Cognitive Psychology: Modes and Integration,* ed. L. Breger, pp. 136-181. Englewood Cliffs, N.J.: Prentice Hall.

Knight, E. H. (1952). Spelling disability as a symptom of emotional disorder. *Bulletin of the Menninger Clinic* 16:84-91.

Koffka, K. (1935). *Principles of Gestalt Psychology.* New York: Harcourt Brace.

Kommerell, V. (1928). Ueber mathematische "Begabung." *Ztschr. f. padagogische Psychol.* 29:143-171.

Kopit, A. L. (1960). *Oh Dad Poor Dad, Momma's Hung You in the Closet and I'm Feeling So Sad.* New York: Hill & Wang.

Kris, E. (1938). Ego development and the comic. *International Journal of Psycho-Analysis* 19:77-90.

———(1944). Art and regression. Translation. *New York Academy of Science* 6:236-250.

———(1947). The nature of psychoanalytic propositions and their validation. In *Freedom and Experience*, ed. S. Hook and M.R. Konwitz. Ithaca, N.Y.: Cornell University Press.

———(1950). On preconscious mental processes. *Psychoanalytic Quarterly* 19:540-550.

———(1951). Ego psychology and interpretation in psychoanalytic therapy. *Psychoanalytic Quarterly* 20:15-30.

———(1952). *Psychoanalytic Explorations in Art.* New York: International Universities Press.

———(1956). The personal myth: A problem in technique. *Journal of the American Psychoanalytic Association* 4:653-681.

Kubie, L. (1934). Body Symbolization and the development of language. *Psychoanalytic Quarterly* 3:430-444.

Laffal, J. (1964). Freud's theory of language. *Psychoanalytic Quarterly* 33:157-175.

———(1965). *Pathological and Normal Language.* New York: Atherton.

LaFora, G. R. (1935). Etude psychologique d'une débile mentale calculatrice du calendrier. *L'Encephale, J. de Neurol. et Psychiat.* 30:309-337.

Langer, S. (1953). *Feeling and Form: A Theory of Art.* New York: Scribner.

———(1957). *Problems of Art.* New York: Scribner.

Launay, C., and Borel-Maisonny (1952). Un cas de dyslexie specifique. *Sem. Hosp., Paris.* 28:1455-1459.

Leitch, M., and Escalona, S. (1949). The reactions of infants to stress. *Psychoanalytic Study of the Child* 3/4:121-140.

Lennenberg, E. H. (1964). A biological perspective of language. In *New Directions in the Study of Language*, ed. E. H. Lennenberg, pp. 65-89. Cambridge: M.I.T. Press, pp. 65-89.

Leopold, W. F. (1952). *Bibliography of Child Language*. Evanston: Northwestern University Press.

Levi-Strauss, C. (1966). *The Savage Mind*. Chicago: University of Chicago Press.

Lewin, B. (1948). The nature of reality and the meaning of nothing. *Psychoanalytic Quarterly* 17:524-528.

Lewis, M. M. (1951). *Infant Speech: A Study of the Beginning of Language*. New York: Humanities Press.

———(1959). *How Children Learn to Speak*. New York: Basic Books.

Lidz, T. (1963). *The Family and Human Adaptation*. New York: International Universities Press.

———(1968) Statements to Panel on Language and the development of the ego. *Journal of the American Psychoanalytic Association* 16:113-122.

Loewald, H. (1960). On the therapeutic action of psychoanalysis. *International Journal of Psycho-Analysis* 41:16-33.

Loewenstein, R. (1951). The problem of interpretation. *Psychoanalytic Quarterly* 20:1-14.

———(1956). Some remarks on the role of speech in psychoanalytic technique. *International Journal of Psycho-Analysis* 37:460-468.

———(1957). Some thoughts on interpretation. *Psychoanalytic Study of the Child* 12:127-150.

———(1972). Ego autonomy and psychoanalytic technique. *Psychoanalytic Quarterly* 41:1-22.

Loomie, L. S.; Rosen, V. H.; and Stein, M. H. (1958). Ernst Kris and the gifted adolescent project. *Psychoanalytic Study of the Child* 13:44-57.

Lorenz, M. (1961). Problems posed by schizophrenic language. *Archives of General Psychiatry* 4:603-610.

Lowry, B., ed. (1960). *Parody, American and British*. New York: Harcourt Brace.

Luria, A. R. (1961). *The Role of Speech in the Regulation of Behavior*. New York: Liveright.

Lynch, B. (1926). *A History of Caricature*. London: Faber and Faber.

MacDonald, D., ed. (1960). *Parodies: An Anthology from Chaucer to Beerbohm — and After.* New York: Random House.

McFie, J. (1952). Cerebral dominance in cases of reading disability. *Journal of Neurology Neurosurgery and Psychiatry* 15:194-199.

McKinnon, D. W. (1967). The study of creative persons: a method and some results. In *Creativity and Learning.* Daedalus Library 8. Boston: Houghton Mifflin.

Mahl, G. F. (1968). Gestures and body movements in interviews. *Res. Psychother.* 3:295-346.

———, and Schulz, G. (1964). Psychological research in the extralinguistic area. In *Approaches to Semiotics,* ed. T. Sebeok et al., pp. 51-124. The Hague: Mouton.

Mahler-Schoenberger, M. (1942). Pseudoimbecility: a magic cap for invisibility. *Psychoanalytic Quarterly* 11:149-164.

Meerloo, J. A. M. (1964). *Unobtrusive Communication: Essays in Psycholinguistics.* Assen, Netherlands: Van Gorcum.

Menzerath, P. (1913). Apropos des calculateurs prodiges. *Bull. de la Soc. Anthropologique* (Brussels) 31:299-234.

Meredith, G. (1888). *Beauchamp's Career.* Boston: Robert.

Michaels, J. J. (1959). Character disorder and acting upon impulse. In *Readings in Psychoanalytic Psychology,* ed. M. Levitt, pp. 181-196. New York: Appleton.

Miller, G. A., and Isard, S. (1963). Some perceptual consequences of linguistic rules. *Journal of Verbal Learning and Verbal Behavior* 2:217-228.

Moebus, P. J. (1907). *Ueber die Anlage zur Mathematik.* 2nd ed. Leipzig.

Morris, C. W. (1938). *Foundations of the Theory of Science,* ed. O. Neurath, R. Carnap, and C. W. Morris. International Encyclopedia of Unified Science. Chicago: University of Chicago Press.

Muensterberger, W. (1951). Roots of primitive art. In *Psychoanalysis and Culture,* ed. G. B. Wilbur and W. Muensterberger. New York: International Universities Press.

———(1961). The creative process: its relation to object loss and fetishism. *Psychoanalytic Study of Society* 2:161-185.

Nagera, H. (1966). *Early Childhood Disturbances, the Infantile Neurosis, and the Adulthood Disturbances: Problems of a Developmental Psychoanalytic Psychology.* New York: International Universities Press.

Needles, W. (1959). Gesticulation and speech. *International Journal of Psycho-Analysis* 40:291-294.

———(1969). The pleasure principle, the constancy principle and the primary autonomous ego. *Journal of the American Psychoanalytic Association* 17:808-825.

Nunberg, H. (1931). The synthetic function of the ego. In *Practice and Theory of Psychoanalysis.* New York: International Universities Press, 1955.

———(1932). *Principles of Psychoanalysis.* New York: International Universities Press, 1955.

Oehl, (1952). Psychologische Untersuchungen uber Zahlendenken Rechnen bei Schulanfangern. *Ztschr. f. angewandte Psychol.* 49:205-351.

Ogden, C. K., and Richards, I. A. (1923). *The Meaning of Meaning.* New York: Harcourt Brace, 1959.

Olinick, S. (1954). Some considerations of the use of questioning as a psychoanalytic technique. *Journal of the American Psychoanalytic Association* 2:57-66.

Orton, S. T. (1937). *Reading, Writing and Speech Problems in Children.* New York: Norton.

———(1939). A neurological explanation of reading disability. *Educational Record* 20:58-68.

Ostrow, M. (1955). A psychoanalytic contribution to the study of brain function. *Psychoanalytic Quarterly* 24:383-423.

Paulson, H. (1966). Language and psychosexual development. Unpublished doctoral dissertation. New York University.

Pearson, G. H. J. (1952). A survey of learning difficulties in children. *Psychoanalytic Study of the Child* 7:322-386.

Peller, L. E. (1954). Libidinal phases, ego development and play. *Psychoanalytic Study of the Child* 11:178-197.

———(1955). Libidinal development as reflected in play. *Psychoanalysis* 3:3-11.

———(1964). Language and its prestages. *Bulletin of the Philadelphia Association for Psychoanalysis* 14:55-76.

———(1966). The functions of language and the functions of mothering. Presented at American Psychoanalytic Association meeting.

———(1967). Freud's contribution of language theory. *Psychoanalytic Study of the Child* 21.

Peter, W. (1905). *Appreciations with an Essay on Style.* New York: Macmillan.

Phillips, A. J. (1934). Relation of left handedness to reversals in reading. *Elementary English Review* 11:97-98.

Piaget, J. (1923). *The Language and Thought of the Child.* London: Routledge & Kegan Paul, 1948.

———(1950). *The Psychology of Intelligence.* New York: Harcourt Brace.

———(1952). *The Child's Conception of Number.* New York: Humanities Press.

———(1953). Logic and Psychology. Manchester: Manchester University Press.

———(1954). *The Construction of Reality in the Child.* New York: Basic Books.

———(1956). *The Child's Conception of Space.* New York: Humanities Press.

Pierce, J. R. (1961). *Symbols, Signals and Noise: The Nature and Process of Communication.* New York: Harper.

Pittenger, R. E. (1966) Minutes of the June 13 meeting of the Study Group in Linguistics and Psychoanalysis. New York Psychoanalytic Institute.

Poincaré, H. (1952). *Science and Hypothesis.* New York: Dover.

———(1952a). *Science and Method.* New York: Dover.

Poponoe, P. B. (1930-31). Rechenkunstler und Vererbung. *Eugenik* (Berlin) 1:152-157.

Ramsey, F. P. (1950). *The Foundations of Mathematics.* New York: Humanities Press.

Rangell, L. (1952). The analysis of a doll phobia. *International Journal of Psycho-Analysis* 33:43-53.

———(1955). Report on Panel: The Borderline Case. *Journal of the American Psychoanalytic Association* 3:285-298.

Ranken, H. B. (1963). Language and thinking. *Science* 141:48-50.

Rapaport, D. (1950). On the psychoanalytic theory of thinking. *International Journal of Psycho-Analysis* 31:1-10.

———(1951a). *Organization and Pathology of Thought.* New York: Columbia University Press.

———(1951b). Paul Schilder's contribution to the theory of thought processes. *International Journal of Psycho-Analysis* 32:291-301

Ravina, A. (1946). Les calculateurs prodiges': leurs méthodes de travail. *Presse Med. d. Paris* 54:1-156.

Reich, A. (1950). The structure of the grotesque-comic sublimation. *Yearbook of Psychoanalysis* 6:194-207. New York: International Universities Press.
Psychiatric Quarterly 37:264-281.

Roe, A. (1952). *The Making of a Scientist.* New York: Dodd, Mead.

Rosen, I. (1955). Defense and Communication in the language of schizophrenia. *Diseases of the Nervous System* 16:315-317.

Rosen, V. H. (1959). Originality and the adolescent group. *Child Study* 36:15-20.

———(1962). The relationship of the Institute to the community. In *The Fruition of an Idea: Fifty Years of Psychoanalysis in New York,* ed. M. Wangh. New York: International Universities Press.

———, and Keschner, M. (1941). Optic neuritis caused by a coal tar hair dye. *Archives of Opthalmology* 25:1020-1040.

Rycroft, C. (1958). An enquiry into the function of words in psychoanalysis. *International Journal of Psycho-Analysis* 39:408-415.

Sapir, E. (1921). *Language: An Introduction to the Study of Speech.* New York: Harcourt Brace.

———(1960). *Culture, Language and Personality.* Berkeley: University of California Press.

Saussure, F. de (1916). *Cours de Linguistique.* Paris: Payot.

Saussure, R. de (1926). Zur psychoanalytischen Auffassung der Intelligenz. *Imago* 12:238-248.

Savitt, R. (1957). Phobic and counterphobic attitudes in a research scientist. *Psychoanalytic Quarterly* 26:150-152.

Schachtel, E. G. (1959). *Metamorphosis. On the Development of Affect, Perception, Attention, and Memory.* New York: Basic Books.

Scherer, M.; Rothman, E.; and Goldstein, K. (1945). A case of idiot savant: an experimental study of personality organization. *Psychol. Mon.* 58:1-62.

Schilder, P. (1936). Zur Psychoanalyse der Geometrie, Arithmetik und Physik. *Imago* 22:389-395.

———(1942). *Mind: Perception and Thought in Their Constructive Aspects.* New York: Columbia University Press.

———(1944). Congenital alexia and its relation to optic perception. *Journal of Genetic Psychology* 65:67-88.

Schnier, J. (1960). Free associations and ego functions in creativity: a study of content and form in art. *American Imago* 17:61-74.

Schur, M. (1966). *The Id and the Regulatory Principles of Mental Functioning.* New York: International Universities Press.

Sebeok, T. A., ed. (1960). *Style in Language.* Cambridge: M.I.T. Press.

———; Hayes, A. S.; and Bateson, M. C. (1964). *Approaches to Semiotics.* The Hague: Mouton.

Selzer, C. A. (1933). *Lateral Dominance and Visual Fusion.* Cambridge, Mass.: Harvard University Press.

Shands, H. C. (1960). *Thinking and Psychotherapy: An Inquiry into the Process of Communication.* Cambridge: Harvard University Press.

Shapiro, T. (1967). Interpretation and the naming process. Paper presented to the Language Study group, New York Psychoanalytic Institute.

———(1970). Interpretation and naming. *Journal of the American Psychoanalytic Association* 18:399-421.

Sharpe, E. F. (1940). Psycho-physical problems revealed in language. *International Journal of Psycho-Analysis* 21:201-213. Also in *Collected Papers on Psycho-Analysis.* London: Hogarth, 1950.

———(1950). Similar and divergent unconscious determinants underlying the sublimation of pure art and pure sciences. *Collected Papers on Psycho-Analysis.* London: Hogarth, pp. 137-154.

Silberer, H. (1951). On symbol formation. In *Organization and Pathology of Thought,* ed. D. Rapaport. New York: Columbia.

Spence, D. (1968). The processing of information in psychotherapy: some links with psycholinguistics and information theory. *Behavioral Science* 13:349-361.

Spoerri, T. H. (1966). The speaking voice of the schizophrenic patient. *Archives of General Psychiatry* 14:581-585.

Stein, M. H. (1958). The cliché: a phenomenon of resistance. *Journal of the American Psychoanalytic Association* 6: 263-277.

Steinberg, S., and Weiss, J. (1954). The art of Edvard Munch and its function in his mental life. *Journal of the American Psychoanalytic Association* 23:409-423.

Sterba, E. (1943). On spelling. *Psychoanalytic Review* 30:273-276.

Stevenson, O. (1954). The first treasured possession. *Psychoanalytic Study of the Child* 9:199-217.

Stewart, W. A. (1961). The development of the therapeutic alliance in borderline patients. *Journal of the American Psychoanalytic Association* 30:165-167.

Stone, L. S. (1954). The widening scope of psychoanalysis. *Journal of the American Psychoanalytic Association* 2:567-594.

———(1961). *The Psychoanalytic Situation.* New York: International Universities Press.

Strachey, J. (1930). Some unconscious factors in reading. *International Journal of Psycho-Analysis* 11:322-331.

Strunk, W., Jr., and White, E. B. (1959). *The Elements of Style.* New York: Macmillan.

Sully, J. (1910). *Studies of Childhood.* New York: Appleton.

Sylvester, E., and Kunst, M. S. (1943). Psychodynamic aspects of the reading problem. *American Journal of Orthopsychiatry* 13:69-76.

Székely, L. (1962). Meaning, meaning schemata, and body schemata in thought. *International Journal of Psycho-Analysis* 43:297-305.

Tarachow, S. (1949). Remarks on the comic process and beauty. *Psychoanalytic Quarterly* 18:215-226.

———(1951). Circuses and clowns. *Psychoanalysis and the Social Sciences* 3:171-185.New York: International Universities Press.

———; Friedman, S.; and Korin, H. (1958). Studies in ambivalence. *Journal of the Hillside Hospital* 7:67-97.

Teitelbaum, H. A. (1958). Defensive verbal communication processes in psychotherapy. In *Psychopathology of Communication,* ed. P.H. Hock and J. Zubin. New York: Grune & Stratton.

Times (London) *Literary Supplement* (1 December 1961). Review of Ogden Nash's *Collected Verse* from 1929 on.

Trilling, L. (1957). Art and neurosis. In *Art and Psychoanalysis*, ed. W. Phillips. New York: Stratford.

Tulchin, S. (1935). Emotional factors in reading disabilities in school children. *Journal of Educational Psychology* 26:443-454.

Ullman, S. (1962). *Semantics.* Oxford: Blackwell.

Voelmy, E. (1949). Psychologisches um kleine und grosse Zahlen. *Schweiz Ztschr. f. Psychol. und ihre Anwendungen* 8:231-253.

Von Neumann, J. (1956). The general and logical theory of automata. In *The World of Mathematics*, ed. J. R. Newman. New York: Simon & Schuster.

Vygotsky, L. S. (1934). *Thought and Language.* Cambridge: M.I.T. Press, 1962.

Waelder, R. (1933). The psychoanalytic theory of play. *Psychoanalytic Quarterly* 2:208-224.

———(1936). The principle of multiple function. *Psychoanalytic Quarterly* 5:45-62.

———(1963). Psychoanalytic contributions to aesthetics. Thirteenth Freud Anniversary Lecture, New York Psychoanalytic Institute.

Webster's New International Dictionary (unabridged) (1953). Springfield, Mass.: Merriam.

Weich, M. J. (1968). Some stages in the development of conceptual language: transitional language, language fetish and language constancy. Minutes of Study Group on Language and Psychoanalysis. New York Psychoanalytic Institute.

Weigl, E. (1941). On the psychology of so-called processes of abstraction. *Journal of Abnormal and Social Psychology* 36:3-33.

Werner, H., and Kaplan, B. (1963b). *Symbol Formation: An Organismic Developmental Approach to Language and the Expression of Thought*. New York: Wiley.

———(1963b). *Symbol Formation*. New York: Wiley.

Whorf, B. L. (1956). *Language, Thought and Reality*. New York: Wiley, and Cambridge: M.I.T. Press.

Wiener, N. (1953). *Ex Prodigy: My Childhood and Youth*. New York: Simon & Schuster.

Wilson, E. (1957). Philoctetes: the wound and the bow in art and psychoanalysis. In *Art and Psychoanalysis*, ed. W. Phillips. New York: Stratford.

Winnicott, D. W. (1953). Transitional objects and transitional phenomena. *International Journal of Psycho-Analysis* 34:89-97.

Wisdom, J. O. (1947). Three dreams of Descartes. *International Journal of Psycho-Analysis* 28:1-18.

Wittels, F. (1952). A contribution to a symposium on religious art and literature. *Journal of the Hillside Hospital* 1:3-6.

Wittgenstein, L. (1953). *Philosophical Investigations*. New York: Macmillan.

Witty, P. A. (1936). Sinistral and mixed manual-ocular behavior in reading disability. *Journal of Educational Psychology* 27:119-134.

———, and Kopel, D. (1936). Factors associated with the etiology of reading disability. *Journal of Educational Research* 29:449-459.

Wolfenstein, M. A. (1951). A phase in the development of children's sense of humor. *Psychoanalytic Study of the Child* 6:336-350.

Wolff, P. (1967). Cognitive considerations for psychoanalytic theory of language acquisition. *Psychological Issues* 5:18-19.

Woody, C., and Phillips, A. J. (1934). The effects of handedness on reversals in reading. *Journal of Educational Research* 27:651-662.

Wulff, M. (1946). Fetishism and object choice in early childhood. *Journal of the American Psychoanalytic Association* 15:450-471.

Young, R. A. (1938). Case studies in reading disability. *American Journal of Orthopsychiatry* 8:230-254.

Index

C

D

E

F

G

H

I

J

K

L

M

N

O

P

R

S

T

U

V

W

Y